CCNA® Data Center

Study Guide

CCNA® Data Center
Introducing Cisco Data Center Networking
Study Guide

Todd Lammle

John Swartz

SYBEX®
A Wiley Brand

Senior Acquisitions Editor: Jeff Kellum
Development Editor: David Clark
Technical Editors: Ryan Lindfield and Isaac Valdez
Production Editor: Christine O'Connor
Copy Editor: Judy Flynn
Editorial Manager: Pete Gaughan
Production Manager: Tim Tate
Vice President and Executive Group Publisher: Richard Swadley
Vice President and Publisher: Neil Edde
Media Project Manager: Laura Moss-Hollister
Media Associate Producer: Shawn Patrick
Media Quality Assurance: Marilyn Hummel
Book Designers: Judy Fung and Bill Gibson
Compositor: Craig Woods, Happenstance Type-O-Rama
Proofreaders: Sarah Kaikini and Daniel Aull, Word One New York
Indexer: Robert Swanson
Project Coordinator, Cover: Katherine Crocker
Cover Designer: Ryan Sneed

Dear Reader,

Thank you for choosing *CCNA Data Center: Introducing Cisco Data Center Networking Study Guide*. This book is part of a family of premium-quality Sybex books, all of which are written by outstanding authors who combine practical experience with a gift for teaching.

Sybex was founded in 1976. More than 30 years later, we're still committed to producing consistently exceptional books. With each of our titles, we're working hard to set a new standard for the industry. From the paper we print on, to the authors we work with, our goal is to bring you the best books available.

I hope you see all that reflected in these pages. I'd be very interested to hear your comments and get your feedback on how we're doing. Feel free to let me know what you think about this or any other Sybex book by sending me an email at nedde@wiley.com. If you think you've found a technical error in this book, please visit http://sybex.custhelp.com. Customer feedback is critical to our efforts at Sybex.

Best regards,

Neil Edde
Vice President and Publisher
Sybex, an Imprint of Wiley

Acknowledgments

I would first like to thank my acquisitions editor, Jeff Kellum. I've worked with Jeff for more years than I can remember, and his experience of working with me and the Cisco certification process is a needed asset for my success. Thanks for hanging in there once again, Jeff!

Working with David Clark as my developmental editor was a first, and it was a smooth, pleasant experience—thank you, David!

In addition, Judy Flynn and Christine O'Connor made the editorial process a breeze. I was very happy when I heard they were working with me once again on this new book! I look forward to many more projects with this great team.

I also want to thank my technical editor, Ryan Lindfield. His dedicated, concise comments have been invaluable and have made this a better book. The technical proofreader is Isaac Valdez, and he has been very detailed, making sure that Ryan, John, and I didn't miss any details. Thank you all!

Thanks also to the Vertical Websites team, whose hard work has resulted in a power-packed, good-looking online test engine. And last but not least, thanks to proofreaders Sarah Kaikini and Dan Aull, indexer Robert Swanson, and compositor Craig Woods at Happenstance Type-O-Rama.

About the Authors

Todd Lammle holds numerous Cisco certifications and is the authority on Cisco certification. He is a world-renowned author, speaker, trainer, and consultant. Todd has over 30 years of experience working with LANs, WANs, large licensed and unlicensed wireless networks, and for the last few years, data center technologies. He is president of GlobalNet Training and Consulting, Inc., a network integration and training firm based in Dallas, San Francisco, and Boulder, Colorado. You can reach Todd through his forum at www.lammle.com.

John Swartz, CCIE No. 4426, is the founder of Boson Software, 3DSNMP, Purple Penguin, Unified Trainers, and Inner Four. He believes the biggest changes in computing are occurring in the data center and with smartphones. He has been a Cisco instructor for 15 years, starting with basic courses and now teaching Unified Computing, Nexus switching, VBLOCK, and other data center technologies. He is also focused on mobile technology; his companies have published over 1,000 apps for the iPhone and Android. John created the original Cisco Press CCNA Network simulator, the Boson Netsim, and numerous practice tests. John lives in Florida with his wife and three kids.

Contents at a Glance

Contents

Introduction

Welcome to the exciting world of Cisco certification! You have picked up this book because you want something better—namely, a better job with more satisfaction. Rest assured that you have made a good decision. Cisco certification can help you get your first networking job or more money and a promotion if you are already in the field.

Cisco certification can also improve your understanding of the internetworking of more than just Cisco products: you will develop a complete understanding of networking and how different network topologies work together to form a network. This is beneficial to every networking job and is the reason Cisco certification is in such high demand, even at companies with few Cisco devices.

Cisco is the king of routing, switching, voice and security, and now data center technology! The Cisco certifications reach beyond the popular certifications, such as those from CompTIA and Microsoft, to provide you with an indispensable factor in understanding today's network—insight into the Cisco world of internetworking and beyond. By deciding that you want to become Cisco certified, you are saying that you want to be the best—the best at routing and the best at switching, and now the best at configuring and administering Nexus and data center technologies. This book will lead you in that direction.

For up-to-the-minute updates covering additions or modifications to the CCNA Data Center certification exams, as well as additional study tools and review questions, be sure to visit the Todd Lammle forum and website found at www.lammle.com.

What Is Nexus and Data Center?

Introducing the Cisco Nexus product line—one of the most significant iterations in how Cisco moves data to occur in the past decade! And it didn't just appear magically either; all things Nexus evolved from a colorfully mixed history of acquisitions, innovation, and a novel business practice Cisco sometimes ventures into known as a spin-in.

A long and storied industry leader, Cisco created some of the earliest routers using IOS, and in the early '90s, it entered the Ethernet switching market by acquiring Crescendo, Grand Junction, and Kalpana. Cisco's now legacy Catalyst switches running the CatOS became the leading data center Ethernet switches in the world!

But sometimes, that's not enough, and Cisco wanted to compete in the Fabric Channel switching market as well. In case you don't know, Fabric Channel is a type of networking used to communicate with storage arrays. Anyway, a select group of Cisco engineers led a startup company, partially funded by Cisco, called Andiamo Systems and created the MDS product line based on the SAN-OS, or Storage Area Network Operating System. After Cisco acquired the newly successful Andiamo Systems in 2004, thereby spinning it back into the fold, the aforementioned group of engineers cum executives retired from Andiamo to lead another startup company called Nuova. This time, they busily went to work on a data center platform that would embrace virtualization and support I/O consolidation and unified fabric with a composite technology from IOS, CatOS, and SAN-OS. History repeated itself with a twist when Cisco acquired Nuova in 2008, and upon spinning back in the company and its technological advances, the Nexus product line running the Nexus Operating System (NX-OS) was soon unveiled. Nuova was then renamed the Server and Virtualization Business Unit, or SAVBU, which has gone on to create a number of wonderful technologies including Nexus as well as the Unified Computing System (UCS) product line.

Okay—so who cares and why does this matter? Well, the answer is everyone does because data center networking covers a vast array of products and technologies! This generation of equipment is totally about unifying technologies from disparate areas like data networking, storage networking, and server management. In short, it's huge!

And NX-OS just happens to be the cornerstone of Cisco's unification strategy. As you'll soon see, both its form and function are majorly based upon the device's heritage.

Cisco Certified Network Associate (CCNA) Data Center

The CCNA Data Center certification includes the first two exams in the Cisco Data Center certification process, and the precursor to all other Cisco Data Center certifications. To become CCNA Data Center certified, you need to pass two exams at $250 a pop:

DCICN: Introducing Cisco Data Center Networking (Exam 640-911)   The 640-911 DCICN Introducing Cisco Data Center Networking exam is the first exam associated with the CCNA Data Center certification. This exam tests a candidate's knowledge of networking concepts for the Data Center environment, based on Nexus-OS (NX-OS). Candidates can prepare for this exam by taking the course DCICN, Introducing Cisco Data Center Networking, where you will learn fundamental information on how a data center network works, how to configure virtualization in the network, addressing schemes, troubleshooting, and configuration skills.

DCICT: Introducing Cisco Data Center Technologies (Exam 640-916)   The 640-916 DCICT Introducing Cisco Data Center Technologies exam is the second exam associated with the CCNA Data Center certification. This exam tests a candidate's knowledge of fundamental data center technologies like network and server virtualization, storage, convergent I/O, and network services like load balancing.

    This book covers the Introducing Cisco Data Center Networking exam.

And once you have your CCNA, you don't have to stop there—you can choose to continue with your studies and achieve a higher certification, called the Cisco Certified Network Professional (CCNP), which requires passing four more exams. Someone with a CCNP has all the skills and knowledge they need to attempt the CCIE Data Center certification, which entails a written exam and a lab exam. But just getting a CCNA Data Center certification can land you that job you've dreamed about.

Why Become CCNA Data Center Certified?

Cisco, not unlike Microsoft and other vendors that provide certification, has created the certification process to give administrators a set of skills and to equip prospective employers with a way to measure those skills or match certain criteria. Obtaining CCNA Data Center certification can be the initial step of a successful journey toward a new, highly rewarding, and sustainable career.

The CCNA program was created to provide a solid introduction not only to the Cisco Nexus operating system and Cisco hardware but also to internetworking in general, making it helpful to you in areas that are not exclusively Cisco's. At this point in the certification process, it's not unrealistic that network managers—even those without Cisco equipment—require Cisco certification for their job applicants.

If you make it through the CCNA and are still interested in Cisco and Data Center technologies, you're headed down a path to certain success.

What Prerequisites Are Required for CCNA Data Center?

None, zippo, nadda! No prior experience needed. Cisco created the Data Center path to stand on its own merits. This might explain to you why this book starts at the very beginning of networking and then moves into Nexus.

This first exam in the CCNA Data Center series is widely considered "CCENT on Nexus," and I have to agree here. Wouldn't it have just been better for Cisco to have the CCENT as a prerequisite and then have just one test on Nexus and UCS instead of putting entry-level networking technologies on this first exam? You bet it would! But please remember that I am the messenger here, trying to help you get your certifications, and Cisco does not inquire about my opinion on the certification process, although I think they should.

 I've known some people to get very frustrated with this first exam because it covers some basic network technologies and then finally gets into Nexus. Please remember that I am just laying down really good study material for you, and for the most part, I don't get to decide what technologies can or cannot go into the book! Please don't shoot the messenger.

How Do You Become CCNA Data Center Certified?

The way to become CCNA Data Center certified is to pass two written tests. Then—poof!—you're CCNA Data Center certified. (Don't you wish it was as easy as that sounds?)

Cisco has only a two-step process that you take to become CCNA Data Center certified—there is not a one-test version as there is for the CCNA Routing and Switching certification.

The two-test method involves passing the following exams:

- Exam 640-911: Introducing Cisco Data Center Networking (DCICN)
- Exam 640-916: Introducing Cisco Data Center Technologies (DCICT)

I can't stress this enough: it's critical that you have some hands-on experience with Cisco Nexus switches. I'll cover how to get hands-on experience with Nexus and UCS next.

> For Cisco Data Center hands-on training with certified expert Todd Lammle, please see www.lammle.com. Each student will get hands-on experience by configuring both Nexus and UCS technologies! In addition, this book includes a free Nexus switch simulator as part of the additional study tools, which you can find at either www.lammle.com or www.sybex.com/go/ccnadatacenternetworking.

Help! I Can't Afford Nexus and UCS Gear!

Unless you're related to Donald Trump, it is unlikely you can build your own data center to study for your CCNA, CCNP, or CCIE Data Center certifications. Gone are the days of having racks in your home office or spare bedroom to study for your certifications in your spare time. The Nexus and UCS equipment is extremely expensive, very large, and unbelievably heavy and will suck enough power and need enough cooling to bankrupt some people. So, what can you do to study for your Data Center certification?

I have the answer for you! When John Swartz and I sat down to start the outline for this book, we also drew out plans for a simple Nexus simulator to help you get through the hands-on labs in both of the CCNA Data Center books we are writing. This simulator isn't a fully functional piece of software that costs hundreds of dollars, but it is very cost effective (free is cost effective, right?) and the software does the job you need it to do. This software provides the hands-on experience you need to build the foundation for the CCNA Data Center exams. I know what you're thinking: what about studying for my CCNP Data Center certifications after I get my CCNA and what about more advanced features? Yes, we're planning those simulators as well, but they are not available as this book goes to press.

> The Nexus switch simulator is part of the additional study tools package for this book. You can find all the study tools at www.lammle.com or www.sybex.com/go/ccnadatacenternetworking.

But wait, there's more! Since I'm providing a Nexus simulator for you, what about the UCS? I've got you covered there as well! I created a new site to help you get started in your Data Center studies, and on this site you will find information on how to download Cisco's free UCS emulator:

http://ucsdatacenter.com/

This is a great emulator and can help get you through the CCNA Data Center certification process, but it's not enough technology for CCNP Data Center studies because you cannot load VMware on the blades. In addition, the website provides information on how to download and install the Nexus 1000v virtual switch, which John and I discuss in our next book in the series.

What Does This Book Cover?

This book covers everything you need to know to pass the CCNA Data Center 640-911 exam. However, taking the time to study and practice is the real key to success.

You will learn the following information in this book:

- Chapter 1, "Understanding Basic Networking," will provide an introduction to basic networking. Starting with what a network is, I'll discuss characteristics of a network and physical topologies. You may be tempted to skip this chapter, but be sure to at least review it and go through the written labs.

- Chapter 2, "Internetworking," introduces you to internetworking. You will learn the basics of the Open Systems Interconnection (OSI) model the way Cisco wants you to learn it. There are written labs and plenty of review questions to help you. Do not skip the fundamental written labs in this chapter!

- Chapter 3, "Ethernet Technologies," will dive into Ethernet networking and standards. Data encapsulation is discussed in detail in this chapter as well. There are written labs and plenty of review questions in this chapter to help you understand the objectives covered in this chapter.

- Chapter 4, "TCP/IP DoD Model," provides you with the background necessary for success on the exam as well as in the real world by discussing TCP/IP. As usual, the written lab and review questions cover the exam objectives.

- Chapter 5, "IP Addressing," is an in-depth chapter that covers the very beginnings of the Internet Protocol stack and then goes all the way to IP addressing and understanding the difference between a network address and a broadcast address. The written lab and review questions cover the exam objectives.

- Chapter 6, "Easy Subnetting," introduces you to subnetting. You will be able to subnet a network in your head after reading this chapter if you really want to. Plenty of help is found in this chapter if you do not skip the written labs and review questions.

Okay—the first six chapters of this book don't cover new technological information. It's likely that you may already have the knowledge covered in these chapters. However, they do cover about 40 percent of the objectives for the exam, which is more than enough to fail you if you don't have them nailed! If you're experienced in networking, then at least go through the review questions for each of the early chapters to refresh your knowledge.

- Chapter 7, "Introduction to Nexus," provides you with the background and an introduction to NX-OS as well as the various hardware used in a Nexus switched network. This is a great chapter, so don't forget to complete the written labs and review questions.

- Chapter 8, "Configuring Nexus," teaches you how to log in and configure NX-OS from the beginning. This is a fun chapter because you will begin to start getting hands-on experience! Hands-on labs, a written lab, and the review questions will help you understand NX-OS to the fullest.

- Chapter 9, "IP Routing," teaches you about IP routing. This is a fun chapter because we will begin to configure our network, add IP addresses, and see basic routing between routers. The written lab and the review questions will help you understand IP routing to the fullest.

- Chapter 10, "Routing Protocols," dives into dynamic routing with Routing Information Protocol (RIP), Enhanced IGRP, and OSPF routing. The hands-on labs, written lab, and review questions will help you master these routing protocols to the extent that the CCNA Data Center 640-911 objectives cover them.

- Chapter 11, "Layer 2 Switching Technologies," gives you background on layer 2 switching and how switches perform address learning and make forwarding and filtering decisions. Chapter 11 also covers Virtual LANs and how you can use them in your internetwork. It also covers the nitty-gritty of VLANs and the different concepts and protocols used with VLANs as well as troubleshooting. Don't skip the written labs, hands-on labs and review questions.

- Chapter 12, "Redundant Switched Technologies," will cover redundant links. We want redundant links, but the Spanning-Tree Protocol (STP) doesn't like them, so we need to understand STP and how to work with this protocol. Network loops and how to avoid them with STP will be discussed as well as the 802.1w RSTP and MSTP versions, and bundling redundant links with Cisco Port Channel. Go through the hands-on lab, written lab, and review questions to make sure you really understand these layer 2 switching technologies.

- Chapter 13, "Security," covers security and access lists, which are created on switches to filter the network. IP standard, extended, and named access lists are covered, but understand that NX-OS only allows configuration of named extended ACLs. Written hands-on labs, along with review questions, will help you study for the security and access-list portion of the CCNA Data Center 640-911 exam.

On the download link, www.sybex.com/go/ccnadatacenternetworking, you'll find the bonus exams, flash cards, and glossary, but also as an added bonus: the Nexus simulator! This free tool will allow you to run through the hands-on labs in this book!

How to Use This Book

If you want a solid foundation for the serious effort of preparing for the 640-911 exam, then look no further. I have spent hundreds of hours putting together this book with the intention of helping you to pass the CCNA exam as well as learning how to configure Nexus switches.

This book is loaded with valuable information, and you will get the most out of your studying time if you understand how it was put together.

To best benefit from this book, I recommend the following study method:

1. Take the assessment test immediately following this introduction. (The answers are at the end of the test.) It's okay if you don't know any of the answers; that's why you bought this book! Carefully read over the explanations for any question you get wrong

and note the chapters in which the material is covered. This information should help you plan your study strategy.

2. Study each chapter carefully, making sure you fully understand the information and the chapter objectives listed at the beginning of each one. Pay extra-close attention to any chapter that includes material covered in questions you missed.

3. Complete the written labs at the end of each chapter. Do *not* skip these written exercises because they directly relate to the CCNA Data Center 640-911 exam and what you must glean from the chapters in which they appear. It's important enough to say it again: do not just skim these labs! Make sure you understand completely the reason for each answer.

4. Complete all hands-on labs in the chapters that have them included, referring to the text of the chapter so that you understand the reason for each step you take. Try to get your hands on some real equipment, but if you don't have Cisco Nexus equipment available, be sure you get the Nexus simulator included with the study tools.

5. Answer all of the review questions related to each chapter. (The answers appear at the end of the chapters.) Note the questions that confuse you and study the topics they cover again. Do not just skim these questions! Make sure you understand completely the reason for each answer. Remember that these will not be the exact questions you find on the exam; they are written to help you understand the chapter material and build foundation.

6. Try your hand at the online practice exams. Also, check out www.lammle.com for more Cisco exam prep questions.

7. Test yourself using all the electronic flashcards. These are brand new and updated flashcard programs to help you prepare for the CCNA Data Center 640-911 exam. They are a great study tool!

To learn every bit of the material covered in this book, you'll have to apply yourself regularly, and with discipline. Try to set aside the same time period every day to study, and select a comfortable and quiet place to do so. If you work hard, you will be surprised at how quickly you learn this material.

If you follow these steps and really study—in addition to using the review questions, the practice exams, the electronic flashcards, and all the written labs, it would be hard to fail the CCNA Data Center exam. However, studying for the CCNA exam is like trying to get in shape—and if you do not go to the gym every day, you won't get in shape.

Additional Study Tools

I worked hard to provide some really great tools to help you with your certification process. All of the following tools should be loaded on your workstation when studying for the test.

Readers can get access to the following tools by visiting www.sybex.com/go/ccnadatacenternetworking.

The Sybex Test Preparation Software

The test preparation software prepares you to pass the CCNA Data Center 640-911 exam. In the test engine, you will find all the review and assessment questions from the book, plus two additional bonus practice exams that appear exclusively with this book.

Additional practice exam questions can be found at www.lammle.com.

Electronic Flashcards

The flashcards include over 50 questions specifically written to hit you hard and make sure you are ready for the exam. Between the review questions, bonus exams, and flashcards, you'll be more than prepared for the exam.

Glossary

The glossary is a handy resource for Cisco Data Center terms. This is a great tool for understanding some of the more obscure terms used in this book.

Nexus Simulator

You can use the Nexus simulator to do all of the hands-on labs included in this book.

Go to www.lammle.com to get additional labs and an upgrade to the simulator included with this book.

Where Do You Take the Exams?

You may take the CCNA Data Center 640-911 exam at any of the Pearson VUE authorized testing centers; visit www.vue.com or call 877-404-EXAM (3926).

To register for the exam, follow these steps:

1. Determine the number of the exam you want to take. (The CCNA Data Center exam number is 640-911.)

2. Register with the nearest Pearson VUE testing center. At this point, you will be asked to pay in advance for the exam. At the time of this writing, the exam is $250 and must be taken within one year of payment. You can schedule exams up to six weeks in advance or as late as the day you want to take it—but if you fail a Cisco exam, you must wait five days before you will be allowed to retake it. If something comes up and you need to cancel or reschedule your exam appointment, contact Pearson VUE at least 24 hours in advance.

3. When you schedule the exam, you'll get instructions regarding all appointment and cancellation procedures, the ID requirements, and information about the testing-center location.

Tips for Taking Your CCNA Exam

The CCNA Data Center 640-911 exam test contains 60 to 75 questions and must be completed in 90 minutes or less. This information can change per exam. You must get a score of about 82 percent to pass this exam, but again, each exam can be different.

Many questions on the exam have answer choices that at first glance look identical—especially the syntax questions! Remember to read through the choices carefully because close doesn't cut it. If you get commands in the wrong order or forget one measly character, you'll get the question wrong. So, to practice, do the hands-on exercises at the end of book's chapters over and over again until they feel natural to you.

Also, never forget that the right answer is the Cisco answer. In many cases, more than one appropriate answer is presented, but the *correct* answer is the one that Cisco recommends. On the exam, it always tells you to pick one, two, or three, never "choose all that apply." The CCNA Data Center 640-911 exam may include the following test formats:

- Multiple-choice single answer
- Multiple-choice multiple answer
- Drag-and-drop
- NX-OS simulations

Cisco-proctored exams will not show the steps to follow in completing a router interface configuration; however, they do allow partial command responses. For example, Switch#show running-config or Switch#sh run would be acceptable.

Here are some general tips for exam success:

- Arrive early at the exam center so you can relax and review your study materials.
- Read the questions *carefully*. Don't jump to conclusions. Make sure you're clear about *exactly* what each question asks. Read twice, answer once is what I always tell my students.
- When answering multiple-choice questions that you're not sure about, use the process of elimination to get rid of the obviously incorrect answers first. Doing this greatly improves your odds if you need to make an educated guess.
- You cannot move forward and backward through the Cisco exams, so double-check your answer before clicking Next since you can't change your mind.

After you complete an exam, you'll get immediate, online notification of your pass or fail status, a printed examination score report that indicates your pass or fail status, and your exam results by section. (The test administrator will give you the printed score report.) Test scores are automatically forwarded to Cisco within five working days after you take the test, so you don't need to send your score to them. If you pass the exam, you'll receive confirmation from Cisco, typically within two to four weeks, sometimes longer.

How to Contact the Authors

You can reach Todd Lammle and John Swartz through Todd's forum found
at www.lammle.com/forum.

CCNA Data Center 640-911 Exam Objectives

The objectives for the Data Center exams are a constant moving target. As of the time
of this writing, the objectives are being updated on www.cisco.com almost weekly. Please
always check Cisco's website for the latest, up-to-date information.

Here are the latest updated objectives as of this writing:

Domain 1.00: Describe How a Network Works (15%)

Exam Objective	Chapters
1.01 Describe the purpose and functions of various network devices	1, 2
(a) interpret a network diagram	1, 2, 3
(b) define physical network topologies	1, 2
1.02 Select the components required to meet a network specification	1, 2
(a) switches	1, 11, 12
1.03 Use the OSI and TCP/IP models and their associated protocols to explain how data flows in a network	4, 6
(a) IP	4, 5
(b) TCP	4
(c) UDP	4
1.04 Describe the purpose and basic operation of the protocols in the OSI and TCP models	4, 6
(a) TCP/IP	4, 5
(b) OSI Layers	2

Domain 2.00: Configure, Verify, and Troubleshoot a Switch with VLANs and Interswitch Communications Using Nexus (21%)

Exam Objective	Chapters
2.01 Explain the technology and media access control method for Ethernet networks	3
(a) IEEE 802 protocols	3
(b) CSMA/CD	3
2.02 Explain basic switching concepts and the operation of Cisco switches	3, 11
(a) Layer 2 addressing	2, 3, 11
(b) MAC table	11
(c) Flooding	11
2.03 Describe and Configure enhanced switching technologies	11
(a) VTP	11
(b) VLAN	11
(c) 802.1q	11, 12
(d) STP	12

Domain 3.00: Implement an IP Addressing Scheme and IP Services to Meet Network Requirements in a Medium-Size Enterprise Branch Office Network Using Nexus (12%)

Exam Objective	Chapters
3.01 Describe the operation and benefits of using private and public IP addressing	5, 6
(a) Classful IP addressing	5

Exam Objective	Chapters
(b) RFC 1918	5
(c) RFC 4193	5
3.02 Describe the difference between IPv4 and IPv6 addressing scheme	5, 6
(a) Comparative address space	5
(b) Host addressing	5

Domain 4.00: Configure, Verify, and Troubleshoot Basic Router Operation and Routing on Cisco Devices Using Nexus (52%)

Exam Objective	Chapters
4.01 Describe and Configure basic routing concepts	8, 9, 10, 11, 12
(a) packet forwarding, router lookup process (e.g., Exec mode, Exec commands, Configuration mode)	8, 9
(b) router lookup process (e.g., Exec mode, Exec commands, Configuration mode)	8, 9
4.02 Describe the operation of Cisco routers	7, 8, 9, 10, 11, 12, 13
(a) router bootup process	7, 8
(b) POST	7, 8
(c) router components	7, 8

Exam objectives are subject to change at any time without prior notice and at Cisco's sole discretion. Please visit Cisco's website (www.cisco.com) for the most current listing of exam objectives.

Assessment Test

1. LAN switching uses a physical and logical topology. Which physical topologies are typically used in today's Ethernet switched networks? (Choose two.)

   A. Bus

   B. Star

   C. Mesh

   D. Extended star

2. Each field in an IPv6 address is how many bits long?

   A. 4

   B. 16

   C. 32

   D. 128

3. Which two advanced spanning-tree protocols does the NX-OS support?

   A. CSTP

   B. RSTP

   C. MSTP

   D. STP

4. Which of the following is true regarding the purpose of flow control?

   A. To ensure that data is retransmitted if an acknowledgment is not received

   B. To reassemble segments in the correct order at the destination device

   C. To provide a means for the receiver to govern the amount of data sent by the sender

   D. To regulate the size of each segment

5. How long is an IPv6 address?

   A. 32 bits

   B. 128 bytes

   C. 64 bits

   D. 128 bits

6. Why is the DSAP field in an 802.3 frame important?

   A. The DSAP field is only used in Ethernet II frames.

   B. The DSAP field specifies the TCP or UDP port that is associated with the transport protocol.

   C. The DSAP field indicates the Network layer protocol so multiple routed protocols can be used.

   D. The DSAP field is only used by the DoD for classified networks.

7. The Internet Protocol (IP) stack has four layers compared to seven for the OSI model. Which layers of the OSI model are combined in the Internet Protocol suite Network Access layer? (Choose two.)

   A. 1

   B. 2

   C. 3

   D. 4

8. UDLD is used with Nexus at the Data Link layer. What does UDLD stand for?

   A. Unified Direct Link Distribution

   B. Unified Data Link Distribution

   C. Unified Direct Link Deployment

   D. UniDirectional Link Detection

9. What will happen if an RFC 1918 assigned address is configured on a public interface that connects to an ISP?

   A. Addresses in a private range will be not routed on the Internet backbone.

   B. Only the ISP router will have the capability to access the public network.

   C. The NAT process will be used to translate this address in a valid IP address.

   D. Several automated methods will be necessary on the private network.

   E. A conflict of IP addresses happens, because other public routers can use the same range.

10. You want to configure your Nexus 7010 so that logically the switch is running three separate NX-OS instances. What is the best way to accomplish this?

   A. VRF

   B. VDC

   C. Storage-operator role

   D. VSANs and VLANs

11. On a Nexus 5010, what type of connector could you use to connect to an Ethernet network? (Choose two.)

 A. SFP

 B. TwinAx

 C. GBIC

 D. GBIC type 2

12. What is the maximum number of IP addresses that can be assigned to hosts on a local subnet that uses a /27 subnet mask?

 A. 14

 B. 15

 C. 16

 D. 30

 E. 31

 F. 62

13. What do the L1 and L2 physical ports provide on a Nexus 5000 series switch?

 A. Database synchronization

 B. Heartbeat

 C. Layer 1 and layer 2 connectivity

 D. Nothing

14. On a new Cisco Nexus switch, you receive an error message when you attempt to create a switch virtual interface (SVI). What is the first command you must use to create the SVI?

 A. `interface vlan (vlanid)`

 B. `vlan (vlanid)`

 C. `feature interface-vlan`

 D. `interface routed`

15. If you wanted to delete the configuration stored in NVRAM, what would you type?

 A. `erase startup`

 B. `erase nvram`

 C. `write erase boot`

 D. `erase running`

16. You want to define a port as a layer 3 port on a Nexus OS. What is the command?

    A. `port routed`

    B. `no switchport`

    C. `switchport`

    D. `port switching`

17. A route update packet is considered invalid with the RIP protocol at what hop count?

    A. Unlimited

    B. 0

    C. 15

    D. 16

    E. 31

    F. 32

18. New VLANs have just been configured on a Nexus switch; however, a directly connected switch is not receiving the VLAN via a summary update. What reasons could cause this problem? (Choose two.)

    A. The VTP passwords are set incorrectly.

    B. The VTP feature has not been enabled.

    C. The VTP domain names do not match.

    D. VTP is not supported on Nexus switches.

19. RSTP is a great protocol if you are not using Port Channel. Which of the following is true regarding RSTP? (Choose three.)

    A. RSTP speeds the recalculation of the spanning tree when the Layer 2 network topology changes.

    B. RSTP is an IEEE standard that redefines STP port roles, states, and BPDUs.

    C. RSTP is extremely proactive and very quick, and therefore it absolutely needs the 802.1 delay timers.

    D. RSTP (802.1w) supersedes 802.1 while remaining proprietary.

    E. All of the 802.1d terminology and most parameters have been changed.

    F. 802.1w is capable of reverting to 802.1 to interoperate with traditional switches on a per-port basis.

20. Which commands would you use to configure an ACL on a Cisco Nexus switch to deny unencrypted web traffic from any source to destination host 10.10.1.110? (Choose two.)

    A. `ip access-list 101, deny tcp any host 10.10.1.110 eq 80`

    B. `ip access-list 101, deny ip any host 10.10.1.110 eq 80`

    C. `permit tcp any any`

    D. `permit ip any any`

Answers to Assessment Test

1. B, D. Physical star and physical extended star are the most popular physical LAN networks today. See Chapter 1 for more information.

2. B. Each field in an IPv6 address is 16 bits long. An IPv6 address is a total of 128 bits. See Chapter 5 for more information.

3. B, C. The NX-OS allows you to configure only the RSTP and MSTP protocols. See Chapter 12 for more information.

4. C. Flow control allows the receiving device to control the transmitter so the receiving device's buffer does not overflow. See Chapter 2 for more information.

5. D. An IPv6 address is 128 bits long, whereas an IPv4 address is only 32 bits long. See Chapter 5 for more information.

6. C. The old Source and Destination Service Access Point fields in a SNAP frame defined the Network Layer protocol that the packet uses. See Chapter 3 for more information.

7. A, B. The OSI Data Link layer (layer 2) and the OSI Physical layer (layer 1) are combined into the Network Access layer of the Internet Protocol suite. See Chapter 4 for more information.

8. D. UniDirectional Link Detection (UDLD) is a Data Link layer protocol used to monitor the physical configuration of the cables and detect when communication is occurring in only one direction. See Chapter 7 for more information.

9. A. Private addresses from RFC 1918 cannot be placed on an interface going to the public Internet. You must configure NAT to translate. See Chapter 5 for more information.

10. B. Virtual device contexts (VDCs) can logically separate a switch into two administrative domains. In this case, one VDC would be assigned all of the Ethernet ports and the other VDC would be assigned all of the storage ports. See Chapter 7 for more information.

11. A, B. Small form-factor pluggable (SPF) modules give you flexibility in selecting what type of cable that you want to use. TwinAx is a copper cable with SFPs embedded in the end and is cost effective. See Chapter 7 for more information.

12. D. A /27 (255.255.255.224) is 3 bits on and 5 bits off. This provides 8 subnets, each with 30 hosts. Does it matter if this mask is used with a Class A, B, or C network address? Not at all. The number of host bits would never change. See Chapter 6 for more information.

13. D. L1 and L2 are not implemented on the Nexus 5010, but they are used on the Fabric Interconnects. See Chapter 7 for more information.

14. C. The feature command turns on a service and enables the commands for that feature. Command will not be visible until enabled. See Chapter 8 for more information.

15. C. The command write erase boot deletes the configuration stored in NVRAM and sets the system back to factory default. See Chapter 8 for more information.

16. B. The switchport command is used to switch between a port being used for layer 2 and layer 3. See Chapter 8 for more information.

17. D. The maximum hop count a route update packet can traverse before considering the route invalid is 15, so 16 hops is invalid for both RIPv1 and RIPv2. See Chapter 10 for more information.

18. A, C. To troubleshoot VTP, you first need to verify that the domain names match, and that they are case sensitive as well. You should also check that the server has a higher revision number than the client or the client won't update the database. Also, if the passwords are set and do not match, the client will reject the update. See Chapter 11 for more information.

19. A, B, F. RSTP helps with convergence issues that plague traditional STP. Rapid PVST+ is based on the 802.1w standard in the same way that PVST+ is based on 802.1. See Chapter 12 for more information.

20. A, D. In solving this business requirement, you first need to create a deny statement from any source to destination host 10.10.1.110 using HTTP with destination port 80. The second line permits all other traffic. See Chapter 13 for more information.

Chapter

1

Understanding Basic Networking

THE FOLLOWING TOPICS ARE COVERED IN THIS CHAPTER:

✓ **Understanding the Functions of Networking**

- What Is a Network?
- Common Physical Components of a Network
- Interpreting a Network Diagram
- Resource-Sharing Functions and Benefits
- Network User Applications
- Impact of User Applications on the Network
- Characteristics of a Network
- Physical Topologies
- Connection to the Internet

You'd have to work pretty hard these days to find someone who would argue that our computers have not become invaluable to us personally and professionally. Our society has become highly dependent on these resources and on sharing them. The ability to communicate with those we need to—whether they're in the same building or in some faraway land—completely hinges on our capacity to create and maintain solid, dependable networks.

And those vitally important networks come in all shapes and sizes—ranging from small and simple to humongous and super complicated. But whatever their flavor, they all need to be maintained properly, and to do that well, you've got to understand networking basics. The various types of devices and technologies that are used to create networks, as well as how they work together, is what this book is about, and I'll go through this critical information one step at a time with you. Understanding all of this will not only equip you with a rock-solid base to build on as you grow in your IT knowledge and career, it will also arm you with what you'll need to move on through this book.

To find up-to-the-minute updates for this chapter, please see www.lammle .com/forum. Also, you may be tempted to skip this chapter, but I advise not to do this. When was the last time you discussed the difference between logical and physical topologies? Remember, this Cisco exam starts from the very beginning of networking, so you must be prepared for anything!

First Things First: What's a Network?

The dictionary defines the word *network* as "a group or system of interconnected people or things." Similarly, in the computer world, the term *network* means two or more connected computers that can share resources like data and applications, office machines, an Internet connection, or some combination of these, as shown in Figure 1.1.

FIGURE 1.1 A basic network

Host   Host   Printer

Okay—Figure 1.1 shows a really basic network made up of only two host computers connected together; they share resources like files and even a printer hooked up to one of the hosts. These two hosts "talk" to each other using a computer language called *binary code*, which consists of lots of 1s and 0s in a specific order that describes exactly what they want to "say."

Next, I'm going to tell you about local area networks (LANs), how they work, and even how we can connect LANs. Then, later in this chapter, I'll describe how to connect remote LANs through something known as a wide area network (WAN).

The Local Area Network (LAN)

Just as the name implies, a *local area network (LAN)* is usually restricted to spanning a particular geographic location like an office building, a single department within a corporate office, or even a home office.

Back in the day, you couldn't put more than 30 workstations on a LAN, and you had to cope with strict limitations on how far those machines could actually be from each other. Because of technological advances, all that's changed now, and we're not nearly as restricted in regard to both a LAN's size and the distance a LAN can span. Even so, it's still best to split a big LAN into smaller logical zones known as *workgroups* to make administration easier.

In a typical business environment, it's a good idea to arrange your LAN's workgroups along department divisions; for instance, you would create a workgroup for Accounting, another one for Sales, and maybe another for Marketing—you get the idea. Figure 1.2 shows two separate LANs, each as its own workgroup.

FIGURE 1.2   A small LAN with two separate LANs (workgroups)

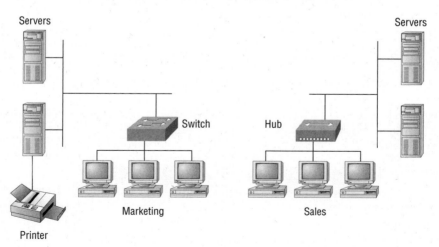

First, don't stress about the devices labeled *hub* and *switch*—these are just connectivity devices that allow hosts to physically connect to resources on a LAN. Trust me; I'll describe them to you in much more detail later in Chapter 2, "Internetworking."

Anyway, back to the figure... Notice that there's a Marketing workgroup and a Sales workgroup. These are LANs in their most basic form. Any device that connects to the Marketing LAN can access the resources of the Marketing LAN—in this case, the servers and printer. If you want to access resources from the Sales LAN, you must connect directly to the Sales LAN.

There are two problems with this:

- You must be physically connected to each LAN to get the resources from that specific workgroup's LAN.

- You can't get from one LAN to the other LAN and use its server data and printing resources remotely.

This is a typical network issue that's easily resolved by using a cool device called a router to connect the two LANs, as shown in Figure 1.3.

FIGURE 1.3   A router connects LANs.

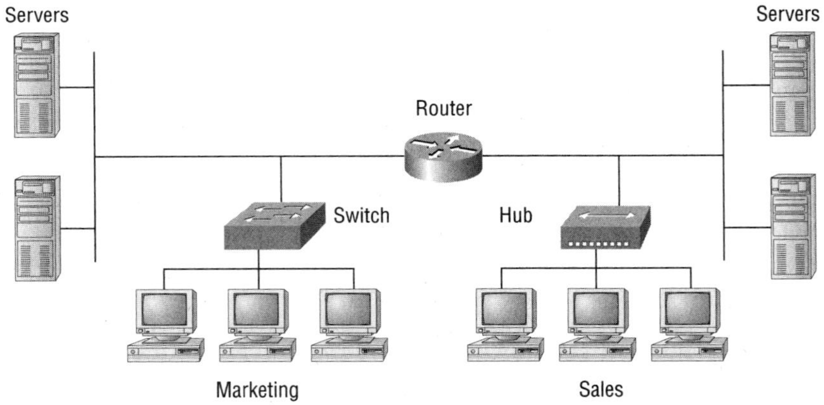

Nice—problem solved! Even though you can use routers for more than just connecting LANs, the router shown in Figure 1.3 is a great solution because the host computers from the Sales LAN can get to the resources (server data and printers) of the Marketing LAN and vice versa.

Now, you might be thinking that we really don't need the router—that we could just physically connect the two workgroups together with a type of cable that would allow the Marketing and Sales workgroups to hook up somehow. True—we could do that, but if we did, we would have only one big, cumbersome workgroup instead of separate workgroups for Marketing and Sales. And that kind of arrangement isn't practical for today's networks.

This is because with smaller, individual yet connected groups, the users on each LAN enjoy much faster response times when accessing resources, and administrative tasks are a lot easier, too. Larger workgroups run more slowly because in them, a legion of hosts are all trying to get to the same resources simultaneously. So the router shown in Figure 1.3, which separates the workgroups while still allowing access between them, is a really great solution after all.

So now, let me define those other terms I've used so far: *workstations*, *servers*, and *hosts*.

Common Network Components

There are a lot of different machines, devices, and media that make up our networks. Right now, I'm going to tell you about three of the most common:

- Workstations
- Servers
- Hosts

Workstations

Workstations are often seriously powerful computers that run more than one central processing unit (CPU) and whose resources are available to other users on the network to access when needed. Don't confuse workstations with client machines, which can be workstations but aren't always. A *client machine* is any device on the network that can ask for access to resources from a workstation—for instance, a printer.

 The terms *workstation* and *host* are used interchangeably because computers have become more and more powerful and the terms have become somewhat fuzzy. The term *host* is used to describe pretty much anything that takes an IP address.

Servers

Servers are also powerful computers. They get their name because they truly are "at the service" of the network and run specialized software for the network's maintenance and control known as the *network operating system.*

In a good design that optimizes the network's performance, servers are highly specialized and are there to handle one important labor-intensive job. This is not to say that a single server can't do many jobs, but more often than not, you'll get better performance if you dedicate a server to a single task. Here's a list of common dedicated servers:

File server   Stores and dispenses files.

Mail server   The network's post office, which handles e-mail functions.

Print server   Manages all printers on the network.

Web server   Manages web-based activities by running Hypertext Transfer Protocol (HTTP) for storing web content and accessing web pages.

Fax server   The "memo maker" that sends and receives paperless faxes over the network.

Application server   Manages network applications.

Telephony server   Handles the call center and call routing and can be thought of as a sophisticated network answering machine.

Remote-access server   Provides remote users with access to the network through modems or an IP connection or wirelessly.

Proxy server   Handles tasks in the place of other machines on the network.

 Now, the idea of Cisco Unified Communication System (UCS) is to virtualize these servers so multiple server applications can run on one powerful machine. You'll see a lot more of this in my upcoming books!

Okay, as I was saying, and at this point in the book, you can think of servers as usually being dedicated to doing one specific important thing within the network. But notice that I said usually—sometimes they have more than one job. But whether servers are designated for one job or are network multi-taskers, they all maintain the network's data integrity by backing up the network's software and hardware. And no matter what, they all serve a number of client machines.

Back in Figure 1.2, I showed you an example of two really simple LAN networks. I want to make sure you know that servers must have considerably superior hard-drive space—a lot more than a simple workstation's capacity—because they serve many client machines and provide any resources they require. Because they're so important, you should always put your servers in a very secure area. My company's servers are in a locked server room because not only are they really pricey workhorses, they also store huge amounts of important and sensitive company data, so they need to be kept safe from any unauthorized access.

In Figure 1.4, you can see a network populated with both workstations and servers. You also see that the hosts can access the servers across the network—pretty much the general idea of having a network.

You probably noticed that there are more workstations here than servers, right? Think of why that is... If you answered that it's because one server can provide resources to what can sometimes be a huge number of individual users at the same time but workstations don't, you've got it!

Hosts

It can be kind of confusing because when people refer to hosts, they really can be referring to almost any type of networking devices—including workstations and servers. But if you dig a bit deeper, you'll find that usually this term comes up when people are talking about resources and jobs that have to do with Transmission Control Protocol/Internet Protocol

(TCP/IP). The scope of possible machines and devices is so broad because, in TCP/IP-speak, a *host* is any network device with an IP address. Yes, you'll hear IT professionals throw this term around pretty loosely, but for the Cisco exams, stick to the definition being network devices, including workstations and servers, with IP addresses.

FIGURE 1.4   A network populated with servers and workstations

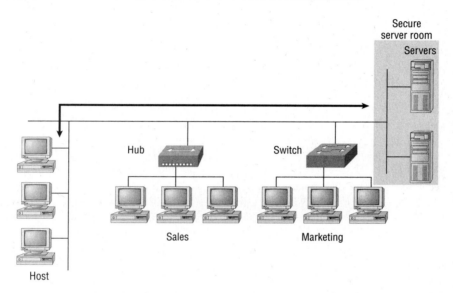

Here's a bit of background: the name *host* harkens back to the Jurassic period of networking when those dinosaurs known as *mainframes* were the only intelligent devices to roam the network. These were called *hosts* whether they had TCP/IP functionality or not. In that bygone age, everything else in the network-scape was referred to as *dumb terminals* because only mainframes—hosts—were given IP addresses. Another fossilized term from way back then is *gateways* when used to refer to any layer 3 machines like routers. We still use these terms today, but they've evolved a bit to refer to the many intelligent devices populating our present-day networks, each of which has an IP address. This is exactly the reason why you hear *host* used so broadly.

Wide Area Network (WAN)

There are legions of people who, if asked to define a *wide area network (WAN)*, couldn't do it. Yet most of them use the Big Dog of all WANs—the Internet—every day! With that in mind, you can imagine that WAN networks are what we use to span large geographic areas and truly go the distance. Like the Internet, WANs usually employ both routers and public links, so that's generally the criteria used to define them.

WANs are covered in more depth in my book, *CCNA: Cisco Certified Network Associate Study Guide, 7th edition* (Sybex, 2011).

Here's a list of some of the important ways that WANs are different from LANs:

- They usually need a router port or ports.
- They span larger geographic areas and/or can link disparate locations.
- They're usually slower.
- We can choose when and how long we connect to a WAN. A LAN is all or nothing—our workstation is either connected permanently to it or not at all, although most of us have dedicated WAN links now.
- WANs can utilize either private or public data transport media like phone lines.

We get the word *Internet* from the term *internetwork*. An internetwork is a type of WAN that connects of a bunch of networks, or *intranets*. In an internetwork, hosts still use hardware addresses to communicate with other hosts on the LAN. However, in an internetwork, hosts use logical addresses (IP addresses) to communicate with hosts on a different LAN (other side of the router).

And *routers* are the devices that make this possible. Each connection into a router is a different logical network. Figure 1.5 demonstrates how routers are employed to create an internetwork and enable our LANs to access WAN resources.

FIGURE 1.5   An internetwork

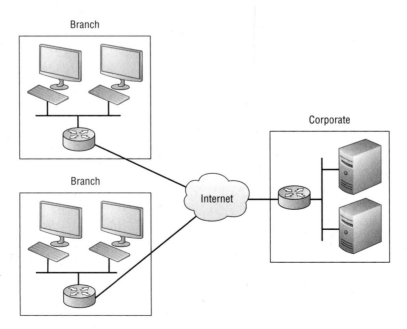

The Internet is a prime example of what's known as a *distributed WAN*—an internetwork that's made up of a lot of interconnected computers located in a lot of different places. There's another kind of WAN, referred to as *centralized*, that's composed of a main, centrally located computer or location that remote computers and devices can connect to. A good example is remote offices that connect to a main corporate office as shown in Figure 1.5.

Network Architecture: Peer-to-Peer or Client/Server?

So, we've developed networking as a way to share resources and information, and how that's achieved directly maps to the particular architecture of the network operating system software. There are two main network types you need to know about: peer-to-peer and client/server. And by the way, it's really tough to tell the difference just by looking at a diagram or even by checking out live video of the network humming along, but the differences between peer-to-peer and client/server architectures are major. They're not just physical; they're logical differences. You'll see what I mean in a bit.

Peer-to-Peer Networks

Computers connected in *peer-to-peer networks* do not have any central, or special authority—they're all *peers*, meaning that when it comes to authority, they're all equals. This means it's up to the computer that has the resource being requested to perform a security check for access rights to its resources.

It also means that the computers existing in a peer-to-peer network can be client machines that access resources and server machines that provide them to other computers. This works really well if there's not a huge number of users on the network, each user handles backing things up locally, and your network doesn't require a lot of security.

If your network is running Windows, Mac, or Unix in a local LAN workgroup, you have a peer-to-peer network. Figure 1.6 gives you a snapshot of a typical peer-to-peer network. Peer-to-peer networks present some challenges. For example, backing up company data becomes an iffy proposition.

It should be clear by now that peer-to-peer networks are not all sunshine—backing up all that super-important data is not only vital, it can be really challenging. What if you forget where you put a badly needed file (haven't we all done that)? And then there's that security issue to tangle with. Because security is not centrally governed, each and every user has to remember and maintain a list of users and passwords on each and every machine. Worse, some of those all-important passwords for the same users change on different machines—even for accessing different resources. Yikes!

Client/Server Networks

Client/server networks are pretty much the polar opposite of peer-to-peer networks because in them, a single server is specified that uses a network operating system for managing the whole network. So instead of the request going directly to the machine with the desired resource, a client machine's request for a resource goes to the main server, which responds by handling security and directing the client to the resource it wants.

FIGURE 1.6   A peer-to-peer network

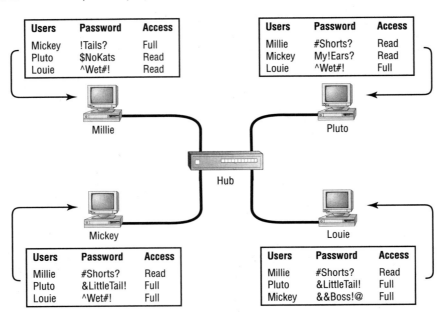

This arrangement definitely has its benefits. First, because the network is much better organized and doesn't depend on users remembering where needed resources are, it's a whole lot easier to find the files you need because everything is stored in one spot on that special server. Your security also gets a lot tighter because all usernames and passwords are on that server (which, by the way, isn't ever used as a workstation). You even gain scalability—client/server networks can have legions of workstations on them. And even with all those demands, their performance is actually optimized.

Check out Figure 1.7. Looking at it, you see a client/server network with a server that has a database of access rights, user accounts, and passwords.

FIGURE 1.7   A client/server network

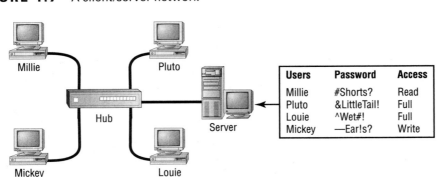

Many of today's networks are a healthy (we hope) combination of the peer-to-peer and client/server architectures with carefully specified servers that permit the simultaneous sharing of resources from devices running workstation operating systems. Even though the supporting machines can't handle as many inbound connections at a time, they still run the server service reasonably well. If this type of mixed environment is designed well, most networks benefit greatly by having the capacity to take advantage of the positive aspects of both worlds.

Physical Network Topologies

Just as a topographical map shows the shape of the terrain, the *physical topology* of a network is also a type of map. It defines the specific characteristics of a network, such as where all the workstations and other devices are located and the precise arrangement of all the physical media like cables. And though these two topologies are usually a lot alike, a particular network can have physical and logical topologies that are very different. But basically, what you want to remember is that a network's physical topology essentially gives you the lay of the land, and the logical topology shows how data navigates through that layout.

Here is a list of the various topologies you're most likely to run into these days:

- Bus
- Star
- Ring
- Mesh
- Point-to-point
- Point-to-multipoint
- Hybrid

Bus Topology

This type of topology is the most basic one of the bunch, and it really does sort of resemble a bus. (Well, okay—actually, it looks more like a bus that's been in a pretty nasty wreck!) Anyway, the *bus topology* consists of two distinct and terminated ends, with each of its computers connecting to one unbroken cable running its entire length. Back in the day, we used to attach computers to that main cable with wiretaps, but this didn't work all that well so we began using drop cables in their place (unless you're dealing with 10Base2 Ethernet, in which case you would slip a "T connector" into the main cable anywhere you wanted to connect a device to it instead of using drop cables).

Figure 1.8 depicts what a typical bus network's physical topology looks like.

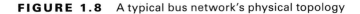

FIGURE 1.8   A typical bus network's physical topology

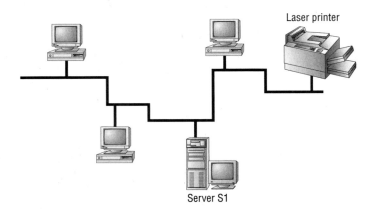

Even though all the computers on this kind of network see all the data flowing through the cable, only the one computer that the data is specifically addressed to actually gets it. Some of the benefits of using a bus topology are that it's easy to install and it's not very expensive, in part because it doesn't require as much cable as the other types of physical topologies. But it also has some drawbacks: for instance, it's hard to troubleshoot, change, or move, and it really doesn't offer much in the way of fault tolerance because everything is connected to that single cable.

The LAN that used a bus topology was replaced with twisted-pair wiring and called 10BaseT Ethernet, and advanced flavors of it are still in use today. 10Base2 and 10BaseT were also referred to as classic "CSMA/CD half-duplex Ethernet," which will be explained in Chapter 3, "Ethernet Technologies."

By the way, *fault tolerance* is the capability of a computer or a network system to respond to a condition automatically, often resolving it, which reduces the impact on the system. If fault-tolerance measures have been implemented correctly on a network, it's highly unlikely that any of that network's users will know that a problem even existed.

Star and Extended-Star Topology

A *star topology's* computers are connected to a central point with their own individual cables or wireless connections. You'll often find that central spot inhabited by a device like a hub, a switch, or an access point.

Star topology offers a lot of advantages over bus topology, making it more widely used even though it obviously requires more physical media. One of its best features is that because each computer or network segment is connected to the central device individually, if the cable fails, it brings down only that particular machine or network segment. That's truly a great benefit because it makes the network much more fault tolerant as well as a lot easier to troubleshoot. Another great thing about a star topology is that it's a lot more scalable—all you have to do if you want to add to it is run a new cable and connect to the machine at the core of the star. In Figure 1.9, you'll find a great example of a typical star topology.

FIGURE 1.9 Typical star topology with a hub

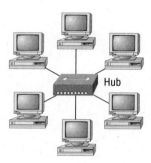

Okay, although it is called *star* topology, it really looks a lot more like the imaginary pictures people draw of the sun. (Yes, the sun is a star—but it definitely doesn't look like how we usually depict it, does it?) You could also get away with saying it looks like a bike wheel with spokes connecting to the hub in the middle of the wheel and extending outward to connect to the rim. And just as with that bike wheel, it's the hub device at the center of a star topology network that can give you the most grief if something goes wrong with it. If that hub in the middle of it all happens to fail, down comes the whole network, so it's a very good thing hubs don't fail often!

Just as it is with pretty much everything, a star topology has its pros and cons. But the good news far outweighs the bad, which is why people are choosing to go with a star topology more and more. Here's a list of benefits gained by opting for a star topology:

- New stations can be added easily and quickly.
- A single cable failure won't bring down the entire network.
- It is relatively easy to troubleshoot.

The star topology has the following disadvantages:

- The total installation cost can be higher because of the larger number of cables (but prices are constantly becoming more competitive).
- It has a single point of failure (the hub or other central device).

There are two more sophisticated implementations of star topology. The first is called *point-to-point link*, where you have not only the device in the center of the spoke acting as a hub but also the one on the other end. This is still an *extended-star* topology, but as I'm sure you can imagine, it gives you a huge amount of scalability!

Another refined version is the wireless flavor, but to understand this version well, you've really got to have a solid grasp of the capabilities and features of all the devices populating the wireless star topology. For now, it's good enough for you to know that access points are pretty much just wireless hubs or switches that behave like their wired counterparts.

Star and extended-star network topologies are the most popular topologies used with switches. Switches are covered in Chapter 2.

Ring Topology

In this type of topology, you'll find that each computer is directly connected to other computers within the same network. Looking at Figure 1.10, you can see that the network's data flows from computer to computer back to the source, with the network's primary cable forming a ring. The problem is, the *ring topology* has a lot in common with the bus topology because if you want to add to the network, you have no choice but to break the cable ring—something that is probably going to bring down the entire network.

FIGURE 1.10   A typical ring topology

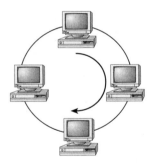

This is one big reason this topology isn't all that popular—you just won't run into it a lot as I did in the 1980s and early 1990s. A few more reasons include the fact that it's pricey because you need several cables to connect each computer; it's really hard to reconfigure; and as you've probably guessed, it's not fault tolerant.

However, with all that being said, if you work at an ISP, you may find a physical ring topology in use for a technology called SONET or possibly some other WAN technology. You just won't find any LANs in physical rings anymore.

The LANs that were used in the 1980s and early 1990s with ring topologies were Token Ring and Fiber Distributed Data Interface (FDDI). These LAN technologies no longer exist but are mentioned in the Data Center CCNA exam objectives.

Mesh Topology

In this type of topology, you'll find that there's a path from every machine to every other one in the network. That's a lot of connections—in fact, the *mesh topology* wins the prize for "most physical connections per device"! You won't find it used in LANs very often (if ever) these days, but you will find a modified version of it known as *hybrid mesh* used in a restrained manner on WANs, including the Internet.

Often, hybrid mesh topology networks will have quite a few connections between certain places to create redundancy (backup). And other types of topologies can sometimes be found in the mix too, which is also why it's dubbed *hybrid*. At any rate, it isn't a full-on full mesh topology if there isn't a connection between all devices in the network. But it's still respectably complicated—Figure 1.11 shows just how much only four connections can complicate things.

FIGURE 1.11   A typical mesh topology

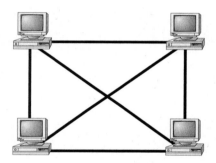

As shown in the figure, things just get more and more complex as both the wiring and the connections multiply. For each *n* location or host, you end up with $n(n-1)/2$ connections. This means that in a network consisting of only 4 computers, you have $4(4-1)/2$, or 6 connections. And if that little network grows to, say, a population of 10 computers, you'll have a whopping 45 connections to cope with—yikes! That's a huge amount of overhead, so only small networks can really use this topology and manage it well. On the bright side, you get a very respectable level of fault tolerance. But it is nice that we don't use these in corporate LANs any longer, because they were very complicated to manage.

A full mesh physical topology has the absolute least likelihood of having a collision.

This is the reason you will usually find the hybrid version in today's WANs. In fact, the mesh topology is actually pretty rare these days. It's mainly used because of the robust fault tolerance it offers—because you've got a multitude of connections, if one goes on the blink, computers and other network devices can simply switch to one of the many redundant connections that are up and running. But as you can imagine, all that cabling the mesh topology requires makes it really costly. Plus, you can make your network management much less insane by using what's known as a *partial mesh topology* solution instead, so why not go that way? You may lose a little fault tolerance, but if you go the partial-mesh route, you still get to use the same technology between all the network's devices. Just remember that with partial mesh, not all devices will be interconnected, so it's very important to choose wisely the ones that are.

Point-to-Point Topology

As its name implies, in a *point-to-point* topology you have a direct connection between two routers, giving you one communication path. The routers in a point-to-point topology can either be linked by a serial cable, making it a physical network, or be far apart and only connected by a circuit within a typical WAN network, making it a logical network.

Figure 1.12 gives you a prime specimen of a T1, or WAN point-to-point connection.

FIGURE 1.12   Three point-to-point connections

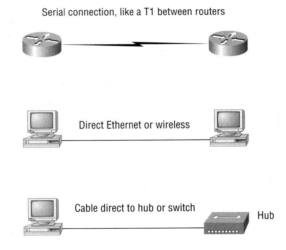

Serial connection, like a T1 between routers

Direct Ethernet or wireless

Cable direct to hub or switch   Hub

What you see here is a lightning bolt and a couple of round things with a bunch of arrows projecting from them, right? Well, the two round things radiating arrows represent our network's two routers, and that lightning bolt represents a WAN link. (These symbols are industry standard and I'll be using them throughout this book, so it would a good idea to get used to them.)

Part two of the diagram shows two computers connected by a cable—a point-to-point link. By the way, this should remind you of something we just went over... remember our talk about peer-to-peer networks? Good! I hope you also happen to remember that a big drawback related to peer-to-peer network sharing is that it is not very scalable. With this in mind, you probably won't be all that surprised that even if both machines have a wireless point-to-point connection, the network won't be very scalable.

You'll usually find point-to-point networks within many of today's WANs, and as you can see in part three of Figure 1.12, a link from a computer to a hub or switch is also a valid point-to-point connection. A common version of this setup consists of a direct wireless link between two wireless bridges that's used to connect computers in two different buildings.

Point-to-Multipoint Topology

Again as the name suggests, a *point-to-multipoint* topology consists of a succession of connections between an interface on one router to multiple destination routers—one point of connection to multiple points of connection. Each of the routers and every one of their interfaces involved in the point-to-multipoint connection are part of the same network.

Figure 1.13 shows a WAN to best demonstrate a point-to-multipoint network that depicts a single corporate router connecting to multiple branches.

FIGURE 1.13   A point-to-multipoint network, example 1

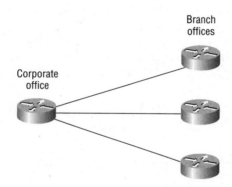

Figure 1.14 shows another prime example of a point-to-multipoint network: a college or corporate campus.

FIGURE 1.14   A point-to-multipoint network, example 2

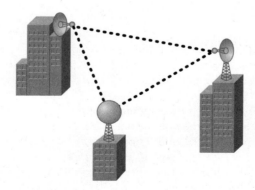

Hybrid Topology

I know I talked about hybrid network topology back in the section about mesh topology, but I didn't give you a picture of it in the form of a figure. I also want to point out that *hybrid topology* means just that—a combination of two or more types of physical or logical network topologies working together within the same network.

Figure 1.15 depicts a simple hybrid network topology. Here you see a LAN switch or hub in a star topology configuration that connects to its hosts via bus topology.

 Real World Scenario

They're Just Cables, Right?

Wrong! Regardless of the type of network you build, you need to start thinking about quality at the bottom and work up.

Think of it as if you were at an electronics store buying the cables for your sweet new home theater system. You've already spent a bunch of time and money getting the right components to meet your needs. In fact, you've probably parted with a respectable chunk of change, so why would you stop there and connect all these great devices with the cable equivalent of twine? No, you're smarter than that. You know that picking out the exact cables that will maximize the sound and picture quality of your specific components can also protect them.

It's the same thing when you're faced with selecting the physical media for a certain network (such as your new client/server network)—you just don't want to cut corners here. Because it's the backbone of the network, you absolutely don't want to be faced with having to dig up everything that's already been installed after the fact. Doing this costs a lot more than taking the time to wisely choose the right cables and spending the money it takes to get them in the first place. The network downtime alone can cost a company a bundle (pun intended). Another reason for choosing the network's physical media correctly is that it's going to be there for a good 5 to 10 years. This means two things: it better be solid quality, and it better be scalable because that network is going to grow and change over the years.

FIGURE 1.15   A simple hybrid network

Hub

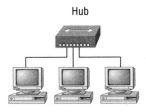

Physical star, Logical bus

Topology Selection, Backbones, and Segments

Okay—now that you're familiar with many different types of network topologies, you're ready for some tips on selecting the right one for your particular network. You also need to know about backbones and segments—the very last part of this chapter.

Selecting the Right Topology

As you now know, not only do you have a buffet of network topologies to choose from, but each one also has pros and cons to implementing it. But it really comes down to that well-known adage, "Ask the right questions." First, how much cash do you have? And how much fault tolerance do you really need? Also, is this network likely to grow like a weed—is it probably going to need to be quickly and easily reconfigured often? In other words, how scalable does your network need to be?

For instance, if your challenge is to design a nice, cost-effective solution that only involves a few computers in a room, getting a wireless access point and some wireless network cards is definitely your best way to go because you won't need to pony up for a bunch of cabling and it's super simple to set up. Alternately, if you're faced with coming up with a solid design for a growing company's already-large network, you're probably good to go using a wired star topology because it will nicely allow for future changes. Remember, a star topology really shines when it comes to making additions to the network, moving things around, and making any kind of changes happen quickly, efficiently, and cost effectively.

If, say, you're hired to design a network for an ISP that needs to be up and running 99.9 percent of the time with no more than eight hours a year allowed downtime, well, you need Godzilla-strength fault tolerance. Do you remember which topology gives that up the best? (Hint—Internet.) Your primo solution is to go with either a hybrid or a partial-mesh topology. Remember that partial mesh leaves you with a subset of $n(n-1)/2$ connections to maintain—a number that could very well blow a big hole in your maintenance budget!

Here's a list of things to keep in mind when you're faced with coming up with the right topology for the right network:

- Cost
- Ease of installation
- Ease of maintenance
- Fault-tolerance requirement

The Network Backbone

Today's networks can get pretty complicated, so we've got to have a standard way of communicating with each other intelligibly about exactly which part of the network we're referring to. This is the reason we divide networks into different parts called *backbones* and *segments*.

Figure 1.16 illustrates a network and shows which part is the backbone and which parts are segments.

FIGURE 1.16   Backbone and segments on a network

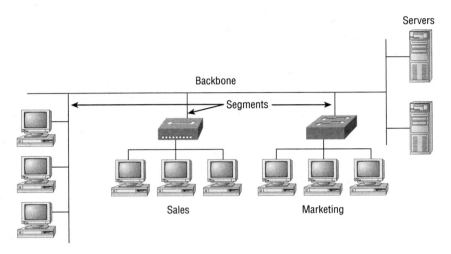

You can see that the network backbone is actually kind of like our own. It's what all the networks segments and servers connect to and what gives the network its structure. As you can imagine, being such an important nerve center, the backbone must use some kind of seriously fast, robust technology—often that's Gigabit Ethernet. And to optimize network performance (that is, speed and efficiency), it follows that you would want to connect all of the network's servers and segments directly to the network's backbone.

Network Segments

When we refer to a segment, we can mean any small section of the network that may be connected to, but isn't actually a piece of, the backbone. The network's workstations connect to its servers, which in turn connect to the network backbone; you can see this by taking another look at Figure 1.16, which displays three segments.

Summary

This chapter created a solid foundation for you to build your networking knowledge on as you go through this book.

In it, you learned what, exactly, a network is, and you got an introduction to some of the components involved in building one—routers, switches, and hubs—as well as the jobs they do in a network.

You also learned that having the components required to build a network isn't all you need—understanding the various types of network connection methods like peer-to-peer and client/server is also vital.

Further, you learned about the various types of logical and physical network topologies and the features and drawbacks of each. We wrapped up the chapter with a short discussion about network backbones and segments and equipped you with the right questions to ask yourself to ensure that you come up with the right network topology for your networking needs.

Exam Essentials

Know your network topologies.   Know the names and descriptions of the topologies. Be aware of the difference between physical networks—(what humans see)—and logical networks—(what the equipment "sees.")

Know the advantages and disadvantages of the topologies.   It is important to know what each topology brings to the table. Knowing the various characteristics of each topology comes in handy during troubleshooting.

Understand the terms *LAN* and *WAN*.   You need to understand when you would use a LAN and when you would use a WAN. A local area network (LAN) is used to connect a group of hosts, and a WAN is used to connect various LANs.

Written Lab

You can find the answers in Appendix A.

Written Lab 1: LAN Topologies

The answers to the written lab can be found in Appendix A.

In this section, you'll complete the following written lab to make sure you've got the information and concepts contained within fully dialed in.

Provide the answers to the following questions:

1. What are the three primary LAN topologies?

2. What network topology is most closely associated with FDDI?

3. What is the term for a device that shares its resources with other network devices?

4. What network model draws a clear distinction between devices that share their resources and devices that do not?

5. Which network topology or connection type can be implemented with only two endpoints?

6. What device is an example of an Ethernet technology implemented as a star topology?

7. Which two network topologies are the most popular with switching?

8. What does VLAN stand for?

9. Will a computer that shares no resources most likely be connected to the backbone or to a segment?

10. Which LAN topology is characterized by all devices being daisy chained together with the devices at each end being connected to only one other device?

Review Questions

You can find the answers in Appendix B.

 NOTE The following questions are designed to test your understanding of this chapter's material. For more information on how to get additional questions, please see this book's introduction.

1. What two network topologies are the most popular in switching? (Choose two.)
   - **A.** Bus
   - **B.** Star
   - **C.** Mesh
   - **D.** Extended star

2. FDDI and Token Ring used which LAN physical topology?
   - **A.** Bus
   - **B.** Ring
   - **C.** Star
   - **D.** Mesh

3. Which of the following physical topologies has the most connections and is the least popular for LANs?
   - **A.** Bus
   - **B.** Star
   - **C.** Ring
   - **D.** Mesh

4. In a physical star topology, what happens when a workstation loses its physical connection to another device?
   - **A.** The ring is broken, so no devices can communicate.
   - **B.** Only that workstation loses its ability to communicate.
   - **C.** That workstation and the device it's connected to lose communication with the rest of the network.
   - **D.** No devices can communicate because there are now two un-terminated network segments.

5. Which network topology is most closely associated with classical CSMA/CD?

   A. Bus

   B. Token passing bus

   C. Star

   D. Extended start

   E. Ring

6. What is a logical grouping of network users and resources called?

   A. WAN

   B. LAN

   C. MPLS

   D. Host

7. Which of the following is a concern when using peer-to-peer networks?

   A. Where to place the server

   B. Whose computer is least busy and can act as the server

   C. The security associated with such a network

   D. Having enough peers to support creating such a network

8. Which of the following is an example of when a point-to-multipoint network is called for?

   A. When a centralized office needs to communicate with many branch offices

   B. When a full mesh of WAN links is in place

   C. When multiple offices are daisy chained to one another in a line

   D. When there are only two nodes in the network to be connected

9. Which of the following is an example of a LAN?

   A. Ten buildings interconnected by Ethernet connections over fiber-optic cabling

   B. Ten routers interconnected by frame-relay circuits

   C. Two routers interconnected with a T1 circuit

   D. A computer connected to another computer so they can share resources

10. Which of the following is a disadvantage of the star topology?

   A. When a port on the central concentrating device fails, the attached end device loses connectivity to the rest of the network.

   B. When the central concentrating device experiences a complete failure, all attached devices lose connectivity to the rest of the network.

   C. In a star topology, a more expensive type of host must be used when compared to the host used when implementing a physical bus.

   D. It is more difficult to add stations and troubleshoot than with other topologies.

11. What is a difference between a LAN and a WAN?

    A. WANs need a special type of router port.

    B. WANs cover larger geographical areas.

    C. WANs can utilize either private or public data transport.

    D. All of the above.

12. What kind of topology do you have if you combine a bus with a star topology?

    A. Extended star

    B. Extended bus

    C. Hybrid

    D. Extended ring

13. Which of the following is the most fault tolerant in a very large enterprise network?

    A. Bus topology

    B. LAN switch

    C. Ring topology

    D. Star topology

14. What advantage does the client/server architecture have over peer-to-peer?

    A. Easier maintenance

    B. Greater organization

    C. Tighter security

    D. All of the above

15. Which of the following is an example of a hybrid network?

    A. Ethernet switch

    B. Ring topology

    C. Bus topology

    D. Star topology

16. You have a network with multiple devices and need to have a smaller broadcast domain while working with a tight budget. Which of the following is the best solution?

    A. Use static IP addresses.

    B. Add more hubs.

    C. Implement more switches.

    D. Install a router.

17. Which type of topology has the greatest number of physical connections?

   A. Point-to-multipoint

   B. Star

   C. Point-to-point

   D. Mesh

18. What type of topology gives you a direct connection between two routers so that there is one communication path?

   A. Point-to-point

   B. Star

   C. Bus

   D. Straight

19. Which network topology is a combination of two or more types of physical or two or more types of logical topologies?

   A. Point-to-multipoint

   B. Hybrid

   C. Bus

   D. Star

20. When designing a network and deciding which type of network topology to use, which item(s) should be considered? (Choose all that apply.)

   A. Cost

   B. Ease of installation

   C. Ease of maintenance

   D. Fault-tolerance requirements

Chapter

2

Internetworking

THE FOLLOWING TOPICS ARE COVERED IN THIS CHAPTER:

✓ **Understanding the Host-to-Host Communications Model**

  ▪ Understanding Host-to-Host Communications

  ▪ OSI Reference Model

  ▪ OSI Model Layers and Their Functions

  ▪ Encapsulation and De-Encapsulation

  ▪ Peer-to-Peer Communication

  ▪ TCP/IP Suite

Welcome to the exciting world of internetworking. This chapter will really help you review your understanding of basic internetworking by focusing on how to connect networks using Cisco routers and switches. First, you need to know exactly what an internetwork is, right? You create an internetwork when you connect two or more networks via a router and configure a logical network addressing scheme with a protocol such as IP or IPv6.

I'll be reviewing the following topics in this chapter:

- Internetworking basics
- Network segmentation
- How bridges, switches, and routers are used to physically and logically segment a network
- How routers are employed to create an internetwork

I'm also going to dissect the Open Systems Interconnection (OSI) model and describe each part to you in detail because you really need a good grasp of it for the solid foundation upon which you'll build your Cisco networking knowledge. The OSI model has seven hierarchical layers that were developed to enable different networks to communicate reliably between disparate systems. Because this book is centering upon all things CCNA, it's crucial for you to understand the OSI model as Cisco sees it, so that's how I'll be presenting the seven layers to you.

After you finish reading this chapter, you'll encounter 20 review questions and three written labs. These are given to you to really lock the information from this chapter into your memory. So don't skip them!

To find up-to-the-minute updates for this chapter, please see www.lammle.com/forum.

Internetworking Basics

It's likely that at some point user response will dwindle to a slow crawl as your network grows and grows. And with all that growth, your LAN's traffic congestion will reach epic proportions. The answer is to break up a really big network into a number of smaller ones—something called *network segmentation*. You do this by using devices like *routers*, *switches*, and *bridges*. Figure 2.1 displays a network that's been segmented with a switch so that each network segment connected to the switch is now a separate collision domain. But make note of the fact that this network is still one broadcast domain.

FIGURE 2.1   A switch can replace the hub, breaking up collision domains.

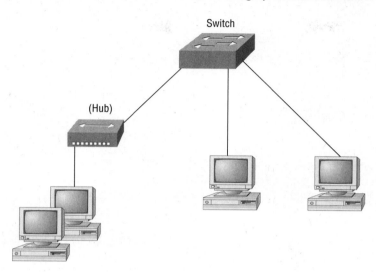

Keep in mind that the hub used in Figure 2.1 just extended the one collision domain from the switch port. Here's a list of some of the things that commonly cause LAN traffic congestion:

- Too many hosts in a broadcast or collision domain
- Broadcast storms
- Too much multicast traffic
- Low bandwidth
- Adding hubs for connectivity to the network

Take another look at Figure 2.1—hubs don't segment a network; they just connect network segments. So basically, it's an inexpensive way to connect a couple of PCs together, which is great for home use and troubleshooting, but that's about it!

Now, routers are used to connect networks and route packets of data from one network to another. Cisco became the de facto standard of routers because of its high-quality router products, great selection, and fantastic service. Routers, by default, break up a *broadcast domain*—the set of all devices on a network segment that hear all the broadcasts sent on that segment. Figure 2.2 shows a router in our little network that creates an internetwork and breaks up broadcast domains.

The network in Figure 2.2 is a pretty cool network. Each host is connected to its own collision domain, and the router has created two broadcast domains. And don't forget that the router provides connections to WAN services as well! The router uses something called a serial interface for WAN connections, specifically, a V.35 physical interface on a Cisco router.

FIGURE 2.2   Routers create an internetwork.

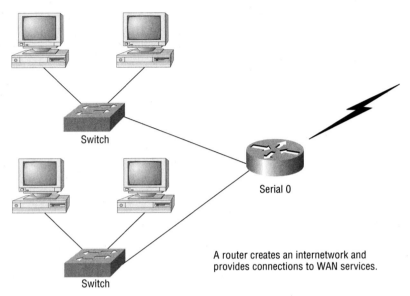

A router creates an internetwork and
provides connections to WAN services.

Breaking up a broadcast domain is important because when a host or server sends a network broadcast, every device on the network must read and process that broadcast—unless you've got a router. When the router's interface receives this broadcast, it can respond by basically saying, "Thanks, but no thanks," and discard the broadcast without forwarding it on to other networks. Even though routers are known for breaking up broadcast domains by default, it's important to remember that they break up collision domains as well.

There are two advantages of using routers in your network:

- They don't forward broadcasts by default.
- They can filter the network based on layer 3 (Network layer) information (e.g., IP address).

Four router functions in your network can be listed as follows:

- Packet switching
- Packet filtering
- Internetwork communication
- Path selection

Unlike layer 2 switches, which forward or filter frames, routers (or layer 3 switches) use logical addressing and provide what is called packet switching. Routers can also provide packet filtering by using access lists, and when routers connect two or more networks together and use logical addressing (IP or IPv6), this is called an internetwork. Last, routers use a routing table (map of the internetwork) to make path selections and to forward packets to remote networks.

Conversely, switches aren't used to create internetworks (they do not break up broadcast domains by default); they're employed to add functionality to a network LAN. The main purpose of a switch is to make a LAN work better—to optimize its performance—providing more bandwidth for the LAN's users. And switches don't forward packets to other networks as routers do. Instead, they only "switch" frames from one port to another within the switched network. Okay, you may be thinking, "Wait a minute, what are frames and packets?" I'll tell you all about them later, in Chapter 3, "Ethernet Technologies," I promise!

By default, switches break up *collision domains*. This is an Ethernet term used to describe a network scenario wherein one particular device sends a packet on a network segment, forcing every other device on that same segment to pay attention to it. If at the same time a different device tries to transmit, leading to a collision, both devices must retransmit, one at a time. Not very efficient! This situation is typically found in a hub environment where each host segment connects to a hub that represents only one collision domain and only one broadcast domain. By contrast, each and every port on a switch represents its own collision domain.

Switches create separate collision domains but a single broadcast domain. Routers provide a separate broadcast domain for each interface.

The term *bridging* was introduced before routers and hubs were implemented, so it's pretty common to hear people referring to bridges as switches and vice versa. That's because bridges and switches basically do the same thing—break up collision domains on a LAN (in reality, you cannot buy a physical bridge these days, only LAN switches, but they use bridging technologies, so Cisco still refers to them as multiport bridges).

So what this means is that a switch is basically just a multiple-port bridge with more brainpower, right? Well, pretty much, but there are differences. Switches do provide this function, but they do so with greatly enhanced management ability and features. Plus, most of the time, bridges had only 2 or 4 ports. Yes, you could get your hands on a bridge with up to 16 ports, but that's nothing compared to the hundreds available on some switches!

You would use a bridge in a network to reduce collisions within broadcast domains and to increase the number of collision domains in your network. Doing this provides more bandwidth for users. And keep in mind that using hubs in your Ethernet network can contribute to congestion. As always, plan your network design carefully!

Figure 2.3 shows how a network would look with all these internetwork devices in place. Remember that the router will not only break up broadcast domains for every LAN interface, it will break up collision domains as well.

FIGURE 2.3   Internetworking devices

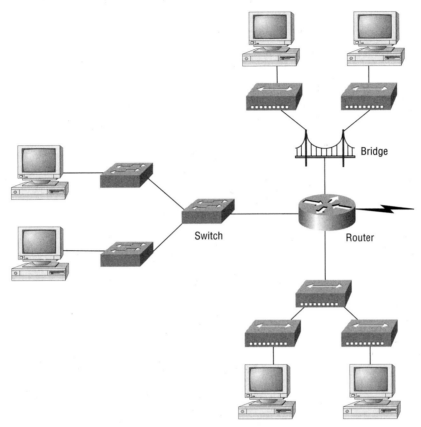

When you looked at Figure 2.3, did you notice that the router is found at center stage and that it connects each physical network together? We have to use this layout because of the older technologies involved—bridges and hubs.

On the top internetwork in Figure 2.3, you'll notice that a bridge was used to connect the hubs to a router. The bridge breaks up collision domains, but all the hosts connected to both hubs are still crammed into the same broadcast domain. Also, the bridge only created two collision domains, so each device connected to a hub is in the same collision domain as every other device connected to that same hub. This is actually pretty lame, but it's still better than having one collision domain for all hosts.

Notice something else: the three hubs at the bottom that are connected also connect to the router, creating one collision domain and one broadcast domain. This makes the bridged network look much better indeed!

 Although bridges/switches are used to segment networks, they will not isolate broadcast or multicast packets.

The best network connected to the router is the LAN switch network on the left. Why? Because each port on that switch breaks up collision domains. But it's not all good—all devices are still in the same broadcast domain. Do you remember why this can be a really bad thing? Because all devices must listen to all broadcasts transmitted, that's why. And if your broadcast domains are too large, the users have less bandwidth and are required to process more broadcasts, and network response time will slow to a level that could cause office riots.

Once we have only switches in our network, things change a lot! Figure 2.4 shows the network that is typically found today.

FIGURE 2.4 Switched networks creating an internetwork

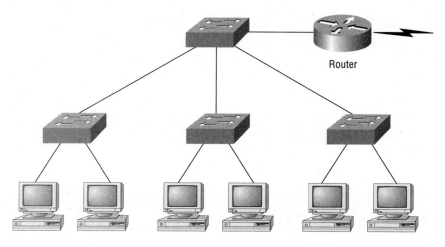

Okay, here I've placed the LAN switches at the center of the network world so the router is connecting only logical networks together. If I implemented this kind of setup, I've created virtual LANs (VLANs), something I'm going to tell you about in Chapter 11, "Layer 2 Switching Technologies." So don't stress. But it is really important to understand that even though you have a switched network, you still need a router (or layer 3 switch) to provide your inter-VLAN communication, or internetworking. Don't forget that!

Obviously, the best network is one that's correctly configured to meet the business requirements of the company it serves. LAN switches with routers, correctly placed in the network, are the best network design. This book will help you understand the basics of routers and switches so you can make good, informed decisions on a case-by-case basis.

Let's go back to Figure 2.3. Looking at the figure, how many collision domains and broadcast domains are in this internetwork? Hopefully, you answered nine collision domains and three broadcast domains! The broadcast domains are definitely the easiest to see because only routers break up broadcast domains by default. And since there are three connections, that gives you three broadcast domains. But do you see the nine collision domains? Just in case that's a no, I'll explain. The all-hub network is one collision domain; the bridge network equals three collision domains. Add in the switch network of five collision domains—one for each switch port—and you've got a total of nine.

Now, in Figure 2.4, each port on the switch is a separate collision domain and each VLAN is a separate broadcast domain. But you still need a router for routing between VLANs. How many collision domains do you see here? I'm counting 10—remember that connections between the switches are considered a collision domain!

🌐 Real World Scenario

Should I Replace My Existing 10/100Mbps Switches?

You're a network administrator at a large company in San Jose. The boss comes to you and says that he got your requisition to buy all new switches and is not sure about approving the expense; do you really need it?

Well, if you can, absolutely! The newest switches really add a lot of functionality to a network that older 10/100Mbps switches just don't have (yes, five-year-old switches are considered just plain old today). But most of us don't have an unlimited budget to buy all new gigabit switches. 10/100Mbps switches can still create a nice network—that is, of course, if you design and implement the network correctly—but you'll still have to replace these switches eventually.

So do you need 1Gbps or better switch ports for all your users, servers, and other devices? Yes, you *absolutely* need new higher-end switches! With the new Windows networking stack and the IPv6 revolution shortly ahead of us, the server and hosts are no longer the bottlenecks of our internetworks. Our routers and switches are! We need at a minimum gigabit to the desktop and on every router interface—10Gbps would be better, or even higher if you can afford it.

So, go ahead! Put that requisition in to buy all new switches. (In Chapter 7 "Introduction to Nexus," I'll talk about Cisco's new Nexus switches!)

So now that you've gotten an introduction to internetworking and the various devices that live in an internetwork, it's time to head into internetworking models.

Internetworking Models

When networks first came into being, computers could typically communicate only with computers from the same manufacturer. For example, companies ran either a complete DECnet solution or an IBM solution—not both together. In the late 1970s, the *Open Systems Interconnection (OSI) reference model* was created by the International Organization for Standardization (ISO) to break this barrier.

The OSI model was meant to help vendors create interoperable network devices and software in the form of protocols so that different vendor networks could work with each other. Like world peace, it'll probably never happen completely, but it's still a great goal.

The OSI model is the primary architectural model for networks. It describes how data and network information are communicated from an application on one computer through the network media to an application on another computer. The OSI reference model breaks this approach into layers.

In the following section, I am going to explain the layered approach and how we can use this approach to help us troubleshoot our internetworks.

The Layered Approach

A *reference model* is a conceptual blueprint of how communications should take place. It addresses all the processes required for effective communication and divides these processes into logical groupings called *layers*. When a communication system is designed in this manner, it's known as *layered architecture*.

Think of it like this: you and some friends want to start a company. One of the first things you'll do is sit down and think through what tasks must be done, who will do them, the order in which they will be done, and how they relate to each other. Ultimately, you might group these tasks into departments. Let's say you decide to have an order-taking department, an inventory department, and a shipping department. Each of your departments has its own unique tasks, keeping its staff members busy and requiring them to focus on only their own duties.

In this scenario, I'm using departments as a metaphor for the layers in a communication system. For things to run smoothly, the staff of each department will have to trust and rely heavily upon the others to do their jobs and competently handle their unique responsibilities. In your planning sessions, you would probably take notes, recording the entire process to facilitate later discussions about standards of operation that will serve as your business blueprint, or reference model.

Once your business is launched, your department heads, each armed with the part of the blueprint relating to their own department, will need to develop practical methods to implement their assigned tasks. These practical methods, or protocols, will need to be compiled into a standard operating procedures manual and followed closely. Each of the various procedures in your manual will have been included for different reasons and have varying degrees of importance and implementation. If you form a partnership or acquire another company, it will be imperative that its business protocols—its business blueprint—match yours (or at least be compatible with it).

Similarly, software developers can use a reference model to understand computer communication processes and see what types of functions need to be accomplished on any one layer. If they are developing a protocol for a certain layer, all they need to concern themselves with is that specific layer's functions, not those of any other layer. Another layer and protocol will handle the other functions. The technical term for this idea is *binding*. The communication processes that are related to each other are bound, or grouped together, at a particular layer.

Advantages of Reference Models

The OSI model is hierarchical, and the same benefits and advantages can apply to any layered model. The primary purpose of all such models, especially the OSI model, is to allow different vendors' networks to interoperate.

Advantages of using the OSI layered model include, but are not limited to, the following:

- It divides the network communication process into smaller and simpler components, thus aiding component development, design, and troubleshooting.

- It allows multiple-vendor development through standardization of network components.

- It encourages industry standardization by defining what functions occur at each layer of the model.

- It allows various types of network hardware and software to communicate.

- It prevents changes in one layer from affecting other layers, so it does not hamper development.

The OSI Reference Model

One of the greatest functions of the OSI specifications is to assist in data transfer between disparate hosts—meaning, for example, that they enable us to transfer data between a Unix host and a PC or a Mac.

The OSI isn't a physical model, though. Rather, it's a set of guidelines that application developers can use to create and implement applications that run on a network. It also provides a framework for creating and implementing networking standards, devices, and internetworking schemes.

The OSI has seven different layers, divided into two groups. The top three layers define how the applications within the end stations will communicate with each other and with users. The bottom four layers define how data is transmitted end to end. Figure 2.5 shows the three upper layers functions, and Figure 2.6 shows the four lower layers functions.

When you study Figure 2.5, understand that the user interfaces with the computer at the Application layer and also that the upper layers are responsible for applications communicating between hosts. Remember that none of the upper layers knows anything about networking or network addresses. That's the responsibility of the four bottom layers.

FIGURE 2.5   The upper layers

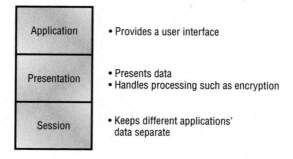

- Application — • Provides a user interface

- Presentation — • Presents data
  • Handles processing such as encryption

- Session — • Keeps different applications' data separate

FIGURE 2.6   The lower layers

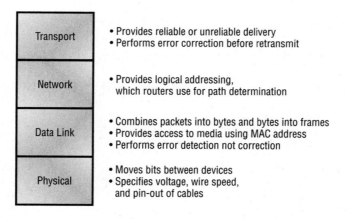

- Transport — • Provides reliable or unreliable delivery
  • Performs error correction before retransmit

- Network — • Provides logical addressing, which routers use for path determination

- Data Link — • Combines packets into bytes and bytes into frames
  • Provides access to media using MAC address
  • Performs error detection not correction

- Physical — • Moves bits between devices
  • Specifies voltage, wire speed, and pin-out of cables

In Figure 2.6, you can see that it's the four bottom layers that define how data is transferred through a physical wire or through switches and routers. These bottom layers also determine how to rebuild a data stream from a transmitting host to a destination host's application.

The following network devices operate at all seven layers of the OSI model:

- Network management stations (NMSs)
- Web and application servers
- Gateways (not default gateways)
- Network hosts

Basically, the ISO is pretty much the Emily Post of the network protocol world. Just as Ms. Post wrote the book setting the standards—or protocols—for human social interaction, the ISO developed the OSI reference model as the precedent and guide for an open network protocol set. Defining the etiquette of communication models, it remains today the most popular means of comparison for protocol suites.

As mentioned, the OSI reference model has the following seven layers:

- Application layer (layer 7)

- Presentation layer (layer 6)

- Session layer (layer 5)

- Transport layer (layer 4)

- Network layer (layer 3)

- Data Link layer (layer 2)

- Physical layer (layer 1)

Figure 2.7 shows a summary of the functions defined in Figure 2.5 and Figure 2.6 at layer of the OSI model.

With this in hand, you're now ready to explore each layer's function in detail.

FIGURE 2.7   Layer functions

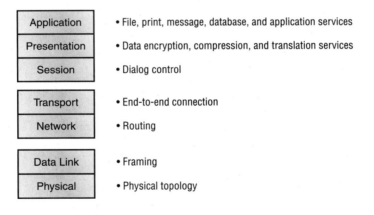

The Application Layer

The *Application layer* of the OSI model marks the spot where users actually communicate to the computer. This layer comes into play only when it's apparent that access to the network is going to be needed soon. Take the case of Internet Explorer (IE). You could uninstall every trace of networking components from a system, such as TCP/IP, NIC card, and so on, and you could still use IE to view a local HTML document—no problem. But things would definitely get messy if you tried to do something like view an HTML document that must be retrieved using HTTP or nab a file with FTP or TFTP. That's because IE will respond to requests such as those by attempting to access the Application layer. And what's happening is that the Application layer is acting as an interface between the actual application program—which isn't at all a part of the layered structure—and the next layer down by providing ways for the application to send information down through the protocol stack. In other words, IE doesn't truly reside within the Application layer—it interfaces with Application layer protocols when it needs to deal with remote resources.

The Application layer is also responsible for identifying and establishing the availability of the intended communication partner and determining whether sufficient resources for the intended communication exist.

These tasks are important because computer applications sometimes require more than only desktop resources. Often, they'll unite communicating components from more than one network application. Prime examples are file transfers and email as well as enabling remote access, network management activities, client/server processes, and information location. Many network applications provide services for communication over enterprise networks, but for present and future internetworking, the need is fast developing to reach beyond the limits of current physical networking.

It's important to remember that the Application layer is acting as an interface between the actual application programs. This means that Microsoft Outlook, for example, does not reside at the Application layer but instead interfaces with the Application layer protocols. Chapter 4, "TCP/IP DoD Model," will present some programs that actually reside at the Application layer—for example, FTP and TFTP.

The Presentation Layer

The *Presentation layer* gets its name from its purpose: it presents data to the Application layer and is responsible for data translation and code formatting.

This layer is essentially a translator and provides coding and conversion functions. A successful data-transfer technique is to adapt the data into a standard format before transmission. Computers are configured to receive this generically formatted data and then convert the data back into its native format for actual reading (for example, EBCDIC to ASCII). By providing translation services, the Presentation layer ensures that data transferred from the Application layer of one system can be read by the Application layer of another one.

The OSI has protocol standards that define how standard data should be formatted. Tasks like data compression, decompression, encryption, and decryption are associated with this layer. Some Presentation layer standards are involved in multimedia operations too.

The Session Layer

The *Session layer* is responsible for setting up, managing, and then tearing down sessions between Presentation layer entities. This layer also provides dialog control between devices, or nodes. It coordinates communication between systems and serves to organize their communication by offering three different modes: *simplex*, *half duplex*, and *full duplex*. To sum up, the Session layer basically keeps different applications' data separate from other applications' data.

The Transport Layer

The *Transport layer* segments and reassembles data into a data stream. Services located in the Transport layer segment and reassemble data from upper-layer applications and unite it into the same data stream. They provide end-to-end data transport services and can establish a logical connection between the sending host and destination host on an internetwork.

Some of you are probably familiar with TCP and UDP already. (But if you're not, no worries—I'll tell you all about them in Chapter 4.) If so, you know that both work at the Transport layer and that TCP is a reliable service and UDP is not. This means that application developers have more options because they have a choice between the two protocols when working with TCP/IP protocols.

The Transport layer is responsible for providing mechanisms for multiplexing upper-layer applications, establishing sessions, and tearing down virtual circuits. It also hides details of any network-dependent information from the higher layers by providing transparent data transfer.

 The term *reliable networking* can be used at the Transport layer. It means that acknowledgments, sequencing, and flow control will be used.

The Transport layer can be connectionless or connection oriented. However, Cisco is mostly concerned with you understanding the connection-oriented portion of the Transport layer. The following sections will provide the skinny on the connection-oriented (reliable) protocol of the Transport layer.

Flow Control

Data integrity is ensured at the Transport layer by maintaining *flow control* and by allowing applications to request reliable data transport between systems. Flow control prevents a sending host on one side of the connection from overflowing the buffers in the receiving host—an event that can result in lost data. Reliable data transport employs a connection-oriented communications session between systems, and the protocols involved ensure that the following will be achieved:

- The segments delivered are acknowledged back to the sender upon their reception.
- Any segments not acknowledged are retransmitted.
- Segments are sequenced back into their proper order upon arrival at their destination.
- A manageable data flow is maintained in order to avoid congestion, overloading, and data loss.

The purpose of flow control is to provide a means for the receiver to govern the amount of data sent by the sender.

Connection-Oriented Communication

In reliable transport operation, a device that wants to transmit sets up a connection-oriented communication session with a remote device by creating a session. The transmitting device first establishes a connection-oriented session with its peer system, which is called a *call setup* or a *three-way handshake*. Data is then transferred; when the transfer is finished, a call termination takes place to tear down the virtual circuit.

Figure 2.8 depicts a typical reliable session taking place between sending and receiving systems. Looking at it, you can see that both hosts' application programs begin by notifying their individual operating systems that a connection is about to be initiated. The two operating systems communicate by sending messages over the network confirming that the transfer is approved and that both sides are ready for it to take place. After all of this required synchronization takes place, a connection is fully established and the data transfer begins (this virtual circuit setup is called overhead!).

While the information is being transferred between hosts, the two machines periodically check in with each other, communicating through their protocol software to ensure that all is going well and that the data is being received properly.

FIGURE 2.8   Establishing a connection-oriented session

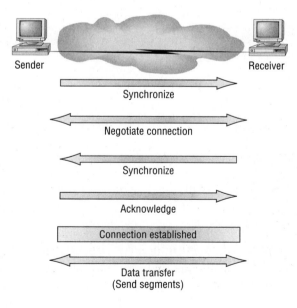

Here's a summary of the steps in the connection-oriented session—the three-way hand-shake—pictured in Figure 2.9:

- The first "connection agreement" segment is a request for synchronization.

- The next segments acknowledge the request and establish connection parameters—the rules—between hosts. These segments request that the receiver's sequencing is synchronized here as well so that a bidirectional connection is formed.

- The final segment is also an acknowledgment. It notifies the destination host that the connection agreement has been accepted and that the actual connection has been established. Data transfer can now begin.

FIGURE 2.9   The three-way handshake

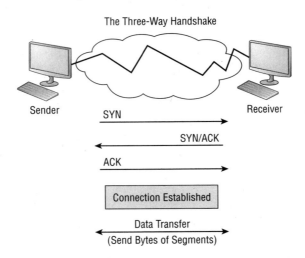

Sounds pretty simple, but things don't always flow so smoothly. Sometimes during a transfer, congestion can occur because a high-speed computer is generating data traffic a lot faster than the network can handle transferring. A bunch of computers simultaneously sending datagrams through a single gateway or destination can also botch things up nicely. In the latter case, a gateway or destination can become congested even though no single source caused the problem. In either case, the problem is basically akin to a freeway bottle-neck—too much traffic for too small a capacity. It's not usually one car that's the problem; there are simply too many cars on that freeway.

Okay, so what happens when a machine receives a flood of datagrams too quickly for it to process? It stores them in a memory section called a *buffer*. But this buffering action can solve the problem only if the datagrams are part of a small burst. If not, and the datagram deluge continues, a device's memory will eventually be exhausted, its flood capacity will be exceeded, and it will react by discarding any additional datagrams that arrive.

No huge worries here, though. Because of the transport function, network flood control systems really work quite well. Instead of dumping data and allowing data to be lost, the transport can issue a "not ready" indicator to the sender, or source, of the flood (as shown in Figure 2.10). This mechanism works kind of like a stoplight, signaling the sending device to stop transmitting segment traffic to its overwhelmed peer. After the peer receiver processes the segments already in its memory reservoir—its buffer—it sends out a "ready" transport indicator. When the machine waiting to transmit the rest of its datagrams receives this "go" indictor, it resumes its transmission.

FIGURE 2.10   Transmitting segments with flow control

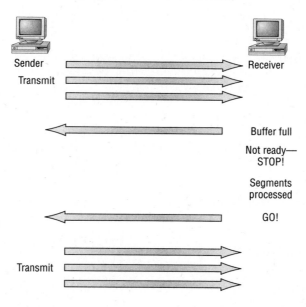

In fundamental, reliable, connection-oriented data transfer, datagrams are delivered to the receiving host in exactly the same sequence they're transmitted—and the transmission fails if this order is breached! If any data segments are lost, duplicated, or damaged along the way, a failure will occur. This problem is solved by having the receiving host acknowledge that it has received each and every data segment.

A service is considered connection-oriented if it has the following characteristics:

- A virtual circuit is set up (e.g., a three-way handshake).
- It uses sequencing.
- It uses acknowledgments.
- It uses flow control.

The types of flow control are buffering, windowing, and congestion avoidance.

Windowing

Ideally, data throughput happens quickly and efficiently. And as you can imagine, it would be slow if the transmitting machine had to wait for an acknowledgment after sending each segment. But because there's time available *after* the sender transmits the data segment and *before* it finishes processing acknowledgments from the receiving machine, the sender uses the break as an opportunity to transmit more data. The quantity of data segments (measured in bytes) that the transmitting machine is allowed to send without receiving an acknowledgment for them is called a *window*.

 Windows are used to control the amount of outstanding, unacknowledged data segments.

So the size of the window controls how much information is transferred from one end to the other. While some protocols quantify information by observing the number of packets, TCP/IP measures it by counting the number of bytes.

As you can see in Figure 2.11, there are two window sizes—one set to 1 and one set to 3.

When you've configured a window size of 1, the sending machine waits for an acknowledgment for each data segment it transmits before transmitting another. If you've configured a window size of 3, it's allowed to transmit three data segments before an acknowledgment is received.

FIGURE 2.11   Windowing

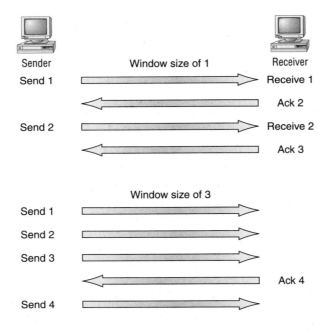

In this simplified example, both the sending and receiving machines are workstations. In reality, this is not done in simple numbers but in the amount of bytes that can be sent.

> If a receiving host fails to receive all the bytes that it should acknowledge, the host can improve the communication session by decreasing the window size.

Acknowledgments

Reliable data delivery ensures the integrity of a stream of data sent from one machine to the other through a fully functional data link. It guarantees that the data won't be duplicated or lost. This is achieved through something called *positive acknowledgment with retransmission*—a technique that requires a receiving machine to communicate with the transmitting source by sending an acknowledgment message back to the sender when it receives data. The sender documents each segment measured in bytes; it then sends and waits for this acknowledgment before sending the next segment round of bytes. When it sends a segment, the transmitting machine starts a timer and retransmits if it expires before an acknowledgment is returned from the receiving end.

In Figure 2.12, the sending machine transmits segments 1, 2, and 3.

FIGURE 2.12   Transport layer reliable delivery

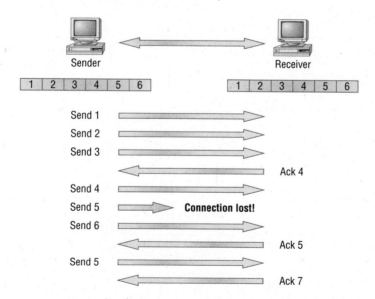

The receiving node acknowledges it has received them by requesting segment 4 with an ACK 4. When it receives the acknowledgment, the sender then transmits segments 4, 5, and 6. If segment 5 doesn't make it to the destination, the receiving node acknowledges that event with a request for the segment to be resent. The sending machine will then resend the lost segment and wait for an acknowledgment, which it must receive in order to move on to the transmission of segment 7.

The Network Layer

The *Network layer* (also called layer 3) manages device addressing, tracks the location of devices on the network, and determines the best way to move data, which means that the Network layer must transport traffic between devices that aren't locally attached. Routers (layer 3 devices) are specified at the Network layer and provide the routing services within an internetwork.

It happens like this: First, when a packet is received on a router interface, the destination IP address is checked. If the packet isn't destined for that particular router, it will look up the destination network address in the routing table. Once the router chooses an exit interface, the packet will be sent to that interface to be framed and sent out on the local network. If the router can't find an entry for the packet's destination network in the routing table, the router drops the packet.

Two types of packets are used at the Network layer: data and route updates.

Data Packets   Used to transport user data through the internetwork. Protocols used to support data traffic are called *routed protocols*; examples of routed protocols are IP and IPv6. You'll learn about IP addressing and IPv6 in Chapter 5.

Route Update Packets   Used to update neighboring routers about the networks connected to all routers within the internetwork. Protocols that send route update packets are called *routing protocols*; examples of some common ones are RIP, RIPv2, EIGRP, and OSPF. Route update packets are used to help build and maintain routing tables on each router.

Figure 2.13 shows an example of two routing tables.

FIGURE 2.13   Routing table used in a router

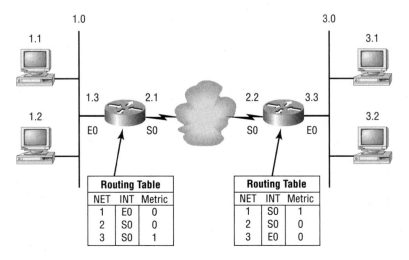

The routing table used in a router includes the following information:

Network Addresses   Protocol-specific network addresses. A router must maintain a routing table for individual routed protocols because each routed protocol keeps track of a network with a different addressing scheme (IP, IPv6, and IPX, for example). Think of it as a street sign in each of the different languages spoken by the residents that live on a particular street. So, if there were American, Spanish, and French folks on a street named Cat, the sign would read Cat/Gato/Chat.

Interface   The exit interface a packet will take when destined for a specific network.

Metric   The distance to the remote network. Different routing protocols use different ways of computing this distance. I'm going to cover routing protocols in Chapter 10, but for now, know that some routing protocols (namely RIP) use something called a *hop count* (the number of routers a packet passes through en route to a remote network), while others use bandwidth, delay of the line, or even tick count (1/18 of a second).

And as I mentioned earlier, routers break up broadcast domains, which means that by default, broadcasts aren't forwarded through a router. Do you remember why this is a good thing? Routers also break up collision domains, but you can also do that using layer 2 (Data Link layer) switches. Because each interface in a router represents a separate network, it must be assigned unique network identification numbers, and each host on the network connected to that router must use the same network number. Figure 2.14 shows how a router works in an internetwork.

FIGURE 2.14   A router in an internetwork

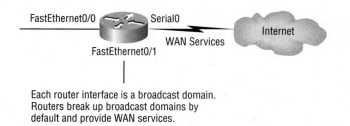

Each router interface is a broadcast domain.
Routers break up broadcast domains by
default and provide WAN services.

Here are some points about routers that you should really commit to memory:

- Routers, by default, will not forward any broadcast or multicast packets.

- Routers use the logical address in a Network layer header to determine the next hop router to forward the packet to.

- Routers can use access lists, created by an administrator, to control security on the types of packets that are allowed to enter or exit an interface.

- Routers can provide layer 2 bridging functions if needed and can simultaneously route through the same interface.

- Layer 3 devices (routers in this case) provide connections between virtual LANs (VLANs).

- Routers can provide quality of service (QoS) for specific types of network traffic.

The Data Link Layer

The *Data Link layer* provides the physical transmission of the data and handles error notification, network topology, and flow control. This means that the Data Link layer will ensure that messages are delivered to the proper device on a LAN using hardware addresses and will translate messages from the Network layer into bits for the Physical layer to transmit.

The Data Link layer formats the message into pieces, each called a *data frame*, and adds a customized header containing the hardware destination and source address. This added information forms a sort of capsule that surrounds the original message in much the same way that engines, navigational devices, and other tools were attached to the lunar modules of the Apollo project. These various pieces of equipment were useful only during certain stages of space flight and were stripped off the module and discarded when their designated stage was complete. Data traveling through networks is similar.

Figure 2.15 shows the Data Link layer with the Ethernet and IEEE specifications. When you check it out, notice that the IEEE 802.2 standard is used in conjunction with and adds functionality to the other IEEE standards.

FIGURE 2.15   Data Link layer

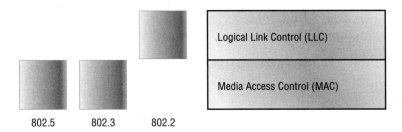

| 802.5 | 802.3 | 802.2 |

It's important for you to understand that routers, which work at the Network layer, don't care at all about where a particular host is located. They're only concerned about where networks are located and the best way to reach them—including remote ones. Routers are totally obsessive when it comes to networks. And for once, this is a good thing! It's the Data Link layer that's responsible for the actual unique identification of each device that resides on a local network.

For a host to send packets to individual hosts on a local network as well as transmit packets between routers, the Data Link layer uses hardware addressing. Each time a packet is sent between routers, it's framed with control information at the Data Link layer, but that information is stripped off at the receiving router and only the original packet is left completely intact. This framing of the packet continues for each hop until the packet is finally delivered to the correct receiving host. It's really important to understand that the packet itself is never altered along the route; it's only encapsulated with the type of control information required for it to be properly passed on to the different media types.

The IEEE Ethernet Data Link layer has two sublayers:

Media Access Control (MAC) 802.3   Defines how packets are placed on the media. Contention media access is "first come/first served" access where everyone shares the same bandwidth—hence the name. Physical addressing is defined here as well as logical topologies. What's a logical topology? It's the signal path through a physical topology. Line discipline, error notification (not correction), ordered delivery of frames, and optional flow control can also be used at this sublayer.

Logical Link Control (LLC) 802.2   Responsible for identifying Network layer protocols and then encapsulating them. An LLC header tells the Data Link layer what to do with a packet once a frame is received. It works like this: a host will receive a frame and look in the LLC header to find out where the packet is destined—say, the IP protocol at the Network layer. The LLC can also provide flow control and sequencing of control bits.

The switches and bridges I talked about near the beginning of the chapter both work at the Data Link layer and filter the network using hardware (MAC) addresses. We will look at these in the following section.

Switches and Bridges at the Data Link Layer

Layer 2 switching is considered hardware-based bridging because it uses specialized hardware called an *application-specific integrated circuit (ASIC)*. ASICs can run up to gigabit speeds with very low latency rates.

Latency is the time measured from when a frame enters a port to when it exits a port.

Bridges and switches read each frame as it passes through the network. The layer 2 device then puts the source hardware address in a filter table and keeps track of which port the frame was received on. This information (logged in the bridge's or switch's filter table) is what helps the machine determine the location of the specific sending device. Figure 2.16 shows a switch in an internetwork.

The real estate business is all about location, location, location, and it's the same way for both layer 2 and layer 3 devices. Though both need to be able to negotiate the network, it's crucial to remember that they're concerned with very different parts of it. Primarily, layer 3 machines (such as routers) need to locate specific networks, whereas layer 2 machines (switches and bridges) need to eventually locate specific devices. So, networks are to routers as individual devices are to switches and bridges. And routing tables that "map" the internetwork are for routers as filter tables that "map" individual devices are for switches and bridges.

After a filter table is built on the layer 2 device, it will forward frames only to the segment where the destination hardware address is located. If the destination device is on the same segment as the frame, the layer 2 device will block the frame from going to any other segments. If the destination is on a different segment, the frame can be transmitted only to that segment. This is called *transparent bridging*.

FIGURE 2.16 A switch in an internetwork

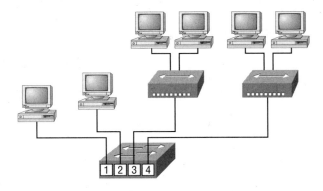

Each segment has its own collision domain.
All segments are in the same broadcast domain.

When a switch interface receives a frame with a destination hardware address that isn't found in the device's filter table, it will forward the frame to all connected segments. If the unknown device that was sent the "mystery frame" replies to this forwarding action, the switch updates its filter table regarding that device's location. But in the event the destination address of the transmitting frame is a broadcast address, the switch will forward all broadcasts to every connected segment by default.

All devices that the broadcast is forwarded to are considered to be in the same broadcast domain. This can be a problem; layer 2 devices propagate layer 2 broadcast storms that choke performance, and the only way to stop a broadcast storm from propagating through an internetwork is with a layer 3 device—a router.

The biggest benefit of using switches instead of hubs in your internetwork is that each switch port is actually its own collision domain. (Conversely, a hub creates one large collision domain.) But even armed with a switch, you still don't break up broadcast domains by default. Neither switches nor bridges will do that. They'll simply forward all broadcasts instead.

Another benefit of LAN switching over hub-centered implementations is that each device on every segment plugged into a switch can transmit simultaneously—at least, they can as long as there is only one host on each port and a hub isn't plugged into a switch port. As you might have guessed, hubs allow only one device per network segment to communicate at a time.

The Physical Layer

Finally arriving at the bottom, we find that the *Physical layer* does two things: it sends bits and receives bits. Bits come only in values of 1 or 0—a Morse code with numerical values. The Physical layer communicates directly with the various types of actual communication media. Different kinds of media represent these bit values in different ways. Some use audio tones, while others employ *state transitions*—changes in voltage from high to low and low to high. Specific protocols are needed for each type of media to describe the proper bit patterns to be used, how data is encoded into media signals, and the various qualities of the physical media's attachment interface.

The Physical layer specifies the electrical, mechanical, procedural, and functional requirements for activating, maintaining, and deactivating a physical link between end systems. This layer is also where you identify the interface between the *data terminal equipment (DTE)* and the *data communication equipment (DCE)*. (Some old phone-company employees still call DCE data circuit-terminating equipment.) The DCE is usually located at the service provider, while the DTE is the attached device. The services available to the DTE are most often accessed via a modem or *channel service unit/data service unit (CSU/DSU)*.

The Physical layer's connectors and different physical topologies are defined by the OSI as standards, allowing disparate systems to communicate. The CCNA objectives are interested only in the IEEE Ethernet standards.

Hubs at the Physical Layer

A *hub* is really a multiple-port repeater. A repeater receives a digital signal and reamplifies or regenerates that signal and then forwards the digital signal out all active ports without looking at any data. An active hub does the same thing. Any digital signal received from a segment on a hub port is regenerated or reamplified and transmitted out all other ports on the hub. This means all devices plugged into a hub are in the same collision domain as well as in the same broadcast domain. Figure 2.17 shows a hub in a network.

FIGURE 2.17   A hub in a network

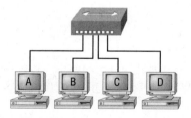

All devices in the same collision domain.
All devices in the same broadcast domain.
Devices share the same bandwidth.

Hubs, like repeaters, don't examine any of the traffic as it enters and is then transmitted out to the other parts of the physical media. Every device connected to the hub, or hubs, must listen if one device transmits. A physical star network—where the hub is a central device and cables extend in all directions out from it—is the type of topology a hub creates. Visually, the design really does resemble a star, whereas Ethernet networks run a logical bus topology, meaning that the signal has to run through the network from end to end.

Hubs and repeaters can be used to enlarge the area covered by a single LAN segment, although I do not recommend this. LAN switches are affordable for almost every situation.

Summary

Whew!—You made it through! You're now armed with a ton of fundamental information; you're ready to build upon it and are well on your way to certification.

I started by discussing simple, basic networking and the differences between collision and broadcast domains.

I then discussed the OSI model—the seven-layer model used to help application developers design applications that can run on any type of system or network. Each layer has its special jobs and select responsibilities within the model to ensure that solid, effective communications do, in fact, occur. I provided you with complete details of each layer and discussed how Cisco views the specifications of the OSI model.

In addition, each layer in the OSI model specifies different types of devices, and I described these different devices used at each layer.

Remember that hubs are Physical layer devices and repeat the digital signal to all segments except the one from which it was received. Switches segment the network using hardware addresses and break up collision domains. Routers break up broadcast domains (and collision domains) and use logical addressing to send packets through an internetwork.

Exam Essentials

Identify the possible causes of LAN traffic congestion.   Too many hosts in a broadcast domain, broadcast storms, multicasting, and low bandwidth are all possible causes of LAN traffic congestion.

Describe the difference between a *collision domain* and a *broadcast domain*.   *Collision domain* is an Ethernet term used to describe a network collection of devices in which one particular device sends a packet on a network segment, forcing every other device on that same segment to pay attention to it. On a *broadcast domain*, a set of all devices on a network segment hears all broadcasts sent on that segment.

Differentiate a MAC address and an IP address and describe how and when each address type is used in a network.   A MAC address is a hexadecimal number identifying the physical connection of a host. MAC addresses are said to operate on layer 2 of the OSI model. IP addresses, which can be expressed in binary or decimal format, are logical identifiers that are said to be on layer 3 of the OSI model. Hosts on the same physical segment locate one another with MAC addresses, while IP addresses are used when they reside on different LAN segments or subnets. Even when the hosts are in different subnets, a destination IP address will be converted to a MAC address when the packet reaches the destination network via routing.

Understand the difference between a hub, a bridge, a switch, and a router. Hubs create one collision domain and one broadcast domain. Bridges break up collision domains but create one large broadcast domain. They use hardware addresses to filter the network. Switches are really just multiple-port bridges with more intelligence. They break up collision domains but create one large broadcast domain by default. Switches use hardware addresses to filter the network. Routers break up broadcast domains and use logical addressing to filter the network.

Identify the functions and advantages of routers. Routers perform packet switching, filtering, and path selection, and they facilitate internetwork communication. One advantage of routers is that they reduce broadcast traffic.

Differentiate connection-oriented and connectionless network services and describe how each is handled during network communications. Connection-oriented services use acknowledgments and flow control to create a reliable session. More overhead is used than in a connectionless network service. Connectionless services are used to send data with no acknowledgments or flow control. This is considered unreliable.

Define the OSI layers, understand the function of each, and describe how devices and networking protocols can be mapped to each layer. You must remember the seven layers of the OSI model and what function each layer provides. The Application, Presentation, and Session layers are upper layers and are responsible for communicating from a user interface to an application. The Transport layer provides segmentation, sequencing, and virtual circuits. The Network layer provides logical network addressing and routing through an internetwork. The Data Link layer provides framing and placing of data on the network medium. The Physical layer is responsible for taking 1s and 0s and encoding them into a digital signal for transmission on the network segment.

Written Labs

In this section, you'll complete the following labs to make sure you've got the information and concepts contained within them fully dialed in:

Lab 2.1: OSI Questions

Lab 2.2: Defining the OSI Layers and Devices

Lab 2.3: Identifying Collision and Broadcast Domains

You can find the answers in Appendix A.

Written Lab 2.1: OSI Questions

Answer the following questions about the OSI model:

1. Which layer chooses and determines the availability of communicating partners along with the resources necessary to make the connection, coordinates partnering applications, and forms a consensus on procedures for controlling data integrity and error recovery?

2. Which layer is responsible for converting data packets from the Data Link layer into electrical signals?

3. At which layer is routing implemented, enabling connections and path selection between two end systems?

4. Which layer defines how data is formatted, presented, encoded, and converted for use on the network?

5. Which layer is responsible for creating, managing, and terminating sessions between applications?

6. Which layer ensures the trustworthy transmission of data across a physical link and is primarily concerned with physical addressing, line discipline, network topology, error notification, ordered delivery of frames, and flow control?

7. Which layer is used for reliable communication between end nodes over the network and provides mechanisms for establishing, maintaining, and terminating virtual circuits; transport-fault detection and recovery; and controlling the flow of information?

8. Which layer provides logical addressing that routers will use for path determination?

9. Which layer specifies voltage, wire speed, and pin-out of cables and moves bits between devices?

10. Which layer combines bits into bytes and bytes into frames, uses MAC addressing, and provides error detection?

11. Which layer is responsible for keeping the data from different applications separate on the network?

12. Which layer is represented by frames?

13. Which layer is represented by segments?

14. Which layer is represented by packets?

15. Which layer is represented by bits?

16. Which layer of the OSI model is associated with the reliable transmission of datagrams?

17. Which layer segments and reassembles data into a data stream?

18. Which layer provides the physical transmission of the data and handles error notification, network topology, and flow control?

19. Which layer manages device addressing, tracks the location of devices on the network, and determines the best way to move data?

20. What is the bit length and expression form of a MAC address?

Written Lab 2.2: Defining the OSI Layers and Devices

Fill in the blanks with the appropriate layer of the OSI or hub, switch, or router device.

Description	Device or OSI Layer
This device sends and receives information about the Network layer.	
This layer creates a virtual circuit before transmitting between two end stations.	
This device uses hardware addresses to filter a network.	
Ethernet is defined at these layers.	
This layer supports flow control, sequencing, and acknowledgments.	
This device can measure the distance to a remote network.	
Logical addressing is used at this layer.	
Hardware addresses are defined at this layer.	
This device creates one big collision domain and one large broadcast domain.	

continues

continued

Description	Device or OSI Layer
This device creates many smaller collision domains, but the network is still one large broadcast domain.	
This device can never run full duplex.	
This device breaks up collision domains and broadcast domains.	

Written Lab 2.3: Identifying Collision and Broadcast Domains

1. In the following exhibit, identify the number of collision domains and broadcast domains in each specified device. Each device is represented by a letter:

    A. Hub

    B. Bridge

    C. Switch

    D. Router

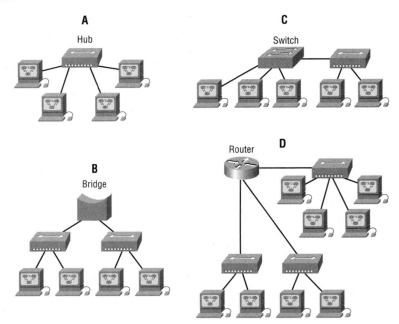

Review Questions

You can find the answers in Appendix B.

 The following questions are designed to test your understanding of this chapter's material. For more information on how to get additional questions, please see this book's introduction.

1. A receiving host has failed to receive all of the segments that it should acknowledge. What can the host do to improve the reliability of this communication session?

    A. Send a different source port number.

    B. Restart the virtual circuit.

    C. Decrease the sequence number.

    D. Decrease the window size.

2. Which layer of the OSI model is associated with the reliable transmission of datagrams?

    A. Transport

    B. Network

    C. Data Link

    D. Physical

3. Which layer 1 devices can be used to enlarge the area covered by a single LAN segment? (Choose two.)

    A. Switch

    B. NIC

    C. Hub

    D. Repeater

    E. RJ45 transceiver

4. Segmentation of a data stream happens at which layer of the OSI model?

    A. Physical

    B. Data Link

    C. Network

    D. Transport

5. Which of the following describe the main router functions? (Choose four.)

   A. Packet switching

   B. Collision prevention

   C. Packet filtering

   D. Broadcast domain enlargement

   E. Internetwork communication

   F. Broadcast forwarding

   G. Path selection

6. Routers operate at layer ___. LAN switches operate at layer ___. Ethernet hubs operate at layer ___. Word processing operates at layer ___.

   A. 3, 3, 1, 7

   B. 3, 2, 1, none

   C. 3, 2, 1, 7

   D. 2, 3, 1, 7

   E. 3, 3, 2, none

7. Which statement describes the function of the OSI Transport layer?

   A. It provides the connectivity and path selection between two host systems that may be located on geographically separated networks.

   B. It defines how data is formatted for transmission and how access to the physical media is controlled.

   C. It establishes, manages, and terminates sessions between two communicating hosts.

   D. It segments data from the system of the sending host and reassembles the data into a data stream on the system of the receiving host.

8. Why does the data communication industry use the layered OSI reference model? (Choose two.)

   A. It divides the network communication process into smaller and simpler components, thus aiding component development and design and troubleshooting.

   B. It enables equipment from different vendors to use the same electronic components, thus saving research and development funds.

   C. It supports the evolution of multiple competing standards and thus provides business opportunities for equipment manufacturers.

   D. It encourages industry standardization by defining what functions occur at each layer of the model.

   E. It provides a framework by which changes in functionality in one layer require changes in other layers.

9. What are two purposes for segmentation with a bridge?

   A. To add more broadcast domains

   B. To create more collision domains

   C. To add more bandwidth for users

   D. To allow more broadcasts for users

10. Which of the following is *not* a cause of LAN congestion?

    A. Too many hosts in a broadcast domain

    B. Adding switches for connectivity to the network

    C. Broadcast storms

    D. Low bandwidth

11. If a switch has three computers connected to it, with no VLANs present, how many broadcast and collision domains is the switch creating?

    A. Three broadcast and one collision

    B. Three broadcast and three collision

    C. One broadcast and three collision

    D. One broadcast and one collision

12. Which two layers of the OSI model relate to the transmission of bits over the wire and packet forwarding based on destination IP address? (Choose two.)

    A. 4

    B. 3

    C. 2

    D. 1

13. Which of the following are types of flow control? (Choose all that apply.)

    A. Buffering

    B. Cut-through

    C. Windowing

    D. Congestion avoidance

    E. VLANs

14. If a hub has three computers connected to it, how many broadcast and collision domains is the hub creating?

    A. Three broadcast and one collision

    B. Three broadcast and three collision

    C. One broadcast and three collision

    D. One broadcast and one collision

15. What is the purpose of flow control?

    A. To ensure that data is retransmitted if an acknowledgment is not received

    B. To reassemble segments in the correct order at the destination device

    C. To provide a means for the receiver to govern the amount of data sent by the sender

    D. To regulate the size of each segment

16. Which definitions are used to describe data at Layers 1, 2, and 4 of the OSI model? (Choose three.)

    A. Best-effort packet delivery

    B. Packets

    C. Frames

    D. Bits

    E. Segments

17. Which of the following is *not* a benefit of reference models such as the OSI model?

    A. It allows changes on one layer to affect operations on all other layers as well.

    B. It divides the network communication process into smaller and simpler components, thus aiding component development, design, and troubleshooting.

    C. It allows multiple-vendor development through standardization of network components.

    D. It allows various types of network hardware and software to communicate.

18. Which of the following devices do *not* operate at all levels of the OSI model?

    A. Network management stations (NMSs)

    B. Routers

    C. Web and application servers

    D. Network hosts

19. When an HTTP document must be retrieved from a location other than the local machine, what layer of the OSI model must be accessed first?

    A. Presentation

    B. Transport

    C. Application

    D. Network

20. Which layer of the OSI model offers three different modes of communication: *simplex*, *half duplex*, and *full duplex*?

    A. Presentation

    B. Transport

    C. Application

    D. Session

Chapter

3

Ethernet Technologies

THE FOLLOWING TOPICS ARE COVERED IN THIS CHAPTER:

✓ **Describing Ethernet Connections**

- Ethernet LAN Hardware
- Ethernet Transceivers and Cables
- UTP Implementation

✓ **Describing Ethernet Communications Standards**

- Definition of a LAN
- Components of a LAN
- Functions of a LAN
- Ethernet
- Ethernet LAN Standards
- Role of CSMA/CD in Ethernet
- Ethernet Frames
- Ethernet Frame Addressing
- Ethernet Addresses
- MAC Addresses and Binary/Hexadecimal Numbers

Before we move on and explore TCP/IP and DoD models, IP addressing, subnetting, and routing in the upcoming chapters, you've got to understand the big picture of LANs and learn the answers to two key questions: How is Ethernet used in today's networks? What are Media Access Control (MAC) addresses and how are they used?

This chapter will answer those questions and more. I'll not only discuss the basics of Ethernet and the way MAC addresses are used on an Ethernet LAN, I'll cover the protocols used with Ethernet at the Data Link layer as well. You'll also learn about the various Ethernet specifications.

As you learned in Chapter 2, "Internetworking," there are a bunch of different types of devices specified at the different layers of the OSI model, and it's very important to understand the many types of cables and connectors used for connecting all those devices to a network. This chapter will review the various cabling used with Cisco devices, describing how to connect to a router or switch and even how to connect a router or switch with a console connection.

Also in this chapter, I'll provide an introduction to encapsulation. Encapsulation is the process of encoding data as it goes down the OSI stack.

After you finish reading this chapter, you'll encounter 20 review questions and four written labs. These are given to you to really lock the information from this chapter into your memory. So don't skip them!

To find up-to-the-minute updates for this chapter, please see: www.lammle.com/forum.

Ethernet Networks in Review

Ethernet is a contention-based media access method that allows all hosts on a network to share the same bandwidth of a link. Ethernet is popular because it's readily scalable, meaning that it's comparatively easy to integrate new technologies, such as upgrading from Fast Ethernet to Gigabit Ethernet, into an existing network infrastructure. It's also relatively simple to implement in the first place, and with it, troubleshooting is reasonably straightforward. Ethernet uses both Data Link and Physical layer specifications, and this chapter will give you both the Data Link layer and Physical layer information you need to effectively implement, troubleshoot, and maintain an Ethernet network.

Collision Domain

As mentioned in Chapter 2, the term *collision domain* is an Ethernet term that refers to a particular network scenario wherein one device sends a packet out on a network segment, thereby forcing every other device on that same physical network segment to pay attention to it. This can be bad because if two devices on one physical segment transmit at the same time, a collision event—a situation where each device's digital signals interfere with another on the wire—occurs and forces the devices to retransmit later. Collisions can have a dramatically negative effect on network performance, so they're definitely something you want to avoid!

The situation I just described is typically found in a hub environment where each host segment connects to a hub that represents only one collision domain and one broadcast domain. This begs the question that we discussed in Chapter 2: What's a broadcast domain?

Broadcast Domain

Here's the written definition: *Broadcast domain* refers a group of devices on a network segment that hear all the broadcasts sent on that network segment.

Even though a broadcast domain is typically a boundary delimited by physical media like switches and routers, it can also reference a logical division of a network segment where all hosts can reach each other via a Data Link layer (hardware address) broadcast.

That's the basic story, so now let's take a look at a collision detection mechanism used in half-duplex Ethernet.

CSMA/CD

Ethernet networking uses *Carrier Sense Multiple Access with Collision Detection (CSMA/CD)*, a protocol that helps devices share the bandwidth evenly without having two devices transmit at the same time on the network medium. CSMA/CD was created to overcome the problem of those collisions that occur when packets are transmitted simultaneously from different nodes. And trust me—good collision management is crucial, because when a node transmits in a CSMA/CD network, all the other nodes on the network receive and examine that transmission. Only bridges and routers can effectively prevent a transmission from propagating throughout the entire network!

So, how does the CSMA/CD protocol work? Let's start by taking a look at Figure 3.1.

When a host wants to transmit over the network, it first checks for the presence of a digital signal on the wire. If all is clear, meaning no carrier is present (no other host is transmitting), the host will then proceed with its transmission. But it doesn't stop there. The transmitting host constantly monitors the wire to make sure no other hosts begin transmitting. If the host detects another signal on the wire, it sends out an extended jam signal that causes all nodes on the segment to stop sending data (think busy signal). The nodes respond to that jam signal by waiting a while before attempting to transmit again. Backoff algorithms determine when the colliding stations can retransmit. If collisions keep occurring after 15 tries, the nodes attempting to transmit will then time out. Pretty clean!

FIGURE 3.1   CSMA/CD

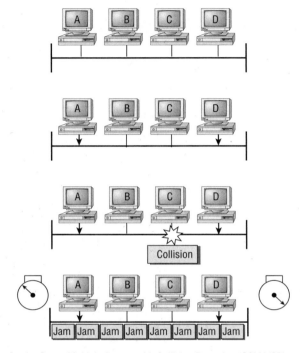

Carrier Sense Multiple Access with Collision Detection (CSMA/CD)

When a collision occurs on an Ethernet LAN, the following happens:

1. A jam signal informs all devices that a collision occurred.

2. The collision invokes a random backoff algorithm.

3. Each device on the Ethernet segment stops transmitting for a short time until their backoff timers expire.

4. All hosts have equal priority to transmit after the timers have expired.

The following are the effects of having a CSMA/CD network sustaining heavy collisions:

▪ Delay

▪ Low throughput

▪ Congestion

Backoff on an Ethernet network is the retransmission delay that's enforced when a collision occurs. When a collision occurs, a host will resume transmission after the forced time delay has expired. After this backoff delay period has expired, all stations have equal priority to transmit data.

In the following sections, I am going to cover Ethernet in detail at both the Data Link layer (layer 2) and the Physical layer (layer 1).

Half- and Full-Duplex Ethernet

Half-duplex Ethernet is defined in the original IEEE 802.3 Ethernet specification; Cisco says it uses only one wire pair with a digital signal running in both directions on the wire. Certainly, the IEEE specifications discuss the process of half duplex somewhat differently, but what Cisco is talking about is a general sense of what is happening here with Ethernet.

It also uses the CSMA/CD protocol to help prevent collisions and to permit retransmitting if a collision does occur. If a hub is attached to a switch, it must operate in half-duplex mode because the end stations must be able to detect collisions. Half-duplex Ethernet is only about 30 to 40 percent efficient because a large 100BaseT network will usually only give you 30Mbps to 40Mbps, at most.

But full-duplex Ethernet uses two pairs of wires at the same time instead of one wire pair like half duplex. And full duplex uses a point-to-point connection between the transmitter of the transmitting device and the receiver of the receiving device. This means that with full-duplex data transfer, you get a faster data transfer compared to half duplex. And because the transmitted data is sent on a different set of wires than the received data, no collisions will occur.

The reason you don't need to worry about collisions is because now it's like a freeway with multiple lanes instead of the single-lane road provided by half duplex. Full-duplex Ethernet is supposed to offer 100 percent efficiency in both directions—for example, you can get 20Mbps with a 10Mbps Ethernet running full duplex or 200Mbps for Fast Ethernet. But this rate is something known as an aggregate rate, which translates as "you're supposed to get" 100 percent efficiency. No guarantees, in networking as in life.

Full-duplex Ethernet can be used in the following typical situations:

- With a connection from a switch to a host
- With a connection from a switch to a switch
- With a connection from a host to a host using a crossover cable
- With a connection from a switch to a router
- With a connection from a router to a router

 Full-duplex Ethernet requires a point-to-point connection when only two nodes are present. You can run full duplex with just about any device except a hub.

Now, if it's capable of all that speed, why wouldn't it deliver? Well, when a full-duplex Ethernet port is powered on, it first connects to the remote end and then negotiates with the other end of the Fast Ethernet link. This is called an *auto detect mechanism*. This mechanism first decides on the exchange capability, which means it checks to see if it can run at 10 Mbps, 100 Mbps, 1,000 Mbps, or even 10,000 Mbps. It then checks to see if it can run full duplex, and if it can't, it will run half duplex.

Remember that half-duplex Ethernet shares a collision domain and provides a lower effective throughput than full-duplex Ethernet, which typically has a private per-port collision domain and a higher effective throughput.

Last, remember these important points:

- There are no collisions in full-duplex mode.
- A dedicated switch port is required for each full-duplex node.
- The host network card and the switch port must be capable of operating in full-duplex mode.

Now let's take a look at how Ethernet works at the Data Link layer.

Ethernet at the Data Link Layer

Ethernet at the Data Link layer is responsible for Ethernet addressing, commonly referred to as hardware addressing or MAC addressing. Ethernet is also responsible for framing packets received from the Network layer and preparing them for transmission on the local network through the Ethernet contention-based media access method. There are four different types of Ethernet frames available:

- Ethernet_II
- IEEE 802.3
- IEEE 802.2
- Sub Network Access Protocol (SNAP)

I'll go over all four of the available Ethernet frames in the upcoming sections, but it's important to remember that networks typically use only the Ethernet_II frame today, but the CCNA Data Center objectives cover all four. Why talk about frames that we don't use? That's a good question. My only thought is "Special Cisco Torture (SCT)." Seriously, though, for Ethernet, we use only Ethernet_II, but the current wireless specifications do use a SNAP frame, so I'll show you that frame in a minute (and it is an exam objective!).

Ethernet Addressing

Here's where we get into how Ethernet addressing works. It uses the *Media Access Control (MAC)* address burned into each and every Ethernet network interface card (NIC), however, this address can be overridden. The MAC, or hardware, address is a 48-bit (6-byte) address written in a hexadecimal format.

Figure 3.2 shows the 48-bit MAC addresses and how the bits are divided.

The *organizationally unique identifier (OUI)* is assigned by the IEEE to an organization. It's composed of 24 bits, or 3 bytes. The organization, in turn, assigns a globally administered address (24 bits, or 3 bytes) that is unique (supposedly, again—no guarantees) to each and every adapter it manufactures. Look closely at the figure. The high-order bit is the Individual/

Group (I/G) bit. When it has a value of 0, we can assume that the address is the MAC address of a device and may well appear in the source portion of the MAC header. When it is a 1, we can assume that the address represents either a broadcast or multi-cast address in Ethernet or a broadcast or functional address in Token Ring and FDDI.

FIGURE 3.2 Ethernet addressing using MAC addresses

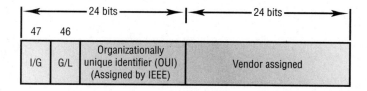

The next bit is the global/local bit, or just G/L bit (also known as U/L, where *U* means *universal*). When set to 0, this bit represents a globally administered address (as by the IEEE). When the bit is a 1, it represents a locally governed and administered address. The low-order 24 bits of an Ethernet address represent a locally administered or manufacturer-assigned code. This portion commonly starts with 24 0s for the first card made and continues in order until there are 24 1s for the last (16,777,216th) card made. You'll find that many manufacturers use these same six hex digits as the last six characters of their serial number on the same card.

Binary to Decimal and Hexadecimal Conversion

Before we get into working with the TCP/IP protocol and IP addressing (covered in Chapter 5, "IP Addressing"), it's really important for you to truly understand the differences between binary, decimal, and hexadecimal numbers and how to convert one format into the other.

So we'll start with binary numbering. It's pretty simple, really. The digits used are limited to either a 1 (one) or a 0 (zero), and each digit is called a *bit* (short for *bi*nary dig*it*). Typically, you count either 4 or 8 bits together, with these being referred to as a nibble and a byte, respectively.

What interests us in binary numbering is the value represented in a decimal format—the typical decimal format being the base-10 number scheme that we've all used since kindergarten. The binary numbers are placed in a value spot: starting at the right and moving left, with each spot having double the value of the previous spot.

Table 3.1 shows the decimal values of each bit location in a nibble and a byte. Remember, a nibble is 4 bits and a byte is 8 bits.

TABLE 3.1 Binary values

Nibble Values	Byte Values
8 4 2 1	128 64 32 16 8 4 2 1

What all this means is that if a one digit (1) is placed in a value spot, then the nibble or byte takes on that decimal value and adds it to any other value spots that have a 1. And if a zero (0) is placed in a bit spot, you don't count that value.

Let me clarify things. If we have a 1 placed in each spot of our nibble, we would then add up 8 + 4 + 2 + 1 to give us a maximum value of 15. Another example for our nibble values would be 1010; that means that the 8-bit and the 2-bit are turned on, which equals a decimal value of 10. If we have a nibble binary value of 0110, then our decimal value would be 6, because the 4 and 2 bits are turned on.

But the byte values can add up to a value that's significantly higher than 15. This is how—If we counted every bit as a one (1), then the byte binary value would look like this (remember, 8 bits equal a byte):

11111111

We would then count up every bit spot because each is turned on. It would look like this, which demonstrates the maximum value of a byte:

128 + 64 + 32 + 16 + 8 + 4 + 2 + 1 = 255

There are plenty of other decimal values that a binary number can equal. Let's work through a few examples:

10010110

Which bits are on? The 128, 16, 4, and 2 bits are on, so we'll just add them up: 128 + 16 + 4 + 2 = 150.

01101100

Which bits are on? The 64, 32, 8, and 4 bits are on, so we just need to add them up: 64 + 32 + 8 + 4 = 108.

11101000

Which bits are on? The 128, 64, 32, and 8 bits are on, so just add the values up: 128 + 64 + 32 + 8 = 232.

Table 3.2 is a table you should memorize before braving the IP sections in Chapter 5.

TABLE 3.2   Binary to decimal memorization chart

Binary Value	Decimal Value
10000000	128
11000000	192
11100000	224
11110000	240

Binary Value	Decimal Value
11111000	248
11111100	252
11111110	254
11111111	255

Hexadecimal addressing is completely different than binary or decimal—it's converted by reading nibbles, not bytes. By using a nibble, we can convert these bits to hex pretty simply. First, understand that the hexadecimal addressing scheme uses only the numbers 0 through 9. And since the numbers 10, 11, 12, and so on can't be used (because they are two-digit numbers), the letters *A*, *B*, *C*, *D*, *E*, and *F* are used to represent 10, 11, 12, 13, 14, and 15, respectively.

NOTE   *Hex* is short for *hexadecimal,* which is a numbering system that uses the first six letters of the alphabet (*A* through *F*) to extend beyond the available 10 digits in the decimal system.

Table 3.3 shows both the binary value and the decimal value for each hexadecimal digit.

TABLE 3.3 Hex to binary to decimal chart

Hexadecimal Value	Binary Value	Decimal Value
0	0000	0
1	0001	1
2	0010	2
3	0011	3
4	0100	4
5	0101	5
6	0110	6
7	0111	7

TABLE 3.3   Hex to binary to decimal chart *(continued)*

Hexadecimal Value	Binary Value	Decimal Value
8	1000	8
9	1001	9
A	1010	10
B	1011	11
C	1100	12
D	1101	13
E	1110	14
F	1111	15

Did you notice that the first 10 hexadecimal digits (0–9) are the same value as the decimal values? If not, look again. This handy fact makes those values super easy to convert.

So suppose you have something like this: 0x6A. (Sometimes Cisco likes to put *0x* in front of characters so you know that they are a hex value. It doesn't have any other special meaning.) What are the binary and decimal values? All you have to remember is that each hex character is one nibble and two hex characters together make a byte. To figure out the binary value, we need to put the hex characters into two nibbles and then put them together into a byte. 6 = 0110 and A (which is 10 in hex) = 1010, so the complete byte would be 01101010, which is 106 in decimal. To convert a longer hexadecimal number, such as 0x718, you'd do the same but the binary would be longer, 111 0001 1000, and you just keep counting from right to left. Let's give it a shot, but first let's look at our possible numbers. Starting on the right, just keep doubling the number and don't stop at 8 bits this time. The valid numbers are 8, 16, 256, 512, and 1024, which equals 1816 in decimal. Let's do one more: 0xC84. In binary it would be 1100 1000 0100. The valid numbers are 4, 128, 1024, and 2048, which equals 3204.

You must be able to convert from hex to decimal on the CCNA Data Center exam! Practice your conversions.

Now, to convert from binary to hex, just take the byte and break it into nibbles. Here's what I mean.

Say you have the binary number 01010101. First, break it into nibbles—0101 and 0101—with the value of each nibble being 5 since the 1 and 4 bits are on. This makes the hex answer

0x55. And in decimal format, the binary number is 01010101, which converts to 64 + 16 + 4 + 1 = 85.

Here's another binary number:

11001100

Your answer would be 1100 = 12 and 1100 = 12 (therefore, it's converted to CC in hex). The decimal conversion answer would be 128 + 64 + 8 + 4 = 204.

One more example, then we need to get working on the Physical layer. Suppose you had the following binary number:

10110101

The hex answer would be 0xB5, since 1011 converts to B and 0101 converts to 5 in hex value. The decimal equivalent is 128 + 32 + 16 + 4 + 1 = 181.

See Written Lab 3.1 for more practice with binary/decimal/hexadecimal conversion.

Ethernet Frames

The Data Link layer is responsible for combining bits into bytes and bytes into frames. Frames are used at the Data Link layer to encapsulate packets handed down from the Network layer for transmission on a type of media access. There are three types of media access methods: contention (Ethernet), token passing (Token Ring and FDDI), and polling (IBM mainframes and 100VG-AnyLAN), although token passing and polling are not typically used in today's networks and are in the objectives just for SCT.

The function of Ethernet stations is to pass data frames between each other using a group of bits known as a MAC frame format. This provides error detection from a *cyclic redundancy check (CRC)*. But remember—this is error detection, not error correction. The 802.3 frames and Ethernet frame are shown in Figure 3.3.

Encapsulating a frame within a different type of frame is called *tunneling*.

Following are the details of the different fields in the 802.3 and Ethernet frame types:

Preamble   An alternating 1,0 pattern provides a 5MHz clock at the start of each packet, which allows the receiving devices to lock the incoming bit stream.

Start Frame Delimiter (SFD)/Synch   The preamble is seven octets and the SFD is one octet (synch). The SFD is 10101011, where the last pair of 1s allows the receiver to come into the alternating 1,0 pattern somewhere in the middle and still sync up and detect the beginning of the data.

FIGURE 3.3   802.3 and Ethernet frame formats

Ethernet_II

Preamble 8 bytes	DA 6 bytes	SA 6 bytes	Type 2 bytes	Data	FCS 4 bytes

802.3_Ethernet

Preamble 8 bytes	DA 6 bytes	SA 6 bytes	Length 2 bytes	Data	FCS

Destination Address (DA)   This transmits a 48-bit value using the least significant bit (LSB) first. The DA is used by receiving stations to determine whether an incoming packet is addressed to a particular node. The destination address can be an individual address or a broadcast or multi-cast MAC address. Remember that a broadcast is all 1s (or *F*s in hex) and is sent to all devices but a multicast is sent only to a similar subset of nodes on a network.

Source Address (SA)   The SA is a 48-bit MAC address used to identify the transmitting device, and it uses the LSB first. Broadcast and multi-cast address formats are illegal within the SA field.

Length or Type   802.3 uses a Length field, but the Ethernet_II frame uses a Type field to identify the Network layer protocol. 802.3 cannot identify the upper-layer protocol and must be used with a proprietary LAN—IPX, for example.

Data   This is a packet sent down to the Data Link layer from the Network layer. The size can vary from 46 to 1,500 bytes.

Frame Check Sequence (FCS)   FCS is a field at the end of the frame that's used to store the cyclic redundancy check (CRC) answer. The CRC is a mathematical algorithm that's run when each frame is built. When a receiving host receives the frame and runs the CRC, the answer should be the same. If not, the frame is discarded, assuming errors have occurred.

Let's pause here for a minute and take a look at some frames caught on our trusty network analyzer. You can see that the frame below has only three fields: Destination, Source, and Type (shown as Protocol Type on this analyzer):

```
Destination:    00:60:f5:00:1f:27
Source:         00:60:f5:00:1f:2c
Protocol Type: 08-00 IP
```

This is an Ethernet_II frame. Notice that the Type field is IP, or 08–00 (mostly just referred to as 0x800) in hexadecimal.

The next frame has the same fields, so it must be an Ethernet_II frame too:

```
Destination:    ff:ff:ff:ff:ff:ff Ethernet Broadcast
Source:         02:07:01:22:de:a4
Protocol Type:  81-37 NetWare
```

I included this one so you could see that the frame can carry more than just IP—it can also carry IPX, or 81-37h. Did you notice that this frame was a broadcast? You can tell because the destination hardware address is all 1s in binary, or all Fs in hexadecimal.

Now, pay special attention to the Length field in the next frame; this must be an 802.3 frame:

```
Flags:          0x80 802.3
Status:         0x00
Packet Length:  64
Timestamp:      12:45:45.192000 06/26/1998
Destination:    ff:ff:ff:ff:ff:ff Ethernet Broadcast
Source:         08:00:11:07:57:28
Length:         34
```

The problem with this frame is this: How do you know which protocol this packet is going to be handed to at the Network layer? It doesn't specify in the frame, so it must be IPX. Why? Because when Novell created the 802.3 frame type (before the IEEE did and called it 802.3 Raw), Novell was pretty much the only LAN server out there. So, the folks at Novell assumed that if you were running a LAN, it must be IPX, and they didn't include any Network layer protocol field information in the 802.3 frame.

Let's take a look at one more Ethernet_II frame. You can see that the Ethernet frame is the same Ethernet_II frame we use with the IPv4 routed protocol. The Type field has 0x86dd when the frame is carrying IPv6 data, and when we have IPv4 data, the frame uses 0x0800 in the protocol field:

```
Destination: IPv6-Neighbor-Discovery_00:01:00:03 (33:33:00:01:00:03)
Source: Aopen_3e:7f:dd (00:01:80:3e:7f:dd)
Type: IPv6 (0x86dd)
```

This is the beauty of the Ethernet_II frame. Because of the Type field, we can run any Network layer routed protocol and it will carry the data because it can identify the Network layer protocol.

802.2 and SNAP

Since the 802.3 Ethernet frame cannot by itself identify the upper-layer (Network) protocol, it obviously needs some help. The IEEE defined the 802.2 LLC specifications to provide this function and more. Figure 3.4 shows the IEEE 802.3 with LLC (802.2) and the SNAP. The LLC header information is added to the data portion of the frame. Now let's take a look at an 802.2 frame and SNAP captured from our analyzer.

FIGURE 3.4   802.2 and SNAP

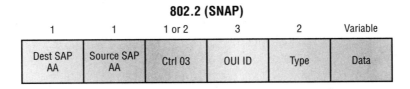

802.2 Frame

The following is an 802.2 frame captured with a protocol analyzer:

```
Flags:        0x80 802.3
Status:       0x02 Truncated
Packet Length:64
Slice Length: 51
Timestamp:    12:42:00.592000 03/26/1998
Destination:  ff:ff:ff:ff:ff:ff Ethernet Broadcast
Source:       00:80:c7:a8:f0:3d
LLC Length:   37
Dest. SAP:    0xe0 NetWare
Source SAP:   0xe0 NetWare Individual LLC
  SublayerManagement Function
Command:      0x03 Unnumbered Information
```

You can see that the first frame has a Length field, so it's probably an 802.3, right? Maybe. Look again. It also has a destination and source service access point (DSAP and an SSAP), so it's not an 802.3. It has to be an 802.2 frame. (Remember, an 802.2 frame is an 802.3 frame with the LLC information in the data field of the header so we know what the upper-layer protocol is.) The SSAP and DSAP define the Network layer protocol source and destination. It would be rare to see these fields define anything but IP and IPv6 in today's networks.

SNAP Frame

The SNAP frame has its own protocol field to identify the upper-layer protocol. This is really a way to allow an Ethernet_II Ether-Type field to be used in an 802.3 frame. Even though the following network trace shows a protocol field, it is actually an Ethernet_II type (Ether-Type) field:

```
Flags:          0x80 802.3
Status:         0x00
Packet Length:78
Timestamp:      09:32:48.264000 01/04/2000
802.3 Header
 Destination:   09:00:07:FF:FF:FF AT Ph 2 Broadcast
 Source:        00:00:86:10:C1:6F
 LLC Length:    60
802.2 Logical Link Control (LLC) Header
 Dest. SAP:     0xAA SNAP
 Source SAP:    0xAA SNAP
 Command:       0x03 Unnumbered Information
 Protocol:      0x080007809B AppleTalk
```

You can identify a SNAP frame because the DSAP and SSAP fields are always AA, and the Command field is always 3.

This frame type was created because not all protocols worked well with the 802.3 Ethernet frame, which didn't have an Ether-Type field. To allow the proprietary protocols created by application developers to be used in the LLC frame, the IEEE defined the SNAP format that uses the exact same codes as Ethernet_II. Up until about 1997 or so, the SNAP frame was on its way out of the corporate market. However, the 802.11 wireless LAN specification uses an Ethernet SNAP field to identify the Network layer protocol. Cisco also still uses a SNAP frame with its proprietary protocol Cisco Discovery Protocol (CDP), but you won't find SNAP in today's Ethernet LAN networks.

Ethernet at the Physical Layer

Ethernet was first implemented by a group called DIX (Digital, Intel, and Xerox). They created and implemented the first Ethernet LAN specification, which the IEEE used to create the IEEE 802.3 committee. This was a 10Mbps network that ran on coax and then eventually twisted-pair and fiber physical media.

The IEEE extended the 802.3 committee to two new committees known as 802.3u (Fast Ethernet) and 802.3ab (Gigabit Ethernet on category 5) and then finally, 802.3ae (10Gbps over fiber and coax).

Figure 3.5 shows the IEEE 802.3 and original Ethernet Physical layer specifications.

FIGURE 3.5   Original Ethernet Physical layer specifications

Data Link (MAC layer)	Ethernet	802.3							
Physical		10Base2	10Base5	10BaseT	10BaseF	100BaseTX	100BaseFX	100BaseT4

When designing your LAN, it's really important to understand the different types of Ethernet media available to you. Sure, it would be great to run Gigabit Ethernet to each desktop and 10Gbps between switches, and you need to figure out how to justify the cost of that network today. But if you mix and match the different types of Ethernet media methods currently available, you can come up with a cost-effective network solution that works great.

The EIA/TIA (which stands for the Electronic Industries Association and the newer Telecommunications Industry Alliance) is the standards body that creates the Physical layer specifications for Ethernet. The EIA/TIA specifies that Ethernet use a *registered jack (RJ) connector* on *unshielded twisted-pair (UTP)* cabling (RJ45). However, this is just called an 8-pin modular connector.

Each Ethernet cable type that is specified by the EIA/TIA has inherent attenuation, which is defined as the loss of signal strength as it travels the length of a cable and is measured in decibels (dB). The cabling used in corporate and home markets is measured in categories. A higher-quality cable will have a higher-rated category and lower attenuation. For example, category 5 is better than category 3 because category 5 cables have more wire twists per foot and therefore less crosstalk. Crosstalk is the unwanted signal interference from adjacent pairs in the cable.

Here are the original IEEE 802.3 standards:

10Base2   10Mbps, baseband technology, up to 185 meters in length. Known as *thinnet* and can support up to 30 workstations on a single segment. Uses a physical and logical bus with BNC connectors and thin coaxial cable. The 10 means 10Mbps, *Base* means baseband technology (which is a digital signaling method for communication on the network), and the 2 means almost 200 meters. 10Base2 Ethernet cards use BNC (British Naval Connector, Bayonet Neill Concelman, or Bayonet Nut Connector), T-connectors, and terminators to connect to a network.

10Base5   10Mbps, baseband technology, up to 500 meters in length using thick coaxial cable. Known as *thicknet*. Uses a physical and logical bus with AUI connectors. Up to 2,500 meters with repeaters and 1,024 users for all segments.

10BaseT   10Mbps using category 3 unshielded twisted-pair (UTP) wiring for runs up to 100 meters. Unlike with the 10Base2 and 10Base5 networks, each device must connect into a hub or switch, and you can have only one host per segment or wire. Uses an RJ45 connector (8-pin modular connector) with a physical star topology and a logical bus.

Each of the 802.3 standards defines an AUI, which allows a one-bit-at-a-time transfer to the Physical layer from the Data Link media-access method. This allows the MAC address to remain constant but means the Physical layer can support both existing and new technologies. The thing is, the original AUI interface was a 15-pin connector, which allowed a transceiver (transmitter/receiver) that provided a 15-pin-to-twisted-pair conversion.

There's an issue, though—the AUI interface can't support 100Mbps Ethernet because of the high frequencies involved. So 100BaseT needed a new interface, and the 802.3u specifications created one called the Media Independent Interface (MII), which provides 100Mbps throughput. The MII uses a nibble, which you of course remember is defined as 4 bits. Gigabit Ethernet uses a Gigabit Media Independent Interface (GMII) and transmits 8 bits at a time. 802.3u (Fast Ethernet) is compatible with 802.3 Ethernet because they share the same physical characteristics. Fast Ethernet and Ethernet use the same maximum transmission unit (MTU) and the same MAC mechanisms, and they both preserve the frame format that is used by 10BaseT Ethernet. Basically, Fast Ethernet is just based on an extension to the IEEE 802.3 specification, and because of that, it offers us a speed increase of 10 times that of 10BaseT.

Here are the expanded IEEE Ethernet 802.3 standards, starting with Fast Ethernet:

100Base-TX (IEEE 802.3u)   100Base-TX, most commonly known as Fast Ethernet, uses EIA/TIA category 5, 5E, or 6 UTP two-pair wiring. One user per segment; up to 100 meters long. It uses an RJ45 connector with a physical star topology and a logical bus.

100Base-FX (IEEE 802.3u)   Uses fiber cabling 62.5/125-micron multi-mode fiber. Point-to-point topology; up to 412 meters long. It uses ST and SC connectors, which are media-interface connectors.

1000Base-CX (IEEE 802.3z)   Copper twisted-pair called twinax (a balanced coaxial pair) that can run only up to 25 meters and uses a special 9-pin connector known as the High Speed Serial Data Connector (HSSDC).

1000Base-T (IEEE 802.3ab)   Category 5, four-pair UTP wiring up to 100 meters long and up to 1Gbps.

1000Base-SX (IEEE 802.3z)   The implementation of 1 Gigabit Ethernet running over multimode fiber-optic cable (instead of copper twisted-pair cable) and using short wavelength laser. Multi-mode fiber (MMF) using 62.5- and 50-micron core; uses an 850 nano-meter (nm) laser and can go up to 220 meters with 62.5-micron, 550 meters with 50-micron.

1000Base-LX (IEEE 802.3z)   Single-mode fiber that uses a 9-micron core and 1300 nm laser and can go from 3 kilometers up to 10 kilometers.

1000Base-ZX (Cisco standard)   1000BaseZX (or 1000Base-ZX) is a Cisco-specified standard for gigabit Ethernet communication. 1000BaseZX operates on ordinary single-mode fiber-optic link with spans up to 43.5 miles (70 km).

10GBase-T   10GBase-T is a standard proposed by the IEEE 802.3an committee to provide 10Gbps connections over conventional UTP cables (category 5e, 6, or 7 cables). 10GBase-T allows the conventional RJ45 used for Ethernet LANs. It can support signal transmission at the full 100-meter distance specified for LAN wiring.

The following are all part of the IEEE 802.3ae standard.

10GBase-Short Range (SR)   An implementation of 10 Gigabit Ethernet that uses short-wavelength lasers at 850 nm over multi-mode fiber. It has a maximum transmission distance of between 2 and 300 meters, depending on the size and quality of the fiber.

10GBase-Long Range (LR)   An implementation of 10 Gigabit Ethernet that uses long-wavelength lasers at 1,310 nm over single-mode fiber. It also has a maximum transmission distance between 2 meters and 10 kilometer, depending on the size and quality of the fiber.

10GBase-Extended Range (ER)   An implementation of 10 Gigabit Ethernet running over single-mode fiber. It uses extra-long-wavelength lasers at 1,550 nm. It has the longest transmission distances possible of the 10-Gigabit technologies: anywhere from 2 meters up to 40 kilometer, depending on the size and quality of the fiber used.

10GBase-Short Wavelength (SW)   10GBase-SW, as defined by IEEE 802.3ae, is a mode of 10GBase-S for MMF with an 850 nm laser transceiver with a bandwidth of 10Gbps. It can support up to 300 meters of cable length. This media type is designed to connect to SONET equipment.

10GBase-Long Wavelength (LW)   10GBase-LW is a mode of 10GBase-L supporting a link length of 10 kilometer on standard single-mode fiber (SMF) (G.652). This media type is designed to connect to SONET equipment.

10GBase-Extra Long Wavelength (EW)   10GBase-EW is a mode of 10GBase-E supporting a link length of up to 40 kilometer on SMF based on G.652 using optical-wavelength 1,550 nm. This media type is designed to connect to SONET equipment.

If you want to implement a network medium that is not susceptible to electromagnetic interference (EMI), fiber-optic cable provides a more secure, long-distance cable that is not susceptible to EMI at high speeds.

Table 3.4 summarizes the cable types.

TABLE 3.4   Common Ethernet cable types

Ethernet Name	Cable Type	Maximum Speed	Maximum Transmission Distance	Notes
10Base5	Coax	10Mbps	500 meters per segment	Also called thicknet, this cable type uses vampire taps to connect devices to cable.

Ethernet Name	Cable Type	Maximum Speed	Maximum Transmission Distance	Notes
10Base2	Coax	10Mbps	185 meters per segment	Also called thinnet, a very popular implementation of Ethernet over coax.
10BaseT	UTP	10Mbps	100 meters per segment	One of the most popular network cabling schemes.
100Base-TX	UTP, STP	100Mbps	100 meters per segment	Two pairs of category 5 UTP.
10Base-FL	Fiber	10Mbps	Varies (ranges from 500 meters to 2,000 meters)	Ethernet over fiber optics to the desktop.
100Base-FX	MMF	100Mbps	2,000 meters	100Mbps Ethernet over fiber optics.
1000Base-T	UTP	1000Mbps	100 meters	Four pairs of category 5e or higher.
1000Base-SX	MMF	1000Mbps	550 meters	Uses SC fiber connectors. Max length depends on fiber size.
1000Base-CX	Balanced, shielded copper	1000Mbps	25 meters	Uses a special connector, the HSSDC. This is very popular in Cisco's UCS implementation, called Twinax.
1000Base-LX	MMF and SMF	1000Mbps	550 meters multimode/ 2,000 meters single mode	Uses longer wavelength laser than 1000Base-SX. Uses SC and LC connectors.
10GBase-T	UTP	10Gbps	100 meters	Connects to the network like a Fast Ethernet link using UTP.
10GBase-SR	MMF	10Gbps	300 meters	850 nm laser. Max length depends on fiber size and quality.
10GBase-LR	SMF	10Gbps	10 kilometers	1,310 nm laser. Max length depends on fiber size and quality.

TABLE 3.4   Common Ethernet cable types *(continued)*

Ethernet Name	Cable Type	Maximum Speed	Maximum Transmission Distance	Notes
10GBase-ER	SMF	10Gbps	40 kilometers	1,550 nm laser. Max length depends on fiber size and quality.
10GBase-SW	MMF	10Gbps	300 meters	850 nm laser transceiver.
10GBase-LW	SMF	10Gbps	10 kilometers	Typically used with SONET.
10GBase-EW	SMF	10Gbps	40 kilometers	1,550 nm optical wavelength.

Armed with the basics covered in this chapter, you're equipped to go to the next level and put Ethernet to work using various Ethernet cabling.

Ethernet Cabling

A discussion about Ethernet cabling is an important one, especially if you are planning on taking the Cisco exams. You need to really understand the following three types of cables:

- Straight-through cable
- Crossover cable
- Rolled cable

We will look at each in the following sections.

Straight-Through Cable

The *straight-through cable* is used to connect the following devices:

- Host to switch or hub
- Router to switch or hub

Four wires are used in straight-through cable to connect Ethernet devices. It is relatively simple to create this type; Figure 3.6 shows the four wires used in a straight-through Ethernet cable.

Notice that only pins 1, 2, 3, and 6 are used. Just connect 1 to 1, 2 to 2, 3 to 3, and 6 to 6 and you'll be up and networking in no time. However, remember that this would be an Ethernet-only cable and wouldn't work with voice or other LAN or WAN technology.

FIGURE 3.6   Straight-through Ethernet cable

Figure 3.6 is used in 10/100Mbps Ethernet. Gigabit Ethernet uses all four pairs.

Crossover Cable

The *crossover cable* can be used to connect the following devices:

- Switch to switch
- Hub to hub
- Host to host
- Hub to switch
- Router direct to host

The same four wires used in the straight-through cable are used in this cable; we just connect different pins together. Figure 3.7 shows how the four wires are used in a crossover Ethernet cable.

FIGURE 3.7   Crossover Ethernet cable

Notice that instead of connecting 1 to 1, 2 to 2, and so on, here we connect pins 1 to 3 and 2 to 6 on each side of the cable.

Rolled Cable

Although *rolled cable* isn't used to connect any Ethernet connections together, you can use a rolled Ethernet cable to connect a host EIA-TIA 232 interface to a router console serial communication (COM) port.

If you have a Cisco router or switch, you would use this cable to connect your PC running HyperTerminal to the Cisco hardware. Eight wires are used in this cable to connect serial devices, although not all eight are used to send information, just as in Ethernet networking. Figure 3.8 shows the eight wires used in a rolled cable.

FIGURE 3.8   Rolled Ethernet cable

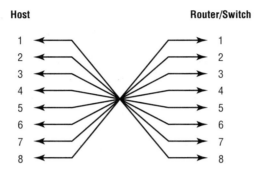

These are probably the easiest cables to make because you just cut the end off on one side of a straight-through cable, turn it over, and put it back on (with a new connector, of course).

Once you have the correct cable connected from your PC to the Cisco router or switch console port, you can start HyperTerminal to create a console connection and configure the device. Typically we'd use a new terminal emulator such as SecureCRT or Putty. Set the configuration as follows:

1. Open HyperTerminal and enter a name for the connection. It is irrelevant what you name it, but I always just use Cisco. Then click OK.

2. Choose the communications port—either COM1 or COM2, whichever is open on your PC.

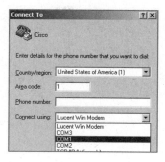

3. Now set the port settings. The default values (2400bps and no flow control hardware) will not work; you must set the port settings as shown in Figure 3.9.

FIGURE 3.9   Port settings for a rolled cable connection

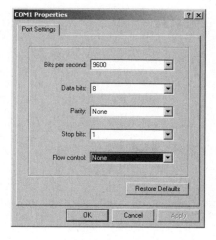

Notice that the bit rate is now set to 9600 and the flow control is set to None. At this point, you can click OK and press the Enter key and you should be connected to your Cisco device console port.

We've taken a look at the various RJ45 unshielded twisted pair (UTP) cables. Keeping this in mind, what cable is used between the switches in Figure 3.10?

In order for host A to ping host B, you need a crossover cable to connect the two switches together. But what types of cables are used in the network shown in Figure 3.11?

In Figure 3.11, there are a variety of cables in use. For the connection between the switches, we'd obviously use a crossover cable like the one we saw in Figure 3.7. The trouble is, we have a console connection that uses a rolled cable. Plus, the connection from the router to the switch is a straight-through cable, as is true for the hosts to the switches. Keep in mind that if we had a serial connection (which we don't), it would be a V.35 that we'd use to connect us to a WAN.

FIGURE 3.10   RJ45 UTP cable question #1

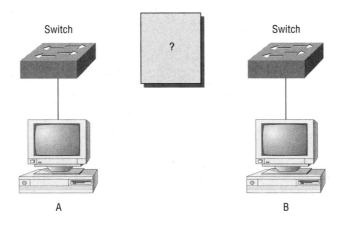

FIGURE 3.11   RJ45 UTP cable question #2

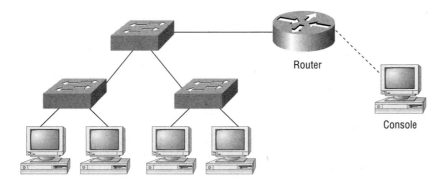

Data Encapsulation

When a host transmits data across a network to another device, the data goes through *encapsulation:* it is wrapped with protocol information at each layer of the OSI model. Each layer communicates only with its peer layer on the receiving device.

To communicate and exchange information, each layer uses *Protocol Data Units (PDUs).* These hold the control information attached to the data at each layer of the model. They are usually attached to the header in front of the data field but can also be at the trailer, or end, of it.

Each PDU attaches to the data by encapsulating it at each layer of the OSI model, and each has a specific name depending on the information provided in each header. This PDU information is read only by the peer layer on the receiving device. After its read, it's stripped off and the data is then handed to the next layer up.

Figure 3.12 shows the PDUs and how they attach control information to each layer. This figure demonstrates how the upper-layer user data is converted for transmission on the network. The data stream is then handed down to the Transport layer, which sets up a virtual circuit to the receiving device by sending over a synch packet. Next, the data stream is broken up into smaller pieces, and a Transport layer header is created and attached to the header of the data field; now the piece of data is called a *segment (a PDU).* Each segment can be sequenced so the data stream can be put back together on the receiving side exactly as it was transmitted.

FIGURE 3.12   Data encapsulation

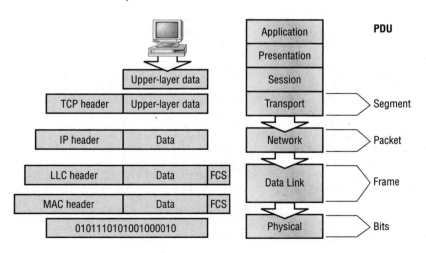

Each segment is then handed to the Network layer for network addressing and routing through the internetwork. Logical addressing (for example, IP) is used to get each segment to the correct network. The Network layer protocol adds a control header to the segment handed down from the Transport layer, and what we have now is called a *packet* or *datagram*. Remember that the Transport and Network layers work together to rebuild a data stream on a receiving host, but it's not part of their work to place their PDUs on a local network segment—which is the only way to get the information to a router or host.

It's the Data Link layer that's responsible for taking packets from the Network layer and placing them on the network medium (cable or wireless). The Data Link layer *encapsulates* each packet in a *frame*, and the frame's header carries the hardware addresses of the source and destination hosts. If the destination device is on a remote network, then the frame is sent to a router to be routed through an internetwork. Once it gets to the destination network, a new frame is used to get the packet to the destination host.

To put this frame on the network, it must first be put into a digital signal. Since a frame is really a logical group of 1s and 0s, the Physical layer is responsible for encoding these digits into a digital signal, which is read by devices on the same local network. The receiving devices will synchronize on the digital signal and extract (decode) the 1s and 0s from the digital signal. At this point, the devices reconstruct the frames, run a CRC, and then check their answer against the answer in the frame's FCS field. If it matches, the packet is pulled from the frame and what's left of the frame is discarded. This process is called *de-encapsulation*. The packet is handed to the Network layer, where the address is checked. If the address matches, the segment is pulled from the packet and what's left of the packet is discarded. The segment is processed at the Transport layer, which rebuilds the data stream and acknowledges to the transmitting station that it received each piece. It then happily hands the data stream to the upper-layer application.

At a transmitting device, the data encapsulation method works like this:

1. User information is converted to data for transmission on the network.

2. Data is converted to segments, and a reliable connection is set up between the transmitting and receiving hosts.

3. Segments are converted to packets or datagrams, and a logical address is placed in the header so each packet can be routed through an internetwork.

4. Packets or datagrams are converted to frames for transmission on the local network. Hardware (Ethernet) addresses are used to uniquely identify hosts on a local network segment.

5. Frames are converted to bits, and a digital encoding and clocking scheme is used.

To explain this in more detail using the layer addressing, I'll use Figure 3.13.

Remember that a data stream is handed down from the upper layer to the Transport layer. As technicians, we really don't care who the data stream comes from because that's really a programmer's problem. Our job is to rebuild the data stream reliably and hand it to the upper layers on the receiving device.

Before we go further in our discussion of Figure 3.13, let's discuss port numbers and make sure we understand them. The Transport layer uses port numbers to define both the virtual circuit and the upper-layer processes, as you can see from Figure 3.14.

FIGURE 3.13   PDU and layer addressing

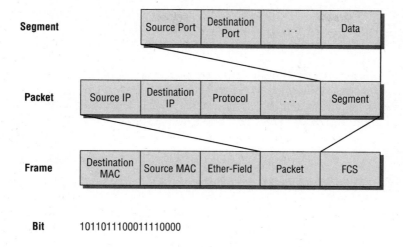

Bit   1011011100011110000

FIGURE 3.14   Port numbers at the Transport layer

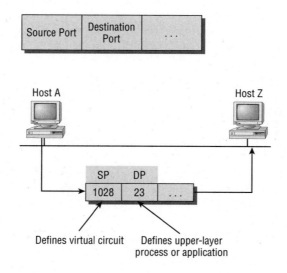

The Transport layer, when using a connection-oriented protocol (that is, TCP), takes the data stream, makes segments out of it, and establishes a reliable session by creating a virtual circuit. It then sequences (numbers) each segment and uses acknowledgments and flow control. If you're using TCP, the virtual circuit is defined by the source and destination port number as well as source and destination IP address (this is called a socket). Remember, the host just makes this up starting at port number 1024 (0 through 1023 are reserved for well-known port numbers). The destination port number defines the upper-layer process (application) that the data stream is handed to when the data stream is reliably rebuilt on the receiving host.

Now that you understand port numbers and how they are used at the Transport layer, let's go back to Figure 3.13. Once the Transport layer header information is added to the piece of data, it becomes a segment and is handed down to the Network layer along with the destination IP address. (The destination IP address was handed down from the upper layers to the Transport layer with the data stream, and it was discovered through a name resolution method at the upper layers—probably DNS.)

The Network layer adds a header, and adds the logical addressing (IP addresses), to the front of each segment. Once the header is added to the segment, the PDU is called a packet. The packet has a protocol field that describes where the segment came from (either UDP or TCP) so it can hand the segment to the correct protocol at the Transport layer when it reaches the receiving host.

The Network layer is responsible for finding the destination hardware address that dictates where the packet should be sent on the local network. It does this by using the Address Resolution Protocol (ARP)—something I'll talk about more in Chapter 4. IP at the Network layer looks at the destination IP address and compares that address to its own source IP address and subnet mask. If it turns out to be a local network request, the hardware address of the local host is requested via an ARP request. If the packet is destined for a remote host, IP will look for the IP address of the default gateway (router) instead.

The packet, along with the destination hardware address of either the local host or default gateway, is then handed down to the Data Link layer. The Data Link layer will add a header to the front of the packet and the piece of data then becomes a frame. (We call it a frame because both a header and a trailer are added to the packet, which makes it resemble bookends or a frame, if you will.) This is shown in Figure 3.13. The frame uses an Ether-Type field to describe which protocol the packet came from at the Network layer. Now a cyclic redundancy check (CRC) is run on the frame, and the answer to the CRC is placed in the Frame Check Sequence field found in the trailer of the frame.

The frame is now ready to be handed down, one bit at a time, to the Physical layer, which will use bit timing rules to encode the data in a digital signal. Every device on the network segment will synchronize with the clock and extract the 1s and 0s from the digital signal and build a frame. After the frame is rebuilt, a CRC is run to make sure the frame is okay. If everything turns out to be all good, the hosts will check the destination MAC and IP addresses to see if the frame is for them.

If all this is making your eyes cross and your brain freeze, don't freak. We'll be going over exactly how data is encapsulated and routed through an internetwork in Chapter 9.

Summary

In this chapter, you learned the fundamentals of Ethernet networking, how hosts communicate on a network, and how CSMA/CD works in an Ethernet half-duplex network. I also talked about the differences between half- and full-duplex modes and discussed the collision detection mechanism CSMA/CD.

Also in this chapter was a description of the common Ethernet cable types used in today's networks. And by the way, you'd be wise to study that section really well!

Four Ethernet frame types were discussed and are part of the CCNA Data Center objectives.

Important enough to not gloss over, this chapter provided an introduction to encapsulation. Encapsulation is the process of encoding data as it goes down the OSI stack. We are now going to move on to the TCP/IP DoD model in the next chapter.

Exam Essentials

Describe the operation of Carrier Sense Multiple Access with Collision Detection (CSMA/CD).   CSMA/CD is a protocol that helps devices share the bandwidth evenly without having two devices transmit at the same time on the network medium. Although it does not eliminate collisions, it helps to greatly reduce them, which reduces retransmissions, resulting in a more efficient transmission of data for all devices.

Differentiate half-duplex and full-duplex communication and define the requirements to utilize each method.   Full-duplex Ethernet uses two pairs of wires instead of one wire pair like half duplex. Full duplex allows for sending and receiving at the same time, using different wires to eliminate collisions, while half duplex can send or receive but not at the same time and still can suffer collisions. To use full duplex, the devices at both ends of the cable must be capable of and configured to perform full duplex.

Describe the sections of a MAC address and the information contained in each section.   The MAC, or hardware, address is a 48-bit (6-byte) address written in a hexadecimal format. The first 24 bits, or 3 bytes, are called the organizationally unique identifier (OUI), which is assigned by the IEEE to the manufacturer of the NIC. The balance of the number uniquely identifies the NIC.

Identify the binary and hexadecimal equivalent of a decimal number.   Any number expressed in one format can also be expressed in the other two. The ability to perform this conversion is critical to understanding IP addressing and subnetting. Be sure to go through the written labs covering binary to decimal to hexadecimal conversion.

Identify the fields in the Data Link portion of an Ethernet frame.   The fields in the Data Link portion of a frame include the Preamble, Start Frame Delimiter, Destination MAC address, Source MAC address, Length or Type, Data, and Frame Check Sequence.

Identify the IEEE physical standards for Ethernet cabling.   These standards describe the capabilities and physical characteristics of various cable types and include but are not limited to 10Base2, 10Base5, and 10BaseT.

Differentiate types of Ethernet cabling and identify their proper application.   The three types of cables that can be created from an Ethernet cable are straight-through (to connect a PC's or a router's Ethernet interface to a hub or switch), crossover (to connect hub to hub, hub to switch, switch to switch, or PC to PC), and rolled (for a console connection from a PC to a router or switch).

Describe the data encapsulation process and the role it plays in packet creation.   Data encapsulation is a process whereby information is added to the frame from each layer of the OSI model. This is also called packet creation. Each layer communicates only with its peer layer on the receiving device.

Written Labs

In this section, you'll complete the following labs to make sure you've got the information and concepts contained within them fully dialed in:

Lab 3.1: Binary/Decimal/Hexadecimal Conversion

Lab 3.2: CSMA/CD Operations

Lab 3.3: Cabling

Lab 3.4: Encapsulation

You can find the answers in Appendix A.

Written Lab 3.1: Binary/Decimal/Hexadecimal Conversion

1. Convert from decimal IP address to binary format.

Complete the following table to express 192.168.10.15 in binary format.

128	64	32	16	8	4	2	1	Binary

Complete the following table to express 172.16.20.55 in binary format.

128	64	32	16	8	4	2	1	Binary

Complete the following table to express 10.11.12.99 in binary format.

128	64	32	16	8	4	2	1	Binary

2. Convert the following from binary format to decimal IP address.

Complete the following table to express 11001100.00110011.10101010.01010101 in decimal IP address format.

128	64	32	16	8	4	2	1	Decimal

Complete the following table to express 11000110.11010011.00111001.11010001 in decimal IP address format.

128	64	32	16	8	4	2	1	Decimal

Complete the following table to express 10000100.11010010.10111000.10100110 in decimal IP address format.

128	64	32	16	8	4	2	1	Decimal

3. Convert the following from binary format to hexadecimal.

Complete the following table to express 11011000.00011011.00111101.01110110 in hexadecimal.

128	64	32	16	8	4	2	1	Hexadecimal

Complete the following table to express 11001010.11110101.10000011.11101011 in hexadecimal.

128	64	32	16	8	4	2	1	Hexadecimal

Complete the following table to express 10000100.11010010.01000011.10110011 in hexadecimal.

128	64	32	16	8	4	2	1	Hexadecimal

Written Lab 3.2: CSMA/CD Operations

Carrier Sense Multiple Access with Collision Detection (CSMA/CD) helps to minimize collisions in the network, thereby increasing data transmission efficiency. Place the following steps of its operation in the order in which they occur.

All hosts have equal priority to transmit after the timers have expired.

Each device on the Ethernet segment stops transmitting for a short time until the timers expire.

The collision invokes a random backoff algorithm.

A jam signal informs all devices that a collision occurred.

Written Lab 3.3: Cabling

For each of the following situations, determine whether a straight-through, crossover, or rolled cable would be used.

1. Host to host

2. Host to switch or hub

3. Router direct to host

4. Switch to switch

5. Router to switch or hub

6. Hub to hub

7. Hub to switch

8. Host to a router console serial communication (COM) port

Written Lab 3.4: Encapsulation

Place the following steps of the encapsulation process in the proper order.

Packets or datagrams are converted to frames for transmission on the local network. Hardware (Ethernet) addresses are used to uniquely identify hosts on a local network segment.

Segments are converted to packets or datagrams, and a logical address is placed in the header so each packet can be routed through an internetwork.

User information is converted to data for transmission on the network.

Frames are converted to bits, and a digital encoding and clocking scheme is used.

Data is converted to segments, and a reliable connection is set up between the transmitting and receiving hosts.

Review Questions

You can find the answers in Appendix B.

 The following questions are designed to test your understanding of this chapter's material. For more information on how to get additional questions, please see this book's introduction.

1. Which fields are contained within an IEEE Ethernet frame? (Choose two.)

   A. Source and destination MAC address

   B. Source and destination network address

   C. Source and destination MAC address and source and destination network address

   D. FCS field

2. Which of the following are unique characteristics of half-duplex Ethernet when compared to full-duplex Ethernet? (Choose two.)

   A. Half-duplex Ethernet operates in a shared collision domain.

   B. Half-duplex Ethernet operates in a private collision domain.

   C. Half-duplex Ethernet has higher effective throughput.

   D. Half-duplex Ethernet has lower effective throughput.

   E. Half-duplex Ethernet operates in a private broadcast domain.

3. You want to implement a network medium that is not susceptible to EMI. Which type of cabling should you use?

   A. Thicknet coax

   B. Thinnet coax

   C. Category 5 UTP cable

   D. Fiber-optic cable

4. In an IEEE 802.3 Ethernet frame, what is the significance of the DSAP field?

   A. The DSAP field is used only in Ethernet II frames.

   B. The DSAP field specifies the TCP or UDP port that is associated with the transport protocol.

   C. The DSAP field indicates the Network layer protocol.

   D. The DSAP field is only used by the DoD for classified networks.

5. What type of RJ45 UTP cable is used between switches?

  A. Straight-through

  B. Crossover cable

  C. Crossover with a CSU/DSU

  D. Crossover with a router in between the two switches

6. How does a host on an Ethernet LAN know when to transmit after a collision has occurred? (Choose two.)

  A. In a CSMA/CD collision domain, multiple stations can successfully transmit data simultaneously.

  B. In a CSMA/CD collision domain, stations must wait until the media is not in use before transmitting.

  C. You can improve the CSMA/CD network by adding more hubs.

  D. After a collision, the station that detected the collision has first priority to resend the lost data.

  E. After a collision, all stations run a random backoff algorithm. When the backoff delay period has expired, all stations have equal priority to transmit data.

  F. After a collision, all stations involved run an identical backoff algorithm and then synchronize with each other prior to transmitting data.

7. What type of RJ45 UTP cable do you use to connect a PC's COM port to a router or switch console port?

  A. Straight-through

  B. Crossover cable

  C. Crossover with a CSU/DSU

  D. Rolled

8. You have the following binary number:10110111. What are the decimal and hexadecimal equivalents?

  A. 69/0x2102

  B. 0x183/B7

  C. 173/A6

  D. 83/0xC5

9. Which of the following contention mechanisms is used by Ethernet?

  A. Token passing

  B. CSMA/CD

  C. CSMA/CA

  D. Host polling

10. In the operation of CSMA/CD, which host(s) have priority after the expiration of the backoff algorithm?

    A. All hosts have equal priority.

    B. The two hosts that caused the collision will have equal priority.

    C. The host that sent the jam signal after the collision has priority.

    D. The host with the highest MAC address has priority.

11. When deploying 10Base2 Ethernet, which is the maximum cable length?

    A. 100 feet

    B. 150 meters

    C. 100 meters

    D. 185 meters

    E. 185 feet

12. Which of the following statements is false with respect to full duplex?

    A. There are no collisions in full-duplex mode.

    B. A dedicated switch port is required for each full-duplex node.

    C. There are few collisions in full-duplex mode.

    D. The host network card and the switch port must be capable of operating in full-duplex mode.

13. Which statement is correct with regard to a MAC address?

    A. A MAC, or logical, address is a 48-bit (6-byte) address written in a hexadecimal format.

    B. A MAC, or hardware, address is a 64-bit (6-byte) address written in a hexadecimal format.

    C. A MAC, or hardware, address is a 48-bit (6-byte) address written in a binary format.

    D. A MAC, or hardware, address is a 48-bit (6-byte) address written in a hexadecimal format.

14. Which part of a MAC address is called the organizationally unique identifier (OUI)?

    A. The first 24 bits, or 3 bytes

    B. The first 12 bits, or 3 bytes

    C. The first 24 bits, or 6 bytes

    D. The first 32 bits, or 3 bytes

15. Which layer of the OSI model is responsible for combining bits into bytes and bytes into frames?

    A. Presentation

    B. Data Link

    C. Application

    D. Transport

16. What is the specific term for the unwanted signal interference from adjacent pairs in the cable?

    A. EMI

    B. RFI

    C. Crosstalk

    D. Attenuation

17. What is the binary value of the decimal number 1263?

    A. 11011101101

    B. 10111101111

    C. 10011101111

    D. 10011101011

    E. 11010001111

18. What is the dotted hexadecimal representation of the IP address 172.13.99.225?

    A. E2.1D.E1.66

    B. AC.0D.63.E1

    C. AB.63.99.D5

    D. BC.0C.C3.1F

19. What is the decimal value of the hexadecimal number 0x718?

    A. 2907

    B. 718

    C. 1816

    D. 3511

20. Which field in an Ethernet II frame performs the same function as the DSAP field in an 802.3 Ethernet frame?

    A. Start of Frame

    B. Frame Check Sequence

    C. Subnetwork Access Protocol

    D. Ether-Type

Chapter

4

TCP/IP DoD Model

THE FOLLOWING TOPICS ARE COVERED IN THIS CHAPTER:

✓ **Describing the TCP/IP Transport Layer**

   ▪ Transport Layer Functions

   ▪ Reliable vs. Best–Effort

   ▪ UDP Characteristics

   ▪ TCP Characteristics

   ▪ TCP/IP Applications

   ▪ Mapping Layer 3 to Layer 4

   ▪ Mapping Layer 4 to Applications

   ▪ Establishing a Connection with a Peer System

   ▪ Flow Control

   ▪ TCP Acknowledgment

   ▪ Windowing

   ▪ TCP Sequence Number and Acknowledgment Numbers

The *Transmission Control Protocol/Internet Protocol (TCP/IP)* suite was created by the Department of Defense (DoD) to ensure and preserve data integrity as well as maintain communications in the event of catastrophic war. So it follows that if designed and implemented correctly, a TCP/IP network can be a truly dependable and resilient one. In this chapter, I'll cover the protocols of TCP/IP, and throughout this book, you'll learn how to create a marvelous TCP/IP network—using Cisco Nexus switches and IOS routers, of course.

We'll begin by taking a look at the DoD's version of TCP/IP and then compare this version and its protocols with the OSI reference model discussed in Chapter 2, "Internetworking."

To find up-to-the minute updates for this chapter, please see
www.lammle.com/forum.

Introducing TCP/IP

Because TCP/IP is so central to working with the Internet and intranets, it's essential for you to understand it in detail. I'll begin by giving you some background on TCP/IP and how it came about and then move on to describing the important technical goals defined by the original designers. After that, you'll find out how TCP/IP compares to a theoretical model—the Open Systems Interconnection (OSI) model.

A Brief History of TCP/IP

TCP/IP first came on the scene in 1973. Later, in 1978, it was divided into two distinct protocols: TCP and IP. Then, in 1983, TCP/IP replaced the Network Control Protocol (NCP) and was authorized as the official means of data transport for anything connecting to ARPAnet, the Internet's ancestor that was created by ARPA, the DoD's Advanced Research Projects Agency, way back in 1957 in reaction to the Soviet's launching of Sputnik. ARPA was soon redubbed DARPA, and it was divided into ARPAnet and MILNET (also in 1983); both were finally dissolved in 1990.

But contrary to what you might think, most of the development work on TCP/IP happened at UC Berkeley in Northern California, where a group of scientists were simultaneously working on the Berkeley version of UNIX, which soon became known as the BSD, or Berkeley Software Distribution, series of Unix versions. Of course, because TCP/IP worked so well, it was packaged into subsequent releases of BSD UNIX and offered to other universities and institutions if they bought the distribution tape. So basically, BSD Unix bundled with TCP/IP began as shareware in the world of academia and, as a result, became the basis of the huge success and exponential growth of today's Internet as well as smaller, private and corporate intranets.

As usual, what may have started as a small group of TCP/IP aficionados evolved, and as it did, the US government created a program to test any new published standards and make sure they passed certain criteria. This was to protect TCP/IP's integrity and to ensure that no developer changed anything too dramatically or added any proprietary features. It's this very quality—this open-systems approach to the TCP/IP family of protocols—that pretty much sealed its popularity because it guarantees a solid connection between myriad hardware and software platforms with no strings attached.

TCP/IP and the DoD Model

The DoD model is basically a condensed version of the OSI model—it's composed of four, instead of seven, layers:

- Process/Application layer
- Host-to-Host layer
- Internet layer
- Network Access layer

Figure 4.1 shows a comparison of the DoD model and the OSI reference model. As you can see, the two are similar in concept, but each has a different number of layers with different names.

FIGURE 4.1   The DoD and OSI models

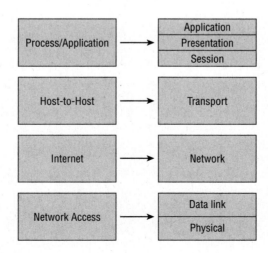

NOTE
When the different protocols in the IP stack are discussed, the layers of the OSI and DoD models are interchangeable. In other words, the Internet layer and the Network layer describe the same thing, as do the Host-to-Host layer and the Transport layer.

A vast array of protocols combine at the DoD model's *Process/Application layer* to integrate the various activities and duties spanning the focus of the OSI's corresponding top three layers (Application, Presentation, and Session). We'll be looking closely at those protocols in the next part of this chapter. The Process/Application layer defines protocols for node-to-node application communication and also controls user-interface specifications.

The *Host-to-Host layer* parallels the functions of the OSI's Transport layer, defining protocols for setting up the level of transmission service for applications. It tackles issues such as creating reliable end-to-end communication and ensuring the error-free delivery of data. It handles packet sequencing and maintains data integrity.

The *Internet layer* corresponds to the OSI's Network layer, designating the protocols relating to the logical transmission of packets over the entire network. It takes care of the addressing of hosts by giving them an IP (Internet Protocol) address, and it handles the routing of packets among multiple networks.

At the bottom of the DoD model, the *Network Access layer* implements the data exchange between the host and the network. The equivalent of the Data Link and Physical layers of the OSI model, the Network Access layer oversees hardware addressing and defines protocols for the physical transmission of data.

The DoD and OSI models are alike in design and concept and have similar functions in similar layers. Figure 4.2 shows the TCP/IP protocol suite and how its protocols relate to the DoD model layers.

FIGURE 4.2   The TCP/IP protocol suite

DoD Model

| Process/Application | Telnet | FTP | LPD | SNMP |
| | TFTP | SMTP | NFS | X Window |

| Host-to-Host | TCP | | UDP | |

| Internet | ICMP | ARP | | RARP |
| | IP | | | |

| Network Access | Ethernet | Fast Ethernet | Token Ring | FDDI |

In the following sections, we will look at the different protocols in more detail, starting with the Process/Application layer protocols.

The Process/Application Layer Protocols

In the following sections, I'll describe the different applications and services typically used in IP networks. The following protocols and applications are covered:

- Telnet
- FTP
- TFTP
- NFS
- SMTP
- POP
- SNMP
- SSH
- HTTP
- HTTPS
- NTP
- DNS
- DHCP/BootP

Telnet

Telnet is the chameleon of protocols—its specialty is terminal emulation. It allows a user on a remote client machine, called the Telnet client, to access the resources of another machine, the Telnet server. Telnet achieves this by pulling a fast one on the Telnet server and making the client machine appears as though it were a terminal directly attached to the local network. This projection is actually a software image—a virtual terminal that can interact with the chosen remote host.

These emulated terminals are of the text-mode type and can execute defined procedures such as displaying menus that give users the opportunity to choose options and access the applications on the duped server. Users begin a Telnet session by running the Telnet client software and then logging into the Telnet server.

File Transfer Protocol (FTP)

File Transfer Protocol (FTP) is the protocol that actually lets us transfer files, and it can accomplish this between any two machines using it. But FTP isn't just a protocol; it's also a program. Operating as a protocol, FTP is used by applications. As a program, it's employed by users to perform file tasks by hand. FTP also allows for access to both directories and files and can accomplish certain types of directory operations, such as relocating into different ones.

Accessing a host through FTP is only the first step, though. Users must then be subjected to an authentication login that's probably secured with passwords and usernames implemented by system administrators to restrict access. You can get around this somewhat by adopting the username *anonymous*—though what you'll gain access to will be limited.

Even when employed by users manually as a program, FTP's functions are limited to listing and manipulating directories, typing file contents, and copying files between hosts. It can't execute remote files as programs.

Trivial File Transfer Protocol (TFTP)

Trivial File Transfer Protocol (TFTP) is the stripped-down, stock version of FTP, but it's the protocol of choice if you know exactly what you want and where to find it, plus it's so easy to use and it's fast too! It doesn't give you the abundance of functions that FTP does, though. TFTP has no directory-browsing abilities; it can do nothing but send and receive files. This compact little protocol also skimps in the data department, sending much smaller blocks of data than FTP, and there's no authentication as with FTP, so it's even more insecure. Few sites support it because of the inherent security risks.

 Real World Scenario

When Should You Use FTP?

The folks at your San Francisco office need a 50GB file emailed to them right away. What do you do? Most email servers would reject the email because they have size limits. Even if there's no size limit on the server, it still would take a while to send this big file to SF. FTP to the rescue!

If you need to give someone a large file or you need to get a large file from someone, FTP is a nice choice. Smaller files (less than 5MB) can just be sent via email if you have the bandwidth of DSL or a cable modem. However, most ISPs don't allow files larger than 5MB or 10MB to be emailed, so FTP is an option you should consider if you are in need of sending and receiving large files (and who isn't these days?). To use FTP, you will need to set up an FTP server on the Internet so that the files can be shared.

Besides, FTP is faster than email, which is another reason to use FTP for sending or receiving large files. In addition, because it uses TCP and is connection-oriented, if the session dies, FTP can sometimes start up where it left off. Try that with your email client!

Network File System (NFS)

Network File System (NFS) is a jewel of a protocol specializing in file sharing. It allows two different types of file systems to interoperate. It works like this: suppose the NFS server software is running on a Windows server and the NFS client software is running on a Unix host.

NFS allows for a portion of the RAM on the Windows server to transparently store Unix files, which can, in turn, be used by Unix users. Even though the Windows file system and Unix file system are unlike—they have different case sensitivity, filename lengths, security, and so on—both Unix users and Windows users can access that same file with their normal file systems, in their normal way.

Simple Mail Transfer Protocol (SMTP)

Simple Mail Transfer Protocol (SMTP), answering our ubiquitous call to email, uses a spooled, or queued, method of mail delivery. Once a message has been sent to a destination, the message is spooled to a device—usually a disk. The server software at the destination posts a vigil, regularly checking the queue for messages. When it detects them, it proceeds to deliver them to their destination. SMTP is used to send mail; POP3 or IMAP is used to receive mail.

Post Office Protocol (POP)

Post Office Protocol (POP) gives us a storage facility for incoming mail, and the latest version is called POP3 (sound familiar?). Basically, how this protocol works is when a client device connects to a POP3 server, messages addressed to that client are released for downloading. It doesn't allow messages to be downloaded selectively, but once they are, the client/server inter-action ends and you can delete and tweak your messages locally at will. Lately we're seeing a newer standard, IMAP, being used more and more in place of POP3.

Simple Network Management Protocol (SNMP)

Simple Network Management Protocol (SNMP) collects and manipulates valuable network information. It gathers data by polling the devices on the network from a management station at fixed or random intervals, requiring them to disclose certain information. When all is well, SNMP receives something called a *baseline*—a report delimiting the operational traits of a healthy network. This protocol can also stand as a watchdog over the network, quickly notifying managers of any sudden turn of events. These network watchdogs are called *agents*, and when aberrations occur, agents send an alert called a *trap* to the management station that contains information such as CPU or interface utilization, up/down status, thermal statistics, and more.

SNMP Versions 1, 2, and 3

SNMP versions 1 and 2 are pretty much obsolete, or should be. This doesn't mean you won't see them in a network at some time because a lot of manufacturers still only support version 2, but v1 is super old and, well, obsolete. SNMPv2 provided improvements, especially in performance. But one of the best additions was what was called GETBULK, which allowed a host to retrieve a large amount of data at once. However, v2 never really caught on in the networking world. SNMPv3 is now the standard and uses both TCP and UDP, unlike v1, which used only UDP. V3 added even more security and message integrity, authentication, and encryption.

Secure Shell (SSH)

Secure Shell (SSH) protocol sets up a secure Telnet session over a standard TCP/IP connection and is employed for doing things like logging into systems, running programs on remote systems, and moving files from one system to another. And it does all of this while maintaining a nice, strong, encrypted connection. You can think of it as the new-generation protocol that's now used in place of `rsh` and `rlogin`—even Telnet.

Hypertext Transfer Protocol (HTTP)

All those snappy websites comprising a mélange of graphics, text, links, and so on—the *Hypertext Transfer Protocol (HTTP)* is making it all possible. It's used to manage communications between web browsers and web servers and opens the right resource when you click a link, wherever that resource may actually reside.

Hypertext Transfer Protocol Secure (HTTPS)

Hypertext Transfer Protocol Secure (HTTPS) is also known as Secure Hypertext Transfer Protocol. It uses Secure Sockets Layer (SSL). Sometimes you'll see it referred to as SHTTP or S-HTTP (which is an extension of HTTP and doesn't use SSL), but no matter—as indicated, it's a secure version of HTTP that arms you with a whole bunch of security tools for keeping transactions between a web browser and a server secure. It's what your browser needs to fill out forms, sign in, authenticate, and encrypt an HTTP message when you make a reservation or buy something online.

Network Time Protocol (NTP)

Kudos to Professor David Mills of the University of Delaware for coming up with this handy protocol that's used to synchronize the clocks on our computers to one standard time source (typically, an atomic clock). *Network Time Protocol (NTP)* works by synchronizing devices to ensure that all computers on a given network agree on the time. This may sound pretty simple, but it's very important because so many of the transactions done today are time- and date-stamped. Think about your precious databases, for one. It can mess up a server pretty badly if it's out of sync with the machines connected to it, even by mere seconds (think crash!). You can't have a transaction entered by a machine at, say, 1:50 a.m. when the server records that transaction as having occurred at 1:45 a.m. So basically, NTP works to prevent "back to the future sans DeLorean" from bringing down the network—very important indeed!

Domain Name Service (DNS)

Domain Name Service (DNS) resolves hostnames—specifically, Internet names, such as www.lammle.com. You don't have to use DNS; you can just type in the IP address of any device you want to communicate with. An IP address identifies hosts on a network and the Internet as well. However, DNS was designed to make our lives easier. Think about this: what would happen if you wanted to move your web page to a different service provider? The IP address would change and no one would know what the new one was. DNS allows you to use a domain name to specify an IP address. You can change the IP address as often as you want and no one will know the difference.

DNS is used to resolve a *fully qualified domain name (FQDN)*—for example, www.lammle.com or todd.lammle.com. An FQDN is a hierarchy that can logically locate a system based on its domain identifier.

If you want to resolve the name *todd*, you either must type in the FQDN of todd.lammle.com or have a device such as a PC or router add the suffix for you. For example, on a Cisco router, you can use the command ip domain-name lammle.com to append each request with the lammle.com domain. If you don't do that, you'll have to type in the FQDN to get DNS to resolve the name.

An important thing to remember about DNS is that if you can ping a device with an IP address but cannot use its FQDN, then you might have some type of DNS configuration failure.

Dynamic Host Configuration Protocol (DHCP)/Bootstrap Protocol (BootP)

Dynamic Host Configuration Protocol (DHCP) assigns IP addresses to hosts. It allows easier administration and works well in small to even very large network environments. All types of hardware can be used as a DHCP server, including a Cisco router.

DHCP differs from BootP in that BootP assigns an IP address to a host but the host's hardware address must be entered manually in a BootP table. You can think of DHCP as a dynamic BootP. But remember that BootP is also used to send an operating system that a host can boot from. DHCP can't do that.

But there is a lot of information a DHCP server can provide to a host when the host is requesting an IP address from the DHCP server. Here's a list of the information a DHCP server can provide:

- IP address
- Subnet mask
- Domain name
- Default gateway (routers)
- DNS server address
- WINS server address

A DHCP server can give us even more information than this, but the items in the list are the most common.

A client that sends out a DHCP Discover message in order to receive an IP address sends out a broadcast at both layer 2 and layer 3.

- The layer 2 broadcast is all *F*s in hex, which looks like this: FF:FF:FF:FF:FF:FF.
- The layer 3 broadcast is 255.255.255.255, which means all networks and all hosts.

DHCP is connectionless, which means it uses User Datagram Protocol (UDP) at the Transport layer, also known as the Host-to-Host layer, which we'll talk about next.

In case you don't believe me, here's an example of output from my trusty analyzer:

```
Ethernet II, Src: 0.0.0.0 (00:0b:db:99:d3:5e),Dst: Broadcast(ff:ff:ff:ff:ff:ff)
Internet Protocol, Src: 0.0.0.0 (0.0.0.0),Dst: 255.255.255.255(255.255.255.255)
```

The Data Link and Network layers are both sending out "all hands" broadcasts saying, "Help—I don't know my IP address!"

Broadcast addresses will be discussed in more detail at the end of this chapter.

Figure 4.3 shows the process of a client/server relationship using a DHCP connection.

FIGURE 4.3   DHCP client four-step process

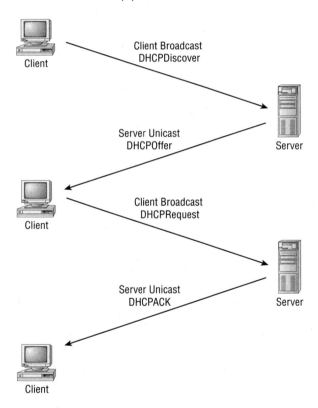

The following is the four-step process a client takes to receive an IP address from a DHCP server:

1. The DHCP client broadcasts a DHCP Discover message looking for a DHCP server (Port 67).

2. The DHCP server that received the DHCP Discover message sends a unicast DHCP Offer message back to the host.

3. The client then broadcasts to the server a DHCP Request message asking for the offered IP address and possibly other information.

4. The server finalizes the exchange with a unicast DHCP Acknowledgment message.

DHCP Conflicts

A DHCP address conflict occurs when two hosts use the same IP address. This sounds bad, doesn't it? Well of course it is!

During IP address assignment, a DHCP server checks for conflicts using the ping program to test the availability of the address before it is assigned from the pool. If no host replies, then the DHCP server assumes that the IP address is not already allocated. This helps the server know that it is providing a good address, but what about the host? To provide extra protection against the all-so-terrible IP conflict issue, the host can broadcast for its own address.

A host uses something called a gratuitous ARP to help avoid a possible duplicate address. The DHCP client sends an ARP broadcast out on the local LAN or VLAN using its newly assigned address to solve conflicts before they occur.

So, if an IP address conflict is detected, the address is removed from the DHCP pool (scope), and it is all-so-important to remember that the address will not be assigned to a host until the administrator resolves the conflict by hand.

Automatic Private IP Addressing (APIPA)

Okay, so what happens if you have a few hosts connected together with a switch or hub and you don't have a DHCP server? You can add IP information by hand (this is called *static IP addressing*), but Windows provides what is called Automatic Private IP Addressing (APIPA), a feature of later Windows operating systems. With APIPA, clients can automatically self-configure an IP address and subnet mask (basic IP information that hosts use to communicate) when a DHCP server isn't available. The IP address range for APIPA is 169.254.0.1 through 169.254.255.254. The client also configures itself with a default Class B subnet mask of 255.255.0.0.

However, when you're in your corporate network working and you have a DHCP server running, and your host shows that it is using this IP address range, this means that either your DHCP client on the host is not working or the server is down or can't be reached because of a network issue. I don't know anyone who's seen a host in this address range and has been happy about it!

Now, let's take a look at the Transport layer, or what the DoD calls the Host-to-Host layer.

The Host-to-Host Layer Protocols

The main purpose of the Host-to-Host layer is to shield the upper-layer applications from the complexities of the network. This layer says to the upper layer, "Just give me your data stream, with any instructions, and I'll begin the process of getting your information ready to send."

The following sections describe the two protocols at this layer:

- Transmission Control Protocol (TCP)
- User Datagram Protocol (UDP)

In addition, we'll look at some of the key host-to-host protocol concepts, as well as the port numbers.

  Remember, this is still considered layer 4, and Cisco really likes the way layer 4 can use acknowledgments, sequencing, and flow control.

Transmission Control Protocol (TCP)

Transmission Control Protocol (TCP) takes large blocks of information from an application and breaks them into segments. It numbers and sequences each segment so that the destination's TCP stack can put the segments back into the order the application intended. After these segments are sent, TCP (on the transmitting host) waits for an acknowledgment of the receiving end's TCP virtual circuit session, retransmitting those that aren't acknowledged.

Before a transmitting host starts to send segments down the model, the sender's TCP stack contacts the destination's TCP stack to establish a connection. What is created is known as a *virtual circuit*. This type of communication is called *connection-oriented*. During this initial handshake, the two TCP layers also agree on the amount of information that's going to be sent before the recipient's TCP sends back an acknowledgment. With everything agreed upon in advance, the path is paved for reliable communication to take place.

TCP is a full-duplex, connection-oriented, reliable, and accurate protocol, but establishing all these terms and conditions, in addition to error checking, is no small task. TCP is very complicated and, not surprisingly, costly in terms of network overhead. And since today's networks are much more reliable than those of yore, this added reliability is often unnecessary. Most programmers use TCP because it removes a lot of programming work; however, real-time video and VoIP use UDP because they can't afford the overhead.

TCP Segment Format

Since the upper layers just send a data stream to the protocols in the Transport layers, I'll demonstrate how TCP segments a data stream and prepares it for the Internet layer. When the Internet layer receives the data stream, it routes the segments as packets through an internetwork. The segments are handed to the receiving host's Host-to-Host layer protocol, which rebuilds the data stream to hand to the upper-layer applications or protocols.

Figure 4.4 shows the TCP segment format. The figure shows the different fields within the TCP header.

FIGURE 4.4   TCP segment format

16-bit source port		16-bit destination port
32-bit sequence number		
32-bit acknowledgment number		
4-bit header length · reserved · flags		16-bit window size
16-bit TCP checksum		16-bit Urgent pointer
options		
data		

The TCP header is 20 bytes long, or up to 24 bytes with options. You need to understand what each field in the TCP segment is:

Source Port   The port number of the application on the host sending the data. (Port numbers will be explained a little later in this section.)

Destination Port   The port number of the application requested on the destination host.

Sequence Number   A number used by TCP that puts the data back in the correct order or retransmits missing or damaged data, a process called sequencing.

Acknowledgment Number   The TCP octet that is expected next.

Header Length   The number of 32-bit words in the TCP header. This indicates where the data begins. The TCP header (even one including options) is an integral number of 32 bits in length.

Reserved   Always set to zero.

Code Bits/Flags   Control functions used to set up and terminate a session.

Window   The window size the sender is willing to accept, in octets.

Checksum   The cyclic redundancy check (CRC), because TCP doesn't trust the lower layers and checks everything. The CRC checks the header and data fields.

Urgent   A valid field only if the Urgent pointer in the code bits is set. If so, this value indicates the offset from the current sequence number, in octets, where the segment of non-urgent data begins.

Options   May be 0 or a multiple of 32 bits, if any. What this means is that no options have to be present (option size of 0). However, if any options are used that do not cause the option field to total a multiple of 32 bits, padding of 0s must be used to make sure the data begins on a 32-bit boundary.

Data Handed down to the TCP protocol at the Transport layer, which includes the upper-layer headers.

Let's take a look at a TCP segment copied from a network analyzer:

```
TCP - Transport Control Protocol
 Source Port:       5973
 Destination Port: 23
 Sequence Number:  1456389907
 Ack Number:       1242056456
 Offset:           5
 Reserved:         %000000
 Code:             %011000
     Ack is valid
     Push Request
Window:            61320
Checksum:          0x61a6
Urgent Pointer:    0
No TCP Options
TCP Data Area:
vL.5.+.5.+.5.+.5  76 4c 19 35 11 2b 19 35 11 2b 19 35 11
  2b 19 35 +. 11 2b 19
Frame Check Sequence: 0x0d00000f
```

Did you notice that everything I talked about earlier is in the segment? As you can see from the number of fields in the header, TCP creates a lot of overhead. Application developers may opt for efficiency over reliability to save overhead, so User Datagram Protocol was also defined at the Transport layer as an alternative.

User Datagram Protocol (UDP)

If you were to compare *User Datagram Protocol (UDP)* with TCP, the former is basically the scaled-down economy model that's sometimes referred to as a thin protocol. Like a thin person on a park bench, a thin protocol doesn't take up a lot of room—or in this case, much bandwidth on a network.

UDP doesn't offer all the bells and whistles of TCP either, but it does do a fabulous job of transporting information that doesn't require reliable delivery—and it does so using far fewer network resources. (UDP is covered thoroughly in Request for Comments 768.)

There are some situations in which it would definitely be wise for developers to opt for UDP rather than TCP. One circumstance is when reliability is already handled at the Process/Application layer. Network File System (NFS) handles its own reliability issues, making the use of TCP both impractical and redundant. But ultimately, it's up to the application developer to decide whether to use UDP or TCP, not the user who wants to transfer data faster.

UDP does *not* sequence the segments and does not care in which order the segments arrive at the destination. But after that, UDP sends the segments off and forgets about them. It doesn't follow through, check up on them, or even allow for an acknowledgment of safe arrival—complete abandonment. Because of this, it's referred to as an unreliable protocol. This does not mean that UDP is ineffective, only that it doesn't handle issues of reliability.

Further, UDP doesn't create a virtual circuit, nor does it contact the destination before delivering information to it. Because of this, it's also considered a *connectionless* protocol. Since UDP assumes that the application will use its own reliability method, it doesn't use any. This gives an application developer a choice when running the Internet Protocol stack: TCP for reliability or UDP for faster transfers.

So, it is important to remember how this works because if the segments arrive out of order (very common in IP networks), they'll just be passed up to the next OSI (DoD) layer in whatever order they're received, possibly resulting in some seriously garbled data. On the other hand, TCP sequences the segments so they get put back together in exactly the right order—something UDP just can't do.

UDP Segment Format

Figure 4.5 clearly illustrates UDP's markedly low overhead as compared to TCP's hungry usage. Look at the figure carefully—can you see that UDP doesn't use windowing or provide for acknowledgments in the UDP header?

FIGURE 4.5 UDP segment

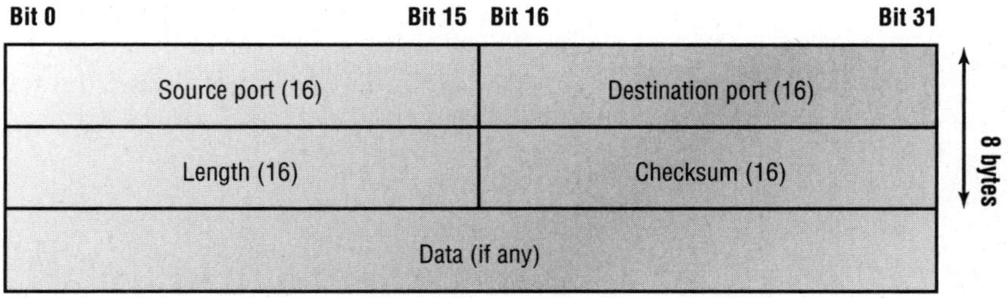

It's important for you to understand what each field in the UDP segment is:

Source Port   Port number of the application on the host sending the data

Destination Port   Port number of the application requested on the destination host

Length   Length of UDP header and UDP data

Checksum   Checksum of both the UDP header and UDP data fields

Data   Upper-layer data

UDP, like TCP, doesn't trust the lower layers and runs its own CRC.

The following shows a UDP segment caught on a network analyzer:

```
UDP - User Datagram Protocol
 Source Port:       1085
 Destination Port: 5136
 Length:           41
 Checksum:         0x7a3c
 UDP Data Area:
 ..Z......00 01 5a 96 00 01 00 00 00 00 00 11 0000 00
 ...C..2._C._C  2e 03 00 43 02 1e 32 0a 00 0a 00 80 43 00 80
Frame Check Sequence: 0x00000000
```

Notice that low overhead! Try to find the sequence number, ack number, and window size in the UDP segment. You can't because they just aren't there!

Key Concepts of Host-to-Host Protocols

Since you've seen both a connection-oriented (TCP) and connectionless (UDP) protocol in action, it would be good to summarize the two here. Table 4.1 highlights some of the key concepts that you should keep in mind regarding these two protocols. You should memorize this table.

TABLE 4.1   Key features of TCP and UDP

TCP	UDP
Sequenced	Unsequenced
Reliable	Unreliable
Connection-oriented	Connectionless
Virtual circuit	Low overhead
Acknowledgments	No acknowledgment
Windowing flow control	No windowing or flow control of any type

A telephone analogy could really help you understand how TCP works. Most of us know that before you speak to someone on a phone, you must first establish a connection with them—wherever they are. This is like a virtual circuit with the TCP protocol. If you were giving someone important information during your conversation, you might say, "You know?" or ask, "Did you get that?" Saying something like this is a lot like a TCP acknowledgment—it's designed to get you verification. From time to time (especially on cell phones), people also ask, "Are you still there?" They end their conversations with a "Goodbye" of some kind, putting closure on the phone call. TCP also performs these types of functions.

Alternately, using UDP is like sending a postcard. To do that, you don't need to contact the other party first. You simply write your message, address the postcard, and mail it. This is analogous to UDP's connectionless orientation. Since the message on the postcard is probably not a matter of life or death, you don't need an acknowledgment of its receipt. Similarly, UDP does not involve acknowledgments.

Let's take a look at another figure, one that includes TCP, UDP, and the applications associated with each protocol, Figure 4.6 (in the next section).

Port Numbers

TCP and UDP must use *port numbers* to communicate with the upper layers because they're what keep track of different conversations crossing the network simultaneously. Originating-source port numbers are dynamically assigned by the source host and will equal some number starting at 1024. 1023 and below are defined in RFC 3232 (or just see www.iana.org), which discusses what are called well-known port numbers.

Virtual circuits that don't use an application with a well-known port number are assigned port numbers randomly from a specific range instead. These port numbers identify the source and destination application or process in the TCP segment.

Figure 4.6 illustrates how both TCP and UDP use port numbers.

FIGURE 4.6   Port numbers for TCP and UDP

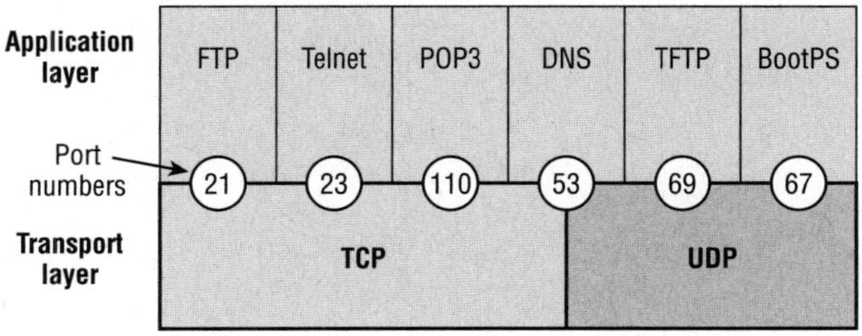

The different port numbers that can be used are explained next:

- Numbers below 1024 are considered well-known port numbers and are defined in RFC 3232.

- Numbers 1024 and above are used by the upper layers to set up sessions with other hosts and by TCP and UDP to use as source and destination addresses in the segment.

In the following sections, we'll take a look at an analyzer output showing a TCP session.

TCP Session: Source Port

The following listing shows a TCP session captured with my analyzer software:

```
TCP - Transport Control Protocol
 Source Port:       5973
 Destination Port: 23
 Sequence Number:   1456389907
 Ack Number:        1242056456
 Offset:            5
 Reserved:          %000000
 Code:              %011000
     Ack is valid
     Push Request
 Window:            61320
 Checksum:          0x61a6
 Urgent Pointer:    0
 No TCP Options
 TCP Data Area:
 vL.5.+.5.+.5.+.5  76 4c 19 35 11 2b 19 35 11 2b 19 35 11
  2b 19 35 +. 11 2b 19
Frame Check Sequence: 0x0d00000f
```

Notice that the source host makes up the source port, which in this case is 5973. The destination port is 23, which is used to tell the receiving host the purpose of the intended connection (Telnet).

By looking at this session, you can see that the source host makes up the source port by using numbers from 1024 to 65535. But why does the source make up a port number? To differentiate between sessions with different hosts, my friend. How would a server know where information is coming from if it didn't have a different number from a sending host? TCP and the upper layers don't use hardware and logical addresses to understand the sending host's address as the Data Link and Network layer protocols do. Instead, they use port numbers.

TCP Session: Destination Port

You'll sometimes look at an analyzer and see that only the source port is above 1024 and the destination port is a well-known port, as shown in the following trace:

```
TCP - Transport Control Protocol
 Source Port:       1144
 Destination Port: 80 World Wide Web HTTP
 Sequence Number:   9356570
 Ack Number:        0
 Offset:            7
 Reserved:          %000000
 Code:              %000010
     Synch Sequence
```

```
Window:             8192
Checksum:           0x57E7
Urgent Pointer:     0
TCP Options:
 Option Type: 2 Maximum Segment Size
   Length:    4
   MSS:       536
 Option Type: 1 No Operation
 Option Type: 1 No Operation
 Option Type: 4
   Length:    2
   Opt Value:
 No More HTTP Data
Frame Check Sequence: 0x43697363
```

And sure enough, the source port is over 1024, but the destination port is 80, or HTTP service. The server, or receiving host, will change the destination port if it needs to.

In the preceding trace, a "syn" packet is sent to the destination device. The syn sequence is what's telling the remote destination device that it wants to create a session.

TCP Session: Syn Packet Acknowledgment

The next trace shows an acknowledgment to the syn packet:

```
TCP - Transport Control Protocol
 Source Port:       80 World Wide Web HTTP
 Destination Port: 1144
 Sequence Number:  2873580788
 Ack Number:       9356571
 Offset:           6
 Reserved:         %000000
 Code:             %010010
      Ack is valid
      Synch Sequence
 Window:            8576
 Checksum:          0x5F85
 Urgent Pointer:    0
 TCP Options:
  Option Type: 2 Maximum Segment Size
    Length:    4
    MSS:       1460
  No More HTTP Data
Frame Check Sequence: 0x6E203132
```

Notice the *Ack is valid*, which means that the source port was accepted and the device agreed to create a virtual circuit with the originating host.

And here again, you can see that the response from the server shows that the source is 80 and the destination is the 1144 sent from the originating host—all's well.

Table 4.2 gives you a list of the typical applications used in the TCP/IP suite, their well-known port numbers, and the Transport layer protocols used by each application or process. It's important that you study and memorize this table.

TABLE 4.2   Key protocols that use TCP and UDP

TCP	UDP
Telnet 23	SNMP 161
SMTP 25	TFTP 69
HTTP 80	DNS 53
FTP 20, 21	BOOTP/DHCP 67
DNS 53	
HTTPS 443	
SSH 22	
POP3 110	
NTP 123	

Notice that DNS uses both TCP and UDP. Whether it opts for one or the other depends on what it's trying to do. Even though it's not the only application that can use both protocols, it's certainly one that you should remember in your studies.

    What makes TCP reliable is sequencing, acknowledgments, and flow control (windowing). UDP does not have reliability.

I want to discuss one more item before we move down to the Internet layer and this is session multiplexing. Session multiplexing is used by both TCP and UDP and basically allows a single computer, with a single IP address, to have multiple sessions occurring simultaneously. Say you go to www.lammle.com and are browsing and then click a link to another page; this opens another session to your host. Now you go to www.cisco.com from another window and that site opens a window as well; now you have three sessions open using one IP address because the Session layer is sorting the separate request based on the Transport layer port number.

The Internet Layer Protocols

In the DoD model, there are two main reasons for the Internet layer's existence: routing and providing a single network interface to the upper layers.

None of the other upper- or lower-layer protocols have any functions relating to routing—that complex and important task belongs entirely to the Internet layer. The Internet layer's second duty is to provide a single network interface to the upper-layer protocols. Without this layer, application programmers would need to write "hooks" into every one of their applications for each different Network Access protocol. This would not only be a pain in the neck, it would lead to different versions of each application—one for Ethernet, another one for wireless, and so on. To prevent this, IP provides one single network interface for the upper-layer protocols. That accomplished, it's then the job of IP and the various Network Access protocols to get along and work together.

All network roads don't lead to Rome—they lead to IP. And all the other protocols at this layer, as well as all those at the upper layers, use it. Never forget that. All paths through the DoD model go through IP. The following sections describe the protocols at the Internet layer:

- Internet Protocol (IP)
- Internet Control Message Protocol (ICMP)
- Address Resolution Protocol (ARP)
- Reverse Address Resolution Protocol (RARP)
- Proxy ARP

Internet Protocol (IP)

Internet Protocol (IP) essentially is the Internet layer. The other protocols found here merely exist to support it. IP holds the big picture and could be said to "see all," in that it's aware of all the interconnected networks. It can do this because all the machines on the network have a software, or logical, address called an IP address.

IP looks at each packet's destination address. Then, using a routing table, it decides where a packet is to be sent next, choosing the best path. The protocols of the Network Access layer at the bottom of the DoD model don't possess IP's enlightened scope of the entire network; they deal only with physical links (local networks).

Identifying devices on networks requires answering these two questions: which network is it on? and what is its ID on that network? The first answer is the *software address*, or *logical address* (the correct street). The second answer is the hardware address (the correct mailbox). All hosts on a network have a logical ID called an IP address. This is the software, or logical, address and contains valuable encoded information, greatly simplifying the complex task of routing. (IP is discussed in RFC 791.)

IP receives segments from the Host-to-Host layer and fragments them into datagrams (packets) if necessary. IP then reassembles datagrams back into segments on the receiving side. Each datagram is assigned the IP address of the sender and of the recipient. Each router (layer 3 device) that receives a datagram makes routing decisions based on the packet's destination IP address.

Figure 4.7 shows an IP header. This will give you an idea of what the IP protocol has to go through every time user data is sent from the upper layers and is to be sent to a remote network.

FIGURE 4.7 IP header

Bit 0		Bit 15 Bit 16		Bit 31	
Version (4)	Header length (4)	Priority and Type of Service (8)	Total length (16)		
Identification (16)			Flags (3)	Fragment offset (13)	
Time to Live (8)		Protocol (8)	Header checksum (16)		
Source IP address (32)					
Destination IP address (32)					
Options (0 or 32 if any)					
Data (varies if any)					

(20 bytes)

The following fields make up the IP header:

Version   IP version number.

Header Length   Header length (HLEN) in 32-bit words.

Priority and Type of Service   Type of Service tells how the datagram should be handled. The first 3 bits are the priority bits.

Total Length   Length of the packet including header and data.

Identification   Each packet sent has a unique IP-packet value called the IP ID; if the packet is fragmented, the receiving host can put it back together by collecting pieces with the same IP ID.

Flags   Specifies whether fragmentation should occur.

Fragment Offset   Provides fragmentation and ordered reassembly if the packet is too large to put in a frame. It also allows different maximum transmission units (MTUs) on the Internet.

Time to Live   The time to live is set into a packet when it is originally generated. If it doesn't get to where it wants to go before the TTL expires, boom—it's gone. This stops IP packets from continuously circling the network looking for a home.

Protocol   Port of upper-layer protocol (TCP is port 6 or UDP is port 17). Also supports Network layer protocols, like ARP and ICMP (this can be called Type field in some analyzers).

We'll talk about this field in more detail in a minute because it is so important, but just understand for now that this tells IP who owns the payload the packet it is carrying (that is, TCP, UDP, ICMP, and so on).

Header Checksum   Cyclic redundancy check (CRC) on header only.

Source IP Address   32-bit IP address of sending station.

Destination IP Address   32-bit IP address of the station this packet is destined for.

Options   Used for network testing, debugging, security, and more.

Data   After the IP option field will be the upper-layer data.

Here's a snapshot of an IP packet caught on a network analyzer (notice that all the header information discussed previously appears here):

```
IP Header - Internet Protocol Datagram
  Version:              4
  Header Length:        5
  Precedence:           0
  Type of Service:      %000
  Unused:               %00
  Total Length:         187
  Identifier:           22486
  Fragmentation Flags:  %010 Do Not Fragment
  Fragment Offset:      0
  Time To Live:         60
  IP Type:              0x06 TCP
  Header Checksum:      0xd031
  Source IP Address:    10.7.1.30
  Dest. IP Address:     10.7.1.10
No Internet Datagram Options
```

The Type field—it's typically a Protocol field, but this analyzer sees it as an IP Type field—is important. If the header didn't carry the protocol information for the next layer, IP wouldn't know what to do with the data carried in the packet. The preceding example tells IP to hand the segment to TCP.

Figure 4.8 demonstrates how the Network layer sees the protocols at the Transport layer when it needs to hand a packet to the upper-layer protocols.

In this example, the Protocol field tells IP to send the data to either TCP port 6 or UDP port 17. But it will only be UDP or TCP if the data is part of a data stream headed for an upper-layer service or application. It could just as easily be destined for Internet Control Message Protocol (ICMP), Address Resolution Protocol (ARP), or some other type of Network layer protocol.

Table 4.3 is a list of some other popular protocols that can be specified in the Protocol field.

FIGURE 4.8   The Protocol field in an IP header

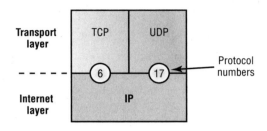

TABLE 4.3   Possible protocols found in the Protocol field of an IP header

Protocol	Protocol Number
ICMP	1
IP in IP (tunneling)	4
TCP	6
IGRP	9
UDP	17
EIGRP	88
OSPF	89
IPv6	41
GRE	47
Layer 2 tunnel (L2TP)	115

You can find a complete list of Protocol field numbers at www.iana.org/ assignments/protocol-numbers.

Internet Control Message Protocol (ICMP)

Internet Control Message Protocol (ICMP) works at the Network layer and is used by IP for many different services. ICMP is a management protocol and messaging service provider for IP. Its messages are carried as IP datagrams. RFC 1256 is an annex to ICMP, which affords hosts' extended capability in discovering routes to gateways.

ICMP packets have the following characteristics:

- They can provide hosts with information about network problems.
- They are encapsulated within IP datagrams.

The following are some common events and messages that ICMP relates to:

Destination Unreachable   If a router can't send an IP datagram any further, it uses ICMP to send a message back to the sender, advising it of the situation. For example, take a look at Figure 4.9, which shows that interface E0 of the Lab_B router is down.

FIGURE 4.9   ICMP error message is sent to the sending host from the remote router.

E0 on Lab B is down. Host A is trying to communicate to Host B. What happens?

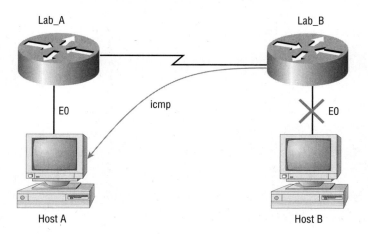

When Host A sends a packet destined for Host B, the Lab_B router will send an ICMP destination unreachable message back to the sending device (Host A in this example).

Buffer Full/Source Quence   If a router's memory buffer for receiving incoming datagrams is full, it will use ICMP to send out this message until the congestion abates.

Hops/Time Exceeded   Each IP datagram is allotted a certain number of routers, called hops, to pass through. If it reaches its limit of hops before arriving at its destination, the last router to receive that datagram deletes it. The executioner router then uses ICMP to send an obituary message, informing the sending machine of the demise of its datagram.

Ping   Packet Internet Groper (Ping) uses ICMP echo request and reply messages to check the physical and logical connectivity of machines on an internetwork.

Traceroute   Using ICMP time-outs, Traceroute is used to discover the path a packet takes as it traverses an internetwork.

Both Ping and Traceroute (also just called Trace; Microsoft Windows uses tracert) allow you to verify address configurations in your internetwork.

The following data is from a network analyzer catching an ICMP echo request:

```
Flags:          0x00
 Status:         0x00
 Packet Length: 78
 Timestamp:      14:04:25.967000 12/20/03
Ethernet Header
 Destination: 00:a0:24:6e:0f:a8
 Source:       00:80:c7:a8:f0:3d
 Ether-Type:  08-00 IP
IP Header - Internet Protocol Datagram
 Version:              4
 Header Length:        5
 Precedence:           0
 Type of Service:     %000
 Unused:              %00
 Total Length:         60
 Identifier:           56325
 Fragmentation Flags: %000
 Fragment Offset:      0
 Time To Live:         32
 IP Type:              0x01 ICMP
 Header Checksum:      0x2df0
 Source IP Address:    100.100.100.2
 Dest. IP Address:     100.100.100.1
 No Internet Datagram Options
ICMP - Internet Control Messages Protocol
 ICMP Type:        8 Echo Request
 Code:             0
 Checksum:         0x395c
 Identifier:       0x0300
 Sequence Number: 4352
 ICMP Data Area:
 abcdefghijklmnop  61 62 63 64 65 66 67 68 69 6a 6b 6c 6d 6e 6f 70
 qrstuvwabcdefghi  71 72 73 74 75 76 77 61 62 63 64 65 66 67 68 69
Frame Check Sequence: 0x00000000
```

Notice anything unusual? Did you catch the fact that even though ICMP works at the Internet (Network) layer, it still uses IP to do the Ping request? The Type field in the IP header is 0x01, which specifies that the data we're carrying is owned by the ICMP protocol. Remember, just as all roads lead to Rome, all segments, or data, *must* go through IP!

> The ping program uses the alphabet in the data portion of the packet as just a payload, typically around 100 bytes by default depending on the operating system, unless, of course, you are pinging from a Windows device, which thinks the alphabet stops at the letter *W* (and doesn't include *X*, *Y*, or *Z*) and then starts at *A* again. Go figure!

If you remember reading about the Data Link layer and the different frame types in Chapter 2, you should be able to look at the preceding trace and tell what type of Ethernet frame this is. The only fields are destination hardware address, source hardware address, and Ether-Type. The only frame that uses an Ether-Type field exclusively is an Ethernet_II frame.

But before we get into the ARP protocol, let's take another look at ICMP in action. Figure 4.10 shows an internetwork (it has a router, so it's an internetwork, right?).

FIGURE 4.10   ICMP in action

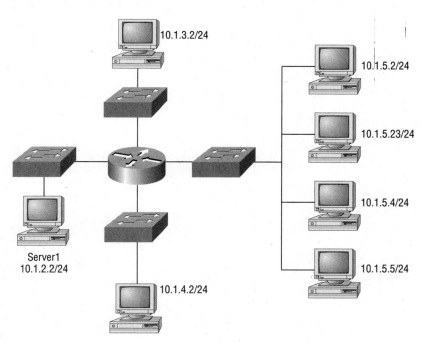

Server1 (10.1.2.24) telnets to 10.1.1.5 from a DOS prompt. What do you think Server1 will receive as a response? Since Server1 will send the Telnet data to the default gateway, which is the router, the router will drop the packet because there isn't a network 10.1.1.0 in the routing table. Because of this, Server1 will receive a destination unreachable back from ICMP.

Address Resolution Protocol (ARP)

Address Resolution Protocol (ARP) finds the hardware address of a host from a known IP address. Here's how it works: when IP has a datagram to send, it must inform a Network Access protocol, such as Ethernet or wireless, of the destination's hardware address on the local network. (It has already been informed by upper-layer protocols of the destination's IP address.) If IP doesn't find the destination host's hardware address in the ARP cache, it uses ARP to find this information.

As IP's detective, ARP interrogates the local network by sending out a broadcast asking the machine with the specified IP address to reply with its hardware address. So basically, ARP translates the software (IP) address into a hardware address—for example, the destination machine's Ethernet board address—and from it, deduces its whereabouts on the LAN by broadcasting for this address. Figure 4.11 shows how an ARP looks to a local network.

 ARP resolves IP addresses to Ethernet (MAC) addresses.

FIGURE 4.11   Local ARP broadcast

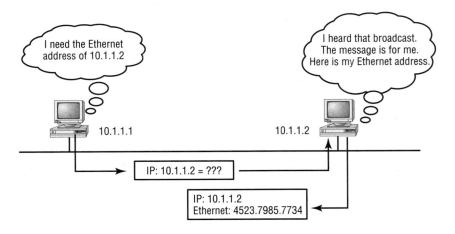

The following trace shows an ARP broadcast—notice that the destination hardware address is unknown and is all *F*s in hex (all 1s in binary)—and is a hardware address broadcast:

```
Flags:          0x00
Status:         0x00
Packet Length: 64
Timestamp:      09:17:29.574000 12/06/03
Ethernet Header
Destination:    FF:FF:FF:FF:FF:FF Ethernet Broadcast
Source:         00:A0:24:48:60:A5
Protocol Type: 0x0806 IP ARP
ARP - Address Resolution Protocol
Hardware:                   1 Ethernet (10Mb)
Protocol:                   0x0800 IP
Hardware Address Length: 6
Protocol Address Length: 4
Operation:                  1 ARP Request
Sender Hardware Address: 00:A0:24:48:60:A5
Sender Internet Address: 172.16.10.3
Target Hardware Address: 00:00:00:00:00:00 (ignored)
Target Internet Address: 172.16.10.10
Extra bytes (Padding):
................ 0A 0A 0A 0A 0A 0A 0A 0A 0A 0A 0A 0A 0A
  0A 0A 0A 0A 0A
Frame Check Sequence: 0x00000000
```

Reverse Address Resolution Protocol (RARP)

When an IP machine happens to be a diskless machine, it has no way of initially knowing its IP address. But it does know its MAC address. *Reverse Address Resolution Protocol (RARP),* as shown in Figure 4.12, discovers the identity of the IP address for diskless machines by sending out a packet that includes its MAC address and a request for the IP address assigned to that MAC address. A designated machine, called a *RARP server*, responds with the answer and the identity crisis is over. RARP uses the information it does know about the machine's MAC address to learn its IP address and complete the machine's ID portrait.

RARP resolves Ethernet (MAC) addresses to IP addresses.

Proxy Address Resolution Protocol (Proxy ARP)

On a network, your hosts can't have more than one default gateway configured. Think about this…What if the default gateway (router) happens to go down? The host won't just start sending to another router automatically—you've got to reconfigure that host. But Proxy ARP can actually help machines on a subnet reach remote subnets without configuring routing or even a default gateway.

FIGURE 4.12   RARP broadcast example

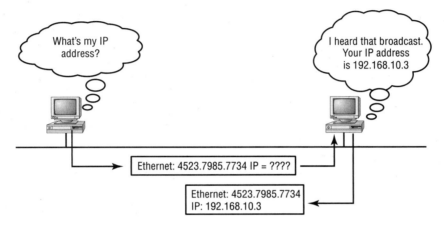

One advantage of using Proxy ARP is that it can be added to a single router on a network without disturbing the routing tables of all the other routers that live there too. But there's a serious downside to using Proxy ARP. Using Proxy ARP will definitely increase the amount of traffic on your network segment, and hosts will have a larger ARP table than usual in order to handle all the IP-to-MAC-address mappings. And Proxy ARP is configured on all Cisco routers by default—you should disable it if you don't think you're going to use it.

One last thought on Proxy ARP: Proxy ARP isn't really a separate protocol. It is a service run by routers on behalf of other devices (usually PCs) that are separated from their query to another device by a router, although they think they share the subnet with the remote device. This lets the router provide its own MAC address in response to ARP queries attempting to resolve a distant IP address to a functional MAC address.

If you can afford it, use Cisco's Hot Standby Router Protocol (HSRP) instead. It means you would have to buy two or more Cisco devices, but it is well worth it. Check out the Cisco website for more information on HSRP.

Summary

If you made it this far and understood everything the first time through, you should be proud of yourself. We really covered a lot of ground in this chapter, but understand that the information in this chapter is key to being able to navigate through the rest of this book.

And even if you didn't get a complete understanding the first time around, don't stress. It really wouldn't hurt you to read this chapter more than once. There is still a lot of ground to cover, so make sure you've got it all down, and get ready for more. What we're doing is building a foundation, and you want a strong foundation, right?

After you learned about the DoD model, the layers, and associated protocols, you learned about the oh-so-important IP addressing. I discussed in detail the difference between each class of address and how to find a network address, broadcast address, and valid host range, which is critical information to understand before going on to Chapter 5.

Since you've already come this far, there's no reason to stop now and waste all those brainwaves and new neurons. So don't stop—go through the written lab and review questions at the end of this chapter and make sure you understand each answer's explanation. The best is yet to come!

Exam Essentials

Differentiate the DoD and the OSI network models. The DoD model is a condensed version of the OSI model, composed of four layers instead of seven, but is nonetheless like the OSI model in that it can be used to describe packet creation and devices and protocols can be mapped to its layers.

Identify Process/Application layer protocols. Telnet is a terminal emulation program that allows you to log into a remote host and run programs. File Transfer Protocol (FTP) is a connection-oriented service that allows you to transfer files. Trivial FTP (TFTP) is a connectionless file transfer program. Simple Mail Transfer Protocol (SMTP) is a sendmail program.

Identify Host-to-Host layer protocols. Transmission Control Protocol (TCP) is a connection-oriented protocol that provides reliable network service by using acknowledgments and flow control. User Datagram Protocol (UDP) is a connectionless protocol that provides low overhead and is considered unreliable.

Identify Internet layer protocols. Internet Protocol (IP) is a connectionless protocol that provides network address and routing through an internetwork. Address Resolution Protocol (ARP) finds a hardware address from a known IP address. Reverse ARP (RARP) finds an IP address from a known hardware address. Internet Control Message Protocol (ICMP) provides diagnostics and destination unreachable messages.

Describe the functions of DNS and DHCP in the network.   Dynamic Host Configuration Protocol (DHCP) provides network configuration information (including IP addresses) to hosts, eliminating the need to perform the configurations manually. Domain Name Service (DNS) resolves hostnames—both Internet names such as www.lammle.com and device names such as Workstation 2—to IP addresses, eliminating the need to know the IP address of a device for connection purposes.

Identify what is contained in the TCP header of a connection-oriented transmission.   The fields in the TCP header include the source port, destination port, sequence number, acknowledgment number, header length, a field reserved for future use, code bits, window size, checksum, Urgent pointer, options field, and finally, the data field.

Identify what is contained in the UDP header of a connectionless transmission.   The fields in the UDP header include only the source port, destination port, length, checksum, and data. The smaller number of fields as compared to the TCP header comes at the expense of providing none of the more advanced functions of the TCP frame.

Identify what is contained in the IP header.   The fields of an IP header include version, header length, priority or type of service, total length, identification, flags, fragment offset, time to live, protocol, header checksum, source IP address, destination IP address, options, and finally, data.

Compare and contrast UDP and TCP characteristics and features.   TCP is connection-oriented, acknowledged, and sequenced and has flow and error control, while UDP is connectionless, unacknowledged, and not sequenced and provides no error or flow control.

Understand the role of port numbers.   Port numbers are used to identify the protocol or service that is to be used in the transmission.

Identify the role of ICMP.   Internet Control Message Protocol (ICMP) works at the Network layer and is used by IP for many different services. ICMP is a management protocol and messaging service provider for IP.

Written Lab 4

In this section, you'll complete the following lab to make sure you've got the information and concepts contained within it fully dialed in:

Lab 4: Internet Protocol (IP) Stack

You can find the answers in Appendix A.

Written Lab 4: Internet Protocol (IP) Stack

Answer the following questions about TCP/IP:

1. Which transport protocol requires a three-way handshake to establish a new connection?

2. What layer of the DoD model is equivalent to the Transport layer of the OSI model?

3. Which protocol at the Transport layer is connectionless?

4. Which protocol at the Transport layer is connection-oriented?

5. What protocol at the Network layer provides management and messaging services for IP?

6. What is used to identify the protocol or service that is to be used in the transmission of frames?

7. The term for data at the Transport layer is what?

8. What is used to identify the protocol or service that is to be used in the transmission of segments?

9. What is used to identify the protocol or service that is to be used in the transmission of packets?

10. Which two layers of the OSI model are combined in the Internet Protocol suite Network Access layer?

Review Questions

You can find the answers in Appendix B.

The following questions are designed to test your understanding of this chapter's material. For more information on how to get additional questions, please see this book's introduction.

1. What must happen if a DHCP IP conflict occurs?

   A. Proxy ARP will fix the issue.

   B. The client uses a gratuitous ARP to fix the issue.

   C. The administrator must fix the conflict by hand at the DHCP server.

   D. DHCE ignores the conflict.

2. Which options describe services that are provided by UDP? (Choose two.)

   A. Session multiplexing

   B. Connection-oriented

   C. Segmentation

   D. Reliable packet delivery

   E. Best effort packet delivery

3. You want to implement a mechanism that automates the IP configuration, including IP address, subnet mask, default gateway, and DNS information. Which protocol will you use to accomplish this?

   A. SMTP

   B. SNMP

   C. DHCP

   D. ARP

4. What protocol is used to find the hardware address of a local device?

   A. RARP

   B. ARP

   C. IP

   D. ICMP

   E. BootP

5. Which of the following are layers in the TCP/IP model? (Choose three.)

   A. Application

   B. Session

   C. Transport

   D. Internet

   E. Data Link

   F. Physical

6. Which layers of the OSI model are combined in the Internet Protocol suite Network Access layer? (Choose two.)

   A. 1

   B. 2

   C. 3

   D. 4

7. Which of the following describe the DHCP Discover message? (Choose two.)

   A. It uses FF:FF:FF:FF:FF:FF as a layer 2 broadcast.

   B. It uses UDP as the Transport layer protocol.

   C. It uses TCP as the Transport layer protocol.

   D. It does not use a layer 2 destination address.

8. Which layer 4 protocol is used for a Telnet connection?

   A. IP

   B. TCP

   C. TCP/IP

   D. UDP

   E. ICMP

9. What protocol does a DHCP client use to verify that there is not a duplicate address assignment?

   A. Acknowledge receipt of a TCP segment.

   B. Ping to its own address to see if a response is detected.

   C. Broadcast a Proxy ARP.

   D. Broadcast a gratuitous ARP.

   E. Telnet to its own IP address.

10. Which of the following services use TCP? (Choose three.)

    A. DHCP

    B. SMTP

    C. SNMP

    D. FTP

    E. HTTP

    F. TFTP

11. Which of the following services use UDP? (Choose three.)

    A. DHCP

    B. SMTP

    C. SNMP

    D. FTP

    E. HTTP

    F. TFTP

12. Which of the following are TCP/IP protocols used at the Application layer of the OSI model? (Choose three.)

    A. IP

    B. TCP

    C. Telnet

    D. FTP

    E. TFTP

13. The following illustration shows a data structure header. What protocol is this header from?

16-bit source port			16-bit destination port	
32-bit sequence number				
32-bit acknowledgment number				
4-bit header length	reserved	flags	16-bit window size	
16-bit TCP checksum			16-bit Urgent pointer	
options				
data				

A. IP

B. ICMP

C. TCP

D. UDP

E. ARP

F. RARP

14. If you use either Telnet or FTP, which is the highest layer you are using to transmit data?

A. Application

B. Presentation

C. Session

D. Transport

15. The DoD model (also called the TCP/IP stack) has four layers. Which layer of the DoD model is equivalent to the Network layer of the OSI model?

A. Application

B. Host-to-Host

C. Internet

D. Network Access

16. Which layers of the OSI model are combined in the Internet Protocol suite Application layer? (Choose two.)

   A. 3

   B. 4

   C. 5

   D. 6

   E. 7

17. What layer in the TCP/IP stack is equivalent to the Transport layer of the OSI model?

   A. Application

   B. Host-to-Host

   C. Internet

   D. Network Access

18. Which statements are true regarding ICMP packets? (Choose two.)

   A. ICMP guarantees datagram delivery.

   B. ICMP can provide hosts with information about network problems.

   C. ICMP is encapsulated within IP datagrams.

   D. ICMP is encapsulated within UDP datagrams.

19. Which layer of the OSI model is associated with Token Ring Media Access Control, FDDI and Ethernet?

   A. 4

   B. 3

   C. 2

   D. 1

20. Which of the following protocols uses both TCP and UDP?

   A. FTP

   B. SMTP

   C. Telnet

   D. DNS

Chapter

5

IP Addressing

THE FOLLOWING TOPICS ARE COVERED IN THIS CHAPTER:

✓ **Describing an IP Addressing Scheme**

- Describing Routing
- Understanding Numbering Systems
- Constructing a Network Addressing Scheme
- Subnetworks

✓ **Transitioning to IPv6**

- Reasons for Using IPv6
- Understanding IPv6 Addresses
- Assigning IPv6 Addresses
- Strategies for Implementing IPv6

In this chapter I'll cover IP addressing and the different classes of IP addresses used in networks today.

Being familiar with the various flavors of IPv4 address types is vital to understanding IP addressing. So is mastering subnetting and being savvy on Variable Length Subnet Masks (VLSMs). I promise you'll understand everything you absolutely must know before we leave the base camp of IPv4 to begin trekking into the fascinating world of Internet Protocol version 6 (IPv6) toward the end of this chapter. Once in that realm, I'll give you a tour of IPv6 features and benefits and then we'll get into dissecting the nuts and bolts of IPv6 addressing itself. After you complete this chapter, I'm certain you'll come to realize that IPv6 just isn't as horrible as many people make it out to be!

To find up-to-the minute updates for this chapter, please see www.lammle.com/forum.

IPv4 Addressing

One of the most important topics in any discussion of TCP/IP is IP addressing. An *IP address* is a numeric identifier assigned to each machine on an IP network. It designates the specific location of a device on the network.

An IP address is a software address, not a hardware address—the latter is hard-coded on a network interface card (NIC) and used for finding hosts on a local network. IP addressing was designed to allow hosts on one network to communicate with a host on a different network regardless of the type of LANs the hosts are participating in.

Before we get into the more complicated aspects of IP addressing, you need to understand some of the basics. First I'm going to explain some of the fundamentals of IP addressing and its terminology. Then you'll learn about the hierarchical IP addressing scheme and private IP addresses.

IP Terminology

Throughout this chapter you'll learn several important terms vital to your understanding of the Internet Protocol. Here are a few to get you started:

Bit   A *bit* is one digit, either a 1 or a 0.

Byte   A *byte* is 7 or 8 bits, depending on whether parity is used. For the rest of this chapter, always assume a byte is 8 bits.

Octet   An octet, made up of 8 bits, is just an ordinary 8-bit binary number. In this chapter, the terms *byte* and *octet* are completely interchangeable.

Network Address   This is the designation used in routing to send packets to a remote network—for example, 10.0.0.0, 172.16.0.0, and 192.168.10.0.

Broadcast Address   The address used by applications and hosts to send information to all nodes on a network is called the *broadcast address*. Examples include 255.255.255.255, which is any network, all nodes; 172.16.255.255, which is all subnets and hosts on network 172.16.0.0; and 10.255.255.255, which broadcasts to all subnets and hosts on network 10.0.0.0.

The Hierarchical IP Addressing Scheme

An IP address consists of 32 bits of information. These bits are divided into four sections, referred to as octets, each containing 1 byte (8 bits). Because an octet contains 1 byte, it's also known as a byte, which is why, as mentioned earlier, the terms byte and octet are completely interchangeable. You can depict an IP address using one of three methods:

- Dotted-decimal, as in 172.16.30.56
- Binary, as in 10101100.00010000.00011110.00111000
- Hexadecimal, as in AC.10.1E.38

All these examples truly represent the same IP address. Hexadecimal isn't used as often as dotted-decimal or binary when IP addressing is discussed, but you still might find an IP address stored in hexadecimal in some programs. The Windows Registry is a good example of a program that stores a machine's IP address in hex.

The 32-bit IP address is a structured or hierarchical address, as opposed to a flat or nonhierarchical address. Although either type of addressing scheme could have been used, *hierarchical addressing* was chosen for a good reason. The advantage of this scheme is that it can handle a large number of addresses, namely 4.3 billion (a 32-bit address space with two possible values for each position—either 0 or 1—gives you 2^{32}, or 4,294,967,296). The disadvantage of the flat addressing scheme, and the reason it's not used for IP addressing, relates to routing. If every address were unique, all routers on the Internet would need to store the address of each and every machine on the Internet. This would make efficient routing impossible, even if only a fraction of the possible addresses were used.

The solution to this problem is to use a two- or three-level hierarchical addressing scheme that is structured by network and host or by network, subnet, and host.

This two- or three-level scheme is comparable to a telephone number. The first section, the area code, designates a very large area. The second section, the prefix, narrows the scope to a local calling area. The final segment, the customer number, zooms in on the specific connection. IP addresses use the same type of layered structure. Rather than all 32 bits being treated as a unique identifier, as in flat addressing, a part of the address is designated as the network address and the other part is designated as either the subnet and host or just the node address.

In the following sections, I'm going to discuss IP network addressing and the different classes of address we can use to address our networks.

Network Addressing

The *network address* (which can also be called the network number) uniquely identifies each network. Every machine on the same network shares that network address as part of its IP address. In the IP address 172.16.30.56, for example, 172.16 is the network address.

The *node address* is assigned to, and uniquely identifies, each machine on a network. This part of the address must be unique because it identifies a particular machine—an individual—as opposed to a network, which is a group. This number can also be referred to as a *host address*. In the sample IP address 172.16.30.56, the 30.56 is the node address.

The designers of the Internet decided to create classes of networks based on network size. For the small number of networks possessing a very large number of nodes, they created the rank *Class A network*. At the other extreme is the *Class C network*, which is reserved for the numerous networks with a small number of nodes. The class distinction for networks between very large and very small is predictably called the *Class B network*.

Subdividing an IP address into a network and node address is determined by the class designation of one's network. Figure 5.1 summarizes the three classes of networks—a subject I'll explain in much greater detail throughout this chapter.

FIGURE 5.1   Summary of the three classes of networks

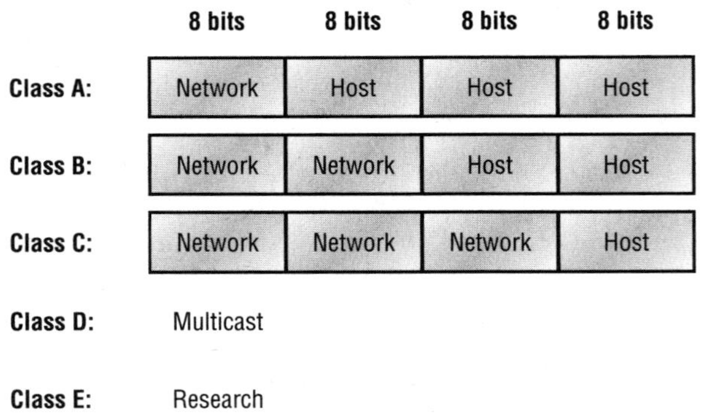

To ensure efficient routing, Internet designers defined a mandate for the leading-bits section of the address for each different network class. For example, since a router knows that a Class A network address always starts with a 0, the router might be able to speed a packet on its way after reading only the first bit of its address. This is where the address schemes define the difference between a Class A, a Class B, and a Class C address. In the next sections, I'll discuss the differences between these three classes, followed by a discussion of the Class D and Class E addresses (Classes A, B, and C are the only ranges that are used to address hosts in our networks).

Network Address Range: Class A

The designers of the IP address scheme said that the first bit of the first byte in a Class A network address must always be off, or 0. This means a Class A address must be between 0 and 127 in the first byte, inclusive.

Consider the following network address:

`0xxxxxxx`

If we turn the other 7 bits all off and then turn them all on, we'll find the Class A range of network addresses:

```
00000000 = 0
01111111 = 127
```

So, a Class A network is defined in the first octet between 0 and 127, and it can't be less or more. (Yes, I know 0 and 127 are not valid in a Class A network. I'll talk about reserved addresses in a minute.)

Network Address Range: Class B

In a Class B network, the RFCs state that the first bit of the first byte must always be turned on but the second bit must always be turned off. If you turn the other 6 bits all off and then all on, you will find the range for a Class B network:

```
10000000 = 128
10111111 = 191
```

As you can see, a Class B network is defined when the first byte is configured from 128 to 191.

Network Address Range: Class C

For Class C networks, the RFCs define the first 2 bits of the first octet as always turned on, but the third bit can never be on. Following the same process as the previous classes, convert from binary to decimal to find the range. Here's the range for a Class C network:

```
11000000 = 192
11011111 = 223
```

So, if you see an IP address that starts at 192 and goes to 223, you'll know it is a Class C IP address.

Network Address Ranges: Classes D and E

The addresses between 224 to 255 are reserved for Class D and E networks. Class D (224–239) is used for multicast addresses and Class E (240–255) for scientific purposes, but I'm not going into these types of addresses in this book (and you don't need to know them).

Network Addresses: Special Purpose

Some IP addresses are reserved for special purposes, so network administrators can't ever assign these addresses to nodes. Table 5.1 lists the members of this exclusive little club and the reasons they're included in it.

TABLE 5.1   Reserved IP addresses

Address	Function
Network address of all 0s	Interpreted to mean "this network or segment."
Network address of all 1s	Interpreted to mean "all networks."
Network 127.0.0.1	Reserved for loopback tests. Designates the local node and allows that node to send a test packet to itself without generating network traffic.
Node address of all 0s	Interpreted to mean "network address" or any host on a specified network.
Node address of all 1s	Interpreted to mean "all nodes" on the specified network; for example, 128.2.255.255 means "all nodes" on network 128.2 (Class B address).
Entire IP address set to all 0s	Used by Cisco routers to designate the default route. Could also mean "any network."
Entire IP address set to all 1s (same as 255.255.255.255)	Broadcast to all nodes on the current network; sometimes called an "all 1s broadcast" or limited broadcast.

Class A Addresses

In a Class A network address, the first byte is assigned to the network address and the three remaining bytes are used for the node addresses. The Class A format is as follows:

network.node.node.node

For example, in the IP address 49.22.102.70, the 49 is the network address and 22.102.70 is the node address. Every machine on this particular network would have the distinctive network address of 49.

Class A network addresses are 1 byte long, with the first bit of that byte reserved and the 7 remaining bits available for manipulation (addressing). As a result, the maximum number of Class A networks that can be created is 128. Why? Because each of the seven bit positions can be either a 0 or a 1, thus 2^7, or 128.

To complicate matters further, the network address of all 0s (0000 0000) is reserved to designate the default route (see Table 5.1 in the previous section). Additionally, the address 127, which is reserved for diagnostics, can't be used either, which means that you can really only use the numbers 1 to 126 to designate Class A network addresses. This means the actual number of usable Class A network addresses is 128 minus 2, or 126.

The IP address 127.0.0.1 is used to test the IP stack on an individual node and cannot be used as a valid host address. However, the loopback address is also used to create a shortcut method for TCP/IP applications and services that run on the same device to communicate with each other.

Each Class A address has 3 bytes (24-bit positions) for the node address of a machine. This means there are 2^{24}—or 16,777,216—unique combinations and, therefore, precisely that many possible unique node addresses for each Class A network. Because node addresses with the two patterns of all 0s and all 1s are reserved, the actual maximum usable number of nodes for a Class A network is 2^{24} minus 2, which equals 16,777,214. Either way, that's a huge amount of hosts on a network segment!

Class A Valid Host IDs

Here's an example of how to figure out the valid host IDs in a Class A network address:

- All host bits off is the network address: 10.0.0.0.
- All host bits on is the broadcast address: 10.255.255.255.

The valid hosts are the numbers in between the network address and the broadcast address: 10.0.0.1 through 10.255.255.254. Notice that 0s and 255s can be valid host IDs. All you need to remember when trying to find valid host addresses is that the host bits can't all be turned off or all be on at the same time.

Class B Addresses

In a Class B network address, the first 2 bytes are assigned to the network address and the remaining 2 bytes are used for node addresses. The format is as follows:

network.network.node.node

For example, in the IP address 172.16.30.56, the network address is 172.16 and the node address is 30.56.

With a network address being 2 bytes (8 bits each), there would be 2^{16} unique combinations. But the Internet designers decided that all Class B network addresses should start with the binary digit 1, then 0. This leaves 14 bit positions to manipulate, therefore 16,384 (that is, 2^{14}) unique Class B network addresses.

A Class B address uses 2 bytes for node addresses. This is 2^{16} minus the two reserved patterns (all 0s and all 1s), for a total of 65,534 possible node addresses for each Class B network.

Class B Valid Host IDs

Here's an example of how to find the valid hosts in a Class B network:

- All host bits turned off is the network address: 172.16.0.0.
- · All host bits turned on is the broadcast address: 172.16.255.255.

The valid hosts would be the numbers in between the network address and the broadcast address: 172.16.0.1 through 172.16.255.254.

Class C Addresses

The first 3 bytes of a Class C network address are dedicated to the network portion of the address, with only 1 measly byte remaining for the node address. Here's the format:

network.network.network.node

Using the example IP address 192.168.100.102, the network address is 192.168.100 and the node address is 102.

In a Class C network address, the first three bit positions are always the binary 110. The calculation is as follows: 3 bytes, or 24 bits, minus 3 reserved positions leaves 21 positions. Hence, there are 2^{21}, or 2,097,152, possible Class C networks.

Each unique Class C network has 1 byte to use for node addresses. This leads to 2^8, or 256, minus the two reserved patterns of all 0s and all 1s, for a total of 254 node addresses for each Class C network.

Class C Valid Host IDs

Here's an example of how to find a valid host ID in a Class C network:

- All host bits turned off is the network ID: 192.168.100.0.
- All host bits turned on is the broadcast address: 192.168.100.255.

The valid hosts would be the numbers in between the network address and the broadcast address: 192.168.100.1 through 192.168.100.254.

Private IP Addresses (RFC 1918)

The people who created the IP addressing scheme also created what we call private IP addresses, found in RFC 1918. These addresses can be used on a private network, but they're not routable through the Internet. This is designed for the purpose of creating a measure of well-needed security, but it also conveniently saves valuable IP address space.

If every host on every network had to have real routable IP addresses, we would have run out of IP addresses to hand out years ago. But by using private IP addresses, ISPs, corporations, and home users need only a relatively tiny group of bona fide IP addresses to connect their networks to the Internet. This is economical because they can use private IP addresses on their inside networks and get along just fine.

To accomplish this task, the ISP and the corporation—the end user, no matter who they are—need to use something called *Network Address Translation (NAT)*, which basically takes a private IP address and converts it for use on the Internet. Many people can use the same real IP address to transmit out onto the Internet. Doing things this way saves megatons of address space—good for us all!

NAT is covered in more depth in my book *CCNA: Cisco Certified Network Associate Study Guide, 7th edition* (Sybex, 2011).

Take a look at Figure 5.2. NAT translation would be configured on the Corporate router and translate public and private IP addresses for the company.

FIGURE 5.2 NAT translation

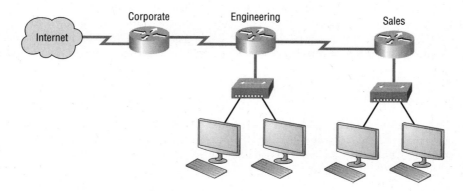

The interface connection to the Internet would be a real, global IP address, and the addresses configured on the Engineering and Sales routers would be private IP addresses.

It's very important to remember the following:

- Private addresses (RFC 1918) are not globally routable on the Internet.
- RFC 1918 specifies that networks must be reserved in each address class: 1 network in Class A, 16 networks in Class B, and 256 in Class C.
- RFC 1918 was created to establish a range of IP addresses that are dedicated to use on internal networks.
- RFC 1918 was created to delay the transition to IPv6.
- The private address must be filtered at Internet border interfaces.
- Private addresses include 10.0.0.0/8, 172.16.0.0/20, and 192.168.0.0/16.
- Network address translation is required on the Internet border device.

The reserved private addresses are listed in Table 5.2.

TABLE 5.2 Reserved IP address space

Address Class	Reserved Address Space
Class A	10.0.0.0 through 10.255.255.255
Class B	172.16.0.0 through 172.31.255.255
Class C	192.168.0.0 through 192.168.255.255

> ### 🌐 Real World Scenario
>
> #### So, What Private IP Address Should I Use?
>
> That's a really great question: Should you use Class A, Class B, or even Class C private addressing when setting up your network? Let's take Acme Corporation in San Francisco as an example. This company is moving into a new building and needs a whole new network (what a treat this is!). It has 14 departments, with about 70 users in each. You could probably squeeze one or two Class C addresses to use, or maybe you could use a Class B, or even a Class A just for fun.
>
> The rule of thumb in the consulting world is, when you're setting up a corporate network—regardless of how small it is—you should use a Class A network address because it gives you the most flexibility and growth options. For example, if you used the 10.0.0.0 network address with a /24 mask, then you'd have 65,536 networks, each with 254 hosts. Lots of room for growth with that network!
>
> But if you're setting up a home network, you'd opt for a Class C address because it is the easiest for people to understand and configure. Using the default Class C mask gives you one network with 254 hosts—plenty for a home network.
>
> With the Acme Corporation, a nice 10.1.*x*.0 with a /24 mask (the *x* is the subnet for each department) makes this easy to design, install, and troubleshoot.

   You must know your private address space to become Cisco Data Center CCNA certified!

IPv4 Address Types

Okay, I've referred to IP addresses throughout Chapters 1 and 2, and even showed you some examples. But I really haven't gone into the different terms and uses associated with them yet, and it's about time I did. So here are the four IPv4 address types that I'd like to define for you:

Loopback (Localhost)   Used to test the IP stack on the local computer. Can be any address from 127.0.0.1 through 127.255.255.254.

Layer 2 Broadcasts   These are sent to all nodes on a LAN.

Broadcasts (Layer 3)   These are sent to all nodes on the network.

Unicast   This is an address for a single interface, and these are used to send packets to a single destination host.

Multicast   These are packets sent from a single source and transmitted to many devices on different networks. Referred to as "one-to-many."

Layer 2 Broadcasts

First, understand that layer 2 broadcasts are also known as hardware broadcasts—they only go out on a LAN, and they don't go past the LAN boundary (router).

The typical hardware address is 6 bytes (48 bits) and looks something like 0c43.a4.f312.c2. The broadcast would be all 1s in binary, which would be all *F*s in hexadecimal, as in FF.FF .FF.FF.FF.FF.

Layer 3 Broadcasts

Then there are the plain old broadcast addresses at layer 3. Broadcast messages are meant to reach all hosts on a broadcast domain. These are the network broadcasts that have all host bits on.

Here's an example that you're already familiar with: the network address of 172.16.0.0 255.255.0.0 would have a broadcast address of 172.16.255.255—all host bits on. Broadcasts can also be "any network and all hosts," as indicated by 255.255.255.255.

Unicast Address

A unicast is an address on a single interface. In IPv4 you can have only one unicast address on an interface, and that address cannot be used anywhere else on the network.

Multicast Address

Multicast is a different beast entirely. At first glance, it appears to be a hybrid of unicast and broadcast communication, but that isn't quite the case. Multicast does allow point-to-multipoint communication, which is similar to broadcasts, but it happens in a different manner. The crux of *multicast* is that it enables multiple recipients to receive messages without flooding the messages to all hosts on a broadcast domain. However, this is not the default behavior—it's what we *can* do with multicasting if it's configured correctly!

Multicast works by sending messages or data to IP *multicast group* addresses. Routers then forward copies (unlike broadcasts, which are not forwarded) of the packet out of every interface that has hosts *subscribed* to that group address. This is where multicast differs from broadcast messages—with multicast communication, copies of packets, in theory, are sent only to subscribed hosts. When I say in theory, this means that the hosts will receive, for example, a multicast packet destined for 224.0.0.9 (this is an EIGRP packet and only a router running the EIGRP protocol will read these). All hosts on the broadcast LAN

(Ethernet is a broadcast multi-access LAN technology) will pick up the frame, read the destination address, and immediately discard the frame, unless they are in the multicast group. This saves PC processing, not LAN bandwidth. Multicasting can cause severe LAN congestion, in some instances, if not implemented carefully.

There are several different groups that users or applications can subscribe to. The range of multicast addresses starts with 224.0.0.0 and goes through 239.255.255.255. As you can see, this range of addresses falls within the IP Class D address space based on the class IP assignment.

IPv6 Addressing

People refer to IPv6 as "the next-generation Internet protocol," and it was originally created as the answer to IPv4's inevitable, looming address-exhaustion crisis. Though you've probably heard a thing or two about IPv6 already, it has been improved even further in the quest to bring us the flexibility, efficiency, capability, and optimized functionality that can truly meet our ever-increasing needs. The capacity of its predecessor, IPv4, pales in comparison—and that's the reason it will eventually fade into history completely.

The IPv6 header and address structure has been completely overhauled, and many of the features that were basically just afterthoughts and addendums in IPv4 are now included as full-blown standards in IPv6. It's seriously well equipped, poised, and ready to manage the mind-blowing demands of the Internet to come.

Why Do We Need IPv6?

Well, the short answer is because we need to communicate and our current system isn't really cutting it anymore—kind of like how the Pony Express can't compete with airmail. Just look at how much time and effort we've invested in coming up with slick new ways to conserve bandwidth and IP addresses. We've even come up with Variable Length Subnet Masks (VLSMs) in our struggle to overcome the worsening address drought.

It's reality—the number of people and devices that connect to networks increases each and every day. That's not a bad thing at all—we're finding new and exciting ways to communicate to more people all the time, and that's a good thing. In fact, it's a basic human need. But the forecast isn't exactly blue skies and sunshine because IPv4, upon which our ability to communicate is presently dependent, is going to run out of addresses for us to use. IPv4 has only about 4.3 billion addresses available, in theory, and we know that we don't even get to use most of those. Sure, the use of Classless Inter-Domain Routing (CIDR) and Network Address Translation (NAT) has helped to extend the inevitable dearth of addresses, but we will run out of them, and it's going to happen within a few years. China is barely online, and we know there's a huge population of people and corporations there that surely want to be. There are a lot of reports that give us all kinds of numbers, but all you really need to think about to convince yourself that I'm not just being an alarmist is the fact that there are about 6.8 billion people in the world today, and it's estimated that just over 10 percent of that population is connected to the Internet—wow!

That statistic is basically screaming at us the ugly truth that based on IPv4's capacity, every person can't even have a computer—let alone all the other IP devices we use with them. I have more than one computer, and it's pretty likely you do too. And I'm not even including in the mix phones, laptops, game consoles, fax machines, routers, switches, and a mother lode of other devices we use every day! So I think I've made it pretty clear that we've got to do something before we run out of addresses and lose the ability to connect with each other as we know it. And that "something" just happens to be implementing IPv6.

The Benefits and Uses of IPv6

So what's so fabulous about IPv6? Is it really the answer to our coming dilemma? Is it really worth it to upgrade from IPv4? All good questions—you may even think of a few more. Of course, there's going to be that group of people with the time-tested and well-known "resistance to change syndrome," but don't listen to them. If we had done that years ago, we'd still be waiting weeks, even months for our mail to arrive via horseback. Instead, just know that the answer is a resounding YES! Not only does IPv6 give us lots of addresses (3.4×10^{38} = definitely enough), but there are many other features built into this version that make it well worth the cost, time, and effort required to migrate to it.

Here are three benefits of migrating from IPv4 to IPv6:

- IPv6 eliminates the requirements for NAT.
- IPv6 includes enough addresses to allocate more than four billion IP address to every person on earth.
- Hosts can be assigned an IP address without DHCP.

Today's networks, as well as the Internet, have a ton of unforeseen requirements that simply were not considerations when IPv4 was created. We've tried to compensate with a collection of add-ons that can actually make implementing them more difficult than they would be if they were required by a standard. By default, IPv6 has improved upon and included many of those features as standard and mandatory. One of these sweet new standards is IPSec—a feature that provides end-to-end security. Another little beauty is known as mobility, and as its name suggests, it allows a device to roam from one network to another without dropping connections.

But it's the efficiency features that are really going to rock the house! For starters, the headers in an IPv6 packet have half the fields, and they are aligned to 64 bits, which gives us some seriously souped-up processing speed—compared to IPv4, lookups happen at light speed! Most of the information that used to be bound into the IPv4 header was taken out, and now you can choose to put it, or parts of it, back into the header in the form of optional extension headers that follow the basic header fields.

And of course there's that whole new universe of addresses (3.4×10^{38}—enough for four billion addresses to be assigned to each person on earth!) we talked about already. But where did we get them? Did that Criss Angel *Mindfreak* dude just show up and, blammo? I mean, that huge proliferation of addresses had to come from somewhere! Well it just so happens that IPv6 gives us a substantially larger address space, meaning the address is a whole lot bigger—four times bigger as a matter of fact! An IPv6 address is actually 128 bits in length, and no worries—I'm going to break down the address piece by piece and show you exactly what it looks like, coming up in the section, "IPv6 Addressing and Expressions." For now, let me just say that all that additional room permits more levels of hierarchy inside the address space and a more flexible addressing architecture. It also makes routing much more efficient and scalable because the addresses can be aggregated a lot more effectively. And IPv6 also allows multiple addresses for hosts and networks. This is especially important for enterprises jonesing for enhanced availability. Plus, the new version of IP now includes an expanded use of multicast communication (one device sending to many hosts or to a select group), which will also join in to boost efficiency on networks because communications will be more specific.

IPv4 uses broadcasts quite prolifically, causing a bunch of problems, the worst of which is of course the dreaded broadcast storm—an uncontrolled deluge of forwarded broadcast traffic that can bring an entire network to its knees and devour every last bit of bandwidth. Another nasty thing about broadcast traffic is that it interrupts each and every device on the network. When a broadcast is sent out, every machine has to stop what it's doing and respond to the traffic whether the broadcast is meant for it or not.

But smile everyone: There is no such thing as a broadcast in IPv6 because it uses multicast traffic instead. And there are two other types of communication as well: unicast, which is the same as it is in IPv4, and a new type called anycast. Anycast communication allows the same address to be placed on more than one device so that when traffic is sent to the device service addressed in this way, it is routed to the nearest host that shares the same address; this is referred to as one-to-nearest. This is just the beginning—we'll get more into the various types of communication in the section called, "Address Types."

IPv6 Addressing and Expressions

Just as understanding how IP addresses are structured and used is critical with IPv4 addressing, it's also vital when it comes to IPv6. You've already read about the fact that at 128 bits, an IPv6 address is much larger than an IPv4 address. Because of this, as well as the new ways the addresses can be used, you've probably guessed that IPv6 will be more complicated to manage. But no worries! As I said, I'll break down the basics and show you what the address looks like, how you can write it, and what many of its common uses are. It's going to be a little weird at first, but before you know it, you'll have it nailed!

So let's take a look at Figure 5.3, which has a sample IPv6 address broken down into sections.

FIGURE 5.3   IPv6 address example

```
2001:0db8:3c4d:0012:0000:0000:1234:56ab
_____|____|_____
Global prefix   Subnet      Interface ID
```

As you can now see, the address is truly much larger—but what else is different? Well, first, notice that it has eight groups of numbers instead of four and also that those groups are separated by colons instead of periods. And hey wait a second... there are letters in that address! Yep, the address is expressed in hexadecimal just as a Mac address is, so you could say this address has eight 16-bit hexadecimal colon-delimited blocks. IPv6 addresses are called 128-bit colon-delimited hexadecimal. That's already quite a mouthful, and you probably haven't even tried to say the address in Figure 5.3 out loud yet!

One other thing I want to point out is for when you set up your test network to play with IPv6, because I know you're going to want to do that. When you use a web browser to make an HTTP connection to an IPv6 device, you have to type the address into the browser with brackets around the literal address. Why? Well, a colon is already being used by the browser for specifying a port number. So basically, if you don't enclose the address in brackets, the browser will have no way to identify the information.

Here's an example of how this looks:

```
http://[2001:0db8:3c4d:0012:0000:0000:1234:56ab]/default.html
```

Now obviously, if you can, you would rather use names to specify a destination (like, www.lammle.com), but even though it's definitely going to be a pain in the rear, we just have to accept the fact that sometimes we have to bite the bullet and type in the address number. So it should be pretty clear that DNS is going to remain extremely important when implementing IPv6.

 There are four hexadecimal characters (16 bits) in each IPv6 field, separated by colons.

Shortened Expression

The good news is that there are a few tricks to help rescue us when writing these monster addresses. For one thing, you can actually leave out parts of the address to abbreviate it, but to get away with doing that you have to follow a couple of rules. First, you can drop any leading zeros in each of the individual blocks. After you do that, the sample address from earlier would then look like this:

```
2001:db8:3c4d:12:0:0:1234:56ab
```

Okay, that's a definite improvement—at least we don't have to write all of those extra zeros! But what about whole blocks that don't have anything in them except zeros? Well, we can kind of lose those too—at least some of them. Again referring to our sample address, we can remove the two consecutive blocks of zeros by replacing them with a double colon, like this:

```
2001:db8:3c4d:12::1234:56ab
```

Cool—we replaced the blocks of all zeros with a double colon. The rule you have to follow to get away with this is that you can replace only one contiguous block of such zeros in an address. So if my address has four blocks of zeros and each of them were separated, I don't get to just replace them all; remember, the rule is that you can replace only one contiguous block with a double colon. Check out this example:

```
2001:0000:0000:0012:0000:0000:1234:56ab
```

And just know that you *can't* do this:

```
2001::12::1234:56ab
```

Instead, this is the best that you can do:

```
2001::12:0:0:1234:56ab
```

The reason the preceding example is our best shot is that if we remove two sets of zeros, the device looking at the address will have no way of knowing where the zeros go back in. Basically, the router would look at the incorrect address and say, "Well, do I place two blocks into the first set of double colons and two into the second set, or do I place three blocks into the first set and one block into the second set?" And on and on it would go because the information the router needs just isn't there.

Address Types

We're all familiar with IPv4's unicast, broadcast, and multicast addresses that basically define who or at least how many other devices we're talking to. But as I mentioned, IPv6 modifies that trio and introduces the anycast. Broadcasts, as we know them, have been eliminated in IPv6 because of their cumbersome inefficiency.

So let's find out what each of these types of IPv6 addressing and communication methods do for us:

Unicast   Packets addressed to a unicast address are delivered to a single interface. There are a few different types of unicast addresses, but we don't need to get into that here.

Global Unicast Addresses   These are your typical publicly routable addresses, and they're the same as they are in IPv4. Global addresses start at 2000::/3.

Link-Local Addresses   These are like the private addresses in IPv4 in that they're not meant to be routed and they start with FE80::/10. Think of them as a handy tool that gives you the ability to throw a temporary LAN together for meetings or to create a small LAN that's not going to be routed but still needs to share and access files and services locally.

Unique Local Addresses (RFC 4193).   These addresses are also intended for non-routing purposes over the Internet, but they are nearly globally unique, so it's unlikely you'll ever have one of them overlap. Unique local addresses were designed to replace site-local addresses, so they basically do almost exactly what IPv4 private addresses do—allow communication throughout a site while being routable to multiple local networks. Site-local addresses were denounced as of September 2004. ULA's contain a 40-bit random number in the prefix and are found in the IPv6 address block of fc00::/7; they are not routable on the Internet.

Multicast   Again, same as in IPv4, packets addressed to a multicast address are delivered to all interfaces tuned into the multicast address. Sometimes people call them one-to-many addresses. It's really easy to spot a multicast address in IPv6 because they always start with *FF*.

Anycast   Like multicast addresses, an anycast address identifies a single unicast address on multiple interfaces, but there's a big difference: the anycast packet is delivered to only one device—actually, to the closest one it finds defined in terms of routing distance. And again, this address is special because you can apply a single address to more than one interface. These are referred to as "one-to-nearest" addresses.

Cisco just added a new objective.

For more information on IPv6 above and beyond the CCNA Data Center objectives, please see my book *CCNA: Cisco Certified Network Associate Study Guide, 7th edition* (Sybex, 2011).

Summary

If you made it this far and understood everything the first time through, you should be proud of yourself. We really covered a lot of ground in this chapter, but understand that the information in this chapter is key to being able to navigate through the rest of this book.

And even if you didn't get a complete understanding the first time around, don't stress. It really wouldn't hurt you to read this chapter more than once. There is still a lot of ground to cover, so make sure you've got it all down, and get ready for more. What we're doing is building a foundation, and you want a strong foundation, right?

After you learned about the DoD model, the layers, and associated protocols, you learned about the oh-so-important IP addressing. I discussed in detail the difference between each class of address and how to find a network address, broadcast address, and valid host range, which is critical information to understand before going on to Chapter 6.

The chapter ended with an introduction to IPv6. I discussed the reason for IPv6, the 128-bit colon-delimited hexadecimal address, and the different types of addresses.

Since you've already come this far, there's no reason to stop now and waste all those brainwaves and new neurons. So don't stop—go through the written lab and review questions at the end of this chapter and make sure you understand each answer's explanation. The best is yet to come!

Exam Essentials

Define the Class A IP address range.   The IP range for a Class A network is 1–126. This provides 8 bits of network addressing and 24 bits of host addressing by default.

Define the Class B IP address range.   The IP range for a Class B network is 128–191. Class B addressing provides 16 bits of network addressing and 16 bits of host addressing by default.

Define the Class C IP address range.   The IP range for a Class C network is 192 through 223. Class C addressing provides 24 bits of network addressing and 8 bits of host addressing by default.

Identify the private IP ranges.   Class A private address range is 10.0.0.0 through 10.255.255.255.

Class B private address range is 172.16.0.0 through 172.31.255.255.

Class C private address range is 192.168.0.0 through 192.168.255.255.

Understand the difference between a broadcast, unicast, and multicast address.   A broadcast is all devices in a subnet, a unicast is one device, and a multicast is some but not all devices.

Remember the IPv6 benefits.   There are enough addresses in IPv6 that we could allocate up to four billion addresses to each person on earth. IPv6 eliminates the need for NAT translation and DHCP servers.

Remember the address format for IPv6.   IPv6 is written in 128-bit colon-delimited hexadecimal, with eight 16-bit fields.

Written Labs

In this section, you'll complete the following written lab to make sure you've got the information and concepts contained within fully dialed in:

Lab 5: TCP/IP

You can find the answers in Appendix A.

Written Lab 5: TCP/IP

Answer the following questions about TCP/IP:

1. Approximately how many IPv6 addresses can be allocated to each person on earth?

2. What is required on Internet border routers if you are using RFC 1918 on your network?

3. What is the valid range of a Class A network address?

4. What is the 127.0.0.1 address used for?

5. How do you find the network address from a listed IP address?

6. How do you find the broadcast address from a listed IP address?

7. What is the Class A private IP address space?

8. What is the Class B private IP address space?

9. What is the Class C private IP address space?

10. What is the format of an IPv6 address?

Review Questions

You can find the answers in Appendix B.

 The following questions are designed to test your understanding of this chapter's material. For more information on how to get additional questions, please see this book's introduction.

1. How many private networks are available with an RFC 1918 Class A reserved IP range?

   A. 1

   B. 16

   C. 256

   D. 16,386

2. Which is true regarding RFC 918? (Choose two.)

   A. RFC 1918 addresses are globally routable on the Internet.

   B. RFC 1918 addresses are not globally routable on the Internet.

   C. RFC 1918 was created to delay the transition to IPv6.

   D. RFC 1918 reserves 2 networks in Class A, 16 networks in Class B, and 256 in Class C.

3. How many private networks are available with an RFC 1918 Class B reserved IP range?

   A. 1

   B. 16

   C. 256

   D. 16,386

4. What is true regarding a benefit of migrating to IPv6?

   A. Multicasts from IPv4 were replaced with broadcasts in IPv6.

   B. DHCP with IPSec in IPv6 is now mandatory.

   C. IPv6 eliminates the requirement for NAT.

   D. IPv6 eliminates the need for VLANs.

5. How many private networks are available with an RFC 1918 Class C reserved IP range?

   A. 1

   B. 16

   C. 256

   D. 16,386

6. Which class of IP address provides a maximum of only 254 host addresses per network ID?

   A. Class A

   B. Class B

   C. Class C

   D. Class D

   E. Class E

7. What will happen if a private IP address is assigned to a public interface connected to an ISP?

   A. Addresses in a private range will be not be routed on the Internet backbone.

   B. Only the ISP router will have the capability to access the public network.

   C. The NAT process will be used to translate this address in a valid IP address.

   D. Several automated methods will be necessary on the private network.

   E. A conflict of IP addresses happens, because other public routers can use the same range.

8. Which of the following describe private addresses? (choose 2)

   A. RFC 4_Private

   B. RFC 1918

   C. RFC 4193

   D. RFC IPv6/IPv4 Private Ranges

   E. RFC 2191

9. Anycast is referred to as what?

   A. One-to-all

   B. One-to-many

   C. One-to-some

   D. One-to-nearest

10. Link-local addresses in IPv6 start with what prefix?

   A. FE80

   B. FE90

   C. 2000

   D. 2E3F

11. Which three are address ranges specified in RFC 1918? (Choose three.)

    A. 10.0.0.0/8

    B. 10.0.0.0/16

    C. 172.16.0.0/24

    D. 172.16.0.0/20

    E. 192.168.0.0/16

    F. 192.168.0.0/24

12. Which is required on your network if you are implementing RFC 1918 and want to connect to the global Internet?

    A. Security

    B. DHCP

    C. NAT

    D. Broadcasts

    E. Multicasts

13. Which are reasons to migrate from IPv4 to IPv6? (Choose three.)

    A. IPv6 eliminates the requirement for NAT.

    B. IPv6 includes enough IP addresses to allocate more than four billion IP addresses to every person on earth.

    C. IPv6 eliminates the need for VLANs.

    D. Hosts can be assigned an IP address without DHCP.

    E. Hosts can be assigned an IP address without DNS.

14. Which two of the following are private IP addresses?

    A. 12.0.0.1

    B. 168.172.19.39

    C. 172.20.14.36

    D. 172.33.194.30

    E. 192.168.24.43

15. What is the address range of a Class B network address in binary?

    A. 01*xxxxxx*

    B. 0*xxxxxxx*

    C. 10*xxxxxx*

    D. 110*xxxxx*

16. What is the addressing format of IPv6?

    A. 48-bit colon-delimited hexadecimal

    B. 48-bit dotted-decimal

    C. 128-bit colon-delimited hexadecimal

    D. 64-bit dotted-decimal

    E. 128-bit dotted-decimal

17. An administrator issues the command `ping 127.0.0.1` from the command-line prompt on a PC. If a reply is received, what does this confirm?

    A. Local network address

    B. APIPA address

    C. Broadcast address

    D. Loopback

18. How do you find the network address from a listed IP address?

    A. Ping the local host.

    B. Use Traceroute on the local IP address.

    C. Turn all host bits off.

    D. Turn all host bits on.

19. How do you find the broadcast address from a listed IP address?

    A. Ping the local host.

    B. Use Traceroute on the local IP address.

    C. Turn all host bits off.

    D. Turn all host bits on.

20. Which IP address can be assigned to an Internet interface?

    A. 10.180.48.224

    B. 9.255.255.10

    C. 192.168.20.223

    D. 172.16.200.18

Chapter

6

Easy Subnetting

THE FOLLOWING TOPICS ARE COVERED IN THIS CHAPTER:

✓ **Describing an IP Addressing Scheme**

- Describing Routing
- Understanding Numbering Systems
- Constructing a Network Addressing Scheme
- Subnetting

This chapter will pick up right where we left off in the last chapter. We will continue our discussion of IP addressing.

We'll start with subnetting an IP network. You're going to have to really apply yourself because it takes time and practice to nail subnetting. So be patient. Do whatever it takes to get this stuff dialed in. This chapter truly is important—possibly the most important chapter in this book for you to understand.

I'll thoroughly cover IP subnetting from the very beginning. I know this might sound weird to you, but I think you'll be much better off if you can try to forget everything you've learned about subnetting before reading this chapter—especially if you've been to a Microsoft class!

So get psyched—you're about to go for quite a ride! This chapter will truly help you understand IP addressing and networking, so don't get discouraged or give up. If you stick with it, I promise that one day you'll look back on this and you'll be really glad you decided to hang on. It's one of those things that after you understand it, you'll wonder why you once thought it was so hard. Ready? Let's go!

For up-to-the-minute updates for this chapter, please see www.lammle.com/forum.

Subnetting Basics

In Chapter 5, you learned how to define and find the valid host ranges used in a Class A, Class B, and Class C network address by turning the host bits all off and then all on. This is very good, but here's the catch: you were defining only one network. What happens if you wanted to take one network address and create six networks from it? You would have to do something called *subnetting*, because that's what allows you to take one larger network and break it into a bunch of smaller networks.

There are loads of reasons in favor of subnetting, including the following benefits:

Reduced Network Traffic We all appreciate less traffic of any kind. Networks are no different. Without trusty routers, packet traffic could grind the entire network down to a near standstill. With routers, most traffic will stay on the local network; only packets destined for other networks will pass through the router. Routers create broadcast domains. The more broadcast domains you create, the smaller the broadcast domains and the less network traffic on each network segment.

Optimized Network Performance   This is a result of reduced network traffic.

Simplified Management   It's easier to identify and isolate network problems in a group of smaller connected networks than within one gigantic network.

Facilitated Spanning of Large Geographical Distances   Because WAN links are considerably slower and more expensive than LAN links, a single large network that spans long distances can create problems in every area previously listed. Connecting multiple smaller networks makes the system more efficient.

In the following sections, I am going to move to subnetting a network address. This is the good part—ready?

IP Subnet-Zero

IP subnet-zero is not a new command, but in the past, Cisco courseware, and Cisco exam objectives, didn't cover it—but it certainly does now! This command allows you to use the first and last subnet in your network design. For example, the Class C mask of 255.255.255.192 provides subnets 64 and 128 (discussed thoroughly later in this chapter), but with the ip subnet-zero command, you now get to use subnets 0, 64, 128, and 192. That is two more subnets for every subnet mask you use. Please understand that this command is on by default on all new routers and all Nexus OS switches.

How to Create Subnets

To create subnetworks, you take bits from the host portion of the IP address and reserve them to define the subnet address. This means fewer bits for hosts, so the more subnets, the fewer bits available for defining hosts.

Later in this chapter, you'll learn how to create subnets, starting with Class C addresses. But before you actually implement subnetting, you need to determine your current requirements as well as plan for future conditions.

Before we move on to designing and creating a subnet mask, you need to understand that in this first section, we will be discussing classful routing, which means that all hosts (all nodes) in the network use the exact same subnet mask. When we move on to Variable Length Subnet Masks (VLSMs), I'll discuss classless routing, which means that each network segment *can* use a different subnet mask.

To create a subnet, follow these steps:

1. Determine the number of required network IDs:

- One for each LAN subnet
- One for each WAN connection

2. Determine the number of required host IDs per subnet:
   - One for each TCP/IP host
   - One for each router interface
3. Based on the above requirements, create the following:
   - One subnet mask for your entire network
   - A unique subnet ID for each physical segment
   - A range of host IDs for each subnet

Understanding the Powers of 2

Powers of 2 are important to understand and memorize for use with IP subnetting. To review powers of 2, remember that when you see a number with another number to its upper right (called an exponent), this means you should multiply the number by itself as many times as the upper number specifies. For example, 2^3 is $2 \times 2 \times 2$, which equals 8. Here's a list of powers of 2 that you should commit to memory:

$2^1 = 2$

$2^2 = 4$

$2^3 = 8$

$2^4 = 16$

$2^5 = 32$

$2^6 = 64$

$2^7 = 128$

$2^8 = 256$

$2^9 = 512$

$2^{10} = 1,024$

$2^{11} = 2,048$

$2^{12} = 4,096$

$2^{13} = 8,192$

$2^{14} = 16,384$

Before you get stressed out about knowing all these exponents, remember that it's helpful to know them, but it's not absolutely necessary. Here's a little trick since you're working with 2s: each successive power of 2 is double the previous one.

For example, all you have to do to remember the value of 2^9 is to first know that $2^8 = 256$. Why? Because when you double 2 to the eighth power (256), you get 2^9 (or 512). To determine the value of 2^{10}, simply start at $2^8 = 256$, and then double it twice.

You can go the other way as well. If you needed to know what 2^6 is, for example, you just cut 256 in half two times: once to reach 2^7 and then one more time to reach 2^6.

Subnet Masks

For the subnet address scheme to work, every machine on the network must know which part of the host address will be used as the subnet address. This is accomplished by assigning a *subnet mask* to each machine. A subnet mask is a 32-bit value that allows the recipient of IP packets to distinguish the network ID portion of the IP address from the host ID portion of the IP address.

The network administrator creates a 32-bit subnet mask composed of 1s and 0s. The 1s in the subnet mask represent the positions that refer to the network or subnet addresses.

Not all networks need subnets, meaning they use the default subnet mask. This is basically the same as saying that a network doesn't have a subnet address. Table 6.1 shows the default subnet masks for Classes A, B, and C. These default masks cannot change. In other words, you can't make a Class B subnet mask read 255.0.0.0. If you try, the host will read that address as invalid and usually won't even let you type it in. For a Class A network, you can't change the first byte in a subnet mask; it must read 255.0.0.0 at a minimum. Similarly, you cannot assign 255.255.255.255, as this is all 1s—a broadcast address. A Class B address must start with 255.255.0.0, and a Class C has to start with 255.255.255.0.

TABLE 6.1   Default subnet mask

Class	Format	Default Subnet Mask
A	*network.node.node.node*	255.0.0.0
B	*network.network.node.node*	255.255.0.0
C	*network.network.network.node*	255.255.255.0

Classless Inter-Domain Routing (CIDR)

Another term you need to familiarize yourself with is *Classless Inter-Domain Routing (CIDR)*. It's basically the method that ISPs (Internet Service Providers) use to allocate a number of addresses to a company, a home—a customer. They provide addresses in a certain block size, something I'll be going into in greater detail later in this chapter.

When you receive a block of addresses from an ISP, what you get will look something like this: 192.168.10.32/28. This is telling you what your subnet mask is. The slash notation (/) means how many bits are turned on (1s). Obviously, the maximum could only be /32 because a byte is 8 bits and there are 4 bytes in an IP address: $(4 \times 8 = 32)$. But keep in mind that the largest subnet mask available (regardless of the class of address) can only be a /30 because you've got to keep at least 2 bits for host bits.

Take, for example, a Class A default subnet mask, which is 255.0.0.0. This means that the first byte of the subnet mask is all ones (1s), or 11111111. When referring to a slash notation, you need to count all the 1 bits to figure out your mask. The 255.0.0.0 is considered a /8 because it has 8 bits that are 1s—that is, 8 bits that are turned on.

A Class B default mask would be 255.255.0.0, which is a /16 because 16 bits are ones (1s): 11111111.11111111.00000000.00000000.

Table 6.2 has a listing of every available subnet mask and its equivalent CIDR slash notation.

TABLE 6.2   CIDR values

Subnet Mask	CIDR Value
255.0.0.0	/8
255.128.0.0	/9
255.192.0.0	/10
255.224.0.0	/11
255.240.0.0	/12
255.248.0.0	/13
255.252.0.0	/14
255.254.0.0	/15
255.255.0.0	/16
255.255.128.0	/17
255.255.192.0	/18
255.255.224.0	/19
255.255.240.0	/20
255.255.248.0	/21
255.255.252.0	/22
255.255.254.0	/23
255.255.255.0	/24
255.255.255.128	/25
255.255.255.192	/26

Subnet Mask	CIDR Value
255.255.255.224	/27
255.255.255.240	/28
255.255.255.248	/29
255.255.255.252	/30

The /8 through /15 can only be used with Class A network addresses. /16 through /23 can be used by Class A and B network addresses. /24 through /30 can be used by Class A, B, and C network addresses. This is a big reason most companies use Class A network addresses. Since they can use all subnet masks, they get the maximum flexibility in network design.

 No, you cannot configure a Cisco IOS router using this slash format, but you can in the NX-OS! Nice! It's *really* important for you to know subnet masks in the slash notation (CIDR).

Subnetting Class C Addresses

There are many different ways to subnet a network. The right way is the way that works best for you. In a Class C address, only 8 bits are available for defining the hosts. Remember that subnet bits start at the left and go to the right, without skipping bits. This means that the only Class C subnet masks can be the following:

```
Binary    Decimal  CIDR
------------------------------------------------------------
00000000 = 0        /24
10000000 = 128      /25
11000000 = 192      /26
11100000 = 224      /27
11110000 = 240      /28
11111000 = 248      /29
11111100 = 252      /30
```

We can't use a /31 or /32 because we have to have at least 2 host bits for assigning IP addresses to hosts.

In the following sections, I'm going to teach you an alternate method of subnetting that makes it easier to subnet larger numbers in no time. Trust me, you need to be able to subnet fast!

Subnetting a Class C Address: The Fast Way!

When you've chosen a possible subnet mask for your network and need to determine the number of subnets, valid hosts, and broadcast addresses of a subnet that the mask provides, all you need to do is answer five simple questions:

- How many subnets does the chosen subnet mask produce?
- How many valid hosts per subnet are available?
- What are the valid subnets?
- What's the broadcast address of each subnet?
- What are the valid hosts in each subnet?

At this point, it's important that you both understand and have memorized your powers of 2. Please refer to the sidebar "Understanding the Powers of 2" earlier in this chapter if you need some help. Here's how you get the answers to those five big questions:

- *How many subnets?* 2^x = number of subnets. x is the number of masked bits, or the 1s. For example, in 11000000, the number of 1s gives us 2^2 subnets. In this example, there are 4 subnets.

- *How many hosts per subnet?* $2^y - 2$ = number of hosts per subnet. y is the number of unmasked bits, or the 0s. For example, in 11000000, the number of 0s gives us $2^6 - 2$ hosts. In this example, there are 62 hosts per subnet. You need to subtract 2 for the subnet address and the broadcast address, which are not valid hosts.

- *What are the valid subnets?* 256 – subnet mask = block size, or increment number. An example would be 256 – 192 = 64. The block size of a 192 mask is always 64. Start counting at zero in blocks of 64 until you reach the subnet mask value and these are your subnets. 0, 64, 128, 192. Easy, huh?

- *What's the broadcast address for each subnet?* Now here's the really easy part. Since we counted our subnets in the last section as 0, 64, 128, and 192, the broadcast address is always the number right before the next subnet. For example, the 0 subnet has a broadcast address of 63 because the next subnet is 64. The 64 subnet has a broadcast address of 127 because the next subnet is 128, and so on. And remember, the broadcast address of the last subnet is always 255.

- *What are the valid hosts?* Valid hosts are the numbers between the subnets, omitting the all 0s and all 1s. For example, if 64 is the subnet number and 127 is the broadcast address, then 65–126 is the valid host range—it's *always* the numbers between the subnet address and the broadcast address.

I know this can truly seem confusing. But it really isn't as hard as it seems to be at first—just hang in there! Why not try a few and see for yourself?

Subnetting Practice Examples: Class C Addresses

Here's your opportunity to practice subnetting Class C addresses using the method I just described. Exciting, isn't it! We're going to start with the first Class C subnet mask and work through every subnet that we can using a Class C address. When we're done, I'll show you how easy this is with Class A and B networks too!

Practice Example #1C: 255.255.255.128 (/25)

Since 128 is 10000000 in binary, there is only 1 bit for subnetting and 7 bits for hosts. We're going to subnet the Class C network address 192.168.10.0.

   192.168.10.0 = Network address

   255.255.255.128 = Subnet mask

Now, let's answer the big five:

- *How many subnets?* Since 128 is 1 bit on (**1**0000000), the answer would be $2^1 = 2$.
- *How many hosts per subnet?* We have 7 host bits off (1**0000000**), so the equation would be $2^7 - 2 = 126$ hosts.
- *What are the valid subnets?* $256 - 128 = 128$ which is your block size. Remember, we'll start at zero and count in our block size, so our subnets are 0, 128.
- *What's the broadcast address for each subnet?* The number right before the value of the next subnet is all host bits turned on and equals the broadcast address. For the zero subnet, the next subnet is 128, so the broadcast of the 0 subnet is 127.
- *What are the valid hosts?* These are the numbers between the subnet and broadcast address. The easiest way to find the hosts is to write out the subnet address and the broadcast address. This way, the valid hosts are obvious. The following table shows the 0 and 128 subnets, the valid host ranges of each, and the broadcast address of both subnets:

Subnet	0	128
First host	1	129
Last host	126	254
Broadcast	127	255

Before moving on to the next example, take a look at Figure 6.1. Okay, looking at a Class C /25, it's pretty clear there are two subnets. But so what—why is this significant? Well actually, it's not, but that's not the right question. What you really want to know is what you would do with this information!

FIGURE 6.1   Implementing a Class C /25 logical network

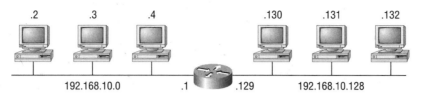

```
Router#show ip route
[output cut]
C 192.168.10.0 is directly connected to Ethernet 0.
C 192.168.10.128 is directly connected to Ethernet 1.
```

I know this isn't exactly everyone's favorite pastime, but it's really important, so just hang in there; we're going to talk about subnetting—period. You need to know that the key to understanding subnetting is to understand the very reason you need to do it. And I'm going to demonstrate this by going through the process of building a physical network—and let's add a router. (We now have an internetwork, as I truly hope you already know!) All right, because we added that router, in order for the hosts on our internetwork to communicate, they must now have a logical network addressing scheme. We could use IPv6, but IPv4 is still the most popular, and it also just happens to be what we're studying at the moment, so that's what we're going with. Okay—now take a look back to Figure 6.1. There are two physical networks, so we're going to implement a logical addressing scheme that allows for two logical networks. As always, it's a really good idea to look ahead and consider likely growth scenarios—both short and long term, but for this example, a /25 will do the trick.

Practice Example #2C: 255.255.255.192 (/26)

In this second example, we're going to subnet the network address 192.168.10.0 using the subnet mask 255.255.255.192.

192.168.10.0 = Network address

255.255.255.192 = Subnet mask

Now, let's answer the big five:

- *How many subnets?* Since 192 is 2 bits on (**11**000000), the answer would be 2^2 = 4 subnets.

- *How many hosts per subnet?* We have 6 host bits off (11**000000**), so the equation would be $2^6 - 2$ = 62 hosts.

- *What are the valid subnets?* 256 – 192 = 64. Remember, we start at zero and count in our block size, so our subnets are 0, 64, 128, and 192.

- *What's the broadcast address for each subnet?* The number right before the value of the next subnet is all host bits turned on and equals the broadcast address. For the zero subnet, the next subnet is 64, so the broadcast address for the zero subnet is 63.

■ *What are the valid hosts?* These are the numbers between the subnet and broadcast address. The easiest way to find the hosts is to write out the subnet address and the broadcast address. This way, the valid hosts are obvious. The following table shows the 0, 64, 128, and 192 subnets, the valid host ranges of each, and the broadcast address of each subnet:

The subnets (do this first)	0	64	128	192
Our first host (perform host addressing last)	1	65	129	193
Our last host	62	126	190	254
The broadcast address (do this second)	63	127	191	255

Okay, again, before getting into the next example, you can see that we can now subnet a /26. And what are you going to do with this fascinating information? Implement it! We'll use Figure 6.2 to practice a /26 network implementation.

FIGURE 6.2   Implementing a Class C /26 logical network

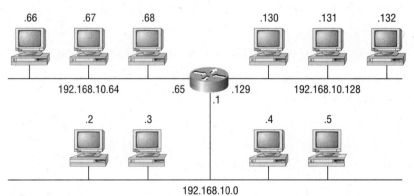

```
Router#show ip route
[output cut]
C 192.168.10.0 is directly connected to Ethernet 0
C 192.168.10.64 is directly connected to Ethernet 1
C 192.168.10.128 is directly connected to Ethernet 2
```

The /26 mask provides four subnetworks, and we need a subnet for each router interface. With this mask, in this example, we actually have room to add another router interface.

Practice Example #3C: 255.255.255.224 (/27)

This time, we'll subnet the network address 192.168.10.0 and subnet mask 255.255.255.224.

> 192.168.10.0 = Network address
>
> 255.255.255.224 = Subnet mask

- *How many subnets?* 224 is 11100000, so our equation would be 2^3 = 8.
- *How many hosts?* $2^5 - 2$ = 30.
- *What are the valid subnets?* 256 – 224 = 32. We just start at zero and count to the subnet mask value in blocks (increments) of 32: 0, 32, 64, 96, 128, 160, 192, and 224.
- *What's the broadcast address for each subnet (always the number right before the next subnet)?*
- *What are the valid hosts (the numbers between the subnet number and the broadcast address)?*

To answer the last two questions, first just write out the subnets, then write out the broadcast addresses—the number right before the next subnet. Last, fill in the host addresses. The following table gives you all the subnets for the 255.255.255.224 Class C subnet mask:

The subnet address	0	32	64	96	128	160	192	224
The first valid host	1	33	65	97	129	161	193	225
The last valid host	30	62	94	126	158	190	222	254
The broadcast address	31	63	95	127	159	191	223	255

Practice Example #4C: 255.255.255.240 (/28)

Let's practice on another one:

> 192.168.10.0 = Network address
>
> 255.255.255.240 = Subnet mask

- *Subnets?* 240 is 11110000 in binary. 2^4 = 16.
- *Hosts?* 4 host bits, or $2^4 - 2$ = 14.
- *Valid subnets?* 256 – 240 = 16. Start at 0: 0 + 16 = 16. 16 + 16 = 32. 32 + 16 = 48. 48 + 16 = 64. 64 + 16 = 80. 80 + 16 = 96. 96 + 16 = 112. 112 + 16 = 128. 128 + 16 = 144. 144 + 16 = 160. 160 + 16 = 176. 176 + 16 = 192. 192 + 16 = 208. 208 + 16 = 224. 224 + 16 = 240.
- *Broadcast address for each subnet?*
- *Valid hosts?*

To answer the last two questions, check out the following table. It gives you the subnets, valid hosts, and broadcast addresses for each subnet. First, find the address of each subnet using the block size (increment). Second, find the broadcast address of each subnet increment (it's always the number right before the next valid subnet), then just fill in the host addresses. The following table shows the available subnets, hosts, and broadcast addresses provided from a Class C 255.255.255.240 mask:

Subnet	0	16	32	48	64	80	96	112	128	144	160	176	192	208	224	240
First host	1	17	33	49	65	81	97	113	129	145	161	177	193	209	225	241
Last host	14	30	46	62	78	94	110	126	142	158	174	190	206	222	238	254
Broadcast	15	31	47	63	79	95	111	127	143	159	175	191	207	223	239	255

Cisco has figured out that most people cannot count in 16s and therefore have a hard time finding valid subnets, hosts, and broadcast addresses with the Class C 255.255.255.240 mask. You'd be wise to study this mask.

Practice Example #5C: 255.255.255.248 (/29)

Let's keep practicing:

192.168.10.0 = Network address

255.255.255.248 = Subnet mask

- *Subnets?* 248 in binary = 11111000. 2^5 = 32.
- *Hosts?* $2^3 - 2 = 6$.
- *Valid subnets?* 256 − 248 = 8. 0, 8, 16, 24, 32, 40, 48, 56, 64, 72, 80, 88, 96, 104, 112, 120, 128, 136, 144, 152, 160, 168, 176, 184, 192, 200, 208, 216, 224, 232, 240, and 248.
- *Broadcast address for each subnet?*
- *Valid hosts?*

Take a look at the following table. It shows some of the subnets (first four and last four only), valid hosts, and broadcast addresses for the Class C 255.255.255.248 mask:

Subnet	0	8	16	24	...	224	232	240	248
First host	1	9	17	25	...	225	233	241	249
Last host	6	14	22	30	...	230	238	246	254
Broadcast	7	15	23	31	...	231	239	247	255

You must be able to subnet to see that the address used in this example is in the zero subnet.

Practice Example #6C: 255.255.255.252 (/30)

Just one more:

> 192.168.10.0 = Network address
>
> 255.255.255.252 = Subnet mask

- *Subnets?* 64.
- *Hosts?* 2.
- *Valid subnets?* 0, 4, 8, 12, etc., all the way to 252.
- *Broadcast address for each subnet (always the number right before the next subnet)?*
- *Valid hosts (the numbers between the subnet number and the broadcast address)?*

The following table shows you the subnet, valid host, and broadcast address of the first four and last four subnets in the 255.255.255.252 Class C subnet:

Subnet	0	4	8	12	...	240	244	248	252
First host	1	5	9	13	...	241	245	249	253
Last host	2	6	10	14	...	242	246	250	254
Broadcast	3	7	11	15	...	243	247	251	255

Subnetting in Your Head: Class C Addresses

It really is possible to subnet in your head. Even if you don't believe me, I'll show you how. And it's not all that hard either—take the following example:

> 192.168.10.33 = Node address
>
> 255.255.255.224 = Subnet mask

First, determine the subnet and broadcast address of the above IP address. You can do this by answering question 3 of the big five questions: 256 – 224 = 32. 0, 32, 64, and so on. The address of 33 falls between the two subnets of 32 and 64 and must be part of the 192.168.10.32 subnet. The next subnet is 64, so the broadcast address of the 32 subnet is 63. (Remember that the broadcast address of a subnet is always the number right before the next subnet.) The valid host range is 33–62 (the numbers between the subnet and broadcast address). This is too easy!

Okay, let's try another one. We'll subnet another Class C address:

> 192.168.10.33 = Node address
>
> 255.255.255.240 = Subnet mask

What subnet and broadcast address is the above IP address a member of? 256 – 240 = 16. 0, 16, 32, 48, and so on. Bingo—the host address is between the 32 and 48 subnets. The subnet is 192.168.10.32, and the broadcast address is 47 (the next subnet is 48). The valid host range is 33–46 (the numbers between the subnet number and the broadcast address).

Okay, we need to do more, just to make sure you have this down.

You have a node address of 192.168.10.174 with a mask of 255.255.255.240. What is the valid host range?

The mask is 240, so we'd do a 256 – 240 = 16. This is our block size. Just keep adding 16 until we pass the host address of 174, starting at zero, of course: 0, 16, 32, 48, 64, 80, 96, 112, 128, 144, 160, 176, and so on. The host address of 174 is between 160 and 176, so the subnet is 160. The broadcast address is 175; the valid host range is 161–174. That was a tough one.

One more—just for fun. This is the easiest one of all Class C subnetting:

192.168.10.17 = Node address

255.255.255.252 = Subnet mask

What subnet and broadcast address is the above IP address a member of? 256 – 252 = 4. 0 (always start at zero unless told otherwise), 4, 8, 12, 16, 20, and so on. You've got it! The host address is between the 16 and 20 subnets. The subnet is 192.168.10.16, and the broadcast address is 19. The valid host range is 17–18.

Now that you're all over Class C subnetting, let's move on to Class B subnetting. But before we do, let's have a quick review.

What Do We Know?

Okay—here's where you can really apply what you've learned so far and begin committing it all to memory. This is a very cool section that I've been using in my classes for years. It will really help you nail down subnetting!

When you see a subnet mask or slash notation (CIDR), you should know the following:

/25 What do we know about a /25?

- 128 mask
- 1 bit on and 7 bits off (10000000)
- Block size of 128
- 2 subnets, each with 126 hosts

/26 What do we know about a /26?

- 192 mask
- 2 bits on and 6 bits off (11000000)
- Block size of 64
- 4 subnets, each with 62 hosts

/27 What do we know about a /27?

- 224 mask
- 3 bits on and 5 bits off (11100000)
- Block size of 32
- 8 subnets, each with 30 hosts

/28   What do we know about a /28?

- 240 mask

- 4 bits on and 4 bits off

- Block size of 16

- 16 subnets, each with 14 hosts

/29   What do we know about a /29?

- 248 mask

- 5 bits on and 3 bits off

- Block size of 8

- 32 subnets, each with 6 hosts

/30   What do we know about a /30?

- 252 mask

- 6 bits on and 2 bits off

- Block size of 4

- 64 subnets, each with 2 hosts

Regardless of whether you have a Class A, Class B, or Class C address, the /30 mask will provide you with only two hosts. This mask is suited almost exclusively—as well as suggested by Cisco—for use on point-to-point links.

If you can memorize this "What Do We Know?" section, you'll be much better off in your day-to-day job and in your studies. Try saying it out loud, which helps you memorize things—yes, your significant other and/or coworkers will think you've lost it, but they probably already do if you are in the networking field. And if you're not yet in the networking field but are studying all this to break into it, you might as well have people start thinking you're an odd bird now since they will eventually anyway.

It's also helpful to write these on some type of flashcards and have people test your skill. You'd be amazed at how fast you can get subnetting down if you memorize block sizes as well as this "What Do We Know?" section.

Subnetting Class B Addresses

Before we dive into this, let's look at all the possible Class B subnet masks first. Notice that we have a lot more possible subnet masks than we do with a Class C network address:

```
255.255.0.0      (/16)
255.255.128.0    (/17)      255.255.255.0    (/24)
255.255.192.0    (/18)      255.255.255.128  (/25)
255.255.224.0    (/19)      255.255.255.192  (/26)
255.255.240.0    (/20)      255.255.255.224  (/27)
255.255.248.0    (/21)      255.255.255.240  (/28)
255.255.252.0    (/22)      255.255.255.248  (/29)
255.255.254.0    (/23)      255.255.255.252  (/30)
```

We know the Class B network address has 16 bits available for host addressing. This means we can use up to 14 bits for subnetting (because we have to leave at least 2 bits for host addressing). Using a /16 means you are not subnetting with Class B, but it is a mask you can use.

By the way, do you notice anything interesting about that list of subnet values—a pattern, maybe? Ah ha! That's exactly why I had you memorize the binary-to-decimal numbers earlier in the chapter. Since subnet mask bits start on the left and move to the right and bits can't be skipped, the numbers are always the same regardless of the class of address. Memorize this pattern.

The process of subnetting a Class B network is pretty much the same as it is for a Class C network, except that you just have more host bits and you start in the third octet.

Use the same subnet numbers for the third octet with Class B that you used for the fourth octet with Class C, but add a zero to the network portion and a 255 to the broadcast section in the fourth octet. The following table shows you an example host range of two subnets used in a Class B 240 (/20) subnet mask:

Subnet Address	16.0	32.0
Broadcast Address	31.255	47.255

Just add the valid hosts between the numbers, and you're set!

The preceding example is true only until you get up to /24. After that, it's numerically exactly like Class C.

Subnetting Practice Examples: Class B Addresses

The following sections will give you an opportunity to practice subnetting Class B addresses. Again, I have to mention that this is the same as subnetting with Class C, except we start in the third octet—with the exact same numbers!

Practice Example #1B: 255.255.128.0 (/17)

172.16.0.0 = Network address

255.255.128.0 = Subnet mask

- *Subnets?* $2^1 = 2$ (same as Class C).
- *Hosts?* $2^{15} - 2 = 32,766$ (7 bits in the third octet, and 8 in the fourth).
- *Valid subnets?* 256 − 128 = 128. 0, 128. Remember that subnetting is performed in the third octet, so the subnet numbers are really 0.0 and 128.0, as shown in the next table.

These are the exact numbers we used with Class C; we use them in the third octet and add a 0 in the fourth octet for the network address.

- *Broadcast address for each subnet?*
- *Valid hosts?*

The following table shows the two subnets available, the valid host range, and the broadcast address of each:

Subnet	0.0	128.0
First host	0.1	128.1
Last host	127.254	255.254
Broadcast	127.255	255.255

Okay, notice that we just added the fourth octet's lowest and highest values and came up with the answers. And again, it's done exactly the same way as for a Class C subnet. We just use the same numbers in the third octet and added 0 and 255 in the fourth octet—pretty simple huh! I really can't say this enough: it's just not hard. The numbers never change; we just use them in different octets!

Practice Example #2B: 255.255.192.0 (/18)

173.16.0.0 = Network address

172.16.0.0 = Network address

255.255.192.0 = Subnet mask

- *Subnets?* 2^2 = 4.
- *Hosts?* $2^{14} - 2$ = 16,382 (6 bits in the third octet, and 8 in the fourth).
- *Valid subnets?* 256 − 192 = 64. 0, 64, 128, 192. Remember that the subnetting is performed in the third octet, so the subnet numbers are really 0.0, 64.0, 128.0, and 192.0, as shown in the next table.
- *Broadcast address for each subnet?*
- *Valid hosts?*

The following table shows the four subnets available, the valid host range, and the broadcast address of each:

Subnet	0.0	64.0	128.0	192.0
First host	0.1	64.1	128.1	192.1
Last host	63.254	127.254	191.254	255.254
Broadcast	63.255	127.255	191.255	255.255

Again, it's pretty much the same as it is for a Class C subnet—we just added 0 and 255 in the fourth octet for each subnet in the third octet.

Practice Example #3B: 255.255.240.0 (/20)

172.16.0.0 = Network address

255.255.240.0 = Subnet mask

- *Subnets?* $2^4 = 16$.
- *Hosts?* $2^{12} - 2 = 4094$.
- *Valid subnets?* $256 - 240 = 16$. 0, 16, 32, 48, etc., up to 240. Notice that these are the same numbers as a Class C 240 mask—we just put them in the third octet and add a 0 and 255 in the fourth octet.
- *Broadcast address for each subnet?*
- *Valid hosts?*

The following table shows the first four subnets, valid hosts, and broadcast addresses in a Class B 255.255.240.0 mask:

Subnet	0.0	16.0	32.0	48.0
First host	0.1	16.1	32.1	48.1
Last host	15.254	31.254	47.254	63.254
Broadcast	15.255	31.255	47.255	63.255

Practice Example #4B: 255.255.254.0 (/23)

172.16.0.0 = Network address

255.255.254.0 = Subnet mask

- *Subnets?* $2^7 = 128$.
- *Hosts?* $2^9 - 2 = 510$.
- *Valid subnets?* $256 - 254 = 2$. 0, 2, 4, 6, 8, etc., up to 254.
- *Broadcast address for each subnet?*
- *Valid hosts?*

The following table shows the first five subnets, valid hosts, and broadcast addresses in a Class B 255.255.254.0 mask:

Subnet	0.0	2.0	4.0	6.0	8.0
First host	0.1	2.1	4.1	6.1	8.1
Last host	1.254	3.254	5.254	7.254	9.254
Broadcast	1.255	3.255	5.255	7.255	9.255

Practice Example #5B: 255.255.255.0 (/24)

Contrary to popular belief, 255.255.255.0 used with a Class B network address is not called a Class B network with a Class C subnet mask. It's amazing how many people see this mask used in a Class B network and think it's a Class C subnet mask. This is a Class B subnet mask with 8 bits of subnetting—it's logically different from a Class C mask. Subnetting this address is fairly simple:

　　172.16.0.0 = Network address

　　255.255.255.0 = Subnet mask

- *Subnets?* $2^8 = 256$.
- *Hosts?* $2^8 - 2 = 254$.
- *Valid subnets?* $256 - 255 = 1$. 0, 1, 2, 3, etc., all the way to 255.
- *Broadcast address for each subnet?*
- *Valid hosts?*

　　The following table shows the first four and last two subnets, the valid hosts, and the broadcast addresses in a Class B 255.255.255.0 mask:

Subnet	0.0	1.0	2.0	3.0	...	254.0	255.0
First host	0.1	1.1	2.1	3.1	...	254.1	255.1
Last host	0.254	1.254	2.254	3.254	...	254.254	255.254
Broadcast	0.255	1.255	2.255	3.255	...	254.255	255.255

Practice Example #6B: 255.255.255.128 (/25)

This is one of the hardest subnet masks you can play with. And worse, it actually is a really good subnet to use in production because it creates over 500 subnets with 126 hosts for each subnet—a nice mixture. So, don't skip over it!

　　172.16.0.0 = Network address

　　255.255.255.128 = Subnet mask

- *Subnets?* $2^9 = 512$.
- *Hosts?* $2^7 - 2 = 126$.
- *Valid subnets?* Okay, now for the tricky part. $256 - 255 = 1$. 0, 1, 2, 3, etc. for the third octet. But you can't forget the one subnet bit used in the fourth octet. Remember when I showed you how to figure one subnet bit with a Class C mask? You figure this the same way. (Now you know why I showed you the 1-bit subnet mask in the Class C section—to make this part easier.) You actually get two subnets for each third octet value, hence the 512 subnets. For example, if the third octet is showing subnet 3, the two subnets would actually be 3.0 and 3.128.

- *Broadcast address for each subnet?*
- *Valid hosts?*

The following table shows how you can create subnets, valid hosts, and broadcast addresses using the Class B 255.255.255.128 subnet mask (the first eight subnets are shown, and then the last two subnets):

Subnet	0.0	0.128	1.0	1.128	2.0	2.128	3.0	3.128	...	255.0	255.128
First host	0.1	0.129	1.1	1.129	2.1	2.129	3.1	3.129	...	255.1	255.129
Last host	0.126	0.254	1.126	1.254	2.126	2.254	3.126	3.254	...	255.126	255.254
Broadcast	0.127	0.255	1.127	1.255	2.127	2.255	3.127	3.255	...	255.127	255.255

Practice Example #7B: 255.255.255.192 (/26)

Now, this is where Class B subnetting gets easy. Since the third octet has a 255 in the mask section, whatever number is listed in the third octet is a subnet number. However, now that we have a subnet number in the fourth octet, we can subnet this octet just as we did with Class C subnetting. Let's try it out:

172.16.0.0 = Network address

255.255.255.192 = Subnet mask

- *Subnets?* 2^{10} = 1024.
- *Hosts?* $2^6 - 2$ = 62.
- *Valid subnets?* 256 – 192 = 64. The subnets are shown in the following table. Do these numbers look familiar?
- *Broadcast address for each subnet?*
- *Valid hosts?*

The following table shows the first eight subnet ranges, valid hosts, and broadcast addresses:

Subnet	0.0	0.64	0.128	0.192	1.0	1.64	1.128	1.192
First host	0.1	0.65	0.129	0.193	1.1	1.65	1.129	1.193
Last host	0.62	0.126	0.190	0.254	1.62	1.126	1.190	1.254
Broadcast	0.63	0.127	0.191	0.255	1.63	1.127	1.191	1.255

Notice that for each subnet value in the third octet, you get subnets 0, 64, 128, and 192 in the fourth octet.

Practice Example #8B: 255.255.255.224 (/27)

This is done the same way as the preceding subnet mask, except that we just have more subnets and fewer hosts per subnet available.

172.16.0.0 = Network address

255.255.255.224 = Subnet mask

- *Subnets?* 2^{11} = 2048.
- *Hosts?* 2^5 − 2 = 30.
- *Valid subnets?* 256 − 224 = 32. 0, 32, 64, 96, 128, 160, 192, 224.
- *Broadcast address for each subnet?*
- *Valid hosts?*

The following table shows the first eight subnets:

Subnet	0.0	0.32	0.64	0.96	0.128	0.160	0.192	0.224
First host	0.1	0.33	0.65	0.97	0.129	0.161	0.193	0.225
Last host	0.30	0.62	0.94	0.126	0.158	0.190	0.222	0.254
Broadcast	0.31	0.63	0.95	0.127	0.159	0.191	0.223	0.255

This next table shows the last eight subnets:

Subnet	255.0	255.32	255.64	255.96	255.128	255.160	255.192	255.224
First host	255.1	255.33	255.65	255.97	255.129	255.161	255.193	255.225
Last host	255.30	255.62	255.94	255.126	255.158	255.190	255.222	255.254
Broadcast	255.31	255.63	255.95	255.127	255.159	255.191	255.223	255.255

Subnetting in Your Head: Class B Addresses

Are you nuts? Subnet Class B addresses in our heads? It's actually easier than writing it out—I'm not kidding! Let me show you how:

Question: What subnet and broadcast address is the IP address 172.16.10.33 255.255.255.224 (/27) a member of?

Answer: The interesting octet (the octet where we count our block size) is the fourth octet. 256 − 224 = 32. 32 + 32 = 64. Bingo: 33 is between 32 and 64. However, remember that the third octet is considered part of the subnet, so the answer would be the 10.32 subnet. The broadcast is 10.63 since 10.64 is the next subnet. That was a pretty easy one.

Question: What subnet and broadcast address is the IP address 172.16.66.10 255.255.192.0 (/18) a member of?

Answer: The interesting octet is the third octet instead of the fourth octet. 256 − 192 = 64. 0, 64, 128. The subnet is 172.16.64.0. The broadcast must be 172.16.127.255 since 128.0 is the next subnet.

Question: What subnet and broadcast address is the IP address 172.16.50.10 255.255.224.0 (/19) a member of?

Answer: 256 − 224 = 0, 32, 64 (remember, we always start counting at zero [0]). The subnet is 172.16.32.0, and the broadcast must be 172.16.63.255 since 64.0 is the next subnet.

Question: What subnet and broadcast address is the IP address 172.16.46.255 255.255.240.0 (/20) a member of?

Answer: 256 − 240 = 16. The third octet is interesting to us. 0, 16, 32, 48. This subnet address must be in the 172.16.32.0 subnet, and the broadcast must be 172.16.47.255 since 48.0 is the next subnet. So, yes, 172.16.46.255 is a valid host.

Question: What subnet and broadcast address is the IP address 172.16.45.14 255.255.255.252 (/30) a member of?

Answer: Where is the interesting octet? 256 − 252 = 4. 0, 4, 8, 12, 16 (in the fourth octet). The subnet is 172.16.45.12, with a broadcast of 172.16.45.15 because the next subnet is 172.16.45.16.

Question: What is the subnet and broadcast address of the host 172.16.88.255/20?

Answer: What is a /20? If you can't answer this, you can't answer this question, can you? A /20 is 255.255.240.0, which gives us a block size of 16 in the third octet, and since no subnet bits are on in the fourth octet, the answer is always 0 and 255 in the fourth octet. 0, 16, 32, 48, 64, 80, 96…bingo. 88 is between 80 and 96, so the subnet is 80.0 and the broadcast address is 95.255.

Question: A router receives a packet on an interface with a destination address of 172.16.46.191/26. What will the router do with this packet?

Answer: Discard it. Do you know why? 172.16.46.191/26 is a 255.255.255.192 mask, which gives us a block size of 64. Our subnets are then 0, 64, 128, 192. 191 is the broadcast address of the 128 subnet, so a router, by default, will discard any broadcast packets.

Subnetting Class A Addresses

Class A subnetting is not performed any differently than Classes B and C, but there are 24 bits to play with instead of the 16 in a Class B address and the 8 in a Class C address.
   Let's start by listing all the Class A masks:

```
255.0.0.0     (/8)
255.128.0.0   (/9)      255.255.240.0  (/20)
255.192.0.0   (/10)     255.255.248.0  (/21)
```

```
255.224.0.0   (/11)          255.255.252.0   (/22)
255.240.0.0   (/12)          255.255.254.0   (/23)
255.248.0.0   (/13)          255.255.255.0   (/24)
255.252.0.0   (/14)          255.255.255.128 (/25)
255.254.0.0   (/15)          255.255.255.192 (/26)
255.255.0.0   (/16)          255.255.255.224 (/27)
255.255.128.0 (/17)          255.255.255.240 (/28)
255.255.192.0 (/18)          255.255.255.248 (/29)
255.255.224.0 (/19)          255.255.255.252 (/30)
```

That's it. You must leave at least 2 bits for defining hosts. And I hope you can see the pattern by now. Remember, we're going to do this the same way as a Class B or C subnet. It's just that, again, we simply have more host bits, and we just use the same subnet numbers we used with Classes B and C, but we start using these numbers in the second octet.

Subnetting Practice Examples: Class A Addresses

When you look at an IP address and a subnet mask, you must be able to distinguish the bits used for subnets from the bits used for determining hosts. This is imperative. If you're still struggling with this concept, please reread the section "IP Addressing" in Chapter 5. It shows you how to determine the difference between the subnet and host bits and should help clear things up.

Practice Example #1A: 255.255.0.0 (/16)

Class A addresses use a default mask of 255.0.0.0, which leaves 22 bits for subnetting since you must leave 2 bits for host addressing. The 255.255.0.0 mask with a Class A address is using 8 subnet bits.

- *Subnets?* $2^8 = 256$.
- *Hosts?* $2^{16} - 2 = 65,534$.
- *Valid subnets?* What is the interesting octet? $256 - 255 = 1$. 0, 1, 2, 3, etc. (all in the second octet). The subnets would be 10.0.0.0, 10.1.0.0, 10.2.0.0, 10.3.0.0, etc., up to 10.255.0.0.
- *Broadcast address for each subnet?*
- *Valid hosts?*

The following table shows the first two and last two subnets, valid host range, and broadcast addresses for the private Class A 10.0.0.0 network:

Subnet	10.0.0.0	10.1.0.0	...	10.254.0.0	10.255.0.0
First host	10.0.0.1	10.1.0.1	...	10.254.0.1	10.255.0.1
Last host	10.0.255.254	10.1.255.254	...	10.254.255.254	10.255.255.254
Broadcast	10.0.255.255	10.1.255.255	...	10.254.255.255	10.255.255.255

Practice Example #2A: 255.255.240.0 (/20)

255.255.240.0 gives us 12 bits of subnetting and leaves us 12 bits for host addressing.

- *Subnets?* $2^{12} = 4096$.
- *Hosts?* $2^{12} - 2 = 4094$.
- *Valid subnets?* What is your interesting octet? $256 - 240 = 16$. The subnets in the second octet are a block size of 1 and the subnets in the third octet are 0, 16, 32, etc.
- *Broadcast address for each subnet?*
- *Valid hosts?*

The following table shows some examples of the host ranges—the first three and the last subnets:

Subnet	10.0.0.0	10.0.16.0	10.0.32.0	...	10.255.240.0
First host	10.0.0.1	10.0.16.1	10.0.32.1	...	10.255.240.1
Last host	10.0.15.254	10.0.31.254	10.0.47.254	...	10.255.255.254
Broadcast	10.0.15.255	10.0.31.255	10.0.47.255	...	10.255.255.255

Practice Example #3A: 255.255.255.192 (/26)

Let's do one more example using the second, third, and fourth octets for subnetting.

- *Subnets?* $2^{18} = 262{,}144$.
- *Hosts?* $2^6 - 2 = 62$.
- *Valid subnets?* In the second and third octet, the block size is 1, and in the fourth octet, the block size is 64.
- *Broadcast address for each subnet?*
- *Valid hosts?*

The following table shows the first four subnets and their valid hosts and broadcast addresses in the Class A 255.255.255.192 mask:

Subnet	10.0.0.0	10.0.0.64	10.0.0.128	10.0.0.192
First host	10.0.0.1	10.0.0.65	10.0.0.129	10.0.0.193
Last host	10.0.0.62	10.0.0.126	10.0.0.190	10.0.0.254
Broadcast	10.0.0.63	10.0.0.127	10.0.0.191	10.0.0.255

The following table shows the last four subnets and their valid hosts and broadcast addresses:

Subnet	10.255.255.0	10.255.255.64	10.255.255.128	10.255.255.192
First host	10.255.255.1	10.255.255.65	10.255.255.129	10.255.255.193
Last host	10.255.255.62	10.255.255.126	10.255.255.190	10.255.255.254
Broadcast	10.255.255.63	10.255.255.127	10.255.255.191	10.255.255.255

Subnetting in Your Head: Class A Addresses

This sounds hard, but as with Class C and Class B, the numbers are the same; we just start in the second octet. What makes this easy? You only need to worry about the octet that has the largest block size (typically called the interesting octet; one that is something other than 0 or 255)—for example, 255.255.240.0 (/20) with a Class A network. The second octet has a block size of 1, so any number listed in that octet is a subnet. The third octet is a 240 mask, which means we have a block size of 16 in the third octet. If your host ID is 10.20.80.30, what is your subnet, broadcast address, and valid host range?

The subnet in the second octet is 20 with a block size of 1, but the third octet is in a block size of 16, so we'll just count them out: 0, 16, 32, 48, 64, 80, 96...voilà! (By the way, you can count by 16s by now, right?) This makes our subnet 10.20.80.0, with a broadcast of 10.20.95.255 because the next subnet is 10.20.96.0. The valid host range is 10.20.80.1 through 10.20.95.254. And yes, no lie! You really can do this in your head if you just get your block sizes nailed!

Okay, let's practice on one more, just for fun!

Host IP: 10.1.3.65/23

First, you can't answer this question if you don't know what a /23 is. It's 255.255.254.0. The interesting octet here is the third one: 256 − 254 = 2. Our subnets in the third octet are 0, 2, 4, 6, etc. The host in this question is in subnet 2.0, and the next subnet is 4.0, so that makes the broadcast address 3.255. And any address between 10.1.2.1 and 10.1.3.254 is considered a valid host.

Summary

Did you read Chapters 5 and 6 and understand everything on the first pass? If so, that is fantastic—congratulations! The thing is, you probably got lost a couple of times—and as I told you, that's what usually happens, so don't stress. Don't feel bad if you have to read each chapter more than once, or even 10 times, before you're truly good to go.

This chapter provided you with an important understanding of IP subnetting. After reading this chapter, you should be able to subnet IP addresses in your head.

This chapter is extremely essential to your Cisco certification process, so if you just skimmed it, please go back and reread it and do all the written labs.

Exam Essentials

Identify the advantages of subnetting.   Benefits of subnetting a physical network include reduced network traffic, optimized network performance, simplified management, and facilitated spanning of large geographical distances.

Describe the effect of the `ip subnet-zero` command.   This command allows you to use the first and last subnet in your network design.

Identify the steps to subnet a classful network.   Understand how IP addressing and subnetting work. First, determine your block size by using the 256-subnet mask math. Then count your subnets and determine the broadcast address of each subnet—it is always the number right before the next subnet. Your valid hosts are the numbers between the subnet address and the broadcast address.

Determine possible block sizes.   This is an important part of understanding IP addressing and subnetting. The valid block sizes are always 2, 4, 8, 16, 32, 64, 128, etc. You can determine your block size by using the 256-subnet mask math.

Describe the role of a subnet mask in IP addressing.   A subnet mask is a 32-bit value that allows the recipient of IP packets to distinguish the network ID portion of the IP address from the host ID portion of the IP address.

Understand and apply the $2^n - 2$ formula.   Use this formula to determine the proper subnet mask for a particular size network given the application of that subnet mask to a particular classful network.

Explain the impact of Classless Inter-Domain Routing (CIDR).   CIDR allows the creation of networks of a size other than those allowed with the classful subnetting by allowing more than the three classful subnet masks.

Written Labs

In this section, you'll complete the following labs to make sure you've got the information and concepts contained within them fully dialed in:

Lab 6.1: Written Subnet Practice #1

Lab 6.2: Written Subnet Practice #2

Lab 6.3: Written Subnet Practice #3

You can find the answers in Appendix A.

Written Lab 6.1: Written Subnet Practice #1

Write the subnet, broadcast address, and valid host range for question 1 through question 6:

1. 192.168.100.25/30
2. 192.168.100.37/28
3. 192.168.100.66/27
4. 192.168.100.17/29
5. 192.168.100.99/26
6. 192.168.100.99/25
7. You have a Class B network and need 29 subnets. What is your mask?
8. What is the broadcast address of 192.168.192.10/29?
9. How many hosts are available with a Class C /29 mask?
10. What is the subnet for host ID 10.16.3.65/23?

Written Lab 6.2: Written Subnet Practice #2

Given a Class B network and the net bits identified (CIDR), complete the following table to identify the subnet mask and the number of host addresses possible for each mask.

Classful Address	Subnet Mask	Number of Hosts per Subnet $(2x - 2)$
/16		
/17		
/18		
/19		
/20		

/21

/22

/23

/24

/25

/26

/27

/28

/29

/30

Written Lab 6.3: Written Subnet Practice #3

Decimal IP Address	Address Class	Number of Subnet and Host Bits	Number of Subnets (2^x)	Number of Hosts ($2^x - 2$)
10.25.66.154/23				
172.31.254.12/24				
192.168.20.123/28				
63.24.89.21/18				
128.1.1.254/20				
208.100.54.209/30				

Review Questions

You can find the answers in Appendix B.

 The following questions are designed to test your understanding of this chapter's material. For more information on how to get additional questions, please see this book's introduction.

1. What is the maximum number of IP addresses that can be assigned to hosts on a local subnet that uses the 255.255.255.224 subnet mask?

   A. 14

   B. 15

   C. 16

   D. 30

   E. 31

   F. 62

2. You have a network that needs 29 subnets while maximizing the number of host addresses available on each subnet. How many bits must you borrow from the host field to provide the correct subnet mask?

   A. 2

   B. 3

   C. 4

   D. 5

   E. 6

   F. 7

3. What is the subnetwork address for a host with the IP address 200.10.5.68/28?

   A. 200.10.5.56

   B. 200.10.5.32

   C. 200.10.5.64

   D. 200.10.5.0

4. The network address of 172.16.0.0/19 provides how many subnets and hosts?

    A. 7 subnets, 30 hosts each

    B. 7 subnets, 2,046 hosts each

    C. 7 subnets, 8,190 hosts each

    D. 8 subnets, 30 hosts each

    E. 8 subnets, 2,046 hosts each

    F. 8 subnets, 8,190 hosts each

5. Which statements describe the IP address 10.16.3.65/23? (Choose two.)

    A. The subnet address is 10.16.3.0 255.255.254.0.

    B. The lowest host address in the subnet is 10.16.2.1 255.255.254.0.

    C. The last valid host address in the subnet is 10.16.2.254 255.255.254.0.

    D. The broadcast address of the subnet is 10.16.3.255 255.255.254.0.

    E. The network is not subnetted.

6. If a host on a network has the address 172.16.45.14/30, what is the subnetwork this host belongs to?

    A. 172.16.45.0

    B. 172.16.45.4

    C. 172.16.45.8

    D. 172.16.45.12

    E. 172.16.45.16

7. Which mask should you use on point-to-point WAN links in order to reduce the waste of IP addresses?

    A. /27

    B. /28

    C. /29

    D. /30

    E. /31

8. What is the subnetwork number of a host with an IP address of 172.16.66.0/21?

    A. 172.16.36.0

    B. 172.16.48.0

    C. 172.16.64.0

    D. 172.16.0.0

9. You have an interface on a router with the IP address of 192.168.192.10/29. Including the router interface, how many hosts can have IP addresses on the LAN attached to the router interface?

   A. 6

   B. 8

   C. 30

   D. 62

   E. 126

10. You need to configure a server that is on the subnet 192.168.19.24/29. The router has the first available host address. Which of the following should you assign to the server?

   A. 192.168.19.0 255.255.255.0

   B. 192.168.19.33 255.255.255.240

   C. 192.168.19.26 255.255.255.248

   D. 192.168.19.31 255.255.255.248

   E. 192.168.19.34 255.255.255.240

11. You have an interface on a router with the IP address of 192.168.192.10/29. What is the broadcast address the hosts will use on this LAN?

   A. 192.168.192.15

   B. 192.168.192.31

   C. 192.168.192.63

   D. 192.168.192.127

   E. 192.168.192.255

12. You need to subnet a network that has 5 subnets, each with at least 16 hosts. Which classful subnet mask would you use?

   A. 255.255.255.192

   B. 255.255.255.224

   C. 255.255.255.240

   D. 255.255.255.248

13. You configure a router interface with the IP address 192.168.10.62 255.255.255.192 and receive the following error:

```
Bad mask /26 for address 192.168.10.62
```

Why did you receive this error?

A. You typed this mask on a WAN link and that is not allowed.

B. This is not a valid host and subnet mask combination.

C. `ip subnet-zero` is not enabled on the router.

D. The router does not support IP.

14. If an Ethernet port on a router were assigned an IP address of 172.16.112.1/25, what would be the valid subnet address of this host?

A. 172.16.112.0

B. 172.16.0.0

C. 172.16.96.0

D. 172.16.255.0

E. 172.16.128.0

15. Using the following illustration, what would be the IP address of E0 if you were using the eighth subnet? The network ID is 192.168.10.0/28 and you need to use the last available IP address in the range. The zero subnet should not be considered valid for this question.

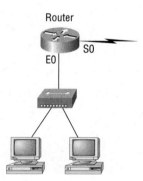

A. 192.168.10.142

B. 192.168.10.66

C. 192.168.100.254

D. 192.168.10.143

E. 192.168.10.126

16. Using the illustration from the previous question, what would be the IP address of S0 if you were using the first subnet? The network ID is 192.168.10.0/28 and you need to use the last available IP address in the range. Again, the zero subnet should not be considered valid for this question.

   A. 192.168.10.24

   B. 192.168.10.62

   C. 192.168.10.30

   D. 192.168.10.127

17. Which configuration command must be in effect to allow the use of 8 subnets if the Class C subnet mask is 255.255.255.224?

   A. Router(config)#`ip classless`

   B. Router(config)#`ip version 6`

   C. Router(config)#`no ip classful`

   D. Router(config)#`ip unnumbered`

   E. Router(config)#`ip subnet-zero`

   F. Router(config)#`ip all-nets`

18. You have a network with a subnet of 172.16.17.0/22. Which is the valid host address?

   A. 172.16.17.1 255.255.255.252

   B. 172.16.0.1 255.255.240.0

   C. 172.16.20.1 255.255.254.0

   D. 172.16.16.1 255.255.255.240

   E. 172.16.18.255 255.255.252.0

   F. 172.16.0.1 255.255.255.0

19. Your router has the following IP address on Ethernet0: 172.16.2.1/23. Which of the following can be valid host IDs on the LAN interface attached to the router? (Choose two.)

   A. 172.16.0.5

   B. 172.16.1.100

   C. 172.16.1.198

   D. 172.16.2.255

   E. 172.16.3.0

   F. 172.16.3.255

20. To test the IP stack on your local host, which IP address would you ping?

    A. 127.0.0.0

    B. 1.0.0.127

    C. 127.0.0.1

    D. 127.0.0.255

    E. 255.255.255.255

Chapter

7

Introduction to Nexus

THE FOLLOWING TOPICS ARE COVERED IN THIS CHAPTER:

✓ **What is Nexus?**

- Hardware

✓ **Describing Cisco NX-OS Software**

- Cisco NX-OS Software Architecture

- Cisco NX-OS Process Recovery

- Cisco NX-OS Conditional Services

✓ **Virtualizing the Network**

- Virtualizing Layer 2 Networks

- Virtualizing Interswitch Links

- Virtualizing Layer 3 Interfaces

- Virtualizing Routing Tables

- Virtualizing Devices

- Virtualizing Everything

In the introduction of this book I talked about the history of Nexus and Cisco's product line and how Cisco's Data Center products, including Nexus and the NX-OS, came into being. In this chapter, we'll take off from the introduction and discuss the Nexus hardware, including the switch interfaces, management ports, and various other hardware pieces of Nexus. We'll then take a look at the NX-OS software architecture and how this software was designed from the ground up and built for the data center.

This chapter will also cover virtualization, including VLANs, Virtual Routing and Forwarding (VRF), virtual device contexts (VDCs), and finally, the Nexus 1000v switch.

NX-OS Hardware

The two hottest hot-button factors in data center networking are speed and reliability, and Nexus hardware answers with high throughput / low latency applications while providing fault tolerance. The hardware is designed to handle high speed 10-, 40-, or even 100-gigabit interfaces—some serious capacity there under the hood! For a little perspective, the first main-stream Ethernet interfaces were 10Mbps and it would take 10,000 of those interfaces to match a single 100Gbps interface. It follows that the design of NX-OS utilizes a plethora of modern networking features key in today's data center, but we're going to focus more on the factors that differ from traditional Cisco switches.

Oh and by the way, the exam objectives zero in on the components and theory but not on the various Nexus model numbers, so we'll be pretty much ignoring them too.

SFP+ Transceivers

Upon taking my small form-Factor pluggable (SFP+), transceiver out of the box for the first time, it hit me that the ports look a lot like little empty boxes. It turns out there's a good reason for that; by default, there's no copper or fiber-optic connection, and that is so the device will be as flexible as possible. This important and very cool feature graciously allows me, the SFP+ transceiver's end user, to pick the type of media I want to use with the Nexus platform.

Figure 7.1 and Figure 7.2 show us two different SFP+ transceivers, one copper and one fiber.

I'm going with fiber optic, so I can implement long-distance or short-distance Ethernet depending on which SFP+ I chose. To connect them, I'll need an SFP+ for each end and a fiberoptic cable. Clearly, the SFP+ also determines the connection's speed—for example, 1Gbps or 10Gbps.

FIGURE 7.1   SFP+ for copper

FIGURE 7.2   SFP+ for fiberoptic Ethernet

For short runs in the data center, I usually opt for a copper cable where the SFPs are part of the cable, as shown in Figure 7.3.

This consolidated cable is known as TwinAx, and these cables are cheap and reliable! Really, their biggest limitation is that they can span only a relatively short distance.

FIGURE 7.3   SFP+ plus copper cable (TwinAx)

Console Port

The day finally comes when your brand-new Nexus switch arrives and you, or you and a buddy or two if it's a big one, install it in the rack, run some power to it, and watch all the pretty lights blink... now what? Fortunately, after a bit of further exploration, you're sure to find the console port, as shown in Figure 7.4.

FIGURE 7.4 Management ports on a Nexus 5000 switch

I'm serious. It is sort of weird, but you actually do have to look around a little because the console port's location really does vary by model! Anyway, once you've found it, just connect the USB to the serial adapter on your laptop and then connect the console cable from the laptop to the Nexus. Make sure the terminal program is set to 8-N-1. If all is well, you should then see a command prompt.

And just so you know, the console port is a specific serial port that's typically used only for the device's initial configuration or when things get really messed up. It's what we've used to manage Cisco devices since the '90s, so if you're experienced in networking, you should feel right at home. Also good to know is that the Nexus platform has other ports dedicated for remote management.

Management Ports

It's important to remember that management ports are not used for data traffic; they're used to connect to the device remotely via Telnet, Secure Shell (SSH), or the web for configuration and monitoring. And while both Telnet and SSH provide remote consoles, I always recommend going with SSH because its traffic is encrypted. Although the web interface is rarely used, it can be a good lens through which a nontechnical user can view information.

We've all been told time and time again to configure management traffic in a separate VLAN on traditional switches. It was a really effective way to isolate management traffic from data traffic and provided some security and fault isolation too. So it's no surprise that the Nexus platform takes this concept up to the next logical step by physically separating the management ports from the data ports.

And isolated it is... That management port has its own IP address, subnet mask, and even its own routing table! We cordon off the management port's routing table with a technology known as Virtual Routing and Forwarding, or VRF, which allows us to have multiple yet separate routing tables on the same device. I'll talk about VRF in more detail later in this chapter.

Okay—take a minute to look back at the Nexus 5010 pictured in Figure 7.4. Can you figure out why there are two management ports shown? That's a good question! We would typically use Management Port 0, and even though Management port 1 appears unused, it's a standard 1Gbps Ethernet port. This means we can connect an RJ-45 Cat-6 cable to it, connect the other end to another Nexus switch, and then use the port for management traffic only.

Never forget that the management port must be configured with IP information from the console, and once it's configured correctly, you can then manage the device remotely through it.

L1/L2 Ports

I'm guessing that you probably noticed the L1/L2 ports on the Nexus 5010 in the figure, right? So what do you think they're for? Well, according to Cisco, these ports are not usable and are therefore disabled at this time. I know I said I wasn't going to talk about specific models in this chapter, but that statement is only mostly true. At the time of this writing, the L1/L2 ports' existence in a disabled state is true for the Nexus 5000s, but this is not so on all devices.

The Cisco UCS Fabric Interconnects—which, for our collective confusion just happen to look exactly like the Nexus 5000 series—work in pairs and use the L1 and L2 ports to communicate management information between the devices—nice!

Ethernet Port Names

Ethernet port names on IOS devices are based on the speed of the port, which is why we have port names like Ethernet 0, FastEthernet 1/1, and GigabitEthernet 2/2. Though crystal clear, this naming system definitely lost its luster when you faced upgrading from a Fast Ethernet switch to a gigabit Ethernet switch because it's not scalable at all. You quickly discovered that pasting the old configuration into the newer device wasn't exactly an option. Besides, the transceiver was typically built into the device so the maximum speed of the port would be recognized.

Not so with Nexus devices because the SFP+ port can handle interfaces of varying speeds. Even better is the fact that to simplify the configuration of these devices, Cisco came up with a super-easy naming standard—no matter what speed the port, the interface is always referred to as, "Ethernet." This means Ethernet 1/2 might be a 1Gbps port and Ethernet 1/3 a 10Gbps port. And just as it is with IOS devices, the numbering indicates the slot number followed by the port number.

Expansion Modules

The entire Nexus concept was designed with flexibility in mind, and there are expansion ports included for different kinds of cards to maximize that quality. As a matter of fact, for the first generation of Nexus switches, the expansion module was the only way to add Fibre Channel connectivity to your storage area network.

This whole idea of a single switch being able to handle both Ethernet data traffic and Fibre Channel storage traffic was really revolutionary. In the not-so-distant past, you had to bankroll a separate Catalyst switch and an MDS switch to be capable of dealing with these two types of traffic!

Expansion modules provide us with additional connectivity for Ethernet and Fibre Channels depending on the module you choose. You will see the color green next to a port, indicating that it's Fibre Channel. Figure 7.5 shows the expansion card.

FIGURE 7.5   Nexus 5020 and expansion cards

The Nexus 7000 series uses line cards for added functionality and ports. Predictably, different models can handle a different number of line cards with a 7010's capacity being 10 and a 7018's being 18, as seen in Figure 7.6.

FIGURE 7.6   Nexus 7010 and line cards

How's that for a huge switch? It's not really too hard to imagine the tremendous connectivity these mammoth devices combined with line cards and a ton of ports can deliver!

Unified Ports

SANs and LANs run parallel in the data center but each uses different types of ports. MDS switches rely on Fibre Channel ports for talking to storage devices, and Catalyst switches need Ethernet ports to talk to data devices.

The first generation of Nexus devices allowed you to add expansion cards for Ethernet, Fibre Channel, or even a combination of ports. But the individual port type was hardwired at the factory, meaning you could only run its specific type of traffic through it or it just wouldn't work.

More recent Nexus switches have taken flexibility to a whole new level by giving us unified ports, or UPs, which can handle both Ethernet and Fibre Channel transceivers. We get to choose which kind of port during the device's configuration, unleashing unprecedented adaptability by allowing us to switch ports between these two, key operational modes!

I don't want you to get confused—there are still separate SFP+ modules for Ethernet and Fibre Channel. It's just that we can now configure them into any UP on the Nexus devices with those supporting this capacity designated clearly with a *UP* suffix. For instance, the Cisco Nexus 5548UP and the 5596UP both offer highly flexible universal ports evidenced by the UP and the color orange next to a port. Figure 7.7 shows the Nexus 5000 family of switches.

FIGURE 7.7   Nexus 5000 family

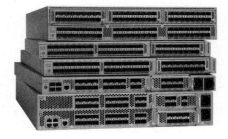

NX-OS Software Overview

The advances regarding the Nexus hardware over the IOS variety are truly significant, but they pale in comparison to the software differences, and it's really the latter that makes the Nexus platform so special. It's also really important to understand NX-OS software and its components if you want to pass the exam!

The NX-OS design makes it ideal for implementation within mission-critical, data center environments where reliability and fault tolerance are vitally important and speed is essential. That's a pretty tall order, but the Nexus and MDS 9000 platforms fill it completely via the powerful NX-OS, offering the most capable data center networking environment around. The MDS platform used a different operating system, called SAN-OS, but NX-OS version 4.1 actually enabled these two different hardware architectures to coexist within a single OS!

NX-OS Architecture

NX-OS architecture is geared to perform three different functions by being able to process layer 2, layer 3, and storage protocols. And like many modern networking products, NX-OS is also based on the Linux kernel to take advantage of this reliable, multitasking OS. Application-specific integrated circuits (ASICs) are added to the mix to create a high-performance cross-system architecture. As a result, NX-OS can amazingly support multiple processors and core CPUs plus line-card processors with ease… but how?

For starters, the control plane and the data plane are separated to provide nonstop forwarding and minimize data disruption. In addition, tasks that require a lot of CPU can be offloaded to dedicated processors.

There are also some ingenious services running in the background, like the ever-vigilant System Manager, which ensures that everything is running smoothly. In NX-OS, services are actually features created as modules, which are individually managed and monitored so that a problem in one module is isolated and doesn't affect other modules.

For example, In-Service Software Upgrades, or ISSU, makes it possible to upgrade images while still forwarding traffic on the data plane. You can see this demonstrated in the following output that zeroes in on some of the processes running on NX-OS:

```
Nexus7K# show processes


PID     State  PC          Start_cnt   TTY   Type  Process
-----   -----  --------    -----------  ----  ----  -------------
[output cut]
3642      S    b7f55be4         1        -     VL   udld
3643      S    b780740d         1        -     VL   cdp
3830      S    b7aaf468         1        -     VL   stp
  -      NR       -             0        -     VL   ospf
  -      NR       -             0        -     VL   hsrp_engine
  -      NR       -             0        -     VL   pim
Nexus7K#
```

By the way, this is only a small, sample portion of the output that shows us that three modular processes, UDLD, CDP, and STP, which operate at layer 2, have all started. The layer 3 processes, OSPF, HSRP, and PIM, have not been started yet.

Process Recovery

By far, one of the coolest things about is NX-OS is that it's basically self-monitoring and self-healing. Each non-kernel process runs in its own protected memory space, providing lots of fault tolerance while isolating any issues that arise. As I said, if one service fails, it does not affect any of the others, and some services like EIGRP can even have two, three, or four separate instances running simultaneously!

As its name implies, Persistent Storage Service, or PSS, is used to store and manage operational information and the configuration of various services. It allows many of them to periodically save their state by using checkpoint, but not all services are designed to do so.

Those that are simply restart and restore their state to the last saved checkpoint if the service fails. If multiple restart attempts also fail, the system switches over to the backup supervisor. All of the information is collected by the system and can be sent to a remote file server.

Here are some key factors to remember:

- Services save state information in a checkpoint that's stored by PSS.
- The system automatically restarts services when they fail.
- The restarted service contacts PSS and resumes from its last checkpoint.
- After multiple failed restarts, the supervisor is switched over.
- All information is logged and can be saved and sent to a remote file server.

But remember, not all services use the PSS checkpoint feature. Some protocols, like IS-IS, OSPF, BGP, and RIP, don't start where they left off in a restart because they're designed to rebuild their information when that happens instead.

Let me clarify this: While a graceful, admin-requested restart is underway, all traffic on the data plane continues based upon the previous information stored in the routing information bases (RIBs). Once the service is restarted, it can proceed to establish adjacencies and rebuild its tables, with the ultimate goal to all of this being to minimize any disruption that can occur at the data plane level.

Let's cause a graceful restart using the `restart` command now:

```
c5020# show processes | include rip
 7261      S  b7a51f43          4    -  rip
   -      NR     -              0    -  rip
   -      NR     -              0    -  rip
   -      NR     -              0    -  rip
```

This output tells us there's one instance of RIP running with the process ID 7261.

Now, if we execute the `restart rip 1` command, we can verify that RIP has restarted because it now has a different process ID:

```
c5020# restart rip 1
c5020# show processes | include rip
 7297      S  b7a51f43          5    -  rip
   -      NR     -              0    -  rip
   -      NR     -              0    -  rip
   -      NR     -              0    -  rip
c5020#
```

Regardless if a module is administratively restarted or restarts due to a problem, downtime is minimized. A high level of availability is maintained by core services like PSS and System Manager as well as Message and Transaction Service (MTS), which are all enabled by default and always running in the background.

Conditional Services

To help Nexus processing and memory requirements, most NX-OS features are not enabled by default, and one simple example of a process you must enable manually is RIP routing. You can run multiple instances of RIP, and you do so via the `router rip process-id` command:

```
c5020# configure
Enter configuration commands, one per line.  End with CNTL/Z.
c5020(config)# router rip 1
                     ^
% Invalid command at '^' marker.
```

This is curious, so let's investigate further why this didn't work:

```
c5020(config)# router ?
                     ^
% Invalid command at '^' marker.
```

Let's start troubleshooting this output by remembering that the Nexus environment is different that the IOS's because in the Nexus world, you've got to enable routing protocols before the routing protocols will work! So, to check and see if the protocol is even up and running, we're going to use the `show feature` command and see what the device tells us:

```
c5020(config)# show feature
Feature Name          Instance  State
--------------------  --------  --------
Flexlink              1         disabled
adapter-fex           1         disabled
assoc_mgr             1         enabled
bgp                   1         disabled
cimserver             1         disabled
dhcp                  1         disabled
eigrp                 1         disabled
eigrp                 2         disabled
eigrp                 3         disabled
eigrp                 4         disabled
fabric-binding        1         disabled
fc-port-security      1         disabled
fcoe                  1         enabled
fcoe-npv              1         disabled
fcsp                  1         disabled
fex                   1         disabled
fport-channel-trunk   1         disabled
```

```
hsrp_engine          1          disabled
interface-vlan       1          disabled
lacp                 1          disabled
ldap                 1          disabled
lldp                 1          enabled
msdp                 1          disabled
npiv                 1          disabled
npv                  1          disabled
ospf                 1          disabled
ospf                 2          disabled
ospf                 3          disabled
ospf                 4          disabled
pim                  1          disabled
poe                  1          disabled
port_track           1          disabled
private-vlan         1          disabled
privilege            1          disabled
rip                  1          disabled
rip                  2          disabled
rip                  3          disabled
rip                  4          disabled
sshServer            1          enabled
tacacs               1          disabled
telnetServer         1          enabled
udld                 1          disabled
vem                  1          disabled
vpc                  1          disabled
vrrp                 1          disabled
vtp                  1          disabled
c5020(config)#
```

Sure enough. RIP is not currently enabled! We'll enable RIP services using the feature RIP command and then try the RIP command again:

```
c5020(config)# feature rip
c5020(config)# show feature | include rip
rip                  1          enabled (not-running)
rip                  2          enabled (not-running)
rip                  3          enabled (not-running)
rip                  4          enabled (not-running)
c5020(config)# router rip 1
```

```
c5020(config-router)# show feature | include rip
rip              1         enabled
rip              2         enabled (not-running)
rip              3         enabled (not-running)
rip              4         enabled (not-running)
```

Okay—this is much better—we can clearly see that RIP is enabled and running. This is really important to remember because there is nothing more frustrating than trying to configure something that hasn't been enabled yet. Nor is there anything more embarrassing if attempted around others, which, worst case, can result in hair loss—even job loss if your boss has no sense of humor! So always make sure you execute a show feature before trying to configure something new.

Virtualizing the Network

It seems you can't go anywhere these days without overhearing someone saying something about virtualization. It's pretty much the biggest thing since Al Gore virtually invented the Internet, but even as hyped as virtualization may seem, this time the hype is earned. It's also true that virtualization is not all that new either because it's actually been around for quite some time.

Before we go any further with this, let me define what I really mean when I say "virtualization" because, well, there are a lot of different definitions out there. For our purposes, from here forward, virtualization is using something logical like software or a protocol to replace something physical like ports, cabling, or a switch. We can do a lot with this new clarification because this concept means we get to replace boatloads of old hardware with considerably less new hardware along with some sophisticated software to make it work!

Let's explore this concept further, starting toward the bottom of the OSI stack and working our way up from there.

Virtualizing Layer 2 Networks

The already familiar VLAN is not generally thought of as real virtualization, but by understanding what VLANs are and by analyzing them we can help everyone understand what we mean by virtualization. Figure 7.8 shows two physically separate layer 2 networks; the Sales and Marketing departments are isolated from each other and using up two separate switches—not good!

Okay, let's say we can make one physical switch into two logical, or virtual, networks. This neatly describes a VLAN, which does this very thing. Individual ports are assigned to a particular VLAN and only share local traffic with other devices on that specific VLAN. This is shown in Figure 7.9.

Effectively, what we've got here is one switch providing two separate networks by logically defining each network as a different VLAN. Now, even if we added another 20 VLANs, we still wouldn't need another switch, that is, until we run out of ports to connect to. So, one of the best gifts virtualization gives us is that it allows us to reduce the amount of hardware we need to accomplish a given task!

With this is mind, let's move on to consider cabling.

FIGURE 7.8   Two physical LANs

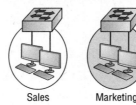

Physical Layer 2 Networks

Sales   Marketing

FIGURE 7.9   Two VLANs

Virtualized Layer 2 Networks VLANs

VLAN 100 / VLAN 200

Sales   Marketing

Virtualizing Interswitch Links

The network semantics gurus have recently redubbed the cables between two switches "interswitch links." If you're new to networking, this probably doesn't bother you a bit, but if you've been around awhile, you remember a protocol called Cisco InterSwitch Link (ISL), making this confusing. So to ensure that everyone is on the same page, understand that in this book, I'm not talking about the ancient protocol; I simply mean a cable running from one switch to another.

The cabling issue gets complicated when you think about a switch with multiple VLANs connecting to another switch with multiple VLANs. Since VLANs don't communicate with each other, you would need to run a separate cable for each VLAN between your two switches. Figure 7.10 demonstrates that if you've have two VLANs, you could need two cables to match.

FIGURE 7.10   Two physical interswitch links

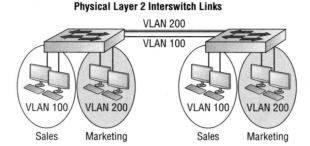

But running many cables for each VLAN ISL will occupy many ports and this is horribly inefficient, so you've got to virtualize to make one cable do the work of the many you would physically need if you didn't. Doing this is commonly known as trunking, where the data frame is tagged, sent across the link, and then untagged. You could split hairs and argue whether this is true virtualization or not, but it's close enough for the purpose of this book, and Figure 7.11 demonstrates how it works.

FIGURE 7.11   Two virtualized interswitch links

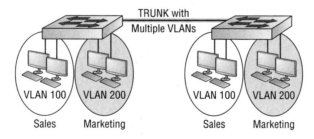

So far we have been talking about what should be some pretty familiar concepts, but next we'll get into Layer 3 and cover some new territory!

Virtualizing Layer 3 Interfaces

We've created layer 2 VLANs that cannot communicate with each other and linked switches connected via trunk links. Each layer 2 VLAN is on its own TCP/IP subnet, or broadcast domain, but to go from one VLAN to another, some routing must occur, so we now need layer 3 interfaces. We can accomplish that goal by connecting a physical layer 3 device's interface to each VLAN, as shown in Figure 7.12.

Now, when someone from the sales VLAN needs to transmit outside of it, the router looks up the destination in the routing table and forwards that traffic out 10.1.2.2.

FIGURE 7.12   Two physical layer 3 interfaces

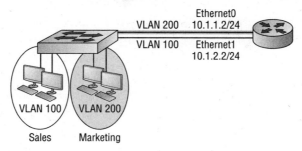

In the figure I used a router to make this work, but I can do this more efficiently by creating a logical layer 3 interface on the switch. These logical interfaces are created for each VLAN and are called switch virtual interfaces, or SVIs. In Figure 7.13, you can see an SVI for VLAN 100 and for VLAN 200.

FIGURE 7.13   Two virtualized layer 3 routable interfaces

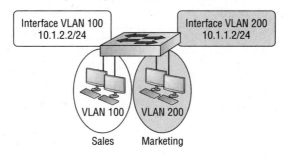

SVIs are often called VLAN interfaces because the command to create them is `interface VLAN`. They provide a default gateway for each VLAN and allow traffic to be routed from it. So, now that we can route traffic using virtual interfaces, how do we control where that traffic goes?

Virtualizing Routing Tables

Most of the time, we assume routers have a routing table, which is used to determine the best path to use to deal with a packet no matter how it got to the router in the first place, right? Figure 7.14 depicts a typical configuration with a default route to the Internet. When a packet destined for the Internet originates on VLAN 100 or VLAN 200, it will be sent out 10.5.5.5.

FIGURE 7.14 Standard layer 3 routing table

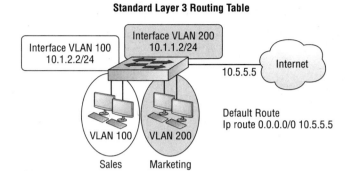

This works great if you want traffic from VLAN 100 to take a different path than traffic from VLAN 200. If you want Internet traffic from VLAN 200 to be sent to 10.5.5.5 and traffic from VLAN 100 to be sent 10.10.10.10, you could just go back to the Stone Age and use two separate physical devices to get that done. But it's definitely better to have a separate routing table used by each VLAN instead, right?

This is where Virtual Routing and Forwarding, or VRF, comes in to play. Each VRF creates a separate routing and forwarding table, and individual ports are then assigned to a particular VRF. After that, each port will use the associated routing table.

Figure 7.15 shows two VRFs we'll call VRF 11 and VRF 22, plus a default route for each. If a packet destined for the internet arrives on an interface that's part of VRF 11, it will be sent to 10.10.10.10, but if it lands on an interface that's part of VRF 22, it will be sent to 10.5.5.5.

Always remember that by default, Nexus switches have two VRFs—management 0 port is in a VRF called Management and all the other ports are in a VRF called Default. We'll talk about this more in the next chapter.

FIGURE 7.15 Virtualized layer 3 routing table - VRF

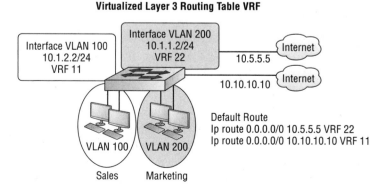

Virtualizing Devices

VRF allows us to create separate routing tables for different interfaces, but all of them are still under the same administrative control. If I'm VLAN 100's administrator and I want to be able to control all the settings that affect it, I need a dedicated device for VLAN 100, as shown in Figure 7.16.

FIGURE 7.16   Physical dedicated devices for separate admin control

Physical Dedicated Device Separate Admin Control, etc.

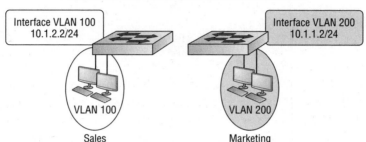

But this is a really inefficient use of resources! The answer? Virtual device contexts (VDCs) will let me logically create separate virtual devices within a single physical device because each VDC runs its own separate copy of NX-OS and provides all the same resources as a dedicated switch! Individual interfaces are associated with a VDC, and the various models of the Nexus 7000 supervisor modules typically permit a range of four to eight VDCs. Figure 7.17 shows two VDCs on a single Nexus device.

FIGURE 7.17   Virtualized dedicated device (VDC)

Virtualized Dedicated Device VDC

So here we've reached the point where we've pretty much virtualized everything except the ports and the physical switch itself. Where do we go from here? Let's take a look at the final step of virtualization now.

Virtualizing Everything

Virtual machines have become a staple of data center design. Just one physical server may actually run hundreds of virtual machines, each with its own operating system and access to the shared resources of the hosts. But how do these virtual machines communicate with each other? Easily, because each virtual machine has a virtual Ethernet interface connecting to a virtual switch, and yes, the entire switch is virtualized!

The virtualized switch is actually a special type of virtual machine that can perform switching and is the brainchild of Cisco and VMware, which got together and created the Nexus 1000V virtual switch.

The Nexus 1000V is purely a software switch with virtual ports that connect to the virtual interfaces of the virtual machine. But for now, it's still running NX-OS, and it's still a real switch moving real data. The virtualization trend will continue to grow and virtual switches will eventually become part of everyone's network, or virtual network if you will!

Summary

In this chapter, you learned the history and basic architecture of Cisco's Nexus product line. We covered some of the fundamental hardware components as well as the basic port types.

You learned that the NX-OS software was designed for the data center and that it has great features, which allow for process recovery. You also discovered how to enable features.

Virtualization was one of the bigger topics we talked about, covering the familiar virtualization methods like VLAN and trunking. We moved on to discuss Virtual Routing and Forwarding called VRFs and virtual device contexts (VDCs). We wrapped the chapter up talking about a truly virtual switch called the Nexus 1000V.

In the next chapter, we will move from theory to configuration of the NX-OS switch, so make sure you've nailed these technologies and concepts before you turn the page!

Exam Essentials

Describe the evolution of SAN-OS to NX-OS. SAN-OS was the original operating system on Cisco MDS devices. NX-OS was developed to run on Nexus switches. NX-OS version 4.1 represented a convergence because it ran not only on Nexus switches but also on the MDS platform.

Define processes that run on NX-OS. NX-OS can run different kinds of processes. At layer 2, it can run processes like Spanning Tree Protocol (STP), UniDirectional Link Detection (UDLD), and Cisco Discovery Protocol. At layer 3, Protocol Independent Multicast (PIM), Hot Standby Routing Protocol (HSRP), and Open Shortest Path First (OSPF) are running.

Describe switch virtual interfaces and their functions.   The switch virtual interface (SVI) is a logical interface that provides routing between VLANs. Typically, there will be one SVI for each VLAN to allow the devices on a subnet access to other VLANs.

Describe core processes in NX-OS.   High availability is provided by core services like Persistent Storage Service (PSS), System Manager, and Message and Transaction Service (MTS). These services ensure a reliable and resilient network operating system.

Written Labs

You can find the answers in Appendix A.

In this section, you'll complete the following labs to make sure you've got the information and concepts contained within them fully dialed in:

Lab 7.1: Ports

Lab 7.2: Virtualization

Lab 7.3: Layers

Lab 7.4: Nexus 1000V

Lab 7.5: VRF and VDC

Written Lab 7.1: Ports

Name the purpose of each of these ports on a Nexus 5010.

1. Console port

2. Management port

3. L1/L2 port

Written Lab 7.2: Virtualization

For each of the following hardware situations, determine the name of the virtualized solution.

1. Separate switches to isolate layer 2 traffic.

2. Multiple interswitch links to allow traffic from multiple VLANs.

3. Physical router ports to route between VLANs.

4. Separate devices to route to different default routes.

5. Separate devices to allow separate administration.

Written Lab 7.3: Layers

Determine which of the following are layer 2 processes and which are layer 3 processes.

1. HSRP

2. STP

3. PIM

4. Cisco Discovery Protocol

5. OSPF

6. UDLD

Written Lab 7.4: Nexus 1000V

A customer asks you to install a Nexus 1000V into his existing VMware environment. He is concerned about how it will fit in his data center. Please determine the following characteristics:

1. Weight

2. Number of additional rack units needed

3. Additional power outlets needed

4. Number of Ethernet ports required

Written Lab 7.5: VRF and VDC

A customer asks you the difference between VRF and VDC. Please explain how they are different and why you might use them.

Review Questions

You will find the answers in Appendix B.

The following questions are designed to test your understanding of this chapter's material. For more information on how to get additional questions, please see this book's introduction.

1. Which version of Cisco Nexus operating system became a common operating system for Cisco Nexus switches and Cisco MDS storage switches?

    A. 2.6

    B. 3.2

    C. 3.8

    D. 4.1

    E. 5.04

    F. 6.1

2. What are three modular layer 2 processes in Cisco's Nexus Operating System? (Choose three.)

    A. UDLD

    B. PIM

    C. HSRP

    D. STP

    E. Cisco Discovery Protocol

    F. OSPF

3. What are three modular layer 3 processes in Cisco's Nexus Operating System? (Choose three.)

    A. UDLD

    B. PIM

    C. HSRP

    D. STP

    E. Cisco Discovery Protocol

    F. OSPF

4. What does UDLD stand for?

    A. Unified Direct Link Distribution

    B. Unified Data Link Distribution

    C. Unified Direct Link Deployment

    D. UniDirectional Link Detection

5. Which statement correctly describes an SVI?

    A. An SVI provides layer 3 routing between VLANs.

    B. An SVI is a layer 2 interface and uses a static MAC address.

    C. An SVI cannot have an IPv6 address assigned to it.

    D. Each switch port requires an SVI assignment.

6. A network administrator wants to have two different administrators on a Nexus 7010, one managing the storage ports and one managing the Ethernet ports. What is the best way to accomplish this?

    A. VRF

    B. VDC

    C. Storage-Operator role

    D. VSANs and VLANs

7. On a Nexus 5010, what could you use to connect to an Ethernet network? (Choose all that apply.)

    A. SFP+

    B. TwinAx

    C. GBIC

    D. GBIC type 2

8. On the Nexus 5010, what does the L1 and L2 provide?

    A. Database synchronization

    B. Heartbeat

    C. Layer 1 and layer 2 connectivity

    D. Nothing

9. When configuring the Nexus device that has a 10-gigabit Ethernet interface located in the first port of slot 3, how would you reference it?

    A. 10G 3/1

    B. Gigabit 3/1

    C. Ethernet 3/1

    D. GBE 3/1

10. A network administrator wants to have two different administrators on a Nexus 7010, one managing the storage ports and one managing the Ethernet ports. What is the best way to accomplish this?

    A. VRF

    B. VDC

    C. Storage-Operator role

    D. VSANs and VLANs

11. A network administrator needs two different VLANs to use different default routes to the Internet. What is the least disruptive way to do this?

    A. VRF

    B. VDC

    C. Unicast balancing

    D. Nothing, this is default behavior.

12. A network administrator tries to configure RIP on a NX-OS device and gets a command not found error. What is the most likely reason for this?

    A. License is not installed.

    B. Only EIGRP is supported.

    C. RIP can only be configured from the GUI.

    D. The RIP feature is not enabled.

13. What is not true of a unified port?

    A. It can support Ethernet SFPs.

    B. It can support Fibre Channel SFPs.

    C. A port can be configured as Ethernet or Fibre Channel.

    D. A port can be configured as Ethernet and Fibre Channel.

14. What is true of the console port?

    A. It is in the default VRF.

    B. It is a serial connection.

    C. It is in the management VRF.

    D. It has its own VDC.

15. What allows a service to periodically save its state?

    A. PSS

    B. OSPF

    C. VSS

    D. UP

Chapter

8

Configuring Nexus

THE FOLLOWING TOPICS ARE COVERED IN THIS CHAPTER:

✓ **Operating Cisco NX-OS Software**

- Describing the Features of the CLI
- Identifying the Help Functions of the CLI
- Describing the Startup Characteristics of the Switch
- Describing Configuration Management

With everything you've learned in Chapters 1 through 7, you're completely ready to be introduced to the Nexus Operating System (NX-OS) command line now. This operating system runs on both Nexus and MDS devices and we'll be using it to explore and configure these exciting, new machines.

If you're already familiar with Cisco's Internetworking Operating System (IOS), you'll certainly encounter lots of similarities. But there are many differences as well, and I'll guide you through them all to successfully complete the configuration of a NX-OS device. Once you're comfortable with the Nexus interface, you'll be ready to configure hostnames, banners, usernames, and more, and I'll close the chapter with the ever-vital verification process. Here's a quick scan of the topics you'll be learning about in this chapter:

- Understanding and configuring the Nexus Operating System (NX-OS)
- Connecting to a device
- Bringing up a device
- Understanding the device prompts
- Understanding the CLI prompts
- Performing editing and help features
- Gathering basic routing information
- Setting administrative functions
- Setting hostnames
- Setting usernames and passwords
- Setting interface descriptions
- Performing interface configurations
- Viewing, saving, and erasing configurations

As always, bear in mind that all the knowledge you gain in this chapter will become a solid foundation to build upon with the skills you'll refine as you move on through this book.

For up-to-the-minute updates for this chapter, please see www.lammle.com/forum.

The NX-OS User Interface

The *Nexus Operating System (NX-OS)* is the kernel of Cisco's newest data center switches and it's designed to be a highly reliable powerhouse of performance. You probably remember that a kernel is the essential part of an operating system that allocates resources and manages things like low-level hardware interfaces and security.

Coming up soon, I'm going to show you the Cisco NX-OS and how to configure a Nexus device using the command-line interface (CLI). Clearly, a good place to start is by telling you about the three ways you can connect to it initially.

Connecting to a Nexus Device

Even though there are other ways to connect to a Nexus device, most of the time, you'll connect via the *console port* for configuration and verification and when checking statistics. This *port* is usually an RJ-45 (8-pin modular) connection located on the device itself. Make a mental note that Nexus Fabric Extenders do not have console ports because they're managed by their parent devices. In one of those similarities I mentioned, Nexus switches are kind of like IOS devices in that they can support out-of-band management from the console port and the Aux port—but not on all platforms!

Another way to connect is called *in-band*, which means configuring the device through the network using a terminal emulation program like Telnet or Secure Shell (SSH.) Most people opt for SSH because it's a more secure way to connect through a network.

The last way to connect is via a dedicated Ethernet management port called *MGMT0*. It's one of the ways Nexus differs from IOS because MGMT0 traffic is separate from the main Ethernet ports. This is referred to as *out-of-band management*. An important point to remember is that after the initial configuration of the device has been completed, most additional configuration is usually completed through this port.

Figure 8.1 shows a Cisco Nexus 5548 switch console port and a management port, but just so you know, the L1 and L2 ports you see to the left of these ports are not currently implemented on the Nexus 5000 series. Take a look.

FIGURE 8.1   Nexus management port

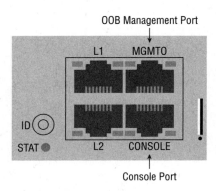

Let's take a look at a Nexus 7000 Supervisor 1 card in Figure 8.2.

FIGURE 8.2 Nexus 7000 Supervisor I card

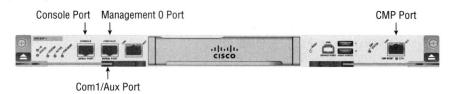

The auxiliary port was traditionally utilized for remote dial-in access so that you could connect via dial-up and manage the switch out-of-band. The auxiliary port exists on the Nexus 7000 Supervisor version 1 but was discontinued in later versions. The CMP Ethernet port is essentially a separate remote access server port that you can connect to remotely even if your management port is down and achieve an out-of-band management connection. As with the Aux port, the CMP port was discontinued after the Nexus 7000 supervisor 1.

Now, let's take a look at a Nexus 7000 Supervisor 2 card in Figure 8.3.

FIGURE 8.3 Nexus 7000 Supervisor 2 card

Notice the clean look and lack of extra, useless management ports such as Aux and CMP. The Supervisor 2 card scales beyond 15 terabits per second (Tbps)! The new Sup2E (enhanced) has two quad-core Intel Xeon processors with 32GB of memory that support more VDC and fabric extenders. The Super2E has four times the CPU and memory power of the Supervisor 1 and is four times the price as well.

You can find more information about all Nexus switches at: www.cisco.com/go/nexus.

Bringing Up an NX-OS Device

When you bring up a Nexus device for the first time, it will look for and then load the kickstart image from flash memory. This program gets the system up and running and loads the system software. After kickstart is loaded and verified, the kernel launches and then executes a power-on self-test (POST) diagnostics session.

Here's how the initial boot looks on my 5040 switch:

```
System Bootstrap, Version 12.4(13r)T, RELEASE SOFTWARE (fc1)

Booting kickstart image: bootflash:/n5000-uk9-kickstart.5.0.3.N2.2.bin....
.........................................................................Image
verification OK
Starting kernel...
Usage: init 0123456SsQqAaBbCcUu
INIT: version 2.85 bootingI2C - Mezz present
Starting Nexus5020 POST...
  Executing Mod 1 1 SEEPROM Test......done
  Executing Mod 1 1 GigE Port Test.......done
  Executing Mod 1 1 Inband GigE Test.....done
  Executing Mod 1 1 NVRAM Test....done
  Executing Mod 1 1 PCIE Test.............................done
  Mod 1 1 Post Completed Successfully
  Executing Mod 1 2 SEEPROM Test....done
  Mod 1 2 Post Completed Successfully
POST is completed
autoneg unmodified, ignoring
autoneg unmodified, ignoring
Checking all filesystems..... done.
```

And by the way, this output would also appear if I were to reboot the Nexus switch.

This initial part of the NX-OS boot process output is all information about kickstart, which first runs the POST and then verifies the file system.

The next part shows us that the system software is being decompressed into RAM and additional plug-in modules are being loaded:

```
Loading system software
Uncompressing system image: bootflash:/n5000-uk9.5.0.3.N2.2.bin


Loading plugin 0: core_plugin...
Loading plugin 1: eth_plugin...
```

Notice that the NX-OS system version showing in the filename is 5.0.3. This is important because the system software contains the majority of the processes the switch uses.

Okay, now the switch will start up initializing processes and begin mounting file systems and loading files. You can see these things happening in the following output:

```
ethernet switching mode
INIT: Entering runlevel: 3Exporting directories for NFS kernel daemon...done.
```

```
Starting NFS kernel daemon:rpc.nfsd.
rpc.mountddone.
Set name-type for VLAN subsystem. Should be visible in /proc/net/vlan/config
Added VLAN with VID == 4042 to IF -:muxif:-
VDC-1 %$ %USER-2-SYSTEM_MSG: CLIS: loading cmd files begin  -
clisVDC-1 %KERN-2-SYSTEM_MSG: Starting kernel... - kernel
VDC-1 %KERN-0-SYSTEM_MSG: platform_type cmdline parameter not
found. Asssuming Oregon. - kernelVDC-1 %KERN-0-SYSTEM_MSG: I2C -
Mezz present  - kernelVDC-1 %KERN-0-SYSTEM_MSG: sprom_drv_init_platform: nuova_
i2c_register_get_card_index  - kernelVDC-1 %USER-2-SYSTEM_MSG:
CLIS: loading cmd files end  - clis
VDC-1 %USER-2-SYSTEM_MSG: CLIS: init begin  - clis
```

Finally, the device tests the application-specific integrated circuits, known as ASICs, and indicates that it's all done:

```
Executing ASIC Power On Self Test..
.............Done
```

At this point, you'll be prompted to log in if the device already has a configuration, but if it's a new device and there isn't one there yet, the System Admin Account Setup will appear.

Command-Line Interface

Initially, an NX-OS device's command-line interface (CLI) seems a lot like IOS, but stay with me for a while and you'll begin to see some key differences pop up as we delve deeper into the configuration!

Entering the CLI

Now again, if you've got a shiny, new device, System Admin Account Setup will appear. Its first request will be for a respectably strong, complex password. The rules for Nexus strong passwords are as follows:

- Must be at least eight characters long.
- Doesn't comprise too many sequential characters, like, "efgh."
- Doesn't contain many of the same characters, such as, "qqqzzz."
- Does not contain common dictionary words.
- Does not contain proper names.
- Comprises uppercase and lowercase characters.
- Contains numbers as well.

Because passwords like this are usually a wise thing to go with anyway, I'd set the administrator password, write it on a sticky note, and plunk it down on my switch for reference, right? You know I'm kidding... No stickies, anywhere, *ever*!

Seriously, I would normally come up with a vault-tight password, but in this learning environment, we're going to go with something much simpler, like this (and just say no to enforcing secure passwords):

```
     ---- System Admin Account Setup ----



Do you want to enforce secure password standard (yes/no): no


  Enter the password for "admin":
  Confirm the password for "admin":
```

The Basic System Configuration dialog now appears; you can get out of it by typing **no** or pressing Ctrl+C.

```
  ---- Basic System Configuration Dialog ----


This setup utility will guide you through the basic configuration of
the system. Setup configures only enough connectivity for management
of the system.


Please register Cisco Nexus 5000 Family devices promptly with your
supplier. Failure to register may affect response times for initial
service calls. Nexus devices must be registered to receive entitled
support services.


Press Enter at anytime to skip a dialog. Use ctrl-c at anytime
to skip the remaining dialogs.


Would you like to enter the basic configuration dialog (yes/no):
Exiting the basic config setup.
```

You'll only see the preceding dialogs when your device doesn't already have a configuration on it. One that does will take you straight to a login prompt with the username *admin* and using the password that was set initially:

```
login: admin
Password:
```

```
Cisco Nexus Operating System (NX-OS) Software
TAC support: http://www.cisco.com/tac
Copyright (c) 2002-2011, Cisco Systems, Inc. All rights reserved.
The copyrights to certain works contained in this software are
owned by other third parties and used and distributed under
license. Certain components of this software are licensed under
the GNU General Public License (GPL) version 2.0 or the GNU
Lesser General Public License (LGPL) Version 2.1. A copy of each
such license is available at
http://www.opensource.org/licenses/gpl-2.0.php and
http://www.opensource.org/licenses/lgpl-2.1.php
switch#
```

Cisco Nexus devices have two main command modes, user exec mode and configuration mode. However, unlike with an IOS device, the pound (#) sign does not indicate privileged mode. There is no "enable" to grant you admin power with NX-OS! The username provides admin or operator powers when you log in. We'll talk about this more later in this chapter.

But for now, I'm just going to type **exit** to leave the console:

```
switch# exit


 login:
```

Next, I'll take you through some basic administrative configurations.

Overview of NX-OS Modes

When configuring from a CLI, you can make global changes to your device by typing config-ure terminal or configure, or even just con. Any of these will get you into global configuration mode and will change the running-config. Never forget that you set a global command from global config mode only once, and doing so affects the entire device.

I just typed type con from the user EXEC prompt. Here's the resulting output:

```
switch# con
Enter configuration commands, one per line.  End with CNTL/Z.
switch(config)#
```

Here, in *global configuration mode*, we'll make changes that will affect the device as a whole. To change the running-config—the current configuration running in dynamic RAM (DRAM)—use the configure command as I just did.

CLI Prompts

It's really important for you to understand the different prompts you'll encounter when configuring an NX-OS device because they serve as a type of compass and will help you navigate where you are at any given point within configuration mode. So next, we'll test the prompts commonly used on a Nexus device and make sure you understand the relevant terms as well. And don't forget to always check your prompts before making any changes to the configuration!

Just so you know, we won't be trying out each and every different command prompt there is because that would be going way beyond the scope of this book. But rest assured that I'll definitely explain all the prompts you'll see throughout this chapter because they're really the ones you'll use most in real life anyway. That, and they also happen to be the ones you absolutely need to know for the exam.

 Now don't freak out on me here because it's not important for you to understand exactly what each of these command prompts do yet. I promise that I'll totally fill you in on all of them really soon, but for now, relax and just focus on becoming familiar with the different prompts available.

Interfaces

I'm going to make changes to an interface now using the interface command from global configuration mode:

```
Enter configuration commands, one per line.  End with CNTL/Z.
switch (config)# interface ?
  ethernet       Ethernet IEEE 802.3z
  loopback       Loopback interface
  mgmt           Management interface
  port-channel   Port Channel interface

switch (config)# interface mgmt 0
switch (config-if)#
```

Did you notice that the prompt changed to (config-if)#? This is important because it tells you that you're in *interface configuration mode*. Of course, it would be really nice if the prompt also told us which interface we're configuring, but for now, we'll have to live without that because sadly, it doesn't. Take this as an omen—you must really pay attention when configuring NX-OS!

At least the NX-OS does offer the command where, and using it will make it tell you the specific interface you're on:

```
switch (config-if)# where
  conf; interface mgmt0      admin@switch
switch (config-if)#
```

Subinterfaces

You can create virtual subinterfaces on a physical interface that are configured as a layer 3 interfaces (not layer 2 ports). Subinterfaces divide a physical interface into two or more virtual interfaces so you can assign unique IP addresses, routing protocols, and more. The IP address for each subinterface must be in a different subnet than any other subinterface, just as they would on any physical interface.

You create a subinterface with a name that consists of the parent interface name (for example, Ethernet 1/1) followed by a period and then by a number that is unique. The prompt then changes to nexus(config-subif)#:

```
switch (config-if)# interface ethernet 1/1.1
switch (config-subif)#
```

Line Commands

You can configure user-mode passwords with the line console command. The prompt will then become (config-console)#:

```
switch (config)# line ?
  com1     Primary terminal line
  console  Primary terminal line
  vty      Virtual terminal line
switch (config)# line console
switch (config-console)#
```

The line console command is a global one that we sometimes also call a major command. Any command typed from the (config-console) prompt is known as a subcommand. The console is used to configure the console port, com1 is for the Aux port, and VTY is for telnet and SSH settings.

Routing Protocol Configurations

Because routing protocols are covered in Chapter 10, "Routing Protocols" I'm just demonstrating how the prompt changes in this one. But just so you know, you can configure routing protocols like RIP, OSPF, and EIGRP using the prompt (config-router#):

```
switch# config t
Enter configuration commands, one per line.  End with CNTL/Z.
switch#(config)# feature eigrp
switch#(config)# router eigrp MyGroup
switch#(config-router)#
```

Defining Terms

As I mentioned, knowing the terms relevant to the technology you're dealing with is vital. Table 8.1 is a good review that lists the most important terms used so far.

TABLE 8.1   Device terms

Mode	Definition
User exec mode	Provides access to all commands
Global configuration mode	Commands that affect the entire system
Specific configuration modes	Commands that affect interfaces/processes only
Setup mode	Interactive configuration dialog

Editing and Help Features

Cisco's advanced editing features can be really helpful when configuring your device. For instance, if you type in a question mark at any prompt, you'll be given a list of all the commands available from that prompt. Check out the output to see what I mean. I just typed a question mark (?) after the switch# prompt:

```
switch# ?
  attach          Connect to a specific linecard
  callhome        Callhome commands
  cd              Change current directory
  cfs             CFS parameters
  checkpoint      Create configuration rollback checkpoint
  city            Set global city params (exec level)
  clear           Reset functions
  cli             CLI commands
  clock           Manage the system clock
  configure       Enter configuration mode
  copy            Copy from one file to another
  csl             CSL
  debug           Debugging functions
  debug-filter    Enable filtering for debugging functions
  delete          Delete a file or directory
  diff-clean      Remove temp files created by '| diff' filters
  dir             List files in a directory
  dos2nxos        DOS to NXOS text file format converter
  echo            Echo argument back to screen (useful for scripts)
  event           Event Manager commands
  find            Find a file below the current directory
```

```
  format             Format disks
-- More --
```

Also very good to know is that at this point, you can simply press the spacebar to gain access to another entire page of information. If that sounds too overwhelming, just press Enter to go one command at a time. You can also press Q to quit and get you back to the prompt.

And if you want even more output and you want to see each and every available command, enter a ? when you're at the More prompt. This is what doing that will get you:

```
Most commands optionally preceded by integer argument k.  Defaults in brackets.
Star (*) indicates argument becomes new default.
--------------------------------------------------------------------
<space>             Display next k lines of text [current screen size]
z                   Display next k lines of text [current screen size]*
<return>            Display next k lines of text [1]*
d or ctrl-D         Scroll k lines [current scroll size, initially 11]*
q or Q or <interrupt>Exit from more
s                   Skip forward k lines of text [1]
f                   Skip forward k screenfuls of text [1]
b or ctrl-B         Skip backwards k screenfuls of text [1]
'                   Go to place where previous search started
=                   Display current line number
/<regular expression>Search for kth occurrence of regular expression [1]
n                   Search for kth occurrence of last r.e [1]
!<cmd> or :!<cmd>    Execute <cmd> in a subshell
v                   Start up /usr/bin/vi at current line
ctrl-L              Redraw screen
:n                  Go to kth next file [1]
:p                  Go to kth previous file [1]
:f                  Display current file name and line number
.                   Repeat previous command
--------------------------------------------------------------------
--More--
```

Okay—we all love these—here's a shortcut that's going to seem completely obvious to you when you read this: To find commands that start with a certain letter, just type the desired letter plus a question mark with no space between them and voilà! Check out what I got when I typed **c?**:

```
switch# c?
  callhome    Callhome commands
  cd          Change current directory
  cfs         CFS parameters
  checkpoint  Create configuration rollback checkpoint
```

```
   city        Set global city params (exec level)
   clear       Reset functions
   cli         CLI commands
   clock       Manage the system clock
   configure   Enter configuration mode
   copy        Copy from one file to another
   csl         CSL
switch#
```

Nice—all I did was enter **c?** and I got an entire list of all the commands that start with the letter *c* in response. And did you happen to notice that the switch# prompt reappeared after the list of commands is displayed? This little trick is super helpful when you have really long commands but all you need is the next possible command. It would be horribly tedious if you had to retype the entire command every time you used a question mark!

So, to find the next command in a string, type the first command and then a question mark like this:

```
switch# clock ?
   set  HH:MM:SS Current Time


switch# clock set ?
   WORD  HH:MM:SS Current Time (Max Size 8)


switch# clock set 12:34:56 ?
   <1-31>  Day of the month


switch# clock set 12:34:56 30 june ?
   <2000-2030>  Enter the year (no abbreviation)


switch# clock set 12:34:56 30 june 2015
Tue Jun 30 12:34:56 UTC 2015
switch#
```

Okay, here you can see that I got a nice little list of the of the next possible parameters *and* what they do by just typing in the clock ? command! To get out of this, you just keep typing a command, a space, and then a question mark until <cr> (carriage return) is your only option.

Now if you're typing commands and receive this,

```
switch# clock set 12:34:56
                          ^
% Incomplete command at '^' marker.
```

you know the command string isn't done yet. Just press the up arrow key to redisplay the last command entered, and then continue with the command by using your question mark.

But if you receive the following error message,

```
switch# clock set 12:34:56 june
                 ^
% Invalid command at '^' marker.
```

it means that you've entered a command incorrectly. See that little caret—the ^? That's a very helpful little marker that highlights the exact spot where you blew it and entered the command incorrectly.

Here's another example of when you'll see that caret:

```
switch# show ethernet 1/1
             ^
% Invalid command at '^' marker.
```

This command looks okay, right? Be careful—it's not! The problem is that the full, proper command is show interface Ethernet 1/1.

Now suppose you receive this error:

```
switch# show v
             ^
% Ambiguous command at '^' marker.
```

It means there are multiple commands that begin with the string you entered and it's not unique. Say the command you're after begins with the letter *v*. Just type **Show v?** after the switch# prompt. That ever-helpful question mark will help you find the command you really need:

```
switch# show v?
  vdc       Show Virtual Device Contexts
  version   Show the software version
  vlan      Vlan commands
  vrf       Display VRF information
```

As you can see, there are four commands beginning with a *v*.

Table 8.2 displays a list of the enhanced editing commands available on a Nexus device.

TABLE 8.2   Enhanced editing commands

Command	Meaning
Ctrl+A	Moves your cursor to the beginning of the line
Ctrl+E	Moves your cursor to the end of the line

Command	Meaning
Esc+B	Moves back one word
Ctrl+B	Moves back one character
Ctrl+F	Moves forward one character
Esc+F	Moves forward one word
Ctrl+D	Deletes a single character
Backspace	Deletes a single character
Ctrl+R	Redisplays a line
Ctrl+U	Erases a line
Ctrl+W	Erases a word
Ctrl+Z	Ends configuration mode and returns to exec
Tab	Finishes typing a command for you

And you can review the command history with the commands shown in Table 8.3.

TABLE 8.3 Command history

Command	Meaning
Ctrl+P or up arrow	Shows last command entered
Ctrl+N or down arrow	Shows previous commands entered
show terminal	Shows terminal configurations

Gathering Basic Information

The show version command will provide you with a view of the basic configuration for the system hardware, plus the software version and the boot images. Here's an example:

```
switch# show version
Cisco Nexus Operating System (NX-OS) Software
```

```
TAC support: http://www.cisco.com/tac
Copyright (c) 2002-2010, Cisco Systems, Inc. All rights reserved.
The copyrights to certain works contained herein are owned by
other third parties and are used and distributed under license.
Some parts of this software are covered under the GNU Public
License. A copy of the license is available at
http://www.gnu.org/licenses/gpl.html.
```

 Real World Scenario

When Do You Use the Cisco Editing Features?

There are some editing features you'll use often and others not so much, if at all. And of course you know that Cisco didn't make these up—they're really just old Unix commands. Still, there's just nothing like Ctrl+A for negating a command!

For example, let's say you entered a really long command and then decide you didn't want to use that command in your configuration after all. Maybe it just didn't work for some reason. Well, all you need to do is use your up arrow key to show the last command entered, press Ctrl+A, type no, then a space, hit Enter—and poof! The command is negated. Keep in mind that this cool little trick doesn't always work on every command, but it does a nice job on a lot of them.

And who can forget the Tab key—it's one of my favorite editing features because it completes a partially entered command if enough characters are present. I love shortcuts, don't you?

If this isn't enough for you, the NX-OS offers us another editing system besides the default Emacs editor and you can enable the Vi editor via terminal edit-mode vi.

The output above describes the Cisco NX-OS running on the device. The next bit of output describes the read-only memory (ROM) employed, which is what is used to boot the device and also holds the POST:

```
ROM: System Bootstrap, Version 12.4(13r)T, RELEASE SOFTWARE (fc1)
```

This section shows us which software versions are running and what the filenames are:

```
Software
  loader:    version N/A
  kickstart: version 5.0(3) [gdb]
  system:    version 5.0(3) [gdb]
  kickstart image file is: bootflash:/titanium-d1-kickstart.5.0.3.gbin
```

```
kickstart compile time:   7/12/2010 18:00:00 [07/24/2010 11:40:20]
system image file is:     bootflash:/titanium-d1.5.0.3.gbin
system compile time:      7/12/2010 18:00:00 [07/24/2010 13:23:40]
```

The next part tells us about the processor, the amount of DRAM and bootflash memory:

```
Hardware
    cisco Nexus5020 Chassis ("40x10GE/Supervisor")
    Intel(R) Celeron(R) M CPU    with 2073408 kB of memory.
    Processor Board ID JAB1243000W


    Device name: switch
    bootflash:    1003520 kB
```

The final section shows us the uptime, reset time, reason for reset, and plug-ins loaded:

```
Kernel uptime is 0 day(s), 1 hour(s), 17 minute(s), 54 second(s)


Last reset at 756736 usecs after  Mon Jan 28 14:21:53 2013
    Reason: Reset Requested by CLI command reload
    System version: 5.0(3)N2(2)
    Service:


plugin
    Core Plugin, Ethernet Plugin
```

In addition to these, the show interfaces and show ip interface brief commands are very useful in verifying and troubleshooting, but we're not going there just yet.

Administrative Configurations

Even though the following sections aren't vital to actually making a switch work on your network, they're still really important. As we move through them, I'm going to reveal configuring commands that will help you administer your network.

First, understand that there are three administrative functions that you can configure on a switch:

- Hostnames
- Passwords
- Interface descriptions

While it's true that none of these will make your switches work better or faster, life will be lot better if you take the time to set these configurations on each of your network devices. This is because they will make troubleshooting and maintaining your network exponentially easier—seriously. So this section will be devoted to demonstrating these administrative functions and their related commands on a Nexus device.

Hostnames

The identity of the devices is set with the `hostname` or `switchname` command. Bear in mind that the hostname is only locally significant, which means that it has no bearing on how the device performs name lookups or even how it works on the internetwork at all.

Here's a sample of the output:

```
switch# conf t
Enter configuration commands, one per line.  End with CNTL/Z.
switch(config)# hostname John
John(config)# hostname Tampa
Tampa(config)# switchname nexus
nexus(config)#
```

Even though it can be kind of tempting to configure the hostname after your own name, it's definitely a better idea to name the device something pertinent to its location. This is because giving it a hostname that's somehow relevant to where the device actually lives will make finding it a whole lot easier later. And well, it also helps confirm that you are, indeed, configuring the right device.

Setting Usernames and Passwords

Nexus authentication requires setting a username and password, and most of the time, that's all you'll need to do. But within some more secure environments, you'll also want to use roles. The two most commonly used built-in roles are network-admin, which gets complete read/write access and write access to the entire NX-OS device, and network-operator, which gets only read access. So you can see that roles come in really handy for specifying what a given user can and can't do, and I'm pretty sure the security benefits gained by using them are crystal clear.

With that, let's start by creating a user from global configuration mode:

```
nexus(config)# username ?
  WORD  User name (Max Size 28)


nexus(config)# username john ?
  <CR>
  expire      Expiry date for this user account
  keypair     Generate SSH User Keys
```

```
password      Password for the user
role          Role which the user is to be assigned to
ssh-cert-dn   Update cert dn
sshkey        Update ssh key for the user for ssh authentication
```

```
nexus(config)# username john password ?
  0     Indicates that the password that follows should be in clear text
  5     Indicates that the password that follows should be encrypted
  WORD  Password for the user (clear text) (Max Size 64)
```

```
nexus(config)# username john password mypassword ?
  <CR>
  expire  Expiry date for this user account
  role    Role which the user is to be assigned to
```

```
nexus(config)# username john password mypassword
```

Okay—you can see that I just created the username *john*, without specifying a role, with the admittedly lame password, *mypassword*. The default username has full administrative control as network-admin. But it doesn't have to stay that way if I go to the next level and assign john a role to limit just what it is he can do.

If you create a user without specifying a role, by default that user will have network-admin as their role. You can change their role as shown here (it is also possible to assign the role and password on a single line):

```
nexus(config)# username john role ?
  network-admin     System configured role
  network-operator  System configured role
  priv-0            Privilege role
  priv-1            Privilege role
  priv-10           Privilege role
  priv-11           Privilege role
  priv-12           Privilege role
  priv-13           Privilege role
  priv-14           Privilege role
  priv-15           Privilege role
  priv-2            Privilege role
  priv-3            Privilege role
  priv-4            Privilege role
  priv-5            Privilege role
  priv-6            Privilege role
```

```
priv-7              Privilege role
priv-8              Privilege role
priv-9              Privilege role
vdc-admin           System configured role
vdc-operator        System configured role
nexus(config)# username john role network-operator
```

There, at the bottom line of the output, you can now see that user *john*'s role has changed to network-operator, meaning he's now prohibited from changing or even viewing the configuration—clearly a security advantage! The various default roles are very helpful when you want to create and enable users without giving them too much access.

Here is an example of providing this level of security in one command line:

```
nexus(config)# username john password Lame0ne role network-operator
```

Now I'll log in as john and we'll try some commands.

```
nexus#
nexus# sh running-config
% Permission denied for the role
nexus# copy run start
% Permission denied for the role


nexus# where
        john@nexus%default
```

Notice that when I logged in as john, which is a network operator, I can neither change nor view the configuration. The default roles are similar to user mode and privileged mode in IOS. Unlike with the IOS, however, you cannot look at the prompt and know where you are, but I can tell who I am logged in as using the where command.

Setting Up Secure Shell

As mentioned earlier, opting for Secure Shell creates a more secure session than the Telnet application, which uses an unencrypted data stream. Instead, Secure Shell uses encryption keys to send data so that your username and password don't travel in clear text.

There are five steps needed to set up SSH:

1. Set your hostname:

```
nexus(config)#hostname John
```

2. Set the domain name—both the hostname and domain name are required for the encryption keys to be generated:

```
John(config)#ip domain-name Lammle.com
```

3. Set the username to allow SSH client access:

```
John(config)#username John password mypass
```

4. Make sure the SSH feature is enabled:

```
John(config)# feature ssh
```

5. Generate the encryption keys for securing the session:

```
John(config)# ssh key ?
  dsa  Generate DSA keys
  rsa  Generate RSA keys
John(config)# ssh key rsa ?
  <CR>
  <768-2048>  Enter number of bits

John(config)# ssh key rsa 1024 ?
  <CR>
  force  Force the generation of keys even if previous ones are present
John(config)# ssh key rsa 1024
```

The process to configure SSH on a Nexus device is somewhat similar than on IOS routers and switches, but you need to start the feature in NX-OS first.

Descriptions

As with the hostname, setting descriptions on an interface is only locally significant and also really helpful for administration purposes. Here's an example where I used the description command to keep track of interface numbers:

```
John(config)# switchname nexus
nexus(config)# int mgmt 0
nexus(config-if)# description connected to the 7010 port 2/1/2
```

And you can view the description of an interface with either the show running-config command or the show interface command:

```
nexus#sh run
[output cut]
interface mgmt0
  description connected to the 7010 port 2/1/2
line console
line vty
```

```
boot kickstart bootflash:/n5000-uk9-kickstart.5.0.3.N2.2.bin
boot system bootflash:/n5000-uk9.5.0.3.N2.2.bin
 [output cut]
```

```
nexus(config-if)# show int mgmt 0
mgmt0 is up
  Hardware: GigabitEthernet, address: 000d.eca4.2fc0 (bia 000d.eca4.2fc0)
  Description: the is connect to the 7010 port 2/1/2
```

Don't Do the *do* Command

Thankfully, beginning with IOS version 12.3, Cisco finally bestowed the do command upon us, which offers a nice view of the configuration and statistics from within configuration mode. But with the Nexus operating system, you don't need it! Just use show commands from within config mode instead:

```
nexus(config-if)# sh clock
16:44:47.067 UTC Mon Jan 28 2013
nexus(config-if)#
```

Okay, you can still use the do command if you really want to, but since you don't have to, why type needlessly?

For those of you resistant to change, here it is:

```
nexus(config-if)# do show clock
16:45:14.057 UTC Mon Jan 28 2013
nexus(config-if)#
```

Just as in an IOS router, you can use the do command to pretty much perform any command within configuration mode. However, with NX-OS you can quickly get used to not having to include the do command. It's a very nice feature!

Device Interfaces

Interface configuration is one of the most important device configurations you can tangle with because without interfaces, a device is a pretty useless thing. Plus, interface configurations require serious precision to enable communication with other devices. Network layer addresses, media type, bandwidth, and more are all on the menu used to configure an interface, but different devices definitely require using specific ways to choose their interfaces.

I know many of us have grown accustomed to using the interface *type number* sequence to configure an interface, but there's an actual, physical slot in Nexus devices. And there's also a port number on the module plugged into that slot. With that in mind, the minimum Nexus configuration would be interface *type slot/port*, as seen here:

```
nexus(config-if)# interface ethernet ?
  <1-255>  Slot/chassis number


nexus(config-if)# interface ethernet 1/?
  <1-128>  Port/slot number


nexus(config-if)# interface ethernet 1/1
nexus(config-if)#
```

An important note here is that some interfaces require three numbers, as when using a fabric extender. In the following example, the 48-port fabric extender has been configured as FEX 100 and the interface number starts with 100 for each port:

```
nexus(config)# int ethernet 100/?
  <1-128>  Port/slot number


nexus(config)# int ethernet 100/1/?
  <1-48>  Port number


nexus(config)# int ethernet 100/1/2
nexus(config-if)#
```

I know this may look a little dicey, but I promise it's not that hard. It helps to remember that you should always view a running-config output first so that you know exactly which interfaces you have to deal with. Here's my only slightly edited 5040 output as an example:

```
nexus# sh run


!Command: show running-config
!Time: Tue Jan 29 12:31:03 2013
 [output cut]
interface Ethernet1/1


interface Ethernet1/2


interface Ethernet1/3
```

```
interface Ethernet1/4
[output cut]
interface mgmt0
  description the is connect to the 7010 port 2/1/2
  ip address 10.10.10.82/16


interface Ethernet100/1/1


interface Ethernet100/1/2


interface Ethernet100/1/3


interface Ethernet100/1/4


[output cut]
```

For the sake of brevity, I didn't include my complete running-config, but I've displayed all you really need to see.

Bringing Up an Interface

Next, I'll show you how to bring up the interface and set an IP address on it.

You can disable an interface with the interface command shutdown and enable it with the no shutdown command.

If an interface is shut down, it'll display administratively down when you use the show interfaces command—sh int for short:

```
nexus# sh int e3/9
Ethernet3/9 is down (Administratively down)[output cut]
```

I've changed devices, so this output is from a Nexus 7010 using line card 3 and port 9 on that card. Another way to check an interface's configuration is via the show running-config command. All interfaces are shut down by default. You can bring up the interface with the no shutdown command—no shut for short:

```
nexus(config)# int e3/9
nexus(config-if)# no shutdown
nexus(config-if)# show int e3/9
Ethernet3/9 is up
[output cut]
```

Configuring IP Addresses

To be able to manage your NX-OS device remotely, you really should attach an IP address to the management interface. To configure IP addresses on an interface, use the ip address command from interface configuration mode:

```
nexus(config)# int e3/9
nexus(config-if)# ip address 172.16.10.2 255.255.255.0
```

This command looks just like it does on IOS devices, but there's another way to do the same thing on a Nexus device using CIDR notation:

```
nexus(config)# int e3/9
nexus(config-if)# ip address 172.16.10.2/24
```

Please don't forget to enable the interface with the no shutdown command, and always remember to use the show interface *int* command to see if the interface is administratively shut down or not! You can also use the show running-config command to get this information.

The ip address *address mask* command starts the IP processing on the interface.

If you want to add a second subnet address to an interface, you have to use the secondary parameter. If you type another IP address and press Enter, it will replace the existing primary IP address and mask. Most of the time, you won't use secondary IP addresses, but doing so can solve some sticky situations.

So let's try it anyway... To add a secondary IP address, just use the secondary parameter:

```
nexus# con
Enter configuration commands, one per line.  End with CNTL/Z.
nexus(config)# int e3/9
nexus(config-if)# ip add 172.16.100.100/24 secondary
nexus(config-if)# show run int e3/9


!Command: show running-config interface Ethernet3/9
!Time: Tue Feb 19 18:29:15 2013


version 5.0(2a)


interface Ethernet3/9
  no ip redirects
  ip address 172.16.10.2/24
```

```
  ip address 172.16.100.100/24 secondary
  no shutdown
```

So now you know how to configure IP addresses on regular interfaces, but what about the management interface? Even though this interface is key and is usually one of the first IP addresses assigned on devices, the management interface is configured just like any other interface:

```
nexus# conf t
Enter configuration commands, one per line.  End with CNTL/Z.
nexus(config)# interface mgmt 0
nexus(config-if)# ip address 10.10.10.82 255.255.255.0
Nexus(config-if)# show run int mgmt0


!Command: show running-config interface mgmt0
!Time: Tue Feb 19 18:32:56 2013


version 5.0(2a)


interface mgmt0
  ip address 10.10.10.82/24
```

Remember that this IP address is accessible only through the management interface and not via the main ports.

Creating a Switched Virtual Interface

The switched virtual interface (SVI) originated from what is actually a very simple idea. We know we can assign IP addresses to an interface, but how do we assign an IP address to a VLAN? Well, let's say that we have a switch with four ports in VLAN 10 and we want to assign an IP address for that VLAN. To achieve this, we would just create an interface for the VLAN because an SVI elegantly provides layer 3 routing between VLANs.

Understand that an SVI or VLAN interface is not a physical interface but a logical one, and it's accessible through any of the ports on that VLAN. On a Nexus device, the Interface-VLAN or SVI feature isn't enabled by default, so if you try to create a VLAN interface, you'll get an error like this one:

```
nexus(config)# interface vlan 300
                    ^
Invalid command (interface name) at '^' marker.
nexus(config)#
```

However, if we enable the feature first, everything works great:

```
nexus(config)# feature interface-vlan
nexus(config)# interface vlan 300
nexus(config-if)# ip address 10.22.33.44 255.255.0.0
nexus(config-if)#
```

Switched virtual interfaces are typically used on devices where layer 3 routing occurs. Most often, each and every single VLAN will have its own interface and layer 3 settings. I've already shown you how to configure a variety of NX-OS interfaces, so I'm not going to be overly repetitive by demonstrating that process again. If you really can't wait and simply must have more information on Nexus layer 3 switching now, you can skip over to Chapter 10, but I recommend sticking with the flow and moving on with the rest of us.

Switchport Settings

Nexus switches have ports that can be configured to behave a lot like the ports on Catalyst switches. Switches with layer 3–capable ports can be either layer 3 or layer 2. The switchport command enables the layer 2 mode and allows for the configuration of various layer 2 settings. In the following example, port e3/9 is currently a layer 3 interface, but I'm going to use the switchport command to configure it as a layer 2 interface:

```
nexus(config)# int e3/9
nexus(config-if)# show int e3/9 switchport
Name: Ethernet3/9
  Switchport: Disabled


nexus(config-if)# switchport
nexus(config-if)# show int e3/9 switchport
Name: Ethernet3/9
  Switchport: Enabled
  Switchport Monitor: Not enabled
  Operational Mode: access
  Access Mode VLAN: 1 (default)
```

Once a port is configured as a switchport, the commands follow the same formula as they would on an IOS device. And even though the port will default to access mode, I'm going to configure a port as an access port and place it into VLAN 10 now using the switchport command:

```
nexus# conf t
Enter configuration commands, one per line.  End with CNTL/Z.
nexus(config)# int e1/20
nexus(config-if)# switchport ?
  <CR>
```

```
access       Set access mode characteristics of the interface
autostate    Include or exclude this port from vlan link up calculation
block        Block specified outbound traffic for all VLANs
description  Enter description of maximum 80 characters
host         Set port host
mode         Enter the port mode
monitor      Monitor session related traffic
monitor      Configures an interface as span-destination
priority     CoS Priority parameter
trunk        Configure trunking parameters on an interface
voice        Set voice mode characterestics of the interface


nexus(config-if)# switchport mode ?
  access      Port mode access
  fex-fabric  Port mode FEX fabric
  trunk       Port mode trunk


nexus(config-if)# switchport mode access
nexus(config-if)# switchport access ?
  vlan  Set VLAN when interface is in access mode


nexus(config-if)# switchport access vlan ?
  <1-3967,4048-4093>  VLAN ID of the VLAN when this port is in access mode


nexus(config-if)# switchport access vlan 10
nexus(config-if)#
```

The switchport mode command is used for configuring the port to be access, trunk, or FEX-fabric. FEX-fabric is required to connect to a Fabric Extender.

To view switchport settings such as VLAN, native trunk mode, and switchport status, I'll use the show interface command followed by the switchport option here:

```
nexus(config)# show int e1/1 switchport
Name: Ethernet1/1
  Switchport: Enabled
  Switchport Monitor: Not enabled
  Operational Mode: trunk
  Access Mode VLAN: 1 (default)
  Trunking Native Mode VLAN: 1 (default)
  Trunking VLANs Enabled: 1,10
  Voice VLAN: none
```

```
Extended Trust State : not trusted [COS = 0]
Administrative private-vlan primary host-association: none
Administrative private-vlan secondary host-association: none
Administrative private-vlan primary mapping: none
Administrative private-vlan secondary mapping: none
Administrative private-vlan trunk native VLAN: none
Administrative private-vlan trunk encapsulation: dot1q
Administrative private-vlan trunk normal VLANs: none
Administrative private-vlan trunk private VLANs: none
Operational private-vlan: none
Unknown unicast blocked: disabled
Unknown multicast blocked: disabled
```

Once a port has been configured as a switchport, only layer 2 commands will be available unless you execute the no switchport command on it to turn it into a layer 3 port:

```
nexus(config-if)# ip add 1.1.1.1 255.255.255.0
                    ^
% Invalid command at '^' marker.
nexus(config-if)# no switchport
nexus(config-if)# ip add 1.1.1.1 255.255.255.0
nexus(config-if)#
```

Notice that the IP address command does not work until the port is switched back to layer 3.

Understand that though layer 2 settings are generally simpler than layer 3 settings, both are equally as important for you to know.

Viewing, Saving, and Erasing Configurations

If you run through setup mode, you'll be asked if you want to use the configuration you just created. If you say yes, then it will copy the configuration running in DRAM, the running-config into NVRAM, and name the file startup-config.

You can manually save the file from DRAM, usually called RAM, to NVRAM by using the copy running-config startup-config command. The cool shortcut for that, which I'm going to use now, is copy run start:

```
nexus# copy running-config startup-config
[########################################] 100%
nexus#
```

You can also copy the running configuration to other locations:

```
nexus# copy running-config ?
  bootflash:      Select destination filesystem
  ftp:            Select destination filesystem
  nvram:          Select destination filesystem
  scp:            Select destination filesystem
  sftp:           Select destination filesystem
  startup-config  Copy from source to startup configuration
  tftp:           Select destination filesystem
  volatile:       Select destination filesystem
```

And if you want to view the files, enter the **show running-config** or **show startup-config** from privileged mode. The sh run command, which is a shortcut for show running-config, tells us that we are viewing the current configuration:

```
nexus# show run


!Command: show running-config
!Time: Tue Jan 29 11:09:20 2013


version 5.0(3)N2(2)
feature telnet
feature lldp


 [output cut]
```

The sh start command—one of the shortcuts for the show startup-config command—shows us the configuration that will be used the next time the device is reloaded. It also tells us how much NVRAM is being used to store the startup-config file. Here's an example:

```
nexus# show start


!Command: show startup-config
!Time: Tue Jan 29 11:09:43 2013
!Startup config saved at: Tue Jan 29 11:06:24 2013


version 5.0(3)N2(2)
feature telnet
feature lldp
 [output cut]
```

Deleting the Configuration and Reloading the Device

If you configure your Nexus device and decide you just want to start over, or you're studying for your CCNA and want to practice setting up a Nexus, then erasing and restarting the device is important to you! You can delete the startup-config file and reset the IP configuration of MGMT0 by using the write erase boot command:

```
nexus# write erase boot
This command will erase the boot variables and the ip configuration
of interface mgmt 0
Do you wish to proceed anyway? (y/n)  [n] y
nexus# show startup-config
No startup configuration
nexus# reload
WARNING: This command will reboot the system
Do you want to continue? (y/n) [n]
```

If you reload or power-cycle the device after using the write erase boot command, you'll be offered setup mode because there's no configuration saved in NVRAM. You can press Ctrl+C to exit setup mode at any time.

Let's say you're remotely connected to a Nexus switch and you want to reset the configuration, and yet maintain a connection to MGMT0. Can't be done? Oh yes it can—just use the write erase command without the boot option and you've nailed it. This is awesome, but you can only do this with Nexus. I dare you to try this with IOS devices!

Verifying Your Configuration

Obviously, show running-config would be the best way to verify your configuration and show startup-config would be the best way to verify the configuration that'll be used the next time the device is reloaded—right?

Well, once you take a look at the running-config and all appears to be good, you can verify your configuration with utilities like ping and Telnet. Ping is a program that uses ICMP echo requests and replies and works by sending a packet to a remote host. If the host on the receiving end responds, you know it's alive, but you don't know if it's alive and also *well*! Just because you can ping a Microsoft server does not mean you can log in! Still, ping is always a great starting point for troubleshooting an internetwork.

When you ping on a Nexus device, it assumes that you want to send the ping out of the main Ethernet interfaces and not the management port. The problem is that we often use the management port to ping, but to be able to do that from this port, you've got to first specify the correct Virtual Routing and Forward, or VRF. VRF maintains a separate routing table for the management port that's different from the other ports. VRFs were covered in detail in Chapter 7, "Introduction to Nexus."

Let's try to ping from our device that has an IP address only on the management port and see what happens:

```
nexus# ping 10.10.1.1
PING 10.10.1.1 (10.10.1.1): 56 data bytes
ping: sendto 10.10.1.1 64 chars, No route to host
Request 0 timed out
ping: sendto 10.10.1.1 64 chars, No route to host
Request 1 timed out
ping: sendto 10.10.1.1 64 chars, No route to host
Request 2 timed out
ping: sendto 10.10.1.1 64 chars, No route to host
Request 3 timed out
ping: sendto 10.10.1.1 64 chars, No route to host
Request 4 timed out


--- 10.10.1.1 ping statistics ---
5 packets transmitted, 0 packets received, 100.00% packet loss
nexus#
```

Okay, by default, it tried to ping from the main Ethernet ports, which do not have an IP address, and because there is no IP address on those ports, it cannot ping. So let's use our ever-handy question mark to explore some other ping options:

```
nexus# ping 10.10.1.1 ?
  <CR>
  count        Number of pings to send
  df-bit       Enable do not fragment bit in IP header
  interval     Wait interval seconds between sending each packet
  packet-size  Packet size to send
  source       Source IP address to use
  timeout      Specify timeout interval
  vrf          Display per-VRF information
```

Most of the options listed here are the same type of options you would have on an IOS router, such as manipulating the number of packets sent, how often to send them, and such. The new output shown here is VRF. The VRF option will allow us to choose Virtual Route Forwarding tables other than the default:

```
nexus# ping 10.10.1.1 vrf ?
  WORD        VRF name (Max Size 32)
  default     Known VRF name
  management  Known VRF name
```

The options listed after VRF will show all of the existing VRFs configured on that device. We should already know that our MGMT0 port is located in the management VRF.

Now let's try pinging using the management VRF:

```
nexus# ping 10.10.1.1 vrf management
PING 10.10.1.1 (10.10.1.1): 56 data bytes
64 bytes from 10.10.1.1: icmp_seq=0 ttl=254 time=2.773 ms
64 bytes from 10.10.1.1: icmp_seq=1 ttl=254 time=3.969 ms
64 bytes from 10.10.1.1: icmp_seq=2 ttl=254 time=3.997 ms
64 bytes from 10.10.1.1: icmp_seq=3 ttl=254 time=4.058 ms
64 bytes from 10.10.1.1: icmp_seq=4 ttl=254 time=4.106 ms


--- 10.10.1.1 ping statistics ---
5 packets transmitted, 5 packets received, 0.00% packet loss
round-trip min/avg/max = 2.773/3.78/4.106 ms
nexus#
```

This output looks very familiar. We see that five pings were successfully sent and replied to. The icmp_seq is indicating which packet in the sequences it is, the ttl is indicating time to live, and the time is showing how long it took round-trip. At the bottom under statistics, it averages the numbers above and shows you the result.

Never forget about that VRF option unless you live for frustration. It can get ugly trying to troubleshoot when you're sending packets out the wrong interfaces!

If you want to find a neighbor's Network layer address, you must either go to the switch itself or enter the **show cdp neighbor detail** command to get the Network layer addresses you need for pinging.

And you can also use an extended ping to change the default variables, as shown here:

```
nexus# ping
Vrf context to use [default] :management
Target IP address or Hostname: 10.10.1.1
Repeat count [5] :
Datagram size [56] :
Timeout in seconds [2] :
Sending interval in seconds [0] :
Extended commands [no] : yes
Source address or interface :
Data pattern [0xabcd] :
Type of service [0] :
Set DF bit in IP header [no] :
Time to live [255] :
Loose, Strict, Record, Timestamp, Verbose [None] :
```

```
Sweep range of sizes [no] :
Sending 5, 56-bytes ICMP Echos to 10.10.1.1
Timeout is 2 seconds, data pattern is 0xABCD


64 bytes from 10.10.1.1: icmp_seq=0 ttl=254 time=2.495 ms
64 bytes from 10.10.1.1: icmp_seq=1 ttl=254 time=3.928 ms
64 bytes from 10.10.1.1: icmp_seq=2 ttl=254 time=4.052 ms
64 bytes from 10.10.1.1: icmp_seq=3 ttl=254 time=4.065 ms
64 bytes from 10.10.1.1: icmp_seq=4 ttl=254 time=4.098 ms


--- 10.10.1.1 ping statistics ---
5 packets transmitted, 5 packets received, 0.00% packet loss
round-trip min/avg/max = 2.495/3.727/4.098 ms
nexus#
```

Notice that the extended ping allows me to set the repeat count higher than the default of 5 and up the datagram size too. Doing this raises the MTU and allows a much better testing of throughput! One last, critical item I want to pull out of the output and highlight is the source address interface line there in the middle. This means you can choose which interface the ping is sourced from, which can be super helpful in certain diagnostic situations!

Traceroute uses ICMP with IP time to live (TTL) time-outs to track the path a packet takes through an internetwork. This is in contrast to ping, which just finds the host and responds. Let's try it and see what we get:

```
nexus# traceroute ?
  A.B.C.D or Hostname  IP address of remote system
  WORD                 Enter Hostname


nexus# traceroute 10.28.254.254
traceroute to 10.28.254.254 (10.28.254.254), 30 hops max, 40 byte packets
 1  10.28.230.1 (10.28.230.1)  0.941 ms  0.676 ms  0.58 ms
 2  10.24.114.213 (10.24.114.213)  0.733 ms  0.7 ms  0.619 ms
 3  10.20.147.46 (10.20.147.46)  0.671 ms  0.619 ms  0.635 ms
 4  10.28.254.254 (10.28.254.254)  0.613 ms  0.628 ms  0.62 ms
```

In this example, we are sending a traceroute to 10.28.254.254. The first router (layer 3 device) that is encountered is 10.28.230.1. That is known at the first hop, and the time for each packet is listed at the end of the line. The second router in the path to 10.28.254.254 (or second hop) is 10.24.114.213. That is followed by the third hop, and the finally we reach 10.28.254.254.

That's all good, but still remember that telnet, ftp, and http are your best tools because they use IP at the Network layer and TCP at the Transport layer to create a session with a remote host. This means that if you can telnet, ftp, or http into a device, your IP connectivity just has to be good:

```
nexus# telnet ?
  A.B.C.D  Enter a valid IPv4 address
  WORD     Enter hostname  (Max Size 64)
```

The syntax for SSH is a little different because you need to specify the username on the command line:

```
nexus# ssh ?
  WORD  Enter hostname or user@hostname (Max Size 64)


nexus# ssh admin@10.10.50.30
```

If you have the choice between Telnet and SSH, always opt for the latter because an SSH session is encrypted. Never forget that anything Telnet is sent in plaintext!

Let's move on and discover how to verify the interface statistics.

Verifying with the *show interface* Command

The show interface commands are a great group to go to for verifying your configuration. The first of these is show interfaces ?, which will reveal all available interfaces to verify and configure. This sleek, highly useful command displays all configurable parameters and statistics about every interface on your device and is also great for troubleshooting an assortment of device and network issues. Let's give it a try and check out the output from a Nexus 5040:

```
nexus# show interface ?
  <CR>
  >                     Redirect it to a file
  >>                    Redirect it to a file in append mode
  brief                 Show brief info of interface
  capabilities          Show interface capabilities information
  counters              Show interface counters
  debounce              Show interface debounce time information
  description           Show interface description
  ethernet              Ethernet IEEE 802.3z
  fcoe (no abbrev)      Show FCoE info for interface
  flowcontrol           Show interface flowcontrol information
  loopback              Loopback interface
  mac-address           Show interface MAC address
  mgmt                  Management interface
```

```
port-channel          Port Channel interface
priority-flow-control Show interface PFC information
snmp-ifindex          Show snmp ifindex list
status                Show interface line status
switchport            Show interface switchport information
transceiver           Show interface transceiver information
trunk                 Show interface trunk information
untagged-cos          Show interface untagged CoS information
|                     Pipe command output to filter
```

We can see that the only "real," physical interfaces are Ethernet and mgmt. The rest are either logical interfaces or additional commands you can use as verification tools.

The next command is show interface ethernet 1/5, which will reveal the hardware address, the encapsulation method, plus a boatload of statistics:

```
nexus# sh int e1/5
Ethernet1/5 is up
  Hardware: 1000/10000 Ethernet, address: 000d.eca4.2fcc (bia 000d.eca4.2fcc)
  MTU 1500 bytes, BW 10000000 Kbit, DLY 10 usec,
      reliability 255/255, txload 1/255, rxload 1/255
  Encapsulation ARPA
  Port mode is access
  full-duplex, 10 Gb/s, media type is 10G
  Beacon is turned off
  Input flow-control is off, output flow-control is off
  Rate mode is dedicated
  Switchport monitor is off
  EtherType is 0x8100
  Last link flapped 21:35:44
  Last clearing of "show interface" counters never
  30 seconds input rate 2624 bits/sec, 328 bytes/sec, 0 packets/sec
  30 seconds output rate 304 bits/sec, 38 bytes/sec, 0 packets/sec
  Load-Interval #2: 5 minute (300 seconds)
    input rate 2.14 Kbps, 0 pps; output rate 192 bps, 0 pps
  RX
    0 unicast packets  25363 multicast packets  0 broadcast packets
    25363 input packets  26732602 bytes
    0 jumbo packets  0 storm suppression packets
    0 giants  0 input error  0 short frame  0 overrun   0 underrun
    0 watchdog  0 if down drop
```

```
   0 input with dribble  0 input discard
   0 Rx pause
TX
   0 unicast packets  42753 multicast packets  0 broadcast packets
   42753 output packets  3701470 bytes
   0 jumbo packets
   0 output errors  0 collision  0 deferred  0 late collision
   0 lost carrier  0 no carrier  0 babble
   0 Tx pause
 0 interface resets
```

This output tells us that the preceding interface is working and appears to be in good shape. You can use the show interfaces command to tell you if you are receiving errors on the interface. This command will also show you the following information:

- The maximum transmission unit (MTU), which is the maximum packet size allowed to transmit on the interface.
- The bandwidth (BW) for use with routing protocols.
- Level of reliability—255/255 means perfect!
- The load—1/255 means no load.

Let's pause for a second and look at the last output again. Can you find the bandwidth of the interface? On a Nexus, Ethernet interfaces are just rather vaguely dubbed "Ethernet," regardless of speed. But there's hope—we can see that the bandwidth is 10000000Kbit, which is really 10,000,000,000 because Kbit means to add three zeros. Thus, the bandwidth equals 10Gbits per second, or 10 Gigabit Ethernet. Problem solved!

The most important output of the show interface command is the first line, which indicates status. If the output reveals that Ethernet 1/1 is up, then the interface is up and running:

```
nexus# show interface ethernet 1/1
Ethernet1/1 is up
```

Here's an example that depicts the most common source of all our networking problems. Type in **sh int e1/22**:

```
nexus(config-if)# sh int e1/22
Ethernet1/22 is down (SFP not inserted)
```

It's telling us that there is no SFP module inserted, meaning, there's nothing plugged in! Happens all the time, right? Let's look at a slightly different example:

```
nexus(config-if)# sh int e1/2
Ethernet1/2 is down (Link not connected)
```

The interface in this scenario does in fact have a cable plugged in, but it's not receiving a signal from the other side. If one end is administratively shut down, as will be displayed next, the remote end would be show up as "administratively down":

```
nexus# sh int e1/1
Ethernet1/1 is down (Administratively down)
```

Sure enough, it is! If you want to enable the interface and bring it up, simply use the command no shutdown from interface configuration mode.

The switch tracks a legion of statistics for the interface, one of which is the number of packets sent and received, known as counters. You can clear the counters on the interface by typing the command clear counters, which will reset all the values to zero. Let's execute this command now:

```
nexus# clear counters ?
  <CR>
  interface  Clear interface counters


nexus# clear counters interface ?
  all           Clear all interface counters
  ethernet      Ethernet IEEE 802.3z
  loopback      Loopback interface
  mgmt          Management interface
  port-channel  Port Channel interface


nexus# clear counters interface ethernet 1/5
nexus#
```

Verifying with the *show ip interface* Command

The show ip interface command gives us loads of information regarding the layer 3 configurations of a device's interfaces:

```
nexus# show ip interface
IP Interface Status for VRF "default"
Vlan10, Interface status: protocol-down/link-down/admin-up, iod: 48,
  IP address: 2.2.2.2, IP subnet: 2.2.2.0/24
  IP broadcast address: 255.255.255.255
  IP multicast groups locally joined: none
  IP MTU: 1500 bytes (using link MTU)
  IP primary address route-preference: 0, tag: 0
```

```
    IP proxy ARP : disabled
    IP Local Proxy ARP : disabled
    IP multicast routing: disabled
    IP icmp redirects: enabled
    IP directed-broadcast: disabled
    IP icmp unreachables (except port): disabled
    IP icmp port-unreachable: enabled
    IP unicast reverse path forwarding: none
    IP load sharing: none
    IP interface statistics last reset: never
    IP interface software stats: (sent/received/forwarded/originated/consumed)
  [output cut]
```

In the resulting output, we can determine the status of the interface, the IP address, and the mask as well as basic IP information.

Using the *show ip interface brief* Command

The show ip interface brief command is one of the most helpful commands you'll ever use on a Nexus device. It will give you a quick overview of all the device's layer 3 interfaces, including the logical address and status. Check it out:

```
nexus# sh ip int brief
IP Interface Status for VRF "default"(1)
Interface         IP Address       Interface Status
Vlan10            2.2.2.2          protocol-up/link-up/admin-up
Vlan40            4.4.4.4          protocol-down/link-down/admin-up
```

This looks good, but where's the management interface? Remember, the management interface is not in the default VRF, so to view management interface information, you must get to the management VRF:

```
nexus# sh ip int brief ?
  <CR>
  >            Redirect it to a file
  >>           Redirect it to a file in append mode
  operational  Display only interfaces that are administratively enabled
  vrf          Display per-VRF information
  |            Pipe command output to filter


nexus# sh ip int brief vrf ?
  WORD         VRF name (Max Size 32)
  all          Display all VRFs
```

```
default      Known VRF name
management   Known VRF name
```

```
nexus# sh ip int brief vrf management
IP Interface Status for VRF "management"(2)
Interface         IP Address      Interface Status
mgmt0             10.10.10.82     protocol-up/link-up/admin-up
nexus#
```

So what's my favorite version of this command? I love the show ip int brief vrf all because it allows me to see all of the IP addresses on the switch even if they are in other VRFs!

Summary

We really got moving in this chapter! In it, I showed you around the Cisco NX-OS and I really hope you gained a lot of insight into the Nexus device world. I began by explaining the Nexus Operating System and how you can use the NX-OS to both run and configure Nexus devices. You learned how to bring a device up and what setup mode does. And because you can now basically configure Nexus devices, you know you should never, ever use setup mode, right?

After I discussed how to connect to a device with a console and LAN connection, I covered the Cisco help features and how to use the CLI to find commands and command parameters. In addition, I discussed a bunch of basic yet powerful show commands, which help you to verify your configurations.

We then explored administrative functions available on a device, which help you manage your network and verify that you're definitely configuring the correct device. You also discovered that setting device passwords properly is one of the most important configurations you can perform. In addition to all that ground, we covered how to use the hostname and interface description to help you administer, verify, and even troubleshoot your device.

And that concludes your introduction to the Cisco NX-OS.

Exam Essentials

Configure NX-OS.   The Nexus OS software can be configured from the command line. The configure command, or con for short, is used to move from user-exec mode to global configuration mode. Ctrl+Z exits any configuration mode and takes you back to user mode.

List the options available to connect to a Nexus device for management purposes.   The three options available are via the console port and auxiliary port and remotely through Telnet or SSH. The remote connection can be in-band though the main Ethernet ports or out-of-band via the management port.

Erase the saved configuration and reboot the switch.   When you want to completely reset the switch, the write erase boot command followed by the reload command will take a switch back to factory defaults. If you wish to preserve the IP configuration on the management port, just use the write erase command to reset the device.

Understand and implement SVI.   To add an IP address to a VLAN requires a switched virtual interface. This provides layer 3 routing between VLANs. SVI necessitates that the feature is enabled via the feature interface-vlan command. Once enabled, an SVI interface is created with the interface vlan command.

Understand and differentiate layer 2 and layer 3 interfaces in NX-OS.   An interface can be configured to behave as a routed port (layer 2) or a switched port (layer 2). The switchport command configures an interface as layer 2 while the no switchport statement makes the interface layer 3.

Recognize roles used for permissions in NX-OS.   NX-OS has two built-in roles for controlling what users can do on the device. The Network-Admin role is unrestricted and can make changes, while the Network-Operator role is read-only.

Access and utilize editing and help features.   Make use of the ability to type a question mark at the end of commands for help in using the commands. Additionally, understand how to filter command help with the same question mark and letters. The Tab key is useful for automatically completing a command.

Identify the information provided by the show interface command.   The show interface command will provide basic interface information. Adding the switchport options will provide additional details like VLAN and trunking information.

Set the hostname of a device.   The command sequence to set the hostname of a device is as follows:

```
enable
config t
hostname Todd
```

Describe the advantages of using Secure Shell and list its requirements.   Secure Shell uses encrypted keys to send data so that usernames and passwords are not sent in the clear. It requires that a hostname and domain name be configured and that encryption keys be generated.

Describe how to view, edit, delete, and save a configuration.   The show running-config command is used to view the current configuration being used by the device. The show startup-config command displays the last configuration that was saved and is the one that will be used at next startup. The copy running-config startup-config command is used to save changes made to the running configuration in NVRAM. The erase startup-config command deletes the saved configuration and will result in the invocation of the setup menu when the device is rebooted because there will be no configuration present.

Written Lab 8.1

You can find the answers in Appendix A.

Write out the command or commands for the following questions:

1. If you type **show inter ethernet 1/1** and notice that the port is administratively down, what commands would you execute to enable the interface?

2. If you wanted to delete the configuration stored in NVRAM and set the system completely back to factory default, what command(s) would you type?

3. If you wanted to create a username of *todd* with a password of *todd*, and the user can change the configuration, what command(s) would you type?

4. If you wanted to create a username of *todd* with a password of *todd*, and the user cannot change the configuration, what command(s) would you type?

5. You want to reinitialize the NX-OS device. What command(s) will you use?

6. How would you set the name of an NX-OS device to *Chicago*?

Hands-on Labs

In this section, you will perform commands on a Nexus device that will help you understand what you learned in this chapter.

You'll need at least one Nexus device—two would be better, three would be outstanding. The hands-on labs in this section are included for use with real Nexus devices.

It is assumed that the device you're going to use has no current configuration present. If necessary, erase any existing configuration with Hands-on Lab 8.1; otherwise, proceed to Hands-on Lab 8.2:

Lab 8.1: Erasing an Existing Configuration

Lab 8.2: Exploring User Exec and Configuration Modes

Lab 8.3: Using the Help and Editing Features

Lab 8.4: Saving an NX-OS Configuration

Lab 8.5: Setting the Hostname, Descriptions, and IP Address

Hands-on Lab 8.1: Erasing an Existing Configuration

The following lab may require the knowledge of a username and password to enter privileged mode. If the device has a configuration with an unknown username and password for privileged mode, this procedure will not be possible:

1. Start the device, and when prompted, enter the username and press Enter. Then enter the correct password and press Enter.

2. At the Switch prompt, type **write erase boot**.

3. At the privileged mode prompt, type **reload**, and when prompted to save the configuration, type **n** for no.

Hands-on Lab 8.2: Exploring User Exec and Configuration Modes

1. Turn the device on. If you just erased the configuration as in Hands-on Lab 8.1, when prompted to continue with the configuration dialog, enter **n** for no and press Enter. When prompted, press Enter to connect to your device. This will put you into user mode.

2. At the switch# prompt, type a question mark (**?**).

3. Notice the -more- at the bottom of the screen.

4. Press the Enter key to view the commands line by line. Press the spacebar to view the commands a full screen at a time. You can type **q** at any time to quit.

5. Type **config** and press Enter.

6. At the switch(config)# prompt, type a question mark (**?**), then **q** to quit, or press the spacebar to view the commands.

7. Type **interface mgmt0** and press Enter. This will allow you to configure the management interface.

8. At the Device(config-if)# prompt, type a question mark (**?**).

9. Type **exit**. Notice how this brings you back one level.

10. Press Ctrl+Z. Notice how this brings you out of configuration mode and places you back into privileged mode.

11. Type **exit**, which will log you out of the device.

Hands-on Lab 8.3: Using the Help and Editing Features

1. Log into the device.

2. Type a question mark (**?**).

3. Type **cl?** and then press Enter. Notice that you can see all the commands that start with *cl*.

4. Type **clock ?** and press Enter.

> Notice the difference between steps 3 and 4. Step 3 has you type letters with no space and a question mark, which will give you all the commands that start with *cl*. Step 4 has you type a command, space, and question mark. By doing this, you will see the next available parameter.

5. Set the router's clock by typing **clock ?** and, following the help screens, setting the device's time and date. The following steps walk you through setting the date and time.

6. Type **clock ?**.

7. Type **clock set ?**.

8. Type **clock set 10:30:30 ?**.

9. Type **clock set 10:30:30 14 May ?**.

10. Type **clock set 10:30:30 14 March 2011**.

11. Press Enter.

12. Type **show clock** to see the time and date.

13. From privileged mode, type **show int e1/1**. Don't press Enter.

14. Press Ctrl+A. This takes you to the beginning of the line.

15. Press Ctrl+E. This should take you back to the end of the line.

16. Press Ctrl+A, then Ctrl+F. This should move you forward one character.

17. Press Ctrl+B, which will move you back one character.

18. Press Enter, then press Ctrl+P. This will repeat the last command.

19. Press the up arrow key on your keyboard. This will also repeat the last command.

20. Type **show terminal** to gather terminal information.

21. Type **sh run**, then press your Tab key. This will finish typing the command for you.

22. Type **sh start**, then press your Tab key. This will finish typing the command for you.

Hands-on Lab 8.4: Saving an NX-OS Configuration

1. Log into the device.

2. To see the configuration stored in NVRAM, type **sh start** and press Tab and Enter, or type **show startup-config** and press Enter. However, if no configuration has been saved, you will get an error message.

3. To save a configuration to NVRAM, which is known as startup-config, you can do one of the following:

   ▪ Type **copy run start** and press Enter.

   ▪ Type **copy running**, press Tab, type **start**, press Tab, and press Enter.

   ▪ Type **copy running-config startup-config** and press Enter.

4. Type **sh start**, press Tab, then press Enter.

5. Type **sh run**, press Tab, then press Enter.

6. Type **write erase**, press Tab, then press Enter.

7. Type **sh start**, press Tab, then press Enter. You should get an error message.

8. Type **reload**, then press Enter. Acknowledge the reload by pressing Enter. Wait for the router to reload.

9. Say no to entering setup mode, or just press Ctrl+C.

Hands-on Lab 8.5: Setting the Hostname, Descriptions, and IP Address

1. Log into the device.

2. Set your hostname on your device by using the hostname command. Notice that it is one word. Here is an example of setting your hostname:

```
switch#config t
switch(config)#hostname switchA
switchA(config)#
```

Notice that the hostname of the switch changed in the prompt as soon as you pressed Enter.

3. You can add an IP address to an interface with the ip address command. You need to get into interface configuration mode first; here is an example of how you do that:

```
config t
int mgmt0
ip address 1.1.1.1 255.255.0.0
```

Notice that the IP address (1.1.1.1) and subnet mask (255.255.0.0) are configured on one line.

4. You can add identification to an interface by using the description command. This is useful for adding information about the connection. Here is an example:

```
config t
int mgmt0
description link to Miami
```

Review Questions

You can find the answers in Appendix B.

 The following questions are designed to test your understanding of this chapter's material. For more information on how to get additional questions, please see this book's introduction.

1. What is the minimum required command to enter global configuration mode on a Cisco Nexus switch?

   A. nexus# con

   B. nexus# configure

   C. nexus# configure global

   D. nexus# configure terminal

2. Which option would you use to exit the Cisco Nexus Operating System interface configuration mode and return to the exec prompt?

   A. nexus(config-if)#Ctrl-C nexus#

   B. nexus(config-if)#Ctrl-Z nexus#

   C. nexus(config-if)#Ctrl-E nexus#

   D. nexus(config-if)#exit nexus#

3. Which two commands would you use to erase the Cisco Nexus Operation System configuration and return the switch to factory defaults'? (Choose two.)

   A. nexus# write erase boot

   B. nexus# erase configuration

   C. nexus# erase running-configuration

   D. nexus# erase startup-configuration

   E. nexus# reboot

   F. nexus# reload

   G. nexus# shutdown

4. On a new Cisco Nexus switch, you receive an error message when you attempt to create an SVI. What is the first command you must use to create the SVI?

   A. interface vlan (vlanid)

   B. vlan (vlanid)

   C. feature interface-vlan

   D. interface routed

5. Which command should you use to configure a Cisco Nexus switch port for layer 2 operation?

    A. `nexus(config)#interface vlan 10 nexus{config-if}#switchport`

    B. `nexus(config-if)#layer-2`

    C. `nexus{config-if}#switchport`

    D. `nexus(config-if)#routed`

6. What is the Cisco Nexus Operating System command to define a port as a layer 3 port?

    A. `port routed`

    B. `no switchport`

    C. `switchport`

    D. `port switching`

7. What are the two default user roles in Cisco Nexus Operating System? (Choose two.)

    A. Admin

    B. Network-Operator

    C. Operator

    D. Storage Operator

    E. Root

    F. System Manager

8. What is the function of the Tab key on the Cisco Nexus Operating System command-line interface?

    A. Redisplays the current command line

    B. Deletes all characters from the cursor to the end of the command line

    C. Clears the terminal screen

    D. Completes a partially entered command if enough characters are present

    E. Moves the cursor one word to the right

9. Which statement correctly describes an SVI?

    A. An SVI provides layer 3 routing between VLANs.

    B. An SVI is a layer 2 interface and uses a dynamic MAC address.

    C. An SVI cannot have an IP address assigned to it.

    D. Each switchport requires an SVI assignment.

10. Which command displays the Trunking Native Mode VLAN on port Ethernet 1/18?

    A. `show running-config switchport e1/18`

    B. `show interface e1/18 native`

    C. `show interface e1/18 switchport`

    D. `show running-config e1/18 switchport`

    E. `show interface e1/18`

11. Which of the following is an example of a static default route on a Nexus device?

    A. `ip route 0.0.0.0/32 10.99.99.2`

    B. `ip route 0.0.0.0/0 Null0`

    C. `ip route 0.0.0.0/32 Null0`

    D. `ip route 0.0.0.0/32 mgmt0 10.99.99.2`

    E. `ip route 0.0.0.0/0 10.99.99.2`

12. Where does Cisco Nexus Operating System store the running configuration file?

    A. NVRAM

    B. Bootflash

    C. Volatile

    D. Flash

    E. RAM

13. Which command will delete the contents of NVRAM on a device?

    A. `delete NVRAM`

    B. `delete startup-config`

    C. `erase NVRAM`

    D. `erase start`

14. Given the following output, what is the most likely reason this interface is not receiving packets?

```
Nexus# sh ip int vlan 11
IP Interface Status for VRF "default"(1)
Vlan11, Interface status: protocol-down/link-down/admin-down, iod: 153,
  IP address: 10.20.20.3, IP subnet: 10.20.20.0/24
  IP broadcast address: 255.255.255.255
  IP multicast groups locally joined:
  224.0.0.9
  IP MTU: 1500 bytes (using link MTU)
  IP primary address route-preference: 0, tag: 0
```

```
IP proxy ARP : disabled
IP Local Proxy ARP : disabled
IP multicast routing: disabled
IP icmp redirects: enabled
IP directed-broadcast: disabled
IP icmp unreachables (except port): disabled
IP icmp port-unreachable: enabled
IP unicast reverse path forwarding: none
IP load sharing: none
IP interface statistics last reset: never
IP interface software stats: (sent/received/forwarded/originated/consumed)
  Unicast packets   : 0/0/0/0/0
  Unicast bytes     : 0/0/0/0/0
  Multicast packets : 0/0/0/0/0
  Multicast bytes   : 0/0/0/0/0
  Broadcast packets : 0/0/0/0/0
  Broadcast bytes   : 0/0/0/0/0
  Labeled packets   : 0/0/0/0/0
  Labeled bytes     : 0/0/0/0/0
```

A. A default access control list is used.

B. The interface is administratively shut down.

C. The interface is in layer 3 mode.

D. This interface is fine; there is not traffic.

15. What command would set the admin password to *cisco*?

A. `enable secret cisco`

B. `enable cisco`

C. `secret cisco`

D. `username admin password cisco`

16. What command would create a switched virtual interface for VLAN 30?

A. `interface SVI 30`

B. `interface SVI 1.30`

C. `interface VLAN 30`

D. `feature SVI 30`

17. You type the following command into the router and receive the following output:

```
switch#show ethernet 1/1
               ^
% Invalid input detected at '^' marker.
```

Why was this error message displayed?

   A. You need to be in config mode.

   B. You cannot have a space between ethernet and 1/1.

   C. You need to be in interface mode.

   D. Part of the command is missing.

18. You type switch#**sh r** and receive a % ambiguous command error. Why did you receive this message?

   A. The command requires additional options or parameters.

   B. There is more than one show command that starts with the letter *r*.

   C. There is no show command that starts with *r*.

   D. The command is being executed from the wrong router mode.

19. Which of the following commands will display the current IP addressing and the layer 1 and 2 status of an interface? (Choose two.)

   A. show version

   B. show interfaces

   C. show controllers

   D. show ip interface

   E. show running-config

20. At which layer of the OSI model would you assume the problem is if you type **show interface serial 1** and receive the following message?

```
Ethernet3/3 is down (Link not connected)
```

   A. Physical layer

   B. Data Link layer

   C. Network layer

   D. None; it is a router problem

Chapter

9

IP Routing

THE FOLLOWING TOPICS ARE COVERED IN THIS CHAPTER:

✓ **Describing the Packet Delivery Process**

- Layer 1 Devices and Their Function

- Layer 2 Devices and Their Function

- Layer 2 Addressing

- Layer 3 Devices and Their Function

- Layer 3 Addressing

- Mapping Layer 2 Addressing to Layer 3 Addressing

- ARP Table

- Host-to-Host Packet Delivery

- Function of the Default Gateway

- Using Common Host Tools to Determine the Path Between Two Hosts Across a Network

In this chapter, I'm going to discuss the IP routing process. This is an important subject to understand since it pertains to all routers and configurations that use IP. IP routing is the process of moving packets from one network to another network using routers. And as before, by routers I mean Cisco routers, of course! However, we are going to use two different devices in this chapter—an IOS router and a Nexus switch with layer 3 capability. Both devices I'll just refer to as a router because we are, well, routing in this chapter by using both devices in the same manner.

But before you read this chapter, you must understand the difference between a routing protocol and a routed protocol. A *routing protocol* is used by routers to dynamically find all the networks in the internetwork and to ensure that all routers have the same routing table. Basically, a routing protocol determines the path of a packet through an internetwork. Examples of routing protocols are RIP, RIPv2, EIGRP, and OSPF.

Once all routers know about all networks, a *routed protocol* can be used to send user data (packets) through the established enterprise. Routed protocols are assigned to an interface and determine the method of packet delivery. Examples of routed protocols are IP and IPv6.

I'm pretty sure that I don't have to tell you that this is definitely important stuff to know. You most likely understand from what I've said so far that IP routing is basically what Cisco routers do, and they do it very well. Again, this chapter is dealing with truly fundamental material—these are things you must know if you want to understand the objectives covered in this book!

In Chapter 10, "Routing Protocols," I'll be moving into dynamic routing with RIP, EIGRP, and OSPF. But first, you've really got to nail down the basics of how packets actually move through an internetwork using routers, so let's get started!

For up-to-the minute updates for this chapter, please see www.lammle.com/forum.

Routing Basics

Once you create an internetwork by connecting your networks to a router, you'll need to configure logical network addresses, such as IP addresses, to all hosts on the internetwork so that they can communicate across that internetwork.

The term *routing* is used for taking a packet from one device and sending it through the network to another device on a different network. Routers don't really care about hosts—they only care about networks and the best path to each network. The logical network address of the destination host is used to get packets to a network through a routed network, and then the hardware address of the host is used to deliver the packet from a router to the correct destination host.

If your network has no routers, then it should be apparent that you are not routing. Routers route traffic to all the networks in your internetwork. To be able to route packets, a router must know, at a minimum, the following:

- Destination address
- Neighbor routers from which it can learn about remote networks
- Possible routes to all remote networks
- The best route to each remote network
- How to maintain and verify routing information

The router learns about remote networks from neighbor routers or from an administrator. The router then builds a routing table (a map of the internetwork) that describes how to find the remote networks. If a network is directly connected, then the router already knows how to get to it.

If a network isn't directly connected to the router, the router must use one of two ways to learn how to get to the remote network: static routing, meaning that someone must hand-type all network locations into the routing table, or something called dynamic routing.

In *dynamic routing*, a protocol on one router communicates with the same protocol running on neighbor routers. The routers then update each other about all the networks they know about and place this information into the routing table. If a change occurs in the network, the dynamic routing protocols automatically inform all routers about the event. If *static routing* is used, the administrator is responsible for updating all changes by hand into all routers. Typically, in a large network, a combination of both dynamic and static routing is used.

Before we jump into the IP routing process, let's take a look at a very simple example that demonstrates how a router uses the routing table to route packets out of an interface. We'll be going into a more detailed study of the process in the next section, but what I am showing now is called the "longest match rule," which means that IP will look through a routing table for the longest match compared to the destination address of a packet. Let's take a look.

Figure 9.1 shows a simple network. Lab_A has four LAN interfaces. Looking at Figure 9.1, can you see which interface you will use to forward an IP datagram to a host with a destination IP address of 10.10.10.30?

FIGURE 9.1   A simple routing example

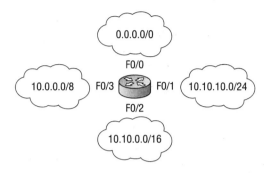

By using the command show ip route on an IOS router we can see the routing table (map of the internetwork) that Lab_A uses to make forwarding decisions:

```
Lab_A#sh ip route
[output cut]
Gateway of last resort is not set
     10.0.0.0/8 is variably subnetted, 3 subnets, 3 masks
S        10.0.0.0/8 is directly connected, FastEthernet0/3
S        10.10.0.0/16 is directly connected, FastEthernet0/2
S        10.10.10.0/24 is directly connected, FastEthernet0/1
S*       0.0.0.0/0 is directly connected, FastEthernet0/0
```

The S in the routing table output means that the networks listed are "statically configured, or administratively configured," and until we add a routing protocol—something like RIP or EIGRP—to the routers in our internetwork, by default we'd have only directly connected networks in our routing table, but in this example four static routes have been configured.

So let's get back to the original question: By looking at the figure and the output of the routing table, can you tell what IP will do with a received packet that has a destination IP address of 10.10.10.30? Well, the answer is that the router will packet-switch the packet to interface FastEthernet 0/1, and this interface will frame the packet and then send it out on the network segment. To reiterate on the longest match rule, IP would look for the destination address 10.10.10.30, and in this example, the packet would match four entries in the output, but IP would use the longest match, which means both IP address and mask, and /24 (f0/1) is the longest match.

Because we can, let's compare the IOS routing table output to a Nexus 7000 output with a similar basic configuration. First we'll configure the 10/100/1000 Ethernet card in slot 3 of the Nexus 7000 with four connections; then we'll display the routing table and discuss it.

```
Nexus7000# config
Enter configuration commands, one per line.  End with CNTL/Z.
```

```
Nexus7000(config)# int e3/1
Nexus7000(config-if)# no switchport
Nexus7000(config-if)# ip address 10.10.10.1 255.255.255.252
Nexus7000(config-if)# no shut
Nexus7000(config-if)# int e3/2
Nexus7000(config-if)# no switchport
Nexus7000(config-if)# ip address 10.10.10.17 255.255.255.240
Nexus7000(config-if)# no shut
Nexus7000(config-if)# int e3/3
Nexus7000(config-if)# no switchport
Nexus7000(config-if)# ip address 10.10.10.66 255.255.255.192
Nexus7000(config-if)# no shut
Nexus7000(config-if)# int e3/4
Nexus7000(config-if)# no switchport
Nexus7000(config-if)# ip address 10.10.1.1 255.255.255.0
Nexus7000(config-if)# no shut
Nexus7000(config-if)# sh ip route
IP Route Table for VRF "default"


'*' denotes best ucast next-hop
'**' denotes best mcast next-hop
'[x/y]' denotes [preference/metric]


10.10.1.0/24, ubest/mbest: 1/0, attached
    *via 10.10.1.1, Eth3/4, [0/0], 00:00:21, direct
10.10.1.1/32, ubest/mbest: 1/0, attached
    *via 10.10.1.1, Eth3/4, [0/0], 00:00:21, local
10.10.10.0/30, ubest/mbest: 1/0, attached
    *via 10.10.10.1, Eth3/1, [0/0], 00:05:16, direct
10.10.10.1/32, ubest/mbest: 1/0, attached
    *via 10.10.10.1, Eth3/1, [0/0], 00:05:16, local
10.10.10.16/28, ubest/mbest: 1/0, attached
    *via 10.10.10.17, Eth3/2, [0/0], 00:04:55, direct
10.10.10.17/32, ubest/mbest: 1/0, attached
    *via 10.10.10.17, Eth3/2, [0/0], 00:04:55, local
10.10.10.64/26, ubest/mbest: 1/0, attached
    *via 10.10.10.66, Eth3/3, [0/0], 00:00:15, direct
10.10.10.66/32, ubest/mbest: 1/0, attached
    *via 10.10.10.66, Eth3/3, [0/0], 00:00:15, local
```

Now that's a different routing table! If you're used to IOS, which most of us are, this is a much different output! However, once you spend some time studying this, you'll get the hang of it. Basically it is the same thing (routing is routing), but it is just displayed differently and one destination network uses four lines in the table. This is easier to understand if I try and display the output on two lines instead of four using the e3/3 interface as an example, but the lines will still wrap because of the length limitation of the book:

```
10.10.10.64/26, ubest/mbest: 1/0, attached*via 10.10.10.66, Eth3/3,
[0/0], 00:00:15, direct
10.10.10.66/32, ubest/mbest: 1/0, attached*via 10.10.10.66, Eth3/3,
[0/0], 00:00:15, local
```

First, you see the attached connected subnet 10.10.10.64/26, via the *exit_ip_address/exit interface*. Pretty much the same as an IOS output.

However, what they have listed next in this output, which is not in an IOS output, is the actual interface IP address, listed as local, in the routing table. When this IP address is the destination IP address of a packet, IP will then parse the routing table and see that this is a locally attached IP address and not forward it out to the interface, e3/3 in this example.

One last thing that is also new. The ubest/mbest:1/0 is the unicast next-hop and multicast next-hop for the listed network. Notice the 1/0, attached *via. This is telling us that there is a single unicast address considered the best next-hop. If there were two routes that were equal to the remote network destination address, then the output would display 2/0. Don't confuse this with the administrative distance/metric—it is not! Administrative distance/metric is covered in the next chapter.

Let's get into this process in more detail.

The IP Routing Process

The IP routing process is fairly simple and doesn't change, regardless of the size of your network. For an example, we'll use Figure 9.2 to describe step-by-step what happens when Host_A wants to communicate with Host_B on a different network.

FIGURE 9.2 IP routing example using two hosts and one router

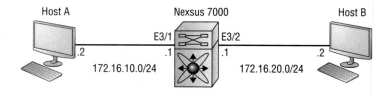

In this example, a user on Host_A pings Host_B's IP address. Routing doesn't get simpler than this, but it still involves a lot of steps. Let's work through them:

1. Internet Control Message Protocol (ICMP) creates an echo request payload (which is just the alphabet in the data field).

2. ICMP hands that payload to Internet Protocol (IP), which then creates a packet. At a minimum, this packet contains an IP source address, an IP destination address, and a Protocol field with 01h. (Remember that Cisco likes to use *0x* in front of hex characters, so this could look like 0x01.) All that tells the receiving host to whom it should hand the payload when the destination is reached—in this example, ICMP.

3. Once the packet is created, IP determines whether the destination IP address is on the local network or a remote one.

4. Since IP determines that this is a remote request, the packet needs to be sent to the default gateway so it can be routed to the remote network. The computer then determines from its configuration the default gateway.

5. The default gateway of host 172.16.10.2 (Host_A) is configured to 172.16.10.1. For this packet to be sent to the default gateway, the hardware address of the router's interface Ethernet 3/1 (configured with the IP address of 172.16.10.1) must be known. Why? So the packet can be handed down to the Data Link layer, framed, and sent to the router's interface that's connected to the 172.16.10.0 network. Because hosts communicate only via hardware addresses on the local LAN, it's important to recognize that for Host_A to communicate to Host_B, it has to send packets to the Media Access Control (MAC) address of the default gateway on the local network.

 MAC addresses are always local on the LAN and never go through and past a router.

6. Next, the Address Resolution Protocol (ARP) cache of the host is checked to see if the IP address of the default gateway has already been resolved to a hardware address:

   - If it has, the packet is then free to be handed to the Data Link layer for framing. (The hardware destination address is also handed down with that packet.) To view the ARP cache on your host, use the following command:

   ```
   C:\>arp -a
   Interface: 172.16.10.2 --- 0x3
     Internet Address      Physical Address      Type
       172.16.10.1         00-15-05-06-31-b0     dynamic
   ```

   - If the hardware address isn't already in the ARP cache of the host, an ARP broadcast is sent out onto the local network to search for the hardware address of 172.16.10.1. The router responds to the request and provides the hardware address of Ethernet 3/1, and the host caches this address.

7. Once the packet and destination hardware address are handed to the Data Link layer, the LAN driver is used to provide media access via the type of LAN being used (in this example, Ethernet). A frame is then generated, encapsulating the packet with control information. Within that frame are the hardware destination and source addresses plus, in this case, an Ether-Type field that describes the Network layer protocol that handed the packet to the Data Link layer—in this instance, IP. At the end of the frame is something called a Frame Check Sequence (FCS) field that houses the result of the cyclic redundancy check. The frame would look something like what I've detailed in Figure 9.3. It contains Host_A's hardware (MAC) address and the destination hardware address of the default gateway. It does not include the remote host's MAC address—remember that!

FIGURE 9.3   Frame used from Host_A to the Lab_A router when Host_B is pinged

Destination MAC (routers E0 MAC address)	Source MAC (Host_A MAC address)	Ether-Type field	Packet	FCS (CRC)

8. Once the frame is completed, it's handed down to the Physical layer to be put on the physical medium (in this example, twisted-pair wire) one bit at a time.

9. Every device in the collision domain receives these bits and builds the frame. They each run a CRC and check the answer in the FCS field. If the answers don't match, the frame is discarded.

   - If the CRC matches, then the hardware destination address is checked to see if it matches too (which, in this example, is the router's interface Ethernet 3/1).
   - If it's a match, then the Ether-Type field is checked to find the protocol used at the Network layer.

10. The packet is pulled from the frame, and what is left of the frame is discarded. The packet is handed to the protocol listed in the Ether-Type field—it's given to IP.

11. IP receives the packet and checks the IP destination address. Since the packet's destination address doesn't match any of the addresses configured on the receiving router itself, the router will look up the destination IP network address in its routing table.

12. The routing table must have an entry for the network 172.16.20.0 or the packet will be discarded immediately and an ICMP message will be sent back to the originating device with a destination network unreachable message.

13. If the router does find an entry for the destination network in its table, the packet is switched to the exit interface—in this example, interface Ethernet 3/2. The output below displays the Lab_A router's routing table. The C means "directly connected." No routing protocols are needed in this network since all networks (all two of them) are directly attached.

```
Nexus7K(config-if)# show ip route
[output cut]
```

```
172.16.10.0/24, ubest/mbest: 1/0, attached
    *via 172.16.10.1, Eth3/1, [0/0], 01:15:59, direct
172.16.10.1/32, ubest/mbest: 1/0, attached
    *via 172.16.10.1, Eth3/1, [0/0], 01:15:59, local
172.16.20.0/24, ubest/mbest: 1/0, attached
    *via 172.16.20.1, Eth3/2, [0/0], 00:00:19, direct
172.16.20.1/32, ubest/mbest: 1/0, attached
    *via 172.16.20.1, Eth3/2, [0/0], 00:00:19, local
```

14. The router packet-switches the packet to the Ethernet 3/2 buffer.

15. The Ethernet 3/2 buffer needs to know the hardware address of the destination host and first checks the ARP cache.

- If the hardware address of Host_B has already been resolved and is in the router's ARP cache, then the packet and the hardware address are handed down to the Data Link layer to be framed. Let's take a look at the ARP cache on the Lab_A router by using the show ip arp command:

```
Nexus7K(config-if)# sh ip arp
IP ARP Table for context default
Total number of entries: 6
Address          Age        MAC Address     Interface
172.16.10.2      00:14:47   0013.1937.e978  Ethernet3/1
172.16.20.2      00:14:40   0015.f9b6.c8a8  Ethernet3/2
```

From the output above, we can see that the router knows the 172.16.10.2 (Host_A) and 172.16.20.2 (Host_B) hardware addresses. Cisco IOS routers will keep an entry in the ARP table for 4 hours, Nexus defaults to 25 minutes.

- If the hardware address has not already been resolved, the router sends an ARP request to E3/2 looking for the hardware address of 172.16.20.2. Host_B responds with its hardware address, and the packet and destination hardware addresses are both sent to the Data Link layer for framing.

16. The Data Link layer creates a frame with the destination and source hardware addresses, Ether-Type field, and FCS field at the end. The frame is handed to the Physical layer to be sent out on the physical medium one bit at a time.

17. Host_B receives the frame and immediately runs a CRC. If the result matches what's in the FCS field, the hardware destination address is then checked. If the host finds a match, the Ether-Type field is then checked to determine the protocol that the packet should be handed to at the Network layer—IP in this example.

18. At the Network layer, IP receives the packet and runs a CRC on the IP header. If that passes, IP then checks the destination address. Since there's finally a match made, the Protocol field is checked to find out to whom the payload should be given to.

19. The payload is handed to ICMP, which understands that this is an echo request. ICMP responds to this by immediately discarding the packet and generating a new payload as an echo reply.

20. A packet is then created including the source and destination addresses, Protocol field, and payload. The destination device is now Host_A.

21. IP then checks to see whether the destination IP address is a device on the local LAN or on a remote network. Since the destination device is on a remote network, the packet needs to be sent to the default gateway.

22. The default gateway IP address is found in the Registry of the Windows device, and the ARP cache is checked to see if the hardware address has already been resolved from an IP address.

23. Once the hardware address of the default gateway is found, the packet and destination hardware addresses are handed down to the Data Link layer for framing.

24. The Data Link layer frames the packet of information and includes the following in the header:
    - The destination and source hardware addresses
    - The Ether-Type field with 0x0800 (IP) in it
    - The FCS field with the CRC result in tow

25. The frame is now handed down to the Physical layer to be sent out over the network medium one bit at a time.

26. The router's Ethernet 3/1 interface receives the bits and builds a frame. The CRC is run, and the FCS field is checked to make sure the answers match.

27. Once the CRC is found to be okay, the hardware destination address is checked. Since the router's interface is a match, the packet is pulled from the frame and the Ether-Type field is checked to see what protocol at the Network layer the packet should be delivered to.

28. The protocol is determined to be IP, so it gets the packet. IP runs a CRC check on the IP header first and then checks the destination IP address.

> IP does not run a complete CRC as the Data Link layer does—it only checks the header for errors.

Since the IP destination address doesn't match any of the router's interfaces, the routing table is checked to see whether it has a route to 172.16.10.0. If it doesn't have a route over to the destination network, the packet will be discarded immediately. (This is the source point of confusion for a lot of administrators—when a ping fails, most people think the packet never reached the destination host. But as we see here, that's not *always* the case. All it takes is for just one of the remote routers to be lacking a route back to the originating host's network and—*poof!*—the packet is dropped on the *return trip*, not on its way to the host.)

> Just a quick note to mention that when (if) the packet is lost on the way back to the originating host, you will typically see a request timed out message because it is an unknown error. If the error occurs because of a known issue, such as if a route is not in the routing table on the way to the destination device, you will see a destination unreachable message. This should help you determine if the problem occurred on the way to the destination or on the way back.

29. In this case, the router does know how to get to network 172.16.10.0—the exit interface is Ethernet 3/1—so the packet is switched to interface Ethernet 3/1.

30. The router checks the ARP cache to determine whether the hardware address for 172.16.10.2 has already been resolved.

31. Since the hardware address to 172.16.10.2 is already cached from the originating trip to Host_B, the hardware address and packet are handed to the Data Link layer.

32. The Data Link layer builds a frame with the destination hardware address and source hardware address and then puts IP in the Ether-Type field. A CRC is run on the frame and the result is placed in the FCS field.

33. The frame is then handed to the Physical layer to be sent out onto the local network one bit at a time.

34. The destination host receives the frame, runs a CRC, checks the destination hardware address, and looks in the Ether-Type field to find out whom to hand the packet to.

35. IP is the designated receiver, and after the packet is handed to IP at the Network layer, it checks the Protocol field for further direction. IP finds instructions to give the payload to ICMP, and ICMP determines the packet to be an ICMP echo reply.

36. ICMP acknowledges that it has received the reply by sending an exclamation point (!) to the user interface. ICMP then attempts to send four more echo requests to the destination host.

You've just experienced Todd's 36 easy steps to understanding IP routing. The key point to understand here is that if you had a much larger network, the process would be the *same*. In a really big internetwork, the packet just goes through more hoops before it finds the destination host.

It's super-important to remember that when Host_A sends a packet to Host_B, the destination hardware address used is the default gateway's Ethernet interface. Why? Because frames can't be placed on remote networks—only local networks. So packets destined for remote networks must go through the default gateway.

Let's take a look at Host_A's ARP cache now:

```
C:\ >arp -a
Interface: 172.16.10.2 --- 0x3
  Internet Address      Physical Address       Type
    172.16.10.1         00-15-05-06-31-b0      dynamic
    172.16.20.1         00-15-05-06-31-b0      dynamic
```

Did you notice that the hardware (MAC) address that Host_A uses to get to Host_B is the Lab_A E3/1 interface? Hardware addresses are *always* local, and they never pass a router's interface. Understanding this process is as important as air to you, so carve this into your memory!

Testing Your IP Routing Understanding

I really want to make sure you understand IP routing because it's super-important. So I'm going to use this section to test your understanding of the IP routing process by having you look at a couple of figures and answer some very basic IP routing questions.

Figure 9.4 shows a LAN connected to RouterA, which is, in turn, connected via a WAN link to RouterB. RouterB has a LAN connected with an HTTP server attached.

FIGURE 9.4 IP routing example 1

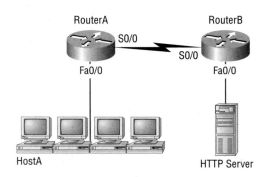

The critical information you need to glean from this figure is exactly how IP routing will occur in this example. Okay—we'll cheat a bit. I'll give you the answer, but then you should go back over the figure and see if you can answer example 2 without looking at my answers.

1. The destination address of a frame, from HostA, will be the MAC address of the Fa0/0 interface of the RouterA router.

2. The destination address of a packet will be the IP address of the network interface card (NIC) of the HTTP server.

3. The destination port number in the segment header will be 80.

That example was a pretty simple one, and it was also very to the point. One thing to remember is that if multiple hosts are communicating to the server using HTTP, they must all use a different source port number. That is how the server keeps the data separated at the Transport layer.

Let's mix it up a little and add another internetworking device into the network and then see if you can find the answers. Figure 9.5 shows a network with only one router but two switches.

FIGURE 9.5   IP routing example 2

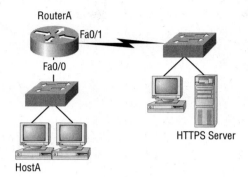

What you want to understand about the IP routing process here is what happens when HostA sends data to the HTTPS server:

1. The destination address of a frame, from HostA, will be the MAC address of the Fa0/0 interface of the RouterA router.

2. The destination address of a packet will be the IP address of the network interface card (NIC) of the HTTPS server.

3. The destination port number in the segment header will have a value of 443.

Notice that the switches weren't used as either a default gateway or another destination. That's because switches have nothing to do with routing. I wonder how many of you chose the switch as the default gateway (destination) MAC address for HostA? If you did, don't feel bad—just take another look with that fact in mind. It's very important to remember that the destination MAC address will always be the router's interface—if your packets are destined for outside the LAN, as they were in these last two examples.

Before we move into some of the more advanced aspects of IP routing, let's discuss ICMP in more detail, as well as how ICMP is used in an internetwork. Take a look at the network shown in Figure 9.6. Ask yourself what will happen if the LAN interface of router Lab_C goes down.

FIGURE 9.6   ICMP error example

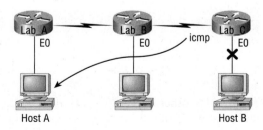

Lab_C will use ICMP to inform Host A that Host B can't be reached, and it will do this by sending an ICMP destination unreachable message. The point of this figure is to help you visualize how ICMP data is routed via IP back to the originating station.

Let's look at another problem. Look at the output of a corporate router's IOS routing table:

```
Corp#sh ip route
[output cut]
R    192.168.215.0 [120/2] via 192.168.20.2, 00:00:23, Serial0/0
R    192.168.115.0 [120/1] via 192.168.20.2, 00:00:23, Serial0/0
R    192.168.30.0 [120/1] via 192.168.20.2, 00:00:23, Serial0/0
C    192.168.20.0 is directly connected, Serial0/0
C    192.168.214.0 is directly connected, FastEthernet0/0
```

What do we see here? If I were to tell you that the corporate router received an IP packet with a source IP address of 192.168.214.20 and a destination address of 192.168.22.3, what do you think the Corp router will do with this packet?

If you said, "The packet came in on the FastEthernet 0/0 interface, but since the routing table doesn't show a route to network 192.168.22.0 (or a default route), the router will discard the packet and send an ICMP destination unreachable message back out interface FastEthernet 0/0," you're a genius! The reason it does this is because that's the source LAN from which the packet originated.

Now, let's check out another figure and talk about the frames and packets in detail. Really, we're not exactly chatting about anything new; we're just making sure that you totally, completely, fully understand basic IP routing. That's because this book, and the exam objectives it's geared toward, are all about IP routing, which means you need to be all over this stuff! We'll use Figure 9.7 for the next few questions.

FIGURE 9.7   Basic IP routing using MAC and IP addresses

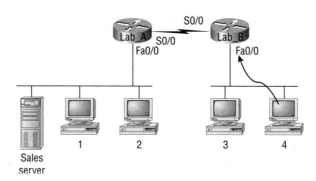

Referring to Figure 9.7, here's a list of all the questions you need the answers to emblazoned in your brain:

1. In order to begin communicating with the Sales server, Host 4 sends out an ARP request. How will the devices exhibited in the topology respond to this request?

2. Host 4 has received an ARP reply. Host 4 will now build a packet, then place this packet in the frame. What information will be placed in the header of the packet that leaves Host 4 if Host 4 is going to communicate to the Sales server?

3. At last, the Lab_A router has received the packet and will send it out Fa0/0 onto the LAN toward the server. What will the frame have in the header as the source and destination addresses?

4. Host 4 is displaying two web documents from the Sales server in two browser windows at the same time. How did the data find its way to the correct browser windows?

The following should probably be written in a teensy font and put upside down in another part of the book so it would be really hard for you to cheat and peek, but since it's actually you who's going to lose out if you peek, here are your answers:

1. In order to begin communicating with the server, Host 4 sends out an ARP request. How will the devices exhibited in the topology respond to this request? Since MAC addresses must stay on the local network, the Lab_B router will respond with the MAC address of the Fa0/0 interface and Host 4 will send all frames to the MAC address of the Lab_B Fa0/0 interface when sending packets to the Sales server.

2. Host 4 has received an ARP reply. Host 4 will now build a packet, then place this packet in the frame. What information will be placed in the header of the packet that leaves Host 4 if Host 4 is going to communicate to the Sales server? Since we're now talking about packets, not frames, the source address will be the IP address of Host 4 and the destination address will be the IP address of the Sales server.

3. Finally, the Lab_A router has received the packet and will send it out Fa0/0 onto the LAN toward the server. What will the frame have in the header as the source and destination addresses? The source MAC address will be the Lab_A router's Fa0/0 interface, and the destination MAC address will be the Sales server's MAC address. (All MAC addresses must be local on the LAN.)

4. Host 4 is displaying two web documents from the Sales server in two different browser windows at the same time. How did the data find its way to the correct browser windows? TCP port numbers are used to direct the data to the correct application window.

Great! But we're not quite done yet. I've got a few more questions for you before you actually get to configure routing in a real network. Ready? Figure 9.8 shows a basic network, and Host 4 needs to get email. Which address will be placed in the destination address field of the frame when it leaves Host 4?

The answer is that Host 4 will use the destination MAC address of the Fa0/0 interface of the Lab_B router—which I'm so sure you knew, right? Look at Figure 9.8 again: Host 4 needs to communicate with Host 1. Which OSI layer 3 source address will be placed in the packet header when it reaches Host 1?

Hopefully you know this: At layer 3, the source IP address will be Host 4 and the destination address in the packet will be the IP address of Host 1. Of course, the destination MAC address from Host 4 will always be the Fa0/0 address of the Lab_B router, right? And since we have more than one router, we'll need a routing protocol that communicates between both of them so that traffic can be forwarded in the right direction to reach the network in which Host 1 is attached.

FIGURE 9.8   Testing basic routing knowledge

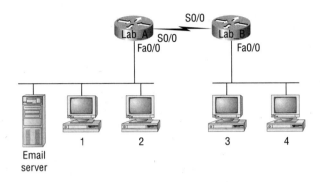

Okay—one more question and you're on your way to being an IP routing genius! Again, using Figure 9.8, Host 4 is transferring a file to the email server connected to the Lab_A router. What would be the layer 2 destination address leaving Host 4? Yes, I've asked this question more than once. But not this one: What will be the source MAC address when the frame is received at the email server?

Hopefully, you answered that the layer 2 destination address leaving Host 4 will be the MAC address of the Fa0/0 interface of the Lab_B router and that the source layer 2 address that the email server will receive will be the Fa0/0 interface of the Lab_A router.

If you did, you're all set to get the skinny on how IP routing is handled in a larger network.

Summary

This chapter covered IP routing in detail. It's extremely important that you really understand the basics we covered in this chapter because everything that's done on a Nexus switch typically will have some type of IP routing configured and running.

You learned in this chapter how IP routing uses frames to transport packets between routers and to the destination host.

In the next chapter, we'll continue on with dynamic routing protocols.

Exam Essentials

Describe the basic IP routing process.   You need to remember that the frame changes at each hop but that the packet is never changed or manipulated in any way until it reaches the destination device (the TTL field in the IP header is decremented for each hop, but that's it!).

List the information required by a router to successfully route packets.   To be able to route packets, a router must know, at a minimum, the destination address, the location of neighboring routers through which it can reach remote networks, possible routes to all remote networks, the best route to each remote network, and how to maintain and verify routing information.

Describe how MAC addresses are used during the routing process.   A MAC (hardware) address will only be used on a local LAN. It will never pass a router's interface. A frame uses MAC (hardware) addresses to send a packet on a LAN. The frame will take the packet to either a host on the LAN or a router's interface (if the packet is destined for a remote network). As packets move from one router to another, the MAC addresses used will change but normally the original source and destination IP addresses within the packet will not.

Written Lab 9

You can find the answers in Appendix A.

Write the answers to the following questions:

1. True/False: To reach a destination host, you must know the MAC address of the remote host.

2. When a PC sends a packet to another PC in a remote network, what destination IP address and MAC address will be in the frame that it sends to its default gateway?

3. True/False: To reach a destination host, you must know the IP address of the remote host.

4. In what situation will a router forward a frame?

5. If a destination IP address in a packet can't be found, what will the IP do with the packet?

Review Questions

You can find the answers in Appendix B.

The following questions are designed to test your understanding of this chapter's material. For more information on how to get additional questions, please see this book's introduction.

1. What destination addresses will be used by HostA to send data to the HTTPS server as shown in the following network? (Choose two.)

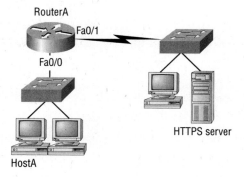

A. The IP address of the switch

B. The MAC address of the remote switch

C. The IP address of the HTTPS server

D. The MAC address of the HTTPS server

E. The IP address of RouterA's Fa0/0 interface

F. The MAC address of RouterA's Fa0/0 interface

2. Which of the following would be true if HostA is trying to communicate to HostB and the interface F0/0 of RouterC goes down, as shown in the following graphic? (Choose two.)

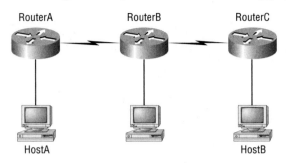

RouterA   RouterB   RouterC

HostA   HostB

   A. RouterC will use an ICMP to inform HostA that HostB cannot be reached.

   B. RouterC will use ICMP to inform RouterB that HostB cannot be reached.

   C. RouterC will use ICMP to inform HostA, RouterA, and RouterB that HostB cannot be reached.

   D. RouterC will send a destination unreachable message type.

   E. RouterC will send a router selection message type.

   F. RouterC will send a source quench message type.

3. What addresses change at each hop a packet takes?

   A. IP addresses

   B. Port numbers

   C. Layer 2 addresses

   D. Segments

4. Your router receives a packet with a destination IP address not found in the routing table. What will the IP do with this packet?

   A. Broadcast it out all interfaces.

   B. Flood it out all interfaces except the one it was received on.

   C. Discard the packet and send an ICMP error message back out the interface it was received on.

   D. Discard the packet and send an ICMP error message back out the interface it was destined for.

5. If your host has a packet destined for a remote network, what local address will your host look for?

    A. The IP address of the closest server

    B. The IP address of the default gateway

    C. The IP address of the closest server

    D. The MAC address of the default gateway

6. What protocols will the IP use when you ping a local address from your host? (Choose two.)

    A. TCP

    B. IP

    C. ARP

    D. ICMP

7. To be able to route a packet, which at a minimum does your router need to know? (Choose two.)

    A. The destination address

    B. The source address

    C. The possible routes to each network

    D. The port number in the segment header

8. When two hosts are trying to communicate across a network, how does the host originating the communication determine the hardware address of the host that it wants to communicate to?

    A. RARP request

    B. Show Network Address request

    C. Proxy ARP request

    D. ARP request

    E. Show Hardware Address request

9. An administrator attempts a traceroute but receives destination unreachable message. Which protocol is responsible for that message?

   A. RARP

   B. RUDP

   C. ICMP

   D. SNMP

10. To be able to route a packet, which of the following does your router need to know? (Choose two.)

   A. The location of neighbor routers

   B. The hardware address of the remote router

   C. How to maintain and verify routing information

   D. The application being used and VLAN information

Chapter

10

Routing Protocols

THE FOLLOWING TOPICS ARE COVERED IN THIS CHAPTER:

✓ **Exploring the Routing Process**

- Routing Tables

- Distance Vector Routing Protocols

✓ **Exploring Routing Protocols**

- Routing Information Protocol

IP routing is essentially the process of moving packets from one network to another network via routers. To be able to forward packets, routers need an accurate map of their internetworks to refer to, called a routing table. Routing tables can be creating manually, a process known as static routing, but going with this method is a lot of work—especially if you're dealing with a decent sized network! The much easier alternative is dynamic routing, which uses protocols to find networks and update routing tables. But in networking as in life, there's no free lunch, and dynamic routing will cost you in bandwidth on your network's links as well as in router CPU processing.

Routing protocols define the set of rules used by a router when it communicates routing information between neighboring routers.

The first dynamic routing protocol I'm going to cover is Routing Information Protocol, or RIP, versions 1 and 2. RIP is only used in small networks now.

Enhanced Interior Gateway Routing Protocol (EIGRP) is a Cisco protocol that predictably runs on Cisco routers and is very important because it's one of the two most popular routing protocols in use today. We'll explore some of the features of EIGRP, and then I'll describe how it works and demonstrate how to configure it with the Nexus operating system, the NX-OS.

After that, you'll be introduced to the Open Shortest Path First (OSPF) routing protocol. OSPF is the most popular routing protocol in use today, especially in data center environments. First, I'll define some vital OSPF terms and then move on by showing you how the protocol works internally. I'll wrap up the chapter by detailing OSPF's advantages over RIP, and finally, you'll learn how to configure OSPF on the NX-OS.

For up-to-the minute updates for this chapter, please see www.lammle.com/forum.

Dynamic Routing

Even though I'm going to show you how to configure static routing on Nexus, dynamic routing will be our focus in this chapter and we're really going to zero in on routing protocols within the NX-OS environment. We'll start with RIP and then move on to EIGRP and OSPF.

But first you need to know that there are two types of routing protocols used in inter-networks: interior gateway protocols (IGPs) and exterior gateway protocols (EGPs). IGPs are used to exchange routing information between routers within the same autonomous system, or AS. An AS is a collection of networks under a common administrative domain in which all routers sharing the same routing table information are included. EGPs, like Border Gateway Protocol (BGP), enable communication between autonomous systems, but that's beyond the scope of this book so I won't be covering it here.

Routing protocols basically drive dynamic routing, so I'm going to give you some foundational information about them next. We'll start with a discussion about administrative distances and the three different kinds of routing protocols.

Routing Protocol Basics

The first and most foundational concept you need to be familiar with is that of administrative distances, referred to as the AD, which is used to rate just how trustworthy the routing information from a neighboring router actually is.

Administrative Distances

An AD is actually an integer ranging from 0 to 255, where 0 is the most trusted and 255 is the least. A value of 255 means no traffic will be passed via this route at all!

If a router receives two updates listing the same remote network, the router will simply check the AD and add the route with the lowest value into the routing table.

Sounds simple, but sometimes both advertised routes to the same network have the same AD. When that happens, then routing protocol metrics like *hop count* and the line's band-width come into play to choose the best path to the remote network. The advertised route with the lowest metric will be placed in the routing table, but if both advertised routes have the same AD as well as the same metrics, then the routing protocol will load-balance to the remote network by sending packets down each equal distance link.

Table 10.1 lists the default administrative distances that a Cisco router uses to decide which route to take to a remote network.

TABLE 10.1 Default administrative distances

Route Source	Default AD
Connected interface	0
Static route	1
EIGRP	90
OSPF	110

TABLE 10.1   Default administrative distances *(continued)*

Route Source	Default AD
RIP	120
External EIGRP	170
Unknown	255 (This route will never be used.)

Always remember that when a network is directly connected, the router will always use the interface connected to that network. Also, if you configure a static route, the router will then believe that route over any other learned routes no matter what. You can change the administrative distance of static routes, but by default, they have an AD of 1. What this means is that if we change the AD of a static route to a higher number, we can then configure routing protocols without having to remove the static routes, which is good because they'll be used as backup routes in case the routing protocol experiences some type of failure. These are typically referred to as floating static routes.

So understand that if you have a static route, a RIP advertised route, and an EIGRP-advertised route all listing the same network, by default, the router will always use the static route unless you change the static route's AD to a value greater than 1.

Routing Protocols

There are three classes of routing protocols:

Distance Vector   The *distance-vector protocols* in use today use distance to determine the best path to a remote network. RIP's strategy for doing this is to keep track of each time a packet goes through a router, known as a *hop*. The route with the least number of hops to the network will be chosen as the best one.

The vector part of the name simply indicates the direction to the remote network. RIP is a very popular distance-vector routing protocols and periodically sends the entire routing table to directly connected neighbors.

Link State   In environments using *link-state protocols*, also called *shortest-path-first protocols*, the routers existing in them each create three separate tables:

- A table to keep track of directly attached neighbors
- A table for referencing the topology of the entire internetwork
- A table to be used as the routing table

As you can see, link-state routers definitely accrue a lot more information and therefore know more about the internetwork than routers using a distance-vector routing protocol ever will. Routers running link-state protocols like OSPF send updates containing the status or state of their own links to all other directly connected routers on the network. This information is then propagated to each of their neighbors.

Hybrid   *Hybrid protocols* like EIGRP use aspects of both distance vector and link state. Cisco typically refers to EIGRP as advanced distance vector, or just distance vector, but in the past they have referred to EIGRP as a hybrid.

There just isn't a set rule for choosing and configuring routing protocols. You really have to do it on a case-by-case basis, so having a working knowledge of exactly how the different routing protocols work will enable you to make solid network design decisions that will fully meet the individual needs of any client and/or business.

Now it's time to go deeper into the specifications of each of these different routing protocols, beginning with a closer examination of the distance-vector class.

Distance-Vector Routing Protocols

The distance-vector routing algorithm works by making routers pass their entire routing table's contents on to neighboring routers. The neighbor routers then incorporate the routing table entries they've received into their own routing tables. This is called routing by rumor because a router that receives an update from a neighbor router totally believes the information about remote networks without confirming it!

As mentioned, it's entirely possible for a network to have multiple links to the same remote network. In this scenario, the administrative distance of each update that a router receives is checked first, and if it's the same, the protocol will then rely on metrics to determine the best path.

RIP simply uses hop count to decide the best path to a network. If it finds more than one link with the same hop count to the same remote network, it will automatically opt to load-balance. RIP can perform round-robin load balancing for up to 16 equal-cost links but only eight by default.

Routing Information Protocol

Routing Information Protocol (RIP) is a true distance-vector routing protocol. It sends the complete routing table out to all active interfaces every 30 seconds and uses only hop count to determine the best way to a remote network. RIP has a maximum allowable hop count of 15 by default, meaning that 16 is viewed as unreachable. RIP works well in small networks, but it's really inefficient on large networks with lots of routers or those with slow WAN links.

RIP version 1 uses only *classful routing*, which means that all devices in the network must use the same subnet mask. This is because RIP version 1 doesn't send updates that include the subnet mask information. RIP version 2 adds a feature called *prefix routing* and includes the subnet mask information along with route updates. This is called *classless routing*.

🌐 Real World Scenario

Should Anyone Really Use RIP in a Modern Internetwork?

Let's say you've been hired as a consultant to install a couple of Cisco Nexus switches into a growing network. Your client just happens to have a couple of old Unix routers that they want to keep installed and that don't support any other routing protocol except RIP. Guess this means you just have to run RIP on the entire network, right?

Well, yes and no. Even though you have to run RIP on a router connecting to that old Unix router network, you certainly don't need to run RIP throughout the whole inter-network! No way... Instead, you're going to opt for *redistribution*, which is basically a means of translating from one type of routing protocol to another. This way, you can support those old routers using RIP and ensure that RIP routes won't be propagated throughout the internetwork, eating up your precious bandwidth. Plus, it lets you implement a more efficient protocol like Enhanced IGRP on the rest of your network!

RIP Version 2

RIP version 2 (RIPv2) is mostly the same as RIP version 1. They're both distance-vector protocols, which means that each router running them will send its complete routing table out to all active interfaces at periodic time intervals. Also, the timers and loop-avoidance schemes, such as hold-down timers and split horizon rules, are the same in both RIP versions. Both RIPv1 and RIPv2 are configured using classful addressing, but as I said, RIPv2 is considered classless because subnet information is included with each route update. Both versions have the same AD of 120.

There are some key differences that make RIPv2 more scalable than RIPv1, but I definitely don't recommend using either RIP version in your network. RIP's big virtue is that it is an open standard and you can use it with any flavor router, as just described in the sidebar "Should Anyone Really Use RIP in a Modern Internetwork?" And remember that RIP is still an exam objective.

It's just that OSPF is worlds better and it also happens to be open standard. RIP requires way too much bandwidth, making it terribly inefficient to use in the vast majority of today's networks. Why go there when you have other, more elegant options available?

Table 10.2 delimits the differences between RIPv1 and RIPv2.

TABLE 10.2   RIPv1 vs. RIPv2

RIPv1	RIPv2
Distance vector	Distance vector
Maximum hop count of 15	Maximum hop count of 15

RIPv1	RIPv2
Classful	Classless
Broadcast based	Uses multicast 224.0.0.9
No support for VLSM	Supports VLSM networks
No authentication	Allows for MD5 authentication
No support for discontiguous networks	Supports discontiguous networks

Don't forget that RIPv2, unlike RIPv1, is a classless routing protocol, meaning that it includes subnet information with route updates even though it is configured as classful, like RIPv1. This is an important distinction because by sending the subnet mask information with the updates, RIPv2 can support Variable Length Subnet Masks (VLSMs) as well as the summarization of network boundaries. By the way, this can and does cause more harm than good in our present day network designs! Another key difference is that RIPv2 can support discontiguous networking if you disable the auto-summarization feature.

RIPv2 is classless and supports VLSM and discontiguous networks. Nexus switches do not run RIPv1. When RIP is enabled on NX-OS, NX-OS runs only RIPv2 and auto-summarization is disabled—wonderful news to all of us!

EIGRP Features and Operation

Enhanced IGRP (EIGRP) is a classless, enhanced distance-vector protocol that uses the concept of an autonomous system, or AS, to describe the set of contiguous routers that run the same routing protocol and share routing information. EIGRP is classless, so it includes the subnet mask in its route updates. And as you now know, the ability to advertise subnet information allows us the freedom to use Variable Length Subnet Masks (VLSMs) and manual summarization when designing our networks!

People sometimes refer to EIGRP as a *hybrid routing protocol, but Cisco typically refers to EIGRP as advanced distance vector* because it has characteristics of both distance-vector and link-state protocols. For example, EIGRP doesn't send link-state packets as OSPF does. Instead, it sends traditional distance-vector updates containing information about networks plus the cost of reaching them from the perspective of the advertising router. But EIGRP synchronizes topology tables between neighbors at startup and then sends specific updates only when topology changes occur, which is a definite link-state characteristic. This flexibility makes EIGRP suitable for huge networks; it has a maximum hop count of 255, with the default set to 100. But please don't get confused by what I just said—EIGRP does *not* use hop count as a metric as RIP does! In EIGRP-speak, *hop count* refers to how many routers an

EIGRP route update packet can pass through before it will be discarded. This effectively limits the size of the AS but has absolutely no bearing whatsoever on how metrics are calculated!

There are a number of powerful features that make EIGRP a real standout from other protocols. The main ones are listed here:

- Support for IP and IPv6 (and some other useless routed protocols) via protocol-dependent modules
- Considered classless (same as RIPv2 and OSPF)
- Support for VLSM/CIDR
- Support for summaries and discontiguous networks
- Efficient neighbor discovery
- Communication via Reliable Transport Protocol (RTP)
- Best path selection via Diffusing Update Algorithm (DUAL)

Another source of confusion is the fact that Cisco often calls EIGRP a distance-vector routing protocol or sometimes even an advanced distance vector. As I said, EIGRP is also called a hybrid routing protocol—don't let this confuse you!

Neighbor Discovery

Before EIGRP routers are willing to exchange routes with each other, they must become neighbors. There are three conditions that must be met for neighborship establishment:

- Hellos received
- AS numbers match
- Identical metrics (K values)

Link-state protocols tend to use Hello messages to establish neighborship (also called adjacency) because they normally do not send out periodic route updates and there has to be some mechanism to help neighbors realize when a new peer has moved in or an old one has left or gone down. To maintain the neighborship relationship, EIGRP routers must also continue receiving Hellos from their neighbors.

EIGRP routers that belong to different autonomous systems (ASes) don't automatically share routing information and they don't become neighbors. This behavior can be a real benefit when used in larger networks to reduce the amount of route information propagated through a specific AS. The only catch is that you might have to take care of redistribution between the different ASes manually.

The only time EIGRP advertises its complete information is when it discovers a new neighbor and forms an adjacency with it through the exchange of Hello packets. When this happens, both neighbors advertise all their information to one another. After each has learned its neighbor's routes, only changes to the routing table are propagated from then on.

When EIGRP routers receive their neighbors' updates, they store them in a local topology table. This table contains all known routes from all known neighbors and serves as the raw material from which the best routes are selected and placed into the routing table.

Let's define some terms before we move on:

Feasible distance (FD)   This is the best metric among all paths to a remote network, including the metric to the neighbor that is advertising that remote network. The route with the lowest FD is the route that you will find in the routing table because it is considered the best path. The metric of a feasible distance is the metric reported by the neighbor (called reported or advertised distance) plus the metric to the neighbor reporting the route.

Reported/advertised distance (AD)   This is the metric of a remote network, as reported by a neighbor. It is also the routing table metric of the neighbor and is the same as the second number in parentheses as displayed in the topology table, the first number being the feasible distance.

Neighbor table   Each router keeps state information about adjacent neighbors. When a newly discovered neighbor is learned, the address and interface of the neighbor are recorded, and this information is held in the neighbor table, stored in RAM. There is one neighbor table for each protocol-dependent module. Sequence numbers are used to match acknowledgments with update packets. The last sequence number received from the neighbor is recorded so that out-of-order packets can be detected.

Topology table   The topology table is populated by the protocol-dependent modules and acted upon by the Diffusing Update Algorithm (DUAL). It contains all destinations advertised by neighboring routers, holding each destination address and a list of neighbors that have advertised the destination. For each neighbor, the advertised metric (distance), which comes only from the neighbor's routing table, is recorded as well as the FD. If the neighbor is advertising this destination, it must be using the route to forward packets.

The neighbor and topology tables are stored in RAM and maintained through the use of Hello and update packets. Yes, the routing table is also stored in RAM, but the information stored in the routing table is gathered only from the topology table.

Feasible successor   A feasible successor is a path whose advertised distance is less than the feasible distance of the current successor, and it is considered a backup route. EIGRP will keep up to 16 feasible successors in the topology table. Only the one with the best metric (the successor) is copied and placed in the routing table. The show ip eigrp topology command will display all the EIGRP feasible successor routes known to a router.

A feasible successor is a backup route and is stored in the topology table. A successor route is stored in the topology table and is copied and placed in the routing table.

Successor   A successor route (think successful!) is the best route to a remote network. A successor route is used by EIGRP to forward traffic to a destination and is stored in the routing table. It is backed up by a feasible successor route that is stored in the topology table—if one is available.

By using the successor, and having feasible successors in the topology table as backup links, the network can converge instantly, and updates to any neighbor make up the only traffic sent from EIGRP.

Reliable Transport Protocol

EIGRP uses a proprietary protocol called *Reliable Transport Protocol (RTP)* to manage the communication of messages between EIGRP-speaking routers. And as the name suggests, reliability is a key concern of this protocol. Cisco has designed a mechanism that leverages multicasts and unicasts to deliver updates quickly and to track the receipt of the data.

When EIGRP sends multicast traffic, it uses the Class D address 224.0.0.10. Each EIGRP router is aware of who its neighbors are, and for each multicast it sends out, it maintains a list of the neighbors who have replied. If EIGRP doesn't get a reply from a neighbor, it will switch to using unicasts to resend the same data. If it still doesn't get a reply after 16 unicast attempts, the neighbor is declared dead. People often refer to this process as *reliable multicast*.

Routers keep track of the information they send by assigning a sequence number to each packet. With this technique, it's possible for them to detect the arrival of old, redundant, or out-of-sequence information.

Being able to do these things is highly important because EIGRP is a quiet protocol. It depends upon its ability to synchronize topology databases at start-up time and then maintain the consistency of databases over time by communicating only when a change occurs.

Diffusing Update Algorithm

EIGRP uses *Diffusing Update Algorithm (DUAL)* for selecting and maintaining the best path to each remote network. This algorithm allows for the following:

- Determining a backup route if one is available
- Support of VLSMs
- Dynamic route recoveries
- Queries for an alternate route if no feasible successor route can be found

DUAL provides EIGRP with possibly the fastest route convergence time among all protocols. The key to EIGRP's speedy convergence is twofold: First, EIGRP routers maintain a copy of all of their neighbors' routes, which they use to calculate their own cost to each remote network. So if the best path goes down, the solution may be as simple as examining the contents of the topology table to select the best replacement route. Second, if there isn't a good alternative in the local topology table, EIGRP routers very quickly ask their neighbors for help finding one. This reliance upon neighbor routers, plus the behavior of leveraging the information obtained from them, accounts for the "diffusing" quality attributed to DUAL.

The EIGRP Hello protocol enables the rapid detection of new or dead neighbors, and RTP provides a reliable mechanism for conveying and sequencing update, query, and query response messages. DUAL then grabs the baton and is responsible for the selection of the best paths and for maintaining relevant information about them.

Route Discovery and Maintenance

The hybrid nature of EIGRP is fully revealed in its approach to route discovery and maintenance. Like many link-state protocols, EIGRP supports the concept of neighbors that are discovered via a Hello process and whose states are monitored. Like many distance-vector protocols, EIGRP uses the routing-by-rumor mechanism I talked about earlier that implies that many routers never hear about a route update firsthand. Instead, they hear about it from another router that may also have heard about it from another one, and so on.

Given the huge amount of information that EIGRP routers have to collect, it makes sense that they have a place to store it, right? Well they do—EIGRP uses a series of tables to store important information about its environment:

Neighborship table   The *neighborship table* (usually referred to as the neighbor table) records information about routers with whom neighborship relationships have been formed.

Topology table   The *topology table* stores the route advertisements received from each neighbor about every route in the internetwork.

Route table   The *route table* stores the routes that are currently used to make routing decisions. There would be separate copies (instances) of each of these tables for each protocol that is actively being supported by EIGRP, whether it's IP or IPv6.

EIGRP Metrics

Another really great thing about EIGRP is that unlike many other protocols, which use a single factor to compare routes and select the best possible path, EIGRP can use a combination of four, called a composite metric. These are the four factors used to build that composite:

- *Bandwidth*
- *Delay*
- *Reliability*
- *Load*

Bear in mind that EIGRP only uses bandwidth and delay of the line to determine the best path to a remote network by default. And just so you know, Cisco sometimes likes to call these factors *path bandwidth value* and *cumulative line delay,* respectively.

Also worth noting is that there's a fifth element to all of this called *maximum transmission unit*, or *MTU*, size. Even though this element is never used in EIGRP calculations, it's a required parameter in some EIGRP-related commands—especially those involving redistribution. The value of the MTU element represents the smallest MTU value found along the path to the destination network.

Open Shortest Path First Basics

Open Shortest Path First (OSPF) is an open standard routing protocol that's been implemented by a wide variety of network vendors, including Cisco. If you have multiple routers and not all of them are species of Cisco, then you can't use EIGRP, now can you? So your remaining CCNA Data Center objective options are basically RIP, RIPv2, and OSPF. If it's a large network, then, really, your only options are OSPF and something called route redistribution—a translation service between routing protocols. And again I personally recommend avoiding both versions of RIP whenever possible!

OSPF works by using the Dijkstra algorithm wherein, first, a shortest path tree is constructed, and then the routing table is populated with the resulting best paths. OSPF converges quickly, although not quite as fast as EIGRP does. It supports multiple, equal-cost routes to the same destination—8 by default, but you can configured up to 16. And like EIGRP, it supports both IP and IPv6 routed protocols.

OSPF offers the following features:

- Supports areas and autonomous systems
- Minimizes routing update traffic
- Allows scalability
- Supports VLSM/CIDR
- Has unlimited hop count
- Is open standard, permitting multi-vendor deployment

OSPF is the first link-state routing protocol that most people are introduced to, so it's good to see how it compares to the traditional distance-vector protocols such as RIPv2 and RIPv1. Table 10.3 displays a comparison of these three protocols.

TABLE 10.3 OSPF and RIP comparison

Characteristic	OSPF	RIPv2	RIPv1
Type of protocol	Link state	Distance vector	Distance vector
Classless support	Yes	Yes	No
VLSM support	Yes	Yes	No
Auto-summarization	No	Yes	Yes
Manual summarization	Yes	No	No
Discontiguous support	Yes	Yes	No

Characteristic	OSPF	RIPv2	RIPv1
Route propagation	Multicast on change	Periodic multicast	Periodic broadcast
Path metric	Bandwidth	Hops	Hops
Hop count limit	None	15	15
Convergence	Fast	Slow	Slow
Peer authentication	Yes	Yes	No
Hierarchical network requirement	Yes (using areas)	No (flat only)	No (flat only)
Updates	Event triggered	Route table updates	Route table updates
Route computation	Dijkstra	Bellman-Ford	Bellman-Ford

OSPF has many features beyond the few I've listed in Table 10.3, and all of them contribute to a fast, scalable, and robust protocol that can be actively deployed in thousands of production networks.

OSPF is supposed to be designed in a hierarchical fashion, which basically means that you can separate the larger internetwork into smaller internetworks called areas. This happens to be the best design for OSPF.

There are three big reasons for creating OSPF in a hierarchical design:

- To decrease routing overhead
- To speed up convergence
- To confine network instability to single areas of the network

Of course, none of these make configuring OSPF easier, only more elaborate and difficult. But it's seriously worth the trouble! However, with all that said, it's important that you understand the drawbacks of link-state routing protocols.

First, understand that in addition to the routing table, link state requires a topology database and a neighbor table, referred to as an adjacency database. This will result in a significant amount of memory and processing in large or complex networks. It's important that your network design is solid, especially in large or complex networks. Let's take a look at the design that OSPF desires—the hierarchical network.

Figure 10.1 shows a typical, though simple OSPF design. Pay particular notice to the fact that some routers connect to the backbone area, called Area 0. When configuring multi-area OSPF, you must have an area 0, and all other areas should connect to this area. (Make a note to yourself that any areas that do not directly connect to Area 0 can still be connected via virtual links. But this is beyond the scope of this book.) Anyway, the routers that connect other areas to the backbone area within an AS are called Area Border Routers (ABRs). And still, at least one interface of the ABR must be in Area 0!

FIGURE 10.1   OSPF design example

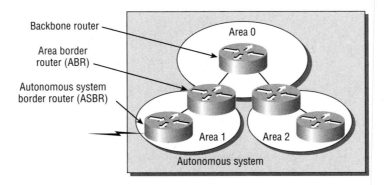

OSPF runs inside an autonomous system, but it can also connect multiple autonomous systems together. The router that connects these autonomous systems is called an Autonomous System Boundary Router, commonly referred to as an ASBR.

Ideally, you would create areas within networks to help keep route updates to a minimum in really large networks. This provides reduced frequency of shortest path first (SPF) calculations. Doing this also keeps problems from propagating throughout the network, isolating them to a single area within it, which makes troubleshooting a lot easier because routing tables are smaller!

OSPF Terminology

Imagine how challenging it would be if you were given a map and compass but had no knowledge of east or west, north or south, river or mountain, lake or desert. You'd probably not get very far putting your new tools to good use without knowing about this stuff. For this reason, you'll begin your exploration of OSPF with a long list of terms that will prevent you from getting lost in the later sections. The following are important OSPF terms to familiarize yourself with before you proceed:

Link   A *link* is a network or router interface assigned to any given network. When an interface is added to the OSPF process, it's considered by OSPF to be a link. This link, or interface, will have state information associated with it (up or down) as well as one or more IP addresses.

Router ID   The *Router ID (RID)* is an IP address used to identify the router. Cisco chooses the Router ID by using the highest IP address of all configured loopback interfaces. If no loopback interfaces are configured with addresses, OSPF will choose the highest IP address of all active physical interfaces.

Neighbor   *Neighbors* are two or more routers that have an interface on a common network, such as two routers connected on a point-to-point serial link.

Adjacency   An *adjacency* is a relationship between two OSPF routers that permits the direct exchange of route updates. OSPF is really picky about sharing routing information—unlike EIGRP, which directly shares routes with all of its neighbors. Instead, OSPF directly shares routes only with neighbors that have also established adjacencies. And not all neighbors will become adjacent—this depends upon both the type of network and the configuration of the routers.

Hello protocol   The OSPF Hello protocol provides dynamic neighbor discovery and maintains neighbor relationships. Hello packets and Link State Advertisements (LSAs) build and maintain the topological database. Hello packets are addressed to multicast address 224.0.0.5.

Neighborship database   The *neighborship database* is a list of all OSPF routers for which Hello packets have been seen. A variety of details, including the Router ID and state, are maintained on each router in the neighborship database.

Topological database   The *topological database* contains information from all of the Link State Advertisement packets that have been received for an area. The router uses the information from the topology database as input into the Dijkstra algorithm that computes the shortest path to every network.

   LSA packets are used to update and maintain the topological database.

Link State Advertisement   A *Link State Advertisement (LSA)* is an OSPF data packet containing link-state and routing information that's shared among OSPF routers. An OSPF router will exchange LSA packets only with routers to which it has established adjacencies.

Designated router   A *designated router (DR)* is elected whenever OSPF routers are connected to the same multi-access network. Cisco likes to call these "broadcast" networks, but really, they are networks that have multiple recipients. Try not to confuse multi-access with multipoint, which can be easy to do sometimes.

A prime example is an Ethernet LAN. To minimize the number of adjacencies formed, a DR is chosen (elected) to disseminate/receive routing information to/from the remaining routers on the broadcast network or link. This ensures that their topology tables are synchronized. All routers on the shared network will establish adjacencies with the DR and backup designated router (BDR)—I'll define this next. The election is won by the router with the highest priority, and the highest Router ID is used as a tiebreaker if the priority of more than one router turns out to be the same.

Backup designated router   A *backup designated router (BDR)* is a hot standby for the DR on multi-access links (remember that Cisco sometimes likes to call these "broadcast" networks). The BDR receives all routing updates from OSPF adjacent routers but doesn't flood LSA updates.

OSPF areas   An *OSPF area* is a grouping of contiguous networks and routers. All routers in the same area share a common Area ID. Because a router can be a member of more than one area at a time, the Area ID is associated with specific interfaces on the router. This would allow some interfaces to belong to area 1 while the remaining interfaces can belong to area 0. All of the routers within the same area have the same topology table. When configuring OSPF, you've got to remember that there must be an area 0 and that this is typically considered the backbone area. Areas also play a role in establishing a hierarchical network organization—something that really enhances the scalability of OSPF!

Broadcast (multi-access)   *Broadcast (multi-access) networks* such as Ethernet allow multiple devices to connect to (or access) the same network as well as provide a *broadcast* ability in which a single packet is delivered to all nodes on the network. In OSPF, a DR and a BDR must be elected for each broadcast multi-access network.

Non-broadcast multi-access   *Non-broadcast multi-access (NBMA) networks* are types such as Frame Relay, X.25, and Asynchronous Transfer Mode (ATM). These networks allow for multi-access but have no broadcast ability like Ethernet. So, NBMA networks require special OSPF configuration to function properly and neighbor relationships must be defined.

DR and BDR are elected on broadcast and non-broadcast multi-access networks. Elections are covered in detail later in this chapter.

Point-to-point   *Point-to-point* refers to a type of network topology consisting of a direct connection between two routers that provides a single communication path. The point-to-point connection can be physical, as in a serial cable directly connecting two routers, or it can be logical, as in two routers that are thousands of miles apart yet connected by a circuit in a Frame Relay network. In either case, this type of configuration eliminates the need for DRs or BDRs—but neighbors are discovered automatically.

Point-to-multipoint   *Point-to-multipoint* refers to a type of network topology consisting of a series of connections between a single interface on one router and multiple destination routers. All of the interfaces on all of the routers sharing the point-to-multipoint connection belong to the same network. As with point-to-point, no DRs or BDRs are needed.

All of these terms play an important part in understanding the operation of OSPF, so again, make sure you're familiar with each of them. Reading through the rest of this chapter will help you to place the terms within their proper context.

So with all of that, let's move on now and get into actually configuring these routing protocols on our Nexus 7000!

Configuring Routing Protocols

Some Nexus devices have the ability to route layer 3 packets but others are strictly layer 2 devices. And implementing the different types of routing protocols is different from doing that on IOS devices. Coming up, I'll cover ground on static, RIP, EIGRP, and OSPF routing protocols plus guide you through configuring each of them. I'll keep the configurations pretty basic, but no worries, I'll include enough for you to understand how they work, how to configure them, even how to verify that each is running properly.

I'm going to use the internetwork pictured in Figure 10.2 as a reference for all configurations throughout this chapter.

FIGURE 10.2   Our sample internetwork

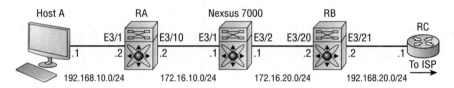

Here you see three Nexus switches, one 7000 series and two 5000 series named RA and RB. RA and RB are preconfigured for this chapter. Also present is RC, which is an ISR router, connecting to an ISP. We're going to focus on configuring the Nexus 7000 in this chapter.

Okay, so let's start by taking a quick look at default routing and then zero in on the routing protocols. But first, let's setup our interface configurations on the Nexus 7000:

```
switch# config
switch(config)# hostname Nexus7k
Nexus7k(config)# int e3/1
Nexus7k(config-if)# no switchport
Nexus7k(config-if)# ip address 172.16.10.1 255.255.255.0
Nexus7k(config-if)# no shutdown
Nexus7k(config-if)# int e3/2
Nexus7k(config-if)# no switchport
Nexus7k(config-if)# ip address 172.16.20.1 255.255.255.0
Nexus7k(config-if)# no shutdown
```

Pretty straightforward. I went to the two Ethernet interfaces and first made them layer 3 ports using the no switchport command; then I added the IP address and enabled the ports with the no shutdown command. Since our other two switches are already configured with IP addressing and routing protocols, we'll start communicating with them as soon as we configure routing on our 7000.

Static Routes

Which type of routing uses the least bandwidth? You guessed it—creating static routes wins! And in small environments, static routes can be just the thing you need. In places where you only have a single possible path to the destination, static routes are ideal. One of the most interesting, cool features is that you can enter the destination subnet mask as dotted-decimal or CIDR notation.

Let's look at the basic NX-OS syntax for static routes:

```
Nexus7K(config)#ip route ?
  A.B.C.D      IP prefix in format i.i.i.i
  A.B.C.D/LEN  IP prefix and network mask length in format x.x.x.x/m
```

The NX-OS allows us to specify a default route by using a network of 0.0.0.0 and a mask of /0, which is different than the IOS configuration. Here's an example:

```
Nexus7K(config)#ip route 0.0.0.0/0 ?
  A.B.C.D       IP next-hop address in format i.i.i.i
  A.B.C.D/LEN   IP next-hop prefix in format i.i.i.i/m
  ethernet      Ethernet IEEE 802.3z
  mgmt          Management interface
  null          Null interface
  port-channel  Port Channel interface
  vlan          Vlan interface
```

The next part of the command specifies the destination, either an IP address of the next hop or our exit interface on the 7000. However, we typically won't bother using the exit interface because even if we configure the default route using the exit interface, unlike in the IOS configs, NX-OS demands that the next hop IP address be configured regardless, so what's the point? It would look something like this:

ip route 0.0.0.0/0 *interface exit_interface*

Okay—using our figure as an example, we'll just simply use our next hop IP address of 172.16.20.2, which is in the direction of our ISP. Here's a typical configuration of a default route that will work great in our example network:

```
Nexus7K(config)#ip route 0.0.0.0/0 172.16.20.2
```

And we can easily verify it via the show ip route command:

```
Nexus7k(config)# sh ip route
IP Route Table for VRF "default"
'*' denotes best ucast next-hop
'**' denotes best mcast next-hop
```

```
'[x/y]' denotes [preference/metric]

0.0.0.0/0, ubest/mbest: 1/0
    *via 172.16.20.2, Eth3/2, [1/0], 00:01:14, static
172.16.10.0/24, ubest/mbest: 1/0, attached
    *via 172.16.10.1, Eth3/1, [0/0], 00:08:32, direct
172.16.10.1/32, ubest/mbest: 1/0, attached
    *via 172.16.10.1, Eth3/1, [0/0], 00:08:32, local
172.16.20.0/24, ubest/mbest: 1/0, attached
    *via 172.16.20.1, Eth3/2, [0/0], 00:08:07, direct
172.16.20.1/32, ubest/mbest: 1/0, attached
    *via 172.16.20.1, Eth3/2, [0/0], 00:08:07, local
Nexus7k(config)#
```

By looking at the route table output, you can see that the single entry on top is our default route, listed as statically configured, with a next hop via 172.16.20.2. This basically instructs that if a packet arrives with a destination address absent from the routing table and matching no entries therein, just pawn it off to the neighbor router. The other entries in the routing table are directly connected interfaces. This demonstration of setting a default static route is vital because it's the most common use of a static route in modern networks. Next, I'll cover RIP and then dig deeper into some dynamic routing protocols.

RIP

As I said, configuring routing protocols with NX-OS is very different from doing it with an IOS. NX-OS is designed as a data center operating system and can run a bunch of instances of various routing protocols simultaneously. But for our purposes, we're only going to use one instance of each routing protocol.

Understand that when we start a routing protocol, NX-OS will require us to confirm that the feature is enabled first. After that, we've got to give the routing protocol an Instance-ID, which we'll just make up, and then enable it on certain interfaces. Then we'll use the address-family command to choose either IPv4 or IPv6 for RIP, and then we'll enable it on certain interfaces. Let's see how our configuration looks on our network:

```
Nexus7k(config)# feature rip
Nexus7k(config)# router rip ToddRIP
Nexus7k(config-router)# address-family ?
  ipv4  Configure IPv4 address-family
  ipv6  Configure IPv6 address-family
Nexus7k(config-router)# address-family ipv4 unicast
Nexus7k(config-router-af)# int e3/1 - 2
Nexus7k(config-if-range)# ip router rip ToddRIP
```

Notice that we ensured that the RIP feature command was enabled first. If we didn't, we'd get an error when trying to configure it! You can see that we then created an instance of RIP called ToddRIP and specified it as IP version 4 with the address-family command. Then we went to our chosen interfaces and enabled RIP for process ToddRIP on each interface that we wanted that process to run on.

And to verify the configuration, we'll use the show ip rip command, which has replaced the show ip protocols command we used in IOS routers:

```
Nexus7k# sh ip rip
Process Name "rip-ToddRIP" VRF "default"
RIP port 520, multicast-group 224.0.0.9
Admin-distance: 120
Updates every 30 sec, expire in 180 sec
Collect garbage in 120 sec
Default-metric: 1
Max-paths: 8
Process is up and running
  Interfaces supported by ipv4 RIP :
    Ethernet3/1
    Ethernet3/2
```

The preceding output shows the following:

- The process's name
- The UDP port number RIP is using (520)
- The multicast group address of 224.0.0.9 (RIPv2 address)
- The AD, multiplied by the maximum path that RIP will load-balance by default, which is 8 by default but can be configured to 16
- The interface running the RIP process ToddRIP

Let's take a look at the routing table using the sh ip route command:

```
Nexus7k# sh ip route
[output cut]
0.0.0.0/0, ubest/mbest: 1/0
    *via 172.16.20.2, Eth3/2, [1/0], 00:22:20, static
172.16.10.0/24, ubest/mbest: 1/0, attached
    *via 172.16.10.1, Eth3/1, [0/0], 00:29:38, direct
172.16.10.1/32, ubest/mbest: 1/0, attached
    *via 172.16.10.1, Eth3/1, [0/0], 00:29:38, local
172.16.20.0/24, ubest/mbest: 1/0, attached
    *via 172.16.20.1, Eth3/2, [0/0], 00:29:13, direct
172.16.20.1/32, ubest/mbest: 1/0, attached
    *via 172.16.20.1, Eth3/2, [0/0], 00:29:13, local
```

```
192.168.10.0/24, ubest/mbest: 1/0
    *via 172.16.10.2, Eth3/1, [120/2], 00:10:47, rip-ToddRIP, rip
192.168.20.0/24, ubest/mbest: 1/0
    *via 172.16.20.2, Eth3/2, [120/2], 00:11:04, rip-ToddRIP, rip
```

Okay, so what can we see here? Well first, the last two entries are RIP found routes. 192.168.10.0 can be reached in two hops via 172.16.10.2, which can be reached out interface e3/1. The [120/2] is the administrative distance and metric, which is 120 for AD and hop count of 2 for metric. Also, network 172.16.20.2 is two hops away via 172.16.20.2, out e3/2. It's important to remember that when you enable RIP on Nexus, it is running version 2 and auto-summary is disabled. This is a good thing! RIP is easy to configure but not widely used in data centers. Let's move on to the other routing protocols now.

EIGRP

The Enhanced Interior Gateway Routing Protocol is used in some data centers, although most enterprise companies are moving toward open-standards protocols.

 Cisco has presented EIGRP to the IETF to make EIGRP nonproprietary. However, at the time of this writing no implementations of EIGRP as an open standard have occurred.

Configuration with EIGRP isn't all that different from the RIP configuration that we just completed except we need to add the autonomous system. Check out this output:

```
Nexus7k(config)# feature eigrp
Nexus7k(config)# router eigrp JohnEIGRP
Nexus7k(config-router)# au?
authentication        autonomous-system
Nexus7k(config-router)# autonomous-system ?
  <1-65535>  Local AS number


Nexus7k(config-router)# autonomous-system 100
Nexus7k(config-router)# int e3/1 - 2
Nexus7k(config-if-range)# ip router eigrp JohnEIGRP
```

See that? This configuration is almost exactly the same as the RIP configuration! It's pretty simple and straightforward—we basically just added the AS number, which has to match all the other routers we want to share routing information with. We'll use the show ip eigrp and show ip route commands to verify the configuration:

```
Nexus7k(config-if-range)# sh ip eigrp
IP-EIGRP AS 100 ID 172.16.10.1 VRF default
```

```
Process-tag: JohnEIGRP
Status: running
Authentication mode: none
Authentication key-chain: none
Metric weights: K1=1 K2=0 K3=1 K4=0 K5=0
IP proto: 88 Multicast group: 224.0.0.10
Int distance: 90 Ext distance: 170
Max paths: 8
Number of EIGRP interfaces: 2 (0 loopbacks)
Number of EIGRP passive interfaces: 0
Number of EIGRP peers: 2
Graceful-Restart: Enabled
Stub-Routing: Disabled
NSF converge time limit/expires: 120/0
NSF route-hold time limit/expires: 240/0
NSF signal time limit/expires: 20/0
Redistributed max-prefix: Disabled
```

The output of show ip eigrp gives us the following:

- The AS number.

- The process-tag, JohnEIGRP.

- The IP protocol field number (88).

- The multicast group address of 224.0.0.10.

- The maximum paths value of 8, the amount of equal cost links EIGRP will load-balance across by default. You can tweak this amount up to 16 links.

Let's check out the routing table now, again using the show ip route command:

```
Nexus7k(config-if-range)# sh ip route
[output cut]
0.0.0.0/0, ubest/mbest: 1/0
    *via 172.16.20.2, Eth3/2, [1/0], 00:26:35, static
172.16.10.0/24, ubest/mbest: 1/0, attached
    *via 172.16.10.1, Eth3/1, [0/0], 00:33:53, direct
172.16.10.1/32, ubest/mbest: 1/0, attached
    *via 172.16.10.1, Eth3/1, [0/0], 00:33:53, local
172.16.20.0/24, ubest/mbest: 1/0, attached
    *via 172.16.20.1, Eth3/2, [0/0], 00:33:28, direct
172.16.20.1/32, ubest/mbest: 1/0, attached
    *via 172.16.20.1, Eth3/2, [0/0], 00:33:28, local
```

```
192.168.10.0/24, ubest/mbest: 1/0
    *via 172.16.10.2, Eth3/1, [90/28416], 00:00:18, eigrp-JohnEIGRP, internal
192.168.20.0/24, ubest/mbest: 1/0
    *via 172.16.20.2, Eth3/2, [90/2170112], 00:00:18, eigrp-JohnEIGRP, internal
Nexus7k(config-if-range)#
```

In the routing table we can see our default route, the two directly connected interfaces configured, and two EIGRP found routes. The [90/28416] is the administrative distance/metric. Now let's get into the most popular routing protocol in data centers—OSPF!

OSPF

The Open Shortest Path First protocol has become the de facto standard in data centers and I won't lie—its configuration can get pretty complex! But don't run away yet, because I promise to keep things simple with this introduction by focusing on the basic configuration using a single area.

Okay—one last time, let's configure our network with OSPF. We're going to place all interfaces within Area 0 since multi-area OSPF is beyond the scope of this book:

```
Nexus7k(config-if-range)# feature ospf
Nexus7k(config)# router ospf TJOSPF
Nexus7k(config-router)# int e3/1 -2
Nexus7k(config-if-range)# ip router ospf TJOSPF area 0
```

First we enabled the feature, then created a process ID called TJOSPF. The process ID name is irrelevant. Last, we added the OSPF process to the interfaces we wanted to route OSPF and configured the area ID. This simplified OSPF configuration for NX-OS is actually very similar to RIP's and EIGRP's, and it's a whole lot simpler than configuring OSPF for an IOS! It's also easy to verify this configuration via the show ip ospf command:

```
Nexus7k(config-if-range)# sh ip ospf
 Routing Process TJOSPF with ID 172.16.10.1 VRF default
 Stateful High Availability enabled
 Graceful-restart is configured
   Grace period: 60 state: Inactive
   Last graceful restart exit status: None
 Supports only single TOS(TOS0) routes
 Supports opaque LSA
 Administrative distance 110
 Reference Bandwidth is 40000 Mbps
 Initial SPF schedule delay 200.000 msecs,
   minimum inter SPF delay of 1000.000 msecs,
   maximum inter SPF delay of 5000.000 msecs
```

```
Initial LSA generation delay 0.000 msecs,
  minimum inter LSA delay of 5000.000 msecs,
  maximum inter LSA delay of 5000.000 msecs
Minimum LSA arrival 1000.000 msec
Maximum paths to destination 8
Number of external LSAs 0, checksum sum 0
Number of opaque AS LSAs 0, checksum sum 0
Number of areas is 0, 0 normal, 0 stub, 0 nssa
Number of active areas is 0, 0 normal, 0 stub, 0 nssa
```

The resulting output doesn't provide as much insight as RIP and EIGRP did, but it did provide the following important information:

- Process ID
- Router ID, which is used to define our router to OSPF neighbors

Now before I can show you the routing table, we'll need to disable the EIGRP feature in the NX-OS because EIGRP has a lower AD than OSPF (90 vs 110), so OSPF routes won't show in the routing table. However, since OSPF's AD is 110, which is lower than RIP, we can keep RIP running on our sample network (never ever keep RIP running in the background on your production network!). We're going to use the no feature eigrp command to bring up the route table and allow OSPF to propagate in the internetwork:

```
Nexus7k(config-if-range)#no feature eigrp
Nexus7K(config)# sh ip route
[output cut]
0.0.0.0/0, ubest/mbest: 1/0
    *via 172.16.20.2, Eth3/2, [1/0], 00:38:05, static
172.16.10.0/24, ubest/mbest: 1/0, attached
    *via 172.16.10.1, Eth3/1, [0/0], 00:45:23, direct
172.16.10.1/32, ubest/mbest: 1/0, attached
    *via 172.16.10.1, Eth3/1, [0/0], 00:45:23, local
172.16.20.0/24, ubest/mbest: 1/0, attached
    *via 172.16.20.1, Eth3/2, [0/0], 00:44:58, direct
172.16.20.1/32, ubest/mbest: 1/0, attached
    *via 172.16.20.1, Eth3/2, [0/0], 00:44:58, local
192.168.10.0/24, ubest/mbest: 1/0
    *via 172.16.10.2, Eth3/1, [110/401], 00:00:48, ospf-TJOSPF, intra
192.168.20.0/24, ubest/mbest: 1/0
    *via 172.16.20.2, Eth3/2, [110/464], 00:01:28, ospf-TJOSPF, intra
Nexus7k(config-if-range)#
```

So while it's true that basic routing protocol configuration on the NX-OS is a bit different from what you're used to, soon you'll be able to do it in your sleep. If not, I'm sure you'll dream about it the night before your test!

Anyway, by looking at the running configuration of our Nexus 7000 using the show run command, we can see that our interfaces are configured with both OSPF and RIP, with only OSPF injected routes in the routing table because of AD (remember, I just disabled EIGRP so that protocol configuration does not show on the interfaces):

```
[output cut]
interface Ethernet3/1
  ip address 172.16.10.1/24
  ip router ospf TJOSPF area 0.0.0.0
  ip router rip ToddRIP
  no shutdown


interface Ethernet3/2
  ip address 172.16.20.1/24
  ip router ospf TJOSPF area 0.0.0.0
  ip router rip ToddRIP
  no shutdown
!
[output cut]
!
router ospf TJOSPF
router rip ToddRIP
  address-family ipv4 unicast
ip route 0.0.0.0/0 172.16.20.2
```

Even though there doesn't seem to be a whole lot to see here, you can use this output to verify the process tags on your interfaces. Doing this has come in really handy when I've had to troubleshoot my networks. By verifying the configurations on my Nexus 7000, I've found typos between the global configuration of the routing protocol and the process tag configured on the interface, which was the reason I wasn't receiving route updates!

Summary

This chapter covered IP routing with default routing and dynamic routing protocols. It's extremely important that you really understand the vital basics we covered in this chapter because everything that's done on a Cisco router typically has some type of IP routing configured and running.

First, you found out how to configure default routing, and then we configured our Nexus lab with a default route. I discussed RIP and how it works within an internetwork, which is not well at all! I demonstrated how to verify RIP and then we added RIP to our little internetwork.

You then learned about EIGRP, a hybrid of link-state routing and distance-vector protocols that Cisco often refers to as an advanced distance-vector protocol. EIGRP allows for unequal-cost load balancing, controlled routing updates, and formal neighbor adjacencies.

You saw how EIGRP uses the capabilities of the Reliable Transport Protocol (RTP) to communicate between neighbors and utilizes the Diffusing Update Algorithm (DUAL) to compute the best path to each remote network.

This chapter also provided you with information about OSPF. It's really difficult to include everything about OSPF because it can be really complex. So much of it falls outside the scope of this chapter and even this book, but you got a good introduction with a few good tips, so you're good to go. (Just make sure you've got what I presented you with completely dialed in!)

Exam Essentials

Differentiate the three types of routing. The three types of routing are static (in which routes are manually configured at the CLI), dynamic (in which the routers share routing information via a routing protocol), and default routing (in which a special route is configured for all traffic without a more specific destination network found in the table).

Compare and contrast static and dynamic routing. Static routing creates no routing update traffic and creates less overhead on the router and network links, but it must be configured manually and does not have the ability to react to link outages. Dynamic routing creates routing update traffic and uses more overhead on the router and network links, but it can both react to link outages and choose the best route when multiple routes exist to the same network.

Understand administrative distance and its role in the selection of the best route.
Administrative distance (AD) is used to rate the trustworthiness of routing information received on a router from a neighbor router. Administrative distance is an integer from 0 to 255, where 0 is the most trusted and 255 means no traffic will be passed via this route. All routing protocols are assigned a default AD, but it can be changed at the CLI.

Differentiate distance-vector, link-state, and hybrid routing protocols. Distance-vector routing protocols make routing decisions based on hop count (think RIP), while link-state routing protocols are able to consider multiple factors such as bandwidth available and delay when selecting the best route. Hybrid routing protocols exhibit characteristics of both types.

Describe the differences between RIPv1 and RIPv2.   RIPv1 sends broadcasts every 30 seconds and has an AD of 120. RIPv2 sends multicasts (224.0.0.9) every 30 seconds and also has an AD of 120. RIPv2 sends subnet mask information with the route updates, which allows it to support classless networking and discontiguous networks. RIPv2 also supports authentication between routers and RIPv1 does not.

Know EIGRP features.   EIGRP is a classless, advanced distance-vector protocol that supports IP, IPX, AppleTalk, and now IPv6. EIGRP uses a unique algorithm, called DUAL, to maintain route information and uses RTP to communicate with other EIGRP routers reliably.

Compare OSPF and RIPv1.   OSPF is a link-state protocol that supports VLSM and classless routing; RIPv1 is a distance-vector protocol that does not support VLSM and supports only classful routing.

Written Lab 10

You can find the answers in Appendix A.

Write the answers to the following questions:

1. What is considered an advanced distance-vector routing protocol?

2. RIP has a maximum hop count of what?

3. RIP sends periodic routing updates at what interval?

4. What is a typical example of a distance-vector routing protocol?

5. When configuring RIP, which mandatory command is used to define the process as IPv4 or IPv6?

Hands-on Labs 10

In this section, you will perform commands on a Nexus device that will help you understand what you learned in this chapter.

You'll need at least one Nexus Device, or the simulator provided with this book.

Lab 10.1: Setting up switch ports for lab

Lab 10.2: Configuring static routing

Lab 10.3: Configuring RIP routing

Lab 10.4: Configuring EIGRP routing

Lab 10.5: Configuring OSPF single area routing

The following graphic will be used in configuring the hands-on labs. Understand that only the Nexus switch can be configured, the other devices are pre-configured for this lab.

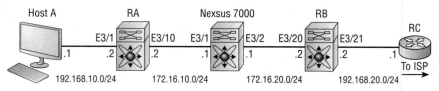

It's important to remember that switches RA and RB are pre-configured for all labs in this chapter. Okay, now let's configure some routing!

Hands-on Lab 10.1: Setting up Ports for Labs

In this first lab you will configure the Nexus switch ports used in this lab as layer 3 ports and with IP addresses.

1. Configure ports e3/1 and e3/2 as layer 3 ports and with IP addresses as shown in the diagram.

```
Nexus7(config-if)# int e3/1
Nexus7(config-if)# no switchport
Nexus7(config-if)# ip address 172.16.10.1/24
Nexus7(config-if)# no shutdown
Nexus7(config-if)# int e3/2
Nexus7(config-if)# no switchport
Nexus7(config-if)# ip address 172.16.20.1/24
Nexus7(config-if)# no shutdown
```

2. Verify the configuration of your directly connected interfaces with the show running-config and the show ip route command.

```
Nexus7# show running-config
[output cut]
!
interface Ethernet3/1
  ip address 172.16.10.1/24
  no shutdown

interface Ethernet3/2
  ip address 172.16.20.1/24
  no shutdown
!
[output cut]

Nexus7# sh ip route
IP Route Table for VRF "default"
'*' denotes best ucast next-hop
'**' denotes best mcast next-hop
'[x/y]' denotes [preference/metric]
'%<string>' in via output denotes VRF <string>
```

```
172.16.10.0/24, ubest/mbest: 1/0, attached
    *via 172.16.10.1, Eth3/1, [0/0], 00:08:32, direct
172.16.10.1/32, ubest/mbest: 1/0, attached
    *via 172.16.10.1, Eth3/1, [0/0], 00:08:32, local
172.16.20.0/24, ubest/mbest: 1/0, attached
    *via 172.16.20.1, Eth3/2, [0/0], 00:08:07, direct
172.16.20.1/32, ubest/mbest: 1/0, attached
    *via 172.16.20.1, Eth3/2, [0/0], 00:08:07, local
```

Notice that there are two directly connected networks in the routing table. We are now ready to move on to configuring routing.

Hands-on Lab 10.2: Configuring Static Routing

In this first lab, you will configure both static routing and default routing on the Nexus switch in order to perform routing. Based on the graphic used for these labs, as well as the output of the routing table shown in lab 10.1, we can see that our Nexus switch is directly connected to Ethernet 3/1, which is directly connected to network 172.16.10.0/24, and to Ethernet 3/2 which is directly connected to network 17.16.20.0/24.

We need to configure one static route and one default route towards the Internet.

1. Configure a static route to remote network 192.168.10.0/24.

```
Nexus7(config)# ip route 192.168.10.0/24 e3/1 172.16.10.2
```

In the above command, I configured a static route to remote network 192.168.10.0/24 with my exit interface e3/1 and a next hop IP address of 172.16.10.2. I didn't need to add the exit interface, but I just used it because I could—there was no value in adding that since I must add the next hop address. Let's verify the route.

```
!
ip route 192.168.10.0/24 Ethernet3/1 172.16.10.2
vrf context management
  ip route 0.0.0.0/0 10.10.1.1
!
```

In the active configuration output above we can see that static route I created on the Nexus switch. Also, the VRF management IP address and default route are displayed. Do not get confused, this default route is not the default route for the default VRF. Let's create a default VRF route.

```
Nexus7(config)# ip route 0.0.0.0/8 172.16.20.2
```

Let's take a look at the routing table.

```
Nexus7(config)# sh ip route
IP Route Table for VRF "default"
'*' denotes best ucast next-hop
'**' denotes best mcast next-hop
'[x/y]' denotes [preference/metric]
'%<string>' in via output denotes VRF <string>


0.0.0.0/8, ubest/mbest: 1/0
    *via 172.16.20.2, [1/0], 00:02:54, static
172.16.10.0/24, ubest/mbest: 1/0, attached
    *via 172.16.10.1, Eth3/1, [0/0], 1d01h, direct
172.16.10.1/32, ubest/mbest: 1/0, attached
    *via 172.16.10.1, Eth3/1, [0/0], 1d01h, local
172.16.20.0/24, ubest/mbest: 1/0, attached
    *via 172.16.20.1, Eth3/2, [0/0], 23:06:39, direct
172.16.20.1/32, ubest/mbest: 1/0, attached
    *via 172.16.20.1, Eth3/2, [0/0], 23:06:39, local
192.168.10.0/24, ubest/mbest: 1/0
    *via 172.16.10.2, Eth3/1, [1/0], 00:00:02, static
Nexus7(config)#
```

We have a static route to network 192.168.10.0, and a default route towards the Internet. Let's take a look at the active configuration file:

```
Nexus7(config)# show running-config
ip route 192.168.10.0/24 Ethernet3/1 172.16.10.2
ip route 0.0.0.0/8 172.16.20.2
vrf context management
  ip route 0.0.0.0/0 10.10.1.1
```

Now we can see the default route for each of our default VRFs. Our Nexus switch is happy running static routing! Now let's make our Nexus switch unhappy by adding the very old RIP routing protocol!

Hands-on Lab 10.3: Configuring RIP Routing

Before we add a routing protocol, I need to remove our static routes. Do you know why? Because of administrative distance! Static routes have an AD of 1 by default and I didn't change the default by adding an AD number at the end of the command, so we have to remove the static route if we want RIP to inject routes into the routing table. RIP has a default AD of 120.

1. Remove the static route, but keep the default route on the default VRF.

```
Nexus7# config
Enter configuration commands, one per line.  End with CNTL/Z.
Nexus7(config)# no ip route 192.168.10.0/24 e3/1 172.16.10.2
Nexus7(config)#
```

2. Verify that your static route is removed from the routing table.

```
Nexus7(config)# sh ip route
IP Route Table for VRF "default"
'*' denotes best ucast next-hop
'**' denotes best mcast next-hop
'[x/y]' denotes [preference/metric]
'%<string>' in via output denotes VRF <string>


0.0.0.0/8, ubest/mbest: 1/0
    *via 172.16.20.2, [1/0], 02:26:04, static
172.16.10.0/24, ubest/mbest: 1/0, attached
    *via 172.16.10.1, Eth3/1, [0/0], 1d01h, direct
172.16.10.1/32, ubest/mbest: 1/0, attached
    *via 172.16.10.1, Eth3/1, [0/0], 1d01h, local
172.16.20.0/24, ubest/mbest: 1/0, attached
    *via 172.16.20.1, Eth3/2, [0/0], 1d01h, direct
172.16.20.1/32, ubest/mbest: 1/0, attached
    *via 172.16.20.1, Eth3/2, [0/0], 1d01h, local
```

Notice our two directly connected networks in the routing table as well as the default route. Now we can add RIP routing.

3. Create a RIP process on the Nexus switch.

```
Nexus7(config)# router rip
                       ^
% Invalid command at '^' marker.
Nexus7(config)# feature rip
```

```
Nexus7(config)# router rip ?
  WORD                    Process ID (Max Size 20)

Nexus7(config)# router rip Todd
Nexus7(config-router)#
```

Notice that I could not configure the RIP process before starting the feature. Since you can create multiple RIP instances I had to name the process ID. This name is irrelevant and only locally significant.

4. Enable either IPv4 or IPv6 routing. This command is mandatory.

```
Nexus7(config-router)# address-family ?
  ipv4  Configure IPv4 address-family
  ipv6  Configure IPv6 address-family

Nexus7(config-router)# address-family ipv4 unicast
Nexus7(config-router-af)#
```

5. Enable the RIP process on the interfaces you want to advertise and receive RIP updates.

```
Nexus7(config-router-af)# int e3/1-2
Nexus7(config-if-range)# ip router rip Todd
```

6. Verify your configuration with the show ip rip command.

```
Nexus7(config-if-range)# sh ip rip
Process Name "rip-Todd" VRF "default"
RIP port 520, multicast-group 224.0.0.9
Admin-distance: 120
Updates every 30 sec, expire in 180 sec
Collect garbage in 120 sec
Default-metric: 1
Max-paths: 8
Process is up and running
  Interfaces supported by ipv4 RIP :
    Ethernet3/1
    Ethernet3/2
```

Notice the process for the default VRF, the UDP port number and multicast group. Also, the AD is 120, updates are every 30 seconds and max-paths is 8, meaning that RIP will auto-load balance across 8 equal cost links by default. Lastly, the interfaces involved in this RIP process are e3/1 and e3/2.

7. Verify with the show ip route command.

```
Nexus7# sh ip route
[output cut]
0.0.0.0/0, ubest/mbest: 1/0
    *via 172.16.20.2, Eth3/2, [1/0], 00:22:20, static
172.16.10.0/24, ubest/mbest: 1/0, attached
    *via 172.16.10.1, Eth3/1, [0/0], 00:29:38, direct
172.16.10.1/32, ubest/mbest: 1/0, attached
    *via 172.16.10.1, Eth3/1, [0/0], 00:29:38, local
172.16.20.0/24, ubest/mbest: 1/0, attached
    *via 172.16.20.1, Eth3/2, [0/0], 00:29:13, direct
172.16.20.1/32, ubest/mbest: 1/0, attached
    *via 172.16.20.1, Eth3/2, [0/0], 00:29:13, local
192.168.10.0/24, ubest/mbest: 1/0
    *via 172.16.10.2, Eth3/1, [120/2], 00:10:47, rip-Todd, rip
192.168.20.0/24, ubest/mbest: 1/0
    *via 172.16.20.2, Eth3/2, [120/2], 00:11:04, rip-Todd, rip
```

You can see the two RIP injected routes to our remote networks. Now let's upgrade to EIGRP.

Hands-on Lab 10.4: Configuring EIGRP Routing

In this lab, we can keep RIP running because EIGRP has a lower AD number of 90.

1. Start the EIGRP process.

```
Nexus7(config)# feature eigrp
Nexus7(config)# router eigrp Todd
```

2. Configure the autonomous system number. This number must be the same on all routers you want to share routing information with.

```
Nexus7(config-router)# autonomous-system ?
  <1-65535>  Local AS number


Nexus7(config-router)# autonomous-system 100
```

3. Configure the interfaces you want to share information in AS 100.

```
Nexus7(config-router)# int e3/1-2
Nexus7(config-if-range)# ip router eigrp Todd
Nexus7(config-if-range)#
```

4. Verify with the show ip eigrp and show ip route commands to verify the configuration.

```
Nexus7(config-if-range)# sh ip eigrp
IP-EIGRP AS 100 ID 172.16.10.1 VRF default
  Process-tag: Todd
  Status: running
  Authentication mode: none
  Authentication key-chain: none
  Metric weights: K1=1 K2=0 K3=1 K4=0 K5=0
  IP proto: 88 Multicast group: 224.0.0.10
  Int distance: 90 Ext distance: 170
  Max paths: 8
  Number of EIGRP interfaces: 2 (0 loopbacks)
  Number of EIGRP passive interfaces: 0
  Number of EIGRP peers: 2
  Graceful-Restart: Enabled
  Stub-Routing: Disabled
  NSF converge time limit/expiries: 120/0
  NSF route-hold time limit/expiries: 240/0
  NSF signal time limit/expiries: 20/0
  Redistributed max-prefix: Disabled


Nexus7(config-if-range)# sh ip route
[output cut]
0.0.0.0/0, ubest/mbest: 1/0
    *via 172.16.20.2, Eth3/2, [1/0], 00:26:35, static
172.16.10.0/24, ubest/mbest: 1/0, attached
    *via 172.16.10.1, Eth3/1, [0/0], 00:33:53, direct
172.16.10.1/32, ubest/mbest: 1/0, attached
    *via 172.16.10.1, Eth3/1, [0/0], 00:33:53, local
172.16.20.0/24, ubest/mbest: 1/0, attached
    *via 172.16.20.1, Eth3/2, [0/0], 00:33:28, direct
172.16.20.1/32, ubest/mbest: 1/0, attached
    *via 172.16.20.1, Eth3/2, [0/0], 00:33:28, local
192.168.10.0/24, ubest/mbest: 1/0
    *via 172.16.10.2, Eth3/1, [90/28416], 00:00:18, eigrp-Todd, internal
```

```
192.168.20.0/24, ubest/mbest: 1/0
   *via 172.16.20.2, Eth3/2, [90/2170112], 00:00:18, eigrp-Todd, internal
Nexus7k(config-if-range)#
```

In the routing table we can see our default route, the two directly connected interfaces configured, and two EIGRP found routes. Let's configure single area OSPF.

Hands-on Lab 10.5: Configuring OSPF Routing

In order to enable OSPF routing and insert OSPF routes into the routing table, we first need to remove EIGRP because it has a lower administrative distance.

1. Disable EIGRP on the Nexus switch.

```
Nexus7(config)# no feature eigrp
```

2. Enable the OSFP feature.

```
Nexus7(config)# feature ospf
```

3. Start the OSPF process.

```
Nexus7(config)# router ospf Todd
```

4. Enable the OSPF process on the interfaces.

```
Nexus7k(config-router)# int e3/1 -2
Nexus7k(config-if-range)# ip router ospf Todd area 0
```

OSPF is very easy to configure compared to IOS.
Verify your configuration with the show ip ospf and show ip route command.

```
Nexus7(config-if-range)# sh ip ospf
 Routing Process Todd with ID 172.16.10.1 VRF default
 Stateful High Availability enabled
 Graceful-restart is configured
   Grace period: 60 state: Inactive
   Last graceful restart exit status: None
 Supports only single TOS(TOS0) routes
 Supports opaque LSA
 Administrative distance 110
 Reference Bandwidth is 40000 Mbps
 Initial SPF schedule delay 200.000 msecs,
   minimum inter SPF delay of 1000.000 msecs,
   maximum inter SPF delay of 5000.000 msecs
```

```
Initial LSA generation delay 0.000 msecs,
  minimum inter LSA delay of 5000.000 msecs,
  maximum inter LSA delay of 5000.000 msecs
Minimum LSA arrival 1000.000 msec
Maximum paths to destination 8
Number of external LSAs 0, checksum sum 0
Number of opaque AS LSAs 0, checksum sum 0
Number of areas is 0, 0 normal, 0 stub, 0 nssa
Number of active areas is 0, 0 normal, 0 stub, 0 nssa


Nexus7(config)# sh ip route
[output cut]
0.0.0.0/0, ubest/mbest: 1/0
    *via 172.16.20.2, Eth3/2, [1/0], 00:38:05, static
172.16.10.0/24, ubest/mbest: 1/0, attached
    *via 172.16.10.1, Eth3/1, [0/0], 00:45:23, direct
172.16.10.1/32, ubest/mbest: 1/0, attached
    *via 172.16.10.1, Eth3/1, [0/0], 00:45:23, local
172.16.20.0/24, ubest/mbest: 1/0, attached
    *via 172.16.20.1, Eth3/2, [0/0], 00:44:58, direct
172.16.20.1/32, ubest/mbest: 1/0, attached
    *via 172.16.20.1, Eth3/2, [0/0], 00:44:58, local
192.168.10.0/24, ubest/mbest: 1/0
    *via 172.16.10.2, Eth3/1, [110/401], 00:00:48, ospf-Todd, intra
192.168.20.0/24, ubest/mbest: 1/0
    *via 172.16.20.2, Eth3/2, [110/464], 00:01:28, ospf-Todd, intra
```

If you are familiar with IOS based routers and how to configure OSPF using OSPF, then this is a welcome upgrade! Configuring OSPF has never been so easy.

Great job on your labs! Let's go through some review questions.

Review Questions

You can find the answers in Appendix B.

> **NOTE**   The following questions are designed to test your understanding of this chapter's material. For more information on how to get additional questions, please see this book's introduction.

1. There are three possible routes for a router to reach a destination network. The first route is from OSPF with a metric of 782. The second route is from RIPv2 with a metric of 4. The third is from EIGRP with a composite metric check of 20514560. Which route will be installed by the router in its routing table?

   A. RIPv2

   B. EIGRP

   C. OSPF

   D. All three

2. Which of the following would be considered an advanced distance-vector routing protocol?

   A. RIP

   B. ARP

   C. OSPF

   D. EIGRP

3. Which of the following describe the instance ID that is used to run a routing protocol on a router? (Choose two.)

   A. It is locally significant.

   B. It is globally significant.

   C. It is needed to identify a unique instance of a routing protocol database.

   D. It is an optional parameter required only if multiple routing processes are running on the router.

4. The maximum hop count for RIP, before considering a route invalid, is which of the following?

   A. Unlimited

   B. 0

   C. 15

   D. 16

   E. 31

   F. 32

5. Which statement are true regarding classless routing protocols? (Choose two.)

   A. The use of discontiguous networks is not allowed.

   B. The use of Variable Length Subnet Masks is permitted.

   C. RIPv1 is a classless routing protocol.

   D. IGRP supports classless routing within the same autonomous system.

   E. RIPv2 supports classless routing.

6. Which of the following are true regarding the distance-vector and link-state routing protocols? (Choose two.)

   A. Link state sends its complete routing table out to all active interfaces at periodic time intervals.

   B. Distance vector sends its complete routing table out to all active interfaces at periodic time intervals.

   C. Link state sends updates containing the state of its own links to all routers in the internetwork.

   D. Distance vector sends updates containing the state of its own links to all routers in the internetwork.

7. A network administrator views the output from the show ip route command. A network that is advertised by both RIP and EIGRP appears in the routing table flagged as an EIGRP route. Why is the RIP route to this network not used in the routing table?

   A. EIGRP has a faster update timer.

   B. EIGRP has a lower administrative distance.

   C. RIP has a higher metric value for that route.

   D. The EIGRP route has fewer hops.

   E. The RIP path has a routing loop.

8. What metric does RIPv2 use to find the best path to a remote network?

   A. Hop count

   B. MTU

   C. Cumulative interface delay

   D. Load

   E. Path bandwidth value

9. If your routing table has a static, a RIP and an EIGRP route to the same network, which route will be used to route packets by default?

   A. Any available route.

   B. RIP route.

   C. Static route.

   D. EIGRP route.

   E. They will all load-balance.

10. Two connected routers are configured only with RIP routing. What will be the result when a router receives a routing update that contains a higher-cost path to a network already in its routing table?

   A. The updated information will be added to the existing routing table.

   B. The update will be ignored and no further action will occur.

   C. The updated information will replace the existing routing table entry.

   D. The existing routing table entry will be deleted from the routing table and all routers will exchange routing updates to reach convergence.

11. Which of the following is true regarding RIPv2?

   A. It has a lower administrative distance than RIPv1.

   B. It converges faster than RIPv1.

   C. It has the same timers as RIPv1.

   D. It is harder to configure than RIPv1.

12. Which of the following protocols support VLSM, summarization, and discontiguous networking? (Choose three.)

   A. RIPv1

   B. IGRP

   C. EIGRP

   D. OSPF

   E. RIPv2

13. Which of the following are true regarding OSPF areas? (Choose three.)

   A. You must have separate loopback interfaces configured in each area.

   B. The numbers you can assign an area go up to 65,535.

   C. The backbone area is also called area 0.

   D. If your design is hierarchical, then you don't need multiple areas.

   E. All areas must connect to area 0.

   F. If you have only one area, it must be called area 1.

14. A network administrator needs to configure a router with a distance-vector protocol that allows classless routing. Which of the following satisfies those requirements?

   A. IGRP

   B. OSPF

   C. RIPv1

   D. EIGRP

   E. IS-IS

15. What are the reasons for creating OSPF in a hierarchical design? (Choose three.)

　A. To decrease routing overhead

　B. To speed up convergence

　C. To confine network instability to single areas of the network

　D. To make configuring OSPF easier

16. What is the administrative distance of OSPF?

　A. 90

　B. 100

　C. 110

　D. 120

17. Which option is an example of a distance-vector routing protocol?

　A. OSPF

　B. ARP

　C. RIP

　D. IS-IS

18. RIP sends it complete routing table out in periodic time intervals. What is the interval?

　A. 15 seconds

　B. 30 seconds

　C. 60 seconds

　D. 90 seconds

19. How often does EIGRP send route updates?

　A. Every 15 seconds

　B. Every 30 seconds

　C. Every 60 seconds

　D. Every 90 seconds

　E. Only when a change occurs

20. What is the administrative distance of EIGRP?

　A. 90

　B. 100

　C. 110

　D. 120

Chapter

11

Layer 2 Switching Technologies

THE FOLLOWING TOPICS ARE COVERED IN THIS CHAPTER:

✓ **Describing Switching**

  ▪ Understanding the Challenges of Shared LANs

  ▪ Solving Network Challenges with Switched LAN Technology

✓ **Implementing VLANs and Trunks**

  ▪ Understanding VLANs

  ▪ Understanding Trunking with 802.1Q

  ▪ Understanding VTP

  ▪ Configuring VTP, Trunks, and VLANs

✓ **Exploring the Routing Process**

  ▪ Traditional Inter-VLAN Routing

  ▪ Multilayer Switching

Layer 2 switching is essentially the process of using the device's hardware address on a LAN to segment a network. Because we've already covered these basic ideas, we're going to get into the finer points of layer 2 switching now, delving deeper into how it works.

Switches have changed networking in a big way, and if a pure switched design is properly implemented, it will certainly result in a clean, cost-effective, and resilient internetwork. Throughout this chapter, we'll survey and compare how networks were designed before and after switching technologies were introduced.

In contrast to the networks of yesterday that were based upon collapsed backbones, today's network design is characterized by a flatter architecture—thanks to switches. So now what? How do we break up broadcast domains in a pure switched internetwork? This challenge is answered by creating VLANs, which are logical collectives of network users and resources connected to administratively defined ports on a switch. When you create VLANs, you gain the ability to create smaller broadcast domains within a layer 2 switched internetwork by assigning different ports on the switch to service different subnetworks. VLANs are treated as their own subnets or broadcast domains, meaning that frames broadcast onto the network are switched only between the ports logically grouped within the same VLAN.

So, does this mean we no longer need routers? Maybe yes; maybe no. It really depends on what you want or what your needs are. By default, hosts existing within a specific VLAN can't communicate with hosts that are members of another VLAN, so if you want inter-VLAN communication, you still need a router.

For up-to-the minute updates for this chapter, please see
www.lammle.com/forum

Switching Services

Unlike bridges, which use software to create and manage a filter table, switches use application-specific integrated circuits, or ASICs, to build and maintain their filter tables. But it's still okay to think of a layer 2 switch as a type of multiport bridge because their basic reason for being is the same: to break up collision domains.

Layer 2 switches and bridges are faster than routers because they don't take up time by looking at the Network layer header information. Instead, they look at the frame's hardware addresses before deciding to forward, flood, or drop the frame.

And unlike hubs, switches create private, dedicated collision domains and provide independent bandwidth on each port. Layer 2 switching provides the following:

- Hardware-based bridging (ASICs)
- Wire speed
- Low latency
- Low cost

What makes layer 2 switching so efficient is that no modification to the data packet takes place. The device only reads the frame encapsulating the packet, which makes the switching process considerably faster and less error prone than routing processes are.

And if you use layer 2 switching for both workgroup connectivity and network segmentation, thereby breaking up collision domains, you can create more network segments than you can with traditional routed networks. Plus, layer 2 switching increases bandwidth for each user because, again, each interface into the switch is its own collision domain.

We'll dive deeper into the layer 2 switching technology soon!

Limitations of Layer 2 Switching

Since layer 2 switching is commonly placed in the same category as bridged networks are, it's easy to assume that it has the same hang-ups and issues that bridged networks do. But switches and bridges are still different devices, and while bridges can be appropriate when integrated into a network correctly, keeping their limitations in mind is critical for a solid, well-functioning network!

While bridged networks break up collision domains, remember that the network is still one large broadcast domain, and neither layer 2 switches nor bridges will break up broadcast domains by default. This not only limits your network's size and growth potential, it also can reduce its overall performance.

Think about growth—broadcasts and multicasts, along with the slow convergence time of legacy spanning trees, can slow your network's performance to a crawl as it expands to handle new demands. This is where Nexus switches really shine! The advanced NX-OS allows us to replace many of the routers we used to employ in our internetwork while mitigating the convergence time issues and other problems the older switches presented.

Bridging vs. LAN Switching

Many people think of layer 2 switches as glorified bridges that just give us a lot more ports. But while a switch is conceptually and functionally similar to a multiport bridge, here are some differences and similarities you should always keep in mind:

- Bridges are software based, while switches are hardware based, using ASIC chips to help make filtering decisions.
- There can be only one spanning-tree instance per bridge, but switches can have many. (I'll cover spanning trees in a bit.)
- Most switches have more ports than most bridges do.
- Both bridges and switches flood layer 2 broadcasts.

- Both bridges and switches learn MAC addresses by examining the source address of each frame received.
- Both bridges and switches make forwarding decisions based on layer 2 addresses.

The Key Three: Switch Functions at Layer 2

Layer 2 switching involves three, distinct functions that are really important for you to remember:

Address Discovery and Retention   Layer 2 switches remember the source hardware address of each frame received on an interface and enter this information into a MAC database called a forward/filter table.

Forward/Filter Decisions   When a frame is received on an interface, the switch analyzes the destination hardware address to determine the appropriate exit interface in the MAC database. The frame will be forwarded out only an appropriate destination port.

Loop Prevention   If multiple connections between switches are created for redundancy purposes, network loops can occur. Spanning Tree Protocol (STP) is used to stop network loops while still permitting redundancy for fault tolerance.

With the basics of our Key Three in mind, let's delve deeper into them now.

Address Discovery and Retention

When a switch is first powered on, the MAC forward/filter table is empty, as shown in Figure 11.1.

FIGURE 11.1   Empty forward/filter table on a switch

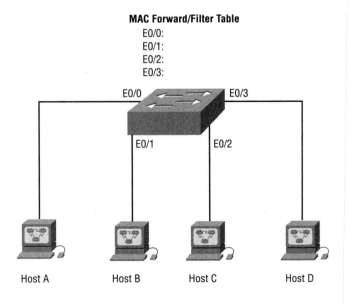

When an interface receives a frame, the switch places the frame's source address in the MAC forward/filter table, allowing it to remember which interface the sending device is located on. The switch then has no choice but to flood the network with this frame out of every port except the source port because it has no idea where the destination device is actually located. This broadcast is actually an attempt to discover the frame's origin. If another device answers this broadcast flood and sends a frame back, then the switch will take the source address from that frame and place that MAC address into its database as well, hereafter associating the address with the interface that received the frame. Since the switch now has both of the relevant MAC addresses in its filtering table, the two devices can now make a point-to-point connection. The switch doesn't need to flood the frame as it did the first time because now the frames can and will be forwarded only between these two, specific devices. This is exactly the thing that makes layer 2 switches better than hubs. When you've got hubs at the helm, all frames will be forwarded out all ports every time—no matter what! Figure 11.2 shows how switches build a MAC database.

FIGURE 11.2 How switches discover hosts' locations

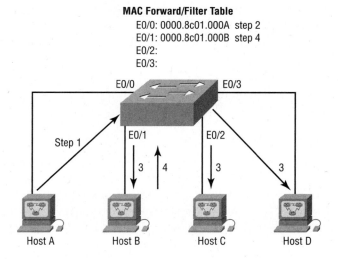

Here, you can see four hosts attached to a switch. When the switch is powered on, there's nothing in its MAC address forward/filter table, but when the hosts start communicating, things begin to change. The switch places the source hardware address of each frame into a table along with the port with which the frame's source address corresponds.

Figure 11.2 demonstrates how a forward/filter table is populated. There are four steps to this process:

1. Host A sends a frame to Host B. Host A's MAC address is 0000.8c01.000A; Host B's MAC address is 0000.8c01.000B.

2. The switch receives the frame on the E0/0 interface and places the source address in the MAC address table.

3. Since the destination address isn't in the MAC database, the frame is forwarded out all interfaces except the source port.

4. Host B receives the frame and responds to Host A. The switch receives this frame on interface E0/1 and places the source hardware address in the MAC database.

Host A and Host B can now make a point-to-point connection and only these two specific devices will receive the frames involved in that communication. Hosts C and D won't see these frames and their MAC addresses won't be found in the database either because they haven't yet sent a frame to the switch.

If Host A and Host B don't communicate to the switch again within a certain amount of time, the switch will flush their entries from the database in effort to keep it as current as possible.

Forward/Filter Decisions

When a frame arrives at a switch interface, the destination hardware address is compared to the forward/filter MAC database. If the destination hardware address is known and therefore listed in the database, the frame will be sent out only the correct exit interface. The switch will transmit the frame out only the destination interface, which preserves bandwidth on the other network segments and is called *frame filtering*.

But if the destination hardware address isn't listed in the MAC database, then the frame will be flooded out all active interfaces except the one the frame was received on. If a device answers the flooded frame, the MAC database is updated with the device's location—its interface.

So again, by default, when a host or server sends a broadcast out on the LAN, the switch will respond by flooding the frame out all active ports except the source port. Remember, although the switch creates smaller collision domains, a network is still one large broadcast domain!

Check out Figure 11.3. In it, Host A sends a data frame to Host D. Here's what our switch will do when it receives the frame from Host A. Since Host A's MAC address is not in the forward/filter table, the switch will add the source address and port to the MAC address table and then forward the frame to Host D. As you know by now, if Host D's MAC address wasn't already in the forward/filter table, the switch would have flooded the frame out all ports except for port Fa0/3!

FIGURE 11.3   Forward/filter table

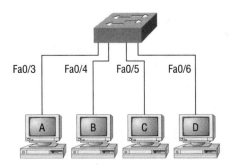

```
Switch#sh mac address-table
Vlan    Mac Address      Ports
----    -----------      -----
   1    0005.dccb.d74b   Fa0/4
   1    000a.f467.9e80   Fa0/5
   1    000a.f467.9e8b   Fa0/6
```

Let's take a look at the output of an IOS-based switch to make sure you've got this foundational concept nailed down before we move to NX-OS. The command on both IOS and NX-OS is show mac address-table:

```
Switch#sh mac address-table
Vlan    Mac Address      Type       Ports
----    -----------      --------   -----
   1    0005.dccb.d74b   DYNAMIC    Fa0/1
   1    000a.f467.9e80   DYNAMIC    Fa0/3
   1    000a.f467.9e8b   DYNAMIC    Fa0/4
   1    000a.f467.9e8c   DYNAMIC    Fa0/3
   1    0010.7b7f.c2b0   DYNAMIC    Fa0/3
   1    0030.80dc.460b   DYNAMIC    Fa0/3
   1    0030.9492.a5dd   DYNAMIC    Fa0/1
   1    00d0.58ad.05f4   DYNAMIC    Fa0/1
```

Let's say our switch receives a frame with the following MAC addresses:

Source MAC: **0005.dccb.d74b**

Destination MAC: **000a.f467.9e8c**

How will it handle this frame? If you answered that because the switch already has the destination MAC address in its MAC address table, the frame will be forwarded out Fa0/3 only, you're right!

Loop prevention/avoidance is covered in detail in Chapter 12, "Redundant Switched Technologies."

VLAN Basics

By default, routers allow broadcasts to occur only within the originating network, while switches forward broadcasts to all segments. The reason it's called a *flat network* is because it's made up of only one *broadcast domain*, not because the actual design is physically flat.

Figure 11.4 illustrates this typical flat network architecture with which layer 2 switched networks are typically designed. In this kind of configuration, every broadcast packet that's transmitted will be seen by every device on the network regardless of whether the device needs to receive that data or not. Take a look.

In Figure 11.4, you can see Host A sending out a broadcast and every port on all switches forwarding it except for the one that originally received it.

Now check out Figure 11.5. It pictures a switched network and shows Host A sending a frame with Host D as its destination. The key factor that's important to note here is that the frame is forwarded out only the port where Host D is located. This is a huge improvement over the old hub networks!

FIGURE 11.4 Flat network structure

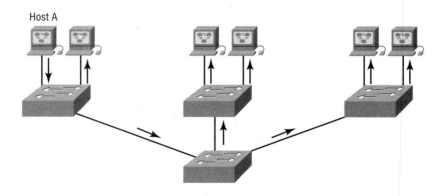

FIGURE 11.5 The benefit of a switched network

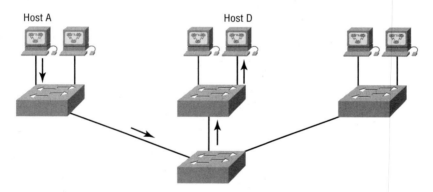

I'm pretty sure it's clear by now that the biggest benefit a layer 2 switched network gives you is that it creates individual collision domain segments for each device plugged into each port on the switch. This scenario frees us from Ethernet density constraints, allowing us to build much larger networks. This is all good, but as usual, each new advance comes with new issues. Relevant to the scenario here is that the larger the number of users and devices on the network, the more broadcasts and packets each switch must handle.

And then there's the ubiquitous security factor, which happens to be particularly troublesome within the typical layer 2 switched internetwork. Issues arise from the fact that by default, all users can see every device and you can't stop devices from broadcasting or users from trying to respond to broadcasts. This means your security options are dismally limited to placing passwords on your servers and other devices.

The answer to this dilemma is the magnificent VLAN, which solves an abundance of problems associated with layer 2 switching.

Here's a short list of ways VLANs simplify network management:

- Network additions, migrations, and other changes are made significantly less painful by just configuring a port into the appropriate VLAN.

- A group of users requiring an unusually high level of security can be corralled into a separate VLAN so that outside users can't communicate with them.

- VLANs are independent from their physical or geographic locations because they are functionally logical.

- VLANs greatly enhance network security.

- VLANs increase the number of broadcast domains while decreasing their size.

Coming up, I'm going to tell you all about switching characteristics and thoroughly describe how switches provide us with better network services than hubs.

Broadcast Control

Broadcasts occur in almost every protocol, but how often they occur depends upon three things:

- The type of protocol
- The application(s) running on the internetwork
- How these services are used

Some older applications have been rewritten to reduce their bandwidth consumption, but the ever-increasing amount of multimedia applications that use both broadcasts and multicasts extensively create a huge burden. Faulty equipment, inadequate segmentation, and poorly designed firewalls seriously compound the problems generated by these broadcast-intensive applications. All of this has brought network design to a whole new level while presenting a host of new challenges for an administrator! This means that it's never been more important to ensure that your network is properly segmented so you can quickly isolate a single segment's problems and prevent them from propagating throughout the internetwork. The most effective way to do that is through strategic switching and routing.

Over the last decade, as switches become more affordable, more companies replaced their flat hub networks with pure switched networks and VLAN environments. All devices within a VLAN are members of the same broadcast domain and receive all broadcasts. By default, these broadcasts are filtered from all ports on a switch that aren't members of the same VLAN. This is great because you get all the benefits you would with a switched design without getting hit with all the problems you'd have if all your users were in the same broadcast domain—sweet!

Security

There's always a catch, though, right? Time to get back to those security issues. A flat internetwork's security used to be tackled by connecting hubs and switches together with routers. So it was basically the router's job to maintain security. This arrangement was pretty ineffective for several reasons: First, anyone connecting to the physical network could access the network resources located on that particular physical LAN. Second, all anyone had to do to observe any and all traffic happening in that network was to plug a network analyzer into the hub. And similar to that last scary fact, users could join a workgroup by just plugging their workstations into the existing hub. Not exactly secure!

But that's exactly what makes VLANs so cool. If you build them and create multiple broadcast groups, you can have total control over each port and user. So the days when anyone could just plug their workstations into any switch port and gain access to network resources are history, because now you get to control each port, plus whatever resources that port can access.

And the good news doesn't end there because VLANs can be created in accordance with the network resources a given user requires. Plus, switches can be configured to inform a network management station of any unauthorized access to network resources. And if you need inter-VLAN communication, you can implement restrictions on a router to make sure that happens securely. You can also place restrictions on hardware addresses, protocols, and applications. Now we're talking—much better!

Flexibility and Scalability

If you were paying attention so far, you know that layer 2 switches only read frames for filtering. This is because they don't check the Network layer protocol. And by default, switches forward broadcasts to all ports, but if you create and implement VLANs, you're essentially creating smaller broadcast domains at layer 2.

This means that broadcasts sent out from a node in one VLAN won't be forwarded to ports configured to belong to a different VLAN. So by assigning switch ports or users to VLAN groups on a switch or group of connected switches, you gain the flexibility to add only the users you want into that broadcast domain regardless of their physical location. This setup can also work to block broadcast storms caused by a faulty network interface card (NIC) as well as preventing an intermediate device from propagating broadcast storms throughout the entire internetwork. Those evils can still happen on the specific VLAN where the problem originated, but the disease will be effectively contained to that particular VLAN.

Another advantage is that when a VLAN gets too big, you can create more of them to keep the broadcasts from consuming too much bandwidth. Always remember—the fewer users in a VLAN, the fewer users affected by broadcasts! This is all good, but you really need to keep network services in mind and have a solid understanding of how the users connect to these services when you create your VLAN.

To understand how a VLAN looks to a switch, it's helpful to begin by looking at a traditional network. Figure 11.6 illustrates how a network was created using hubs to connect physical LANs to a router:

Here you can see that each network is attached with a hub port to the router. Make a note to self that each segment also has its own logical network number even though this isn't obvious when looking at the figure. Moving on, each node attached to a particular physical network has to match that network's number in order to be able to communicate on the internetwork. Each department has its own LAN, so if you needed to add new users to, let's say, Sales, you would just plug them into the Sales LAN to automatically include them in the Sales collision and broadcast domain. This design really did work well for many years!

FIGURE 11.6 Physical LANs connected to a router

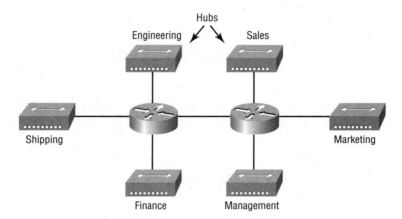

But there was one major flaw: What happens if the hub for Sales is full but we need to add another user into the Sales LAN? Or, what do we do if there's no more physical space where the Sales team is located for this new employee? Is the answer to simply stick the new Sales team member over on the same side of the building as the Finance people and plug them in there because there's room? Doing this would obviously make the new user part of the Finance LAN, which is very bad for many reasons. First and foremost, we now have a major security problem! Because the new Sales employee is a member of the Finance broadcast domain, our newbie can openly see all the same servers and freely access the potentially sensitive network services that the Finance folks can. The second issue is, for this user to access the appropriate Sales network services they actually do need to do their job, and they would have to go through the router to log in to the Sales server, which is not exactly efficient.

Now let's look at what a switch accomplishes for us. Figure 11.7 shows how switches totally solve our problem by removing the physical boundary and demonstrates how six VLANs, numbered 2 through 7, are used to create a broadcast domain for each department. Each switch port is then administratively assigned a VLAN membership, depending on the host and which broadcast domain it's to be placed in.

So now if we need to add another user to the Sales VLAN 7, we can simply assign the port to VLAN 7 regardless of where the new Sales team member is physically located—nice! This illustrates one of the greatest advantages to designing your network with VLANs over the old collapsed backbone design.

Notice that I started assigning VLANs with VLAN number 2. The number is actually irrelevant, but you might be wondering what happened to VLAN 1? Well that VLAN is an administrative VLAN, and even though it can be used for a workgroup, Cisco recommends that you use it for administrative purposes only. You shouldn't ever delete or change the name of VLAN 1, and by default, all ports on a switch are members of VLAN 1 until you change them.

FIGURE 11.7   Switches removing the physical boundary

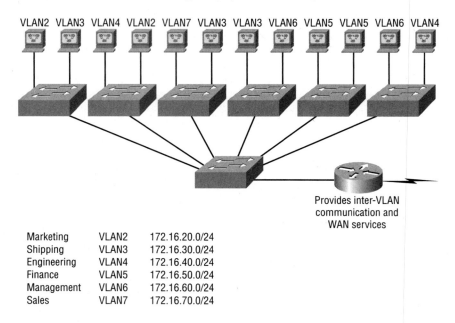

Marketing	VLAN2	172.16.20.0/24
Shipping	VLAN3	172.16.30.0/24
Engineering	VLAN4	172.16.40.0/24
Finance	VLAN5	172.16.50.0/24
Management	VLAN6	172.16.60.0/24
Sales	VLAN7	172.16.70.0/24

Look at Figure 11.7 again. Because each VLAN is considered a broadcast domain, it must also have its own subnet number. And if you're using IPv6, then each VLAN must also be assigned its own IPv6 network number. So you don't get confused, just keep thinking of VLANs as separate subnets, or even separate networks.

Now let's get back to that "because of switches, we don't need routers anymore" misconception. Referring to Figure 11.7, notice that there are seven VLANs, or broadcast domains, counting VLAN 1. The nodes within each VLAN can communicate with each other but not with anything in a different VLAN because the nodes in any given VLAN "think" that they're actually in a collapsed backbone, as illustrated back in Figure 11.6.

So what do we use to enable the hosts in Figure 11.7 to communicate to a node or host on a different VLAN? You guessed it—a router! Those nodes absolutely must to go through a router, or some other layer 3 device, just as they do when they're configured for internetwork communication, as shown in Figure 11.6. It works the exact same way that it would if we were trying to connect different physical networks. Communication between VLANs must go through a layer 3 device!

Identifying VLANs

Know that switch ports are layer 2-only interfaces that are associated with a physical port. If it's an access port on a switch, it can belong to only one single VLAN, but if it's a trunk port, in can belong to all VLANs. You can manually configure a port as either an access or trunk port, or you can just let the Dynamic Trunking Protocol (DTP) operate on a per-port basis to set the switchport mode. DTP does this by negotiating with the port on the other end of the link.

Switches are definitely pretty busy devices. As frames are switched throughout the network, they've got to be able to keep track of all the different types plus understand what to do with them depending on the hardware address. And remember—frames are handled differently according to the type of link they're traversing.

There are two basic different types of ports in a NX-OS switched environment covered in this book:

Access Ports   On access ports, which can belong to and carry the traffic of only one VLAN, data is received and sent in native formats with no VLAN tagging whatsoever. Anything arriving on an access port is simply assumed to belong to the particular VLAN assigned to the port. So, what do you think will happen if an access port receives a tagged packet, say, IEEE 802.1Q tagged? Right—that packet would simply be dropped. But why? Well, because an access port doesn't look at the source address, so tagged traffic can be forwarded and received only on trunk ports.

With an access link, this can be referred to as the port's *configured VLAN*. Any device attached to an *access link* is unaware of a VLAN membership. The device basically assumes it's part of some broadcast domain, but since it doesn't have the big picture, it doesn't understand the physical network topology at all.

Also good to know is that switches remove any VLAN information from the frame before it's forwarded out to an access-link device. Remember that access-link devices can't communicate with devices outside their VLAN unless the packet is routed. And you can only create a switch port to be either an access port or a trunk port—not both. So you've got to choose one or the other and know that if you make it an access port, that port can be assigned to only one VLAN!

Trunk Ports   Believe it or not, the term trunk port was inspired by the telephone system trunks, which carry multiple telephone conversations at a time. So it follows that trunk ports can similarly carry multiple VLANs at a time.

A *trunk link* is a 100Mbps or 1000Mbps or 10000Mbps point-to-point link between two switches, between a switch and router, or even between a switch and server, and it carries the traffic of multiple VLANs—from 1 to 4,094 at a time. But make a note that it's really only up to 1,005 unless you're going with extended VLANs.

Trunking can be a real advantage because with it, you get to make a single port part of a whole group of different VLANs at the same time. This is a great feature because you can actually set ports up to have a server in two separate broadcast domains simultaneously so your users won't have to cross a layer 3 device like a router to log in for access. Another benefit to trunking comes into play when you're connecting switches. Trunk links can carry the frames of various VLANs across the link, but by default, if the links between your switches aren't trunked, only information from the configured access VLAN will be switched across that link.

Check out Figure 11.8. It illustrates how the different links are used within a switched network.

FIGURE 11.8   Access and trunk links in a switched network

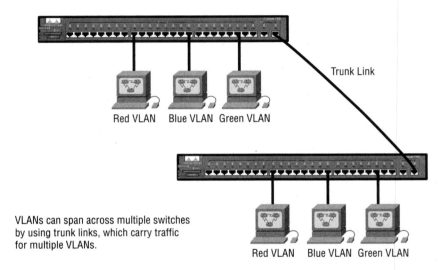

VLANs can span across multiple switches by using trunk links, which carry traffic for multiple VLANs.

All hosts connected to the switches can communicate to all ports in their VLAN because of the trunk link between them. Remember, if we used an access link between the switches instead, only one VLAN would be able to communicate across the switches. As you can see, these hosts are using access links to connect to the switch, so they're communicating in one VLAN only. That means that without a router, no host can communicate outside its own VLAN, but they can send data over trunked links to hosts on another switch configured within their same VLAN.

Okay—it's finally time to tell you about frame tagging and the VLAN identification methods used in it.

Frame Tagging

As you now know, you can set up your VLANs to span more than one connected switch. You can see that going on in Figure 11.8, which depicts hosts from various VLANs spread across a bunch of switches. This flexible, power-packed capability is probably the main advantage to implementing VLANs.

But it can get kind of complicated—even for a switch—so there needs to be a way for each one to keep track of all the users and frames as they travel over the switch fabric and VLANs. When I say "switch fabric," I'm just referring to a group of switches that share the same VLAN information. Anyway, this just happens to be where *frame tagging* enters the scene. This frame identification method uniquely assigns a user-defined VLAN ID to each frame. Sometimes people refer to it as a VLAN ID or even VLAN color.

Here's how it works: Once within the switch fabric, each switch that the frame reaches must first identify the VLAN ID from the frame tag. It then finds out what to do with the frame by looking at the information in what's known as the filter table. If the frame reaches a switch that has another trunked link, the frame will be forwarded out the trunk-link port.

Once the frame reaches an exit that's determined by the forward/filter table to be an access link matching the frame's VLAN ID, the switch will remove the VLAN identifier. This is so the destination device can receive the frames without being required to understand their VLAN identification information.

Another important fact about trunk ports is that they will support tagged and untagged traffic simultaneously—if you're using 802.1Q trunking, which I'll cover later. The trunk port is assigned a default port VLAN ID (PVID) for a VLAN on which all untagged traffic will travel. This VLAN is also called the native VLAN, and is always VLAN 1 by default, but you can change it to any VLAN number you want.

Similarly, any untagged or tagged traffic with a NULL, or unassigned VLAN ID, is assumed to belong to the VLAN with the port default PVID—again, VLAN 1, by default. A packet with a VLAN ID equal to the outgoing port native VLAN is sent untagged and can communicate only to hosts or devices within the same VLAN. All other VLAN traffic has to be sent with a VLAN tag to communicate within a particular VLAN that corresponds with that specific tag.

VLAN Identification Methods

VLAN identification is the tool switches use to keep track of all those frames as they're traversing a switch fabric. It's how switches identify which frames belong to which VLANs, and there's more than one trunking method, which I'll cover next.

Inter-Switch Link (ISL)

Inter-Switch Link (ISL) is a way of explicitly tagging VLAN information onto an Ethernet frame. This tagging information allows VLANs to be multiplexed over a trunk link through an external encapsulation method (ISL), which allows the switch to identify the VLAN membership of a frame received over the trunked link.

By running ISL, you can interconnect multiple switches and still maintain VLAN information as traffic travels between switches on trunk links. ISL functions at layer 2 by encapsulating a data frame with a new header and a new cyclic redundancy check, or CRC.

Of note is that this is proprietary to Cisco switches, and it's used for Fast Ethernet and Gigabit Ethernet links only. *ISL routing* is pretty versatile and can be used on a switch port, router interfaces, and server interface cards to trunk a server. But ISL is a legacy Cisco proprietary protocol that's not supported on Nexus, so why even bring this up to you then? Because I don't want you to have confusion when you hear the term ISL. Cisco's new use for the term ISL means a trunk link between two switches. So let's take a look at the only protocol in use today for frame tagging an ISL with Nexus.

IEEE 802.1q

Created by the IEEE as a standard method of frame tagging, IEEE 802.1q actually inserts a field into the frame to identify the VLAN. If you're trunking between a Cisco switched link and a different brand of switch, you've got to use 802.1q for the trunk to work.

And it works like this: you first designate each port that is going to be a trunk with 802.1q encapsulation. In order for them to be able to communicate, these ports must be assigned a specific VLAN ID, making them the native VLAN. Understand that VLAN 1 is the default, native VLAN and all traffic for a native VLAN when using 802.1q is untagged. The ports that populate the same trunk create a group with this native VLAN and each port gets tagged with an identification number reflecting that membership, with the default again being VLAN 1. The native VLAN allows the trunks to accept information received without any VLAN identification or frame tag.

Unlike ISL, which encapsulates trunking information to an Ethernet frame, 802.1q actually inserts fields into the frame and runs a new CRC. Figure 11.9 shows how 802.1q frame tagging information is added into the Ethernet frame between the source MAC address and EtherType Field.

> The basic purpose of ISL and 802.1q frame-tagging methods is to provide inter-switch VLAN communication. Also, remember that any 802.1q frame tagging is removed if a frame is forwarded out an access link—tagging is used internally and across trunk links only. Last, if you want to pass management traffic such as CDP and VTP, the native VLAN ID must match on both ends of the trunk link.

VLAN Trunking Protocol (VTP)

Cisco created this one too. The basic goals of *VLAN Trunking Protocol (VTP)* are to manage all configured VLANs across a switched internetwork and to maintain consistency throughout that network. VTP allows you to add, delete, and rename VLANs with any of this information being propagated to all other switches within the VTP domain.

Here's a list of some of the cool features VTP has to offer:

- Consistent VLAN configuration across all switches in the network
- VLAN trunking over mixed networks, such as Ethernet to ATM LANE or even FDDI

- Accurate tracking and monitoring of VLANs
- Dynamic reporting of any added VLANs to all switches in the VTP domain
- Adding VLANs using Plug and Play

FIGURE 11.9　Ethernet frame without and with 802.1q tagging

Header Without and With 802.1Q Tag

Preamble (7-bytes)	Start Frame Delimiter (1-byte)	Dest. MAC Address (6-bytes)	Source MAC Address (6-bytes)	Length /Type (2-bytes)	MAC Client Data (0-n bytes)	Pad (0-p bytes)	Frame Check Sequence (4-bytes)

Preamble (7-bytes)	Start Frame Delimiter (1-byte)	Dest. MAC Address (6-bytes)	Source MAC Address (6-bytes)	Length/Type = 802.1Q Tag Type (2-bytes)	Tag Control Information (2-bytes)	Length/type (2-bytes)	MAC Client Data (0-n bytes	Pad (0-p bytes)	Frame Check Sequence (4- bytes)

3 bits = User Priority field
1 bit = Canonical Format Identifier (CFI)
12 bits - VLAN Identifier (VLAN ID)

Very nice, but before you can get VTP to manage your VLANs across the network, you have to create a VTP server. Actually, you don't need to even do that since all switches default to VTP server mode, so really, you just need to make sure you have a server. Anyway, all servers that need to share VLAN information must use the same domain name. Because a switch can be in only one domain at a time, this means that a switch can share VTP domain information with other switches only if they're configured into the same VTP domain. You can use a VTP domain if you have more than one switch connected in a network, but if you've got all your switches in only one VLAN, you don't need to use VTP. Do keep in mind that VTP information is sent between switches only via a trunk port.

Switches advertise VTP management domain information, a configuration revision number, and all known VLANs with any specific parameters. But there's also something called *VTP transparent mode*. In it, you can configure switches to forward VTP information through trunk ports and yet not to accept information updates or update their VTP databases.

If you've got sneaky users adding switches to your VTP domain behind your back, you can include passwords, but don't forget that every switch must be set up with the same password. And as you can imagine, this little precaution can be a serious hassle administratively.

Switches detect any added VLANs within a VTP advertisement and then prepare to send information on their trunk ports with the newly defined VLAN in tow. Updates are sent out as revision numbers that consist of summary advertisements. Anytime a switch sees a higher revision number, it knows the information it's getting is more current, so it will overwrite the existing VLAN database with the latest information.

It would be good to memorize these three requirements for VTP to communicate VLAN information between switches:

▪ The VTP management domain name of both switches must be set the same.

▪ One of the switches has to be configured as a VTP server.

▪ Set a consistent VTP password if you choose to use one.

And now that you've got that down, we're going to delve deeper into the world of VTP by exploring VTP modes and VTP pruning.

VTP Modes of Operation

Figure11.10 depicts all different modes of operation within a VTP domain using NX-OS.

FIGURE 11.10   VTP modes

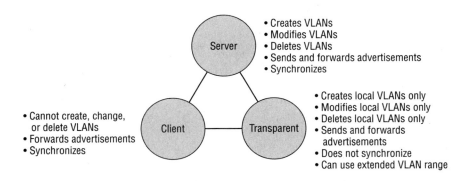

Server   This is the default mode for all Catalyst switches. You need at least one server in your VTP domain to propagate VLAN information throughout that domain. Also important: the switch must be in server mode to be able to create, add, and delete VLANs in a VTP domain. VLAN information must be changed in server mode, and any change made to VLANs on a switch in server mode will be advertised to the entire VTP domain. In VTP server mode, VLAN configurations are saved in NVRAM on the switch.

Client   In client mode, switches receive information from VTP servers, but they also receive and forward updates. In this way, they behave like VTP servers. The difference is that they can't create, change, or delete VLANs. Also, none of the ports on a client switch can be added to a new VLAN until the VTP server notifies the client switch about the new VLAN, which is then added into the client's VLAN database. Also important is that VLAN information sent from a VTP server isn't stored in NVRAM. This is key because it means that if the switch is reset or reloaded, the VLAN information will be deleted. So here's a really helpful hint: if you want a switch to become a server, first make it a client so it will receive all the correct VLAN information, then change it to a server—so much easier!

Okay, so basically, a switch in VTP client mode will forward VTP summary advertisements and process them. This switch will learn the information, but it won't save the VTP configuration in the running configuration. And it won't save it in NVRAM either, because switches in VTP client mode will only learn about and pass along VTP information—that's it!

 Real World Scenario

So, When Do I Need to Consider Using VTP?

Here's a scenario for you. Bob, a senior network administrator at Acme Corporation in San Francisco, has about 25 switches all connected together, and he wants to configure VLANs to break up broadcast domains. When do you think he should start to consider using VTP?

If you answered that he should have used VTP the moment he had more than one switch and multiple VLANs, you're right—congratulations! If you have only one switch, then VTP is irrelevant. It also isn't a player if you're not configuring VLANs in your network. But if you do have multiple switches that use multiple VLANs, you'd better configure your VTP server and clients, and you better do it right.

When you first bring up your unconfigured switched network, verify that your main switch is a VTP server and that all the other ones are VTP clients. When you create VLANs on the main VTP server, all switches will receive the VLAN database.

If you have an existing switched network and you want to add a new switch, make sure to configure it as a VTP client before you install it. If you don't, it's possible—okay, highly probable—that your new little beauty will send out a new VTP database to all your other switches, effectively wiping out all your existing VLANs like a nuclear blast. No one needs that!

Transparent   Switches in transparent mode don't participate in the VTP domain or share its VLAN database, but they'll still forward VTP advertisements through any configured trunk links. They can create, modify, and delete VLANs because they keep their own database—one they keep secret from all the other switches! Of note is that despite being kept in NVRAM, the VLAN database in transparent mode is only locally significant. The whole purpose of transparent mode is to allow remote switches to receive the VLAN database from a VTP server-configured switch via a switch that's not participating in the same VLAN assignments.

VTP only learns about normal-range VLANs with VLAN IDs 1 to 1005. VLANs with IDs greater than 1005 are called extended-range VLANs and they're not stored in the VLAN database. The switch must be in VTP transparent mode when you create VLAN IDs from 1006 to 4094, so it would be pretty rare that you'd ever use these. One more thing: VLAN IDs 1 and 1002 to 1005 are automatically created on all switches and can't be removed!

Off   The off mode in VTP is only in the newer version of NX-OS and is an additional tool you can use with VTP. This is not available with IOS at the time of this writing. Off mode doesn't really turn VTP off as you would think, because the switch will still receive and store updates but never send them out trunk links. This is different than transparent mode, which just receives and forwards advertisements but does not learn from the updates. Basically the off mode was created for your SNMP manager to monitor VLANs.

Where Did I Get My VLAN and VTP Databases?

The answer to this question depends on a few factors, but understand that NX-OS is different than an IOS-based switch. In an IOS-based switch the VLAN and VTP databases were stored in the vlan.dat file found in flash memory. Deleting this file would set the VLAN configurations back to factory default. We want to take a different approach when configuring our VLANs and VTP on our NX-OS switches and understanding where the information is stored.

First, the default configuration file for NX-OS is vlan.dat in bootflash but also the VLANs and VTP information is stored in startup-config. Let's take a look:

```
Nexus7k# dir
     12377     Feb 11 23:12:21 2013   1.t
    124967     Mar 06 17:38:05 2013   20130306_173342_poap_4477_init.log
      3923     Feb 28 19:16:42 2013   ftp
     49152     Feb 28 19:31:31 2013   lost+found/
 107369112     Oct 14 01:23:54 2011   n7000-s1-dk9.5.0.2a.bin
 207655044     Feb 28 19:27:08 2013   n7000-s1-dk9.6.1.3.bin
  23613440     Oct 14 01:24:07 2011   n7000-s1-kickstart.5.0.2a.bin
    110592     Jan 08 01:18:41 2013   n7000-s1-kickstart.5.2.1.bin
  29704704     Feb 28 19:28:59 2013   n7000-s1-kickstart.6.1.3.bin
      4096     Feb 28 19:47:13 2013   scripts/
  65124480     Mar 14 22:36:42 2013   t.txt
      4096     Mar 05 23:03:02 2013   vdc_2/
      4096     Mar 06 17:56:37 2013   vdc_3/
      4096     Mar 05 23:07:56 2013   vdc_4/
       508     Mar 18 20:30:23 2013   vlan.dat


Usage for bootflash://
  561324032 bytes used
 1277534208 bytes free
 1838858240 bytes total


Nexus7k#show run
[output cut]
```

```
vlan 1,44,70,99,1003,1006-1007,2323
vlan 44
  name freddy
vlan 70
  name Pod41
vlan 99
  name fred
```

We can see from the preceding output that the vlan.dat is indeed in bootflash, but what's different from an IOS switch is that the vlan.dat file does not override the active configuration file but instead mirrors the VTP configuration and the VLAN database in active configuration.

When a switch first boots up, the switch will look in the startup-config for the VTP/VLAN information and will use that configuration. If the switch is a VTP server and there is no configuration in startup-config, the server will get the VLAN database from the vlan.dat file. If there is no vlan.dat or the information cannot be retrieved, then a default configuration will be used. The default allows only VLANs 1 to 1001 to be used, and the VTP revision number will be zero (0).

If a switch boots up and the startup-config has the VTP mode as client, the switch will expect a VLAN database within 5 seconds of sending a VTP request to the server. If an update is not received, it will use the VLAN configuration in the startup-config until an update is received.

When a switch boots up in transparent mode, the VTP database in vlan.dat is not used. The VLAN and VTP configuration in the startup-config are placed in the active configuration file and used as the current active database.

You can try to delete the vlan.dat file as we do with IOS switches, but look what happens when I deleted the file:

```
Nexus7k# sh vlan brief


VLAN Name                             Status    Ports
---- -------------------------------- --------- -------------------------------
1    default                          active    Eth3/4
44   freddy                           active
70   Pod41                            active    Eth3/41, Eth3/42
99   fred                             active
1003 VLAN1003                         active
1006 VLAN1006                         active
1007 VLAN1007                         active
2323 VLAN2323                         active
```

```
Nexus7# delete bootflash:vlan.dat
Do you want to delete "/vlan.dat" ? (yes/no/abort)   [y]
Nexus7k# sh vlan brief


VLAN Name                             Status     Ports
---- -------------------------------- ---------- -------------------------------
1    default                          active     Eth3/4
44   freddy                           active
70   Pod41                            active     Eth3/41, Eth3/42
99   fred                             active
1003 VLAN1003                         active
1006 VLAN1006                         active
1007 VLAN1007                         active
2323 VLAN2323                         active


Nexus7#
```

The vlan.dat file gets the information from the current configuration. Deleting this file does nothing, and Cisco recommends in its documentation not to delete the file.

Configuring VLANs, VTP, and IVR

This may come as a surprise, but configuring VLANs is actually pretty easy. It's just that figuring out which users you want in each VLAN is not. But once you've decided on the number of VLANs you want to create, and once you've established the group of users you want to belong to each of them, it's time to bring your first VLAN into the world.

To configure VLANs on a Cisco Catalyst switch, use the global config vlan command. In the following example, I'm going to demonstrate how to configure VLANs on the S1 switch by creating three VLANs for three different departments. Always remember that by default, VLAN 1 is the native, administrative VLAN, and in the NX-OS, the VLANs are stored in the configuration and copied to the vlan.dat file.

Let's take a look at the following output to see this in motion:

```
Nexus7k(config)# vlan ?
  <1-3967,4048-4093>  VLAN ID 1-4094 or range(s): 1-5, 10 or 2-5,7-19
  access-map          Configure a VLAN access map
  dot1Q               IEEE 802.1Q Virtual LAN
  filter              Specify access control for packets
Nexus7k(config)# vlan 2
```

```
Nexus7k(config-vlan)# name Sales
Nexus7k(config-vlan)# vlan 3
Nexus7k(config-vlan)# name Marketing
Nexus7k(config-vlan)# vlan 4
Nexus7k(config-vlan)# name Accounting
```

From the preceding commands, it appears that you can create VLANs and number them whatever you want to from 2 to 4094. But this is only mostly true. VLANs numbered above 1005 are called extended VLANs, and VLANs numbered from 3968 to 4047 can never be configured at all! To configure VLANs 1002 through 1005, you need to set your switch to transparent mode, but there is no value in using these VLANs. To get a clear picture of all that, here's what happens when I try to set my Nexus switch to reserved VLAN 1002 and VLAN 4000 while my switch is in VTP server mode:

```
Nexus7k(config)# vlan 1002
ERROR: 1002 cannot be configured when VTP is in CLIENT or SERVER mode


Nexus7k(config)# vlan 4000
                     ^
invalid vlans (reserved values) at '^' marker.
```

Let's take a look at a command that shows the switches' internal VLANs and their usage:

```
Nexus7# sh vlan internal usage

VLANs                   DESCRIPTION
-------------------     ------------------
3968-4031               Multicast
4032-4035,4048-4059     Online Diagnostic
4036-4039,4060-4087     ERSPAN
4042                    Satellite
3968-4095               Current
Nexus7#
```

If you want to find VLANs that have been created within the extended range, you can use the command show vlan, show vlan brief, or the easiest one, and my personal favorite, show vlan summary:

```
Nexus7k# sh vlan summary
```

```
Number of existing VLANs          : 7
 Number of existing user VLANs    : 4
 Number of existing extended VLANs : 3
```

Make sure you understand how to verify configured VLANs and extended VLANs for the exam objectives!

After you create the VLANs that you want, you can use the show vlan command to check them out. But take notice of the following output. By default, all ports on the switch are in VLAN 1. Also, it's really important to remember that to change the VLAN associated with a port, you must go to each interface and tell it which VLAN to be a member of.

Always remember that a created VLAN is unused until it's assigned to a switch port or ports. Also, all ports are always assigned in VLAN 1 unless set otherwise!

Okay, so once the VLANs have been created, you can verify your configuration with the show vlan command—sh vlan for short:

```
Nexus7k# sh vlan
VLAN Name                             Status    Ports
---- -------------------------------- --------- -------------------------------
1    default                          active    Eth3/20, Eth3/21, Eth3/22
                                                Eth3/23, Eth3/24, Eth3/25
                                                Eth3/26, Eth3/27, Eth3/28
                                                Eth3/29


2    Sales                            active
3    Marketing                        active
4    Accounting                       active
 [output cut]
```

Just so you know, the output you get could vary from what you see here depending on your specific switch's default behavior. For instance, Nexus 7000 switches default to layer 3 ports, and these ports won't show up as an available port for a VLAN. If you have layer 2 ports, as demonstrated in the output you see here, those ports will be listed under VLAN 1 by default until you change the port membership. But my output is from a Nexus switch, not from an IOS-based one, and this will display both trunk ports and access ports under each VLAN!

So now that we can actually see the VLANs we've created, we can specifically assign switch ports to them. And even though each port can only be part of one VLAN, we can use trunking to make a port available to traffic from all VLANs.

Assigning Switch Ports to VLANs

As you probably guessed, there's more than one way to configure a port. But we're still going to start by joining the port to a particular VLAN. After that, we can assign a membership mode that will determine the type of traffic the port carries. We can even tweak the number of VLANs to which the port can belong.

To configure each port on a switch to belong to a specific VLAN or access port, I'm going to enter the interface switchport command. We can also configure multiple ports at the same time by using a comma or dash. And notably, to assign multiple ports to a VLAN, we no longer need the range command we used when configuring multiple ports in the IOS!

Alright, so in the following example, I'm going to configure interface e3/29 to VLAN 3:

```
Nexus7k(config)# int e3/29
Nexus7k(config-if)# switchport mode access
Nexus7k(config-if)# switchport access ?
  vlan  Set VLAN when interface is in access mode


Nexus7k(config-if)# switchport access vlan 3
Nexus7k(config-if)# sh vlan


VLAN Name                             Status    Ports
---- -------------------------------- --------- -------------------------------
1    default                          active    Eth3/20, Eth3/21, Eth3/22
                                                Eth3/23, Eth3/24, Eth3/25
                                                Eth3/26, Eth3/27, Eth3/28
2    Sales                            active
3    Marketing                        active    Eth3/29
4    Accounting                       active
```

By starting with the switchport mode access command, I ensured that this would be a non-trunking layer 2 port. We can now assign a VLAN to the port with the switchport access command.

We're almost done! Do remember that if you plugged devices into each VLAN port, they can only talk to other devices within the same VLAN. But since we really want inter-VLAN communication to happen, it's a great time to get into a more in-depth look at trunking, which will move us nicely into VTP and inter-VLAN communication. I'll also demonstrate how to do this along the way.

Configuring Trunk Ports

Because the NX-OS switch only runs the IEEE 802.1q encapsulation method, we don't need to set the encapsulation command as we did with IOS-based switches because ISL just isn't an option. And unlike IOS-based switches, Nexus OS switches do not auto-detect trunking, meaning that if you want to trunk a port, you've got to configure it manually. To configure trunking on an Ethernet port, I'm going to use the interface command `switchport mode trunk`.

The following switch output shows the trunk configuration on interface e3/28 as set to `trunk`:

```
Nexus7k(config-if)# where
  conf; interface Ethernet3/29       admin@Nexus7k-Nexus20%default


Nexus7k(config-if)# int e3/28
Nexus7k(config-if)# switchport mode ?
  access        Port mode access
  dot1q-tunnel  Port mode dot1q tunnel
  fex-fabric    Port mode FEX fabric
  trunk         Port mode trunk


Nexus7k(config-if)# switchport mode trunk
```

Pretty simple and straightforward. To disable trunking on an interface, use the `switchport mode access` command, which sets the port back to a dedicated layer 2 access switch port. Take a look at the `show vlan` output now:

```
Nexus7k(config-if)# sh vlan


VLAN Name                             Status    Ports
---- -------------------------------- --------- --------------------------------
1    default                          active    Eth3/20, Eth3/21, Eth3/22
                                                Eth3/23, Eth3/24, Eth3/25
                                                Eth3/26, Eth3/27, Eth3/28
2    Sales                            active    Eth3/28
3    Marketing                        active    Eth3/28, Eth3/29
4    Accounting                       active    Eth3/28
```

I mentioned that trunk links show up in the `show vlan` output, and we can see that port e3/28 is now listed under each VLAN. But to me, this output can get kind of annoying if you have a lot of trunk links. As far as I'm concerned, this is what the `show interface trunk` command is for!

Defining the Allowed VLANs on a Trunk

Because trunk ports send and receive information from all VLANs by default, if a frame is untagged, it will be sent to the management VLAN. This applies to the extended range VLANs too.

But we can remove VLANs from the allowed list to prevent traffic from certain VLANs from traversing a trunked link. I'm going to do that now using the switchport trunk allowed vlan command:

```
Nexus7k(config-if)# switchport trunk ?
  allowed  Set allowed VLAN characteristics when interface is in trunking mode
  native   Set trunking native characteristics when interface is in trunking
           mode


Nexus7k(config-if)# switchport trunk allowed vlan ?
  <1-3967,4048-4093>  VLAN IDs of the allowed VLANs when this port in trunking
                      mode
  add                 Add VLANs to the current list
  all                 All VLANs
  except              All VLANs except the following
  none                No VLANs
  remove              Remove VLANs from the current list


Nexus7k(config-if)# switchport trunk allowed vlan remove 3
Nexus7k(config-if)# show int trunk


Port       Native  Status      Port
           Vlan                Channel
Eth3/28    1       trunking    --


Port       Vlans Allowed on Trunk
Eth3/28    1-2, 4-3967,4048-4093
```

Presto...VLAN 3 is no longer allowed across e3/28's trunk link. But that's not all that can be done using this command. With it, we can do the following:

- Add and remove individual VLANs to the link
- Allow all VLANs across the trunk link (the default) or allow none at all
- Allow all VLANs excluding the ones you chose by hand

Most of the time, people use this command to remove individual VLANs from links. Next up, I'm going to show you how to configure a native VLAN for a trunk before we get into routing between VLANs.

Changing or Modifying the Trunk Native VLAN

As I said, you might not want to change the trunk port native VLAN from VLAN 1, but you can, and some people do it for security reasons. To change the native VLAN, use the following command:

```
Nexus7k(config-if)# switchport trunk native vlan ?
  <1-3967,4048-4093>  VLAN ID of the native VLAN when this port is in trunking
                      mode
```

```
Nexus7k(config-if)# switchport trunk native vlan 600
```

You can see that I've changed my native VLAN on my trunk link to 600. I can verify this action using the show running-config command; we can now see the configuration under the trunk link:

```
!
interface Ethernet3/28
  switchport
  switchport mode trunk
  switchport trunk native vlan 600
  switchport trunk allowed vlan 1-2,4-3967,4048-4093
```

In addition to the show run command, the show interface *interface* switchport command is an exam objective and displays the trunking native mode VLAN for port Ethernet 3/28. Here's an example:

```
Nexus7k#  sh int e3/28 switchport
Name: Ethernet3/28
  Switchport: Enabled
  Switchport Monitor: Not enabled
  Operational Mode: trunk
  Access Mode VLAN: 1 (default)
  Trunking Native Mode VLAN: 600 (Vlan not created)
  Trunking VLANs Enabled: 1-2,4-3967,4048-4093
  Administrative private-vlan primary host-association: none
  Administrative private-vlan secondary host-association: none
  Administrative private-vlan primary mapping: none
  Administrative private-vlan secondary mapping: none
  Administrative private-vlan trunk native VLAN: none
  Administrative private-vlan trunk encapsulation: dot1q
  Administrative private-vlan trunk normal VLANs: none
  Administrative private-vlan trunk private VLANs: none
  Operational private-vlan: none
```

The show interface *interface* switchport command reveals the native VLAN for that interface, as does the show interface trunk command. Make sure you remember both commands! And don't forget that all switches on a given trunk must use the same native VLAN or you won't be able to send management traffic down that link.

Configuring VTP

All Cisco IOS switches are configured to be VTP servers by default, so it's easy to assume that this is consistent throughout the NX-OS, but it's not. Whether this is true or not depends upon the specific NX-OS version you're dealing with. Some NX-OS versions are set as VTP servers by default, but some versions default to transparent.

Okay, now to configure VTP, you've got to enable the VTP feature on the NX-OS first. And of course, once you configure the VTP information on a switch, you need to verify it.

When you configure VTP, you have a few options, including setting the domain name, password, operating mode, and pruning capabilities of the switch. I'm going to use the vtp global configuration mode command to configure all these settings. In the following example, I'll set the S1 switch to vtp server, the VTP domain to Lammle, and the VTP password to todd:

```
Nexus7k(config)# feature vtp
Nexus7k(config)# vtp mode server
Nexus7k(config)# vtp domain Lammle
Nexus7k(config)# vtp password todd
Nexus7k(config)# vtp version 2
Nexus7k(config)# vtp pruning
Pruning switched on.Nexus7k(config)# sh vtp password
VTP password: todd
Nexus7k(config)# sh vtp status
VTP Status Information
----------------------

VTP Version                    : 2 (capable)
Configuration Revision         : 0
Maximum VLANs supported locally : 1005
Number of existing VLANs       : 5
VTP Operating Mode             : Server
VTP Domain Name                : Lammle
VTP Pruning Mode               : Enabled (Operationally Enabled))
VTP V2 Mode                    : Disabled
VTP Traps Generation           : Disabled
MD5 Digest                     : 0x02 0x11 0x18 0x4B 0x36 0xC5 0xF4 0x1F
```

```
Configuration last modified by 0.0.0.0 at 0-0-00 00:00:00
Local updater ID is 0.0.0.0
VTP version running            : 2
```

Please make sure that if you want to change and distribute any VLAN information on a switch, you absolutely must be in VTP server mode. In the preceding example, I had used just about every VTP command there is; there are not a lot of commands to configure VTP and only one to verify it, which can make it tough for troubleshooting. VTP pruning is helpful in stopping a VLAN broadcast from traversing a trunked link if there are no ports in that VLAN on the receiving switch. However, not all switches support VTP pruning.

After you configure the VTP information, you can verify it with the show vtp status command as shown in the preceding output. The preceding switch output shows the VTP domain, the VTP mode, and the switch's VTP password.

Let's go to the Nexus 7K and 5K switches that I connected together and set them into the Lammle VTP domain. It is very important to remember that the VTP domain name is case sensitive! VTP is not forgiving—one teeny small mistake and it just won't work. Let's take a look:

```
Nexus7k# sh vtp stat
VTP Version                       : 2 (capable)
Configuration Revision            : 4
Maximum VLANs supported locally : 1005
Number of existing VLANs          : 8
VTP Operating Mode                : Server
VTP Domain Name                   : Lammle
VTP Pruning Mode                  : Enabled (Operationally Enabled)
VTP V2 Mode                       : Disabled
VTP Traps Generation              : Disabled
MD5 digest                        : 0x0F 0xC9 0x98 0xAC 0x87 0xF7 0x1E 0x74
Configuration last modified by 0.0.0.0 at 5-15-11 00:03:29
Local updater ID is 0.0.0.0
VTP version running               : 2


Nexus5k# show vtp status
VTP Version                       : 2
Configuration Revision            : 4
Maximum VLANs supported locally : 1005
Number of existing VLANs          : 8
VTP Operating Mode                : Client
VTP Domain Name                   : Lammle
```

```
VTP Pruning Mode               : Disabled
VTP V2 Mode                    : Disabled
VTP Traps Generation           : Disabled
MD5 digest                     : 0x0F 0xC9 0x98 0xAC 0x87 0xF7 0x1E 0x74
Configuration last modified by 0.0.0.0 at 0-0-00 00:00:00
```

First, I want you to notice that there are two switches and that each is running VTP version 2. The next line is one of the most important lines because it reveals the VTP database revision number. The server's database number must be higher than a client's or regular server's in order for the database device to even receive and process the database because if the number is the same or lower, the switches will just discard the summary advertisement as though it was nothing! Okay, next up we see the number of existing VLANs—a total of eight, including five default VLANs, VLAN 1 and 1002 through 1005. So we clearly have three configured VLANs. Moving on, we see that our VTP mode is client, but it could show up as server, client or transparent or even off. The domain name, Lammle, is very important as well, and it absolutely must be the same on all switches. In case you're wondering, the answer is yes—it's case sensitive!

The last two lines represent the MD5 digest used for the VTP password and the IP address (if shown) of the specific server that we received the VLAN database from. Did you notice that the MD5 hash matches exactly on both switches? This means our VTP passwords match on both of them. By the way, this just happens to be a great troubleshooting tool because if your domain names and passwords don't match, VTP summary advertisements will be rejected! So don't forget to run the show vtp password command on both switches to verify that the MD5 matches.

Let's mix things up now by connecting a router into our switched network and configuring inter-VLAN communication!

Configuring Inter-VLAN Routing

Hosts in a VLAN live in their own broadcast domain and can communicate freely. VLANs create network partitioning and traffic separation at layer 2 of the OSI, and as I said when I told you why we still need routers, if you want hosts or any other IP-addressable device to communicate between VLANs, you just have to have a layer 3 device to provide routing—period.

For this, you can use a router that has an interface for each VLAN or a router that supports 802.1q routing.

As shown in Figure 11.11, if you have only two or three VLANs, you can get by with a router equipped with two or three Fast Ethernet connections. And unless you're someone housing a huge, multi-department staff, 10BaseT is perfectly okay for home use—but *only* for home use because for anything else, you need serious power, and I'd recommend Fast Ethernet or Gigabit interfaces for that!

FIGURE11.11:   Router with individual VLAN associations

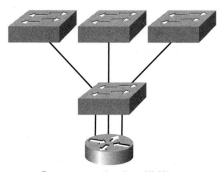

Router connecting three VLANs
together for inter-VLAN communication,
one interface for each VLAN.

In Figure 11.11, you can see that each router interface is plugged into an access link. This means that each router's interface IP address would become the default gateway address for each host in each respective VLAN.

If you have more VLANs available than router interfaces, you'll need to either configure trunking on one Fast Ethernet interface or buy a layer 3 device, such as a Nexus switch are. But if you go with the latter option, do remember that not all Nexus switches support layer 3 routing—choose carefully! If you're short on cash, you can use one Fast Ethernet interface and run 802.1q trunking instead of using a router interface for each VLAN. Figure 11.12 shows how a Fast Ethernet interface on a router will look when configured with 802.1q trunking. Doing this allows all VLANs to communicate through one interface. Cisco calls this a "router on a stick."

FIGURE 11.12   "Router on a stick"

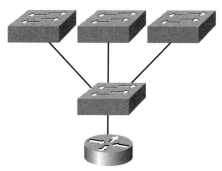

Router connecting all VLANs together
allowing for inter-VLAN communication,
using only one router interface
(router on a stick).

I've got to say that to really nail this well, you're much better off using a higher-end switch and routing on the backplane!

When you're dealing with a large or enterprise network, deploying inter-VLAN routing (IVR) on to the switch fabric is the way to go because it's a lot faster for basic VLAN connectivity. This is known as a switched virtual interface (SVI), and it's logically configured on the switch. But it's rare to be able to replace your external routers in all circumstances because every network is different, with different needs, so design each accordingly.

Differences aside, let's take a look at a typical VLAN network now and then configure NX-OS with SVIs to provide layer 3 routing between VLANs. Figure 11.13 shows a Nexus with three VLANs configured.

FIGURE 11.13   Nexus with three VLANs

VLAN 10: 172.16.10.0/24
VLAN 20: 172.16.20.0/24
VLAN 30: 172.16.30.0/24

As you know, the hosts in these three VLANs can't communicate to hosts outside their own VLAN by default. I just addressed this issue by connecting a router port into each VLAN and then configuring "router on a stick."

Let's get inside the Nexus 7000 workhorse and configure SVIs for each VLAN to enable inter-VLAN routing:

```
Nexus7k(config)# feature interface-vlan
Nexus7k(config)# interface vlan 10
Nexus7k(config-if)# ip address 172.16.10.1/24
Nexus7k(config-if)# int vlan 20
Nexus7k(config-if)# ip address 172.16.20.1/24
Nexus7k(config-if)# int vlan 30
Nexus7k(config-if)# ip address 172.16.30.1/24
```

And you thought this would be hard, right? First, I enabled the SVI feature and then the interface for each VLAN, followed by the IP address that will become the default gateway address for each VLAN. Each VLAN's host can now communicate with the others through the switch fabric. One last thing—it's really important that you don't get the commands vlan 10 and interface vlan 10 confused. Instead, remember that the first configures the VLAN in the active configuration file and the second configures the *routed interface* for that specific VLAN.

Summary

This chapter introduced you to the world of virtual LANs and described how Cisco switches can use them. You saw how VLANs break up broadcast domains in a switched internetwork—a very important, necessary thing because layer 2 switches only break up collision domains and, by default, all switches make up one large broadcast domain. I also described access links to you, and we went over how trunked VLANs work across a Fast Ethernet or faster link.

You now know that you really shouldn't ever change, delete, or rename VLAN 1 because it's the default, native VLAN. This means that any layer 2 ports that aren't specifically assigned to a different VLAN will be sent down to the native VLAN—VLAN 1. You would want to mess with this arrangement only to meet some pretty unusual security requirements!

Trunking is a crucial technology to understand well when you're dealing with a network populated by multiple switches that are running several VLANs. I also talked at length about VLAN Trunk Protocol (VTP), which in reality has nothing to do with trunking. You learned that it does send VLAN information down a trunked link but that the trunk configuration in and of itself isn't part of VTP.

This chapter also provided important troubleshooting and configuration examples of VTP, trunking, and VLAN configurations, including inter-VLAN routing.

Exam Essentials

Understand the term *frame tagging*.   *Frame tagging* refers to VLAN identification; this is what switches use to keep track of all those frames as they're traversing a switch fabric. It's how switches identify which frames belong to which VLANs.

Understand the 802.1Q VLAN identification method.   This is a non-proprietary IEEE method of frame tagging. Nexus uses only 802.1q frame tagging.

Remember how to set a trunk port on a Nexus switch.   To set a port to trunking on a Nexus switch, use the `switchport mode trunk` command. Same command as used on IOS-based switches, but the encapsulation command is not available because Nexus doesn't support ISL.

Remember to check a switch port's VLAN assignment when plugging in a new host.   If you plug a new host into a switch, then you must verify the VLAN membership of that port. If the membership is different than what is needed for that host, the host will not be able to reach the needed network services, such as a workgroup server.

Understand the purpose and configuration of VTP.   VTP provides propagation of the VLAN database throughout your switched network. All switches must be in the same VTP domain in order to exchange this information.

Understand the VTP modes.   VTP provides three different modes of operation: server, client, and transparent. Server mode can add, delete and modify VLANs as well as send summary advertisements and synchronize with clients. Client synchronizes the VLAN database with a server and forward summary advertisements downstream to other switches. Client cannot add, delete, or modify VLANs. Transparent mode receives and forwards only summary advertisements and has a local database only. The last mode, used for monitoring of VLANs only, is off.

Remember how to create a Cisco "router on a stick" to provide inter-VLAN communication. You can use a Cisco Fast Ethernet or Gigabit Ethernet interface to provide inter-VLAN routing. The switch port connected to the router must be a trunk port; then you must create virtual interfaces (subinterfaces) on the router port for each VLAN connecting to it. The hosts in each VLAN will use this subinterface address as their default gateway address.

Remember what an SVI is.   Switched virtual interfaces are virtual interfaces that you create virtually on the Nexus switch; they provide inter-VLAN communication.

Remember how to configure an SVI.   To create an SVI, it's rather simple. Go to *global config* and enable the SVI process, then type the interface VLAN #, and finally, add the IP address for that VLAN, as in this example:

```
feature interface-vlan
interface vlan 10
ip address 192.168.10.0/24
```

Written Lab 11

You can find the answers in Appendix A. In this section, write the answers to the following questions:

1. What VTP mode can only accept VLAN information and not change it?

2. What command will show us where we received our VLAN database from?

3. VLANs break up _____ domains.

4. Switches, by default, break up only _____ domains.

5. What VTP mode has a local database and does not synchronize with servers?

6. What does trunking provide?

7. What is frame tagging?

8. True/False: The 802.1q encapsulation is removed from the frame if the frame is forwarded out an access link.

9. What type of link on a switch is a member of only one VLAN?

10. What feature do you enable in order to create an SVI?

Hands-On Labs 11

In this section, you will perform commands on a Nexus switch that will help you understand what you learned in this chapter.

You'll need at least one Nexus device. The hands-on labs in this section are included for use with a real Nexus device or the Nexus simulator included with this book.

Here are the hands-on labs for chapter 11:

Lab 11.1: Creating VLANs on NX-OS

Lab 11.2: Verifying VLANs on NX-OS

Lab 11.3: Assigning switch ports to VLANs

Lab 11.4: Creating and verifying trunk links

Hands-on Lab 11.1: Creating VLANs

In this first lab you will create three VLANs and name them Sales, Marketing, and Accounting. Use VLAN numbers 2, 3, and 4, respectively. Then you will create three extended VLANs.

Log in to your switch and open the console.

Configure three VLANs named Sales, Marketing and Accounting, using VLAN numbers 2, 3, and 4.

```
Nexus7k(config)# vlan ?
  <1-3967,4048-4093>   VLAN ID 1-4094 or range(s): 1-5, 10 or 2-5,7-19
  access-map           Configure a VLAN access map
  dot1Q                IEEE 802.1Q Virtual LAN
  filter               Specify access control for packets
Nexus7k(config)# vlan 2
Nexus7k(config-vlan)# name Sales
Nexus7k(config-vlan)# vlan 3
Nexus7k(config-vlan)# name Marketing
Nexus7k(config-vlan)# vlan 4
Nexus7k(config-vlan)# name Accounting
```

Create three new VLANs in the extended range using numbers 2000, 2001, and 2002, with the names as Engineering1, Engineering2, and Engineering3.

```
Nexus7k(config-vlan)# vlan 2000
Nexus7k(config-vlan)# name Engineering1
Nexus7k(config-vlan)# vlan 2001
Nexus7k(config-vlan)# name Engineering2
Nexus7k(config-vlan)# vlan 2002
Nexus7k(config-vlan)# name Engineering3
```

Great job, now let's verify our VLAN's!

Hands-on Lab 11.2: Verifying VLANs

In this lab, you will verify your VLAN database by using the show vlan and show vlan summary commands.

From the command prompt, use the show vlan command to verify the newly created VLANs.

```
Nexus7k# sh vlan
VLAN Name                             Status    Ports
---- -------------------------------- --------- --------------------------------
1    default                          active    Eth3/20, Eth3/21, Eth3/22
                                                Eth3/23, Eth3/24, Eth3/25
                                                Eth3/26, Eth3/27, Eth3/28
                                                Eth3/29

2    Sales                            active
```

```
3       Marketing                       active
4       Accounting                      active
2000    Engineering1                    active
2001    Engineering2                    active
2002    Engineering3                    active
```

If you want to find out how many VLANs you have configured on your Nexus switch, as well as how many are configured in the extended range, then use the show vlan summary command.

```
Nexus7k# sh vlan summary
Number of existing VLANs        : 7
 Number of existing user VLANs    : 4
 Number of existing extended VLANs : 3
```

Notice there are seven VLANs configured with three of them being extended VLANs.

Hands-on Lab 11.3: Assigning Switch Ports to VLANs

Now that we have our seven VLANs configured, this lab will have you assign these VLANs to ports on the switch.

Configure interface Ethernet 3/20 into VLAN 2. The ports must be layer 2 ports.

```
Nexus7k(config)# int e3/20-22
Nexus7k(config-if-range)# switchport
Nexus7k(config-if-range)# int e3/20
Nexus7k(config-if)# switchport mode access
Nexus7k(config-if)# switchport access ?
  vlan   Set VLAN when interface is in access mode


Nexus7k(config-if)# switchport access vlan 2
```

Configure interface Ethernet 3/21 into VLAN 3.

```
Nexus7k(config-if)# int e3/21
Nexus7k(config-if)# switchport mode access
Nexus7k(config-if)# switchport access vlan 3
```

Configure interface Ethernet 3/22 into VLAN 4.

```
Nexus7k(config)# int e3/22
Nexus7k(config-if)# switchport mode access
Nexus7k(config-if)# switchport access vlan 4
```

Verify your configuration with the `show vlan` command.

```
Nexus7k(config-if)# sh vlan
```

VLAN	Name	Status	Ports
1	default	active	Eth3/20, Eth3/21, Eth3/22
			Eth3/23, Eth3/24, Eth3/25
			Eth3/26, Eth3/27, Eth3/28
2	Sales	active	Eth3/20
3	Marketing	active	Eth3/21
4	Accounting	active	Eth3/22

Let's create and verify a trunk link.

Hands-on Lab 11.4: Creating and Verifying Trunk Links

In this lab, you will configure a trunk port and then verify the configuration.

1. On port Ethernet 3/28 configure the command to make the port a trunk port so it can pass traffic for all VLANs.

```
Nexus7k(config-if)# int e3/28
Nexus7k(config-if)# switchport mode ?
  access        Port mode access
  dot1q-tunnel  Port mode dot1q tunnel
  fex-fabric    Port mode FEX fabric
  trunk         Port mode trunk


Nexus7k(config-if)# switchport mode trunk
```

2. Pretty simple and straightforward. To disable trunking on an interface, use the `switchport mode access` command, which sets the port back to a dedicated layer 2 access switch port.

3. Take a look at the `show vlan` output now:

```
Nexus7k(config-if)# sh vlan
```

VLAN	Name	Status	Ports
1	default	active	Eth3/20, Eth3/21, Eth3/22
			Eth3/23, Eth3/24, Eth3/25
			Eth3/26, Eth3/27, Eth3/28

2	Sales	active	Eth3/20, Eth3/28
3	Marketing	active	Eth3/21, Eth3/28
4	Accounting	active	Eth3/22, Eth3/28

4. Notice in the above output that the trunk link is now listed on every port in the output of the show vlan command.

5. You can also verify the trunk link with the show running-config command.

```
Nexus7k(config-if)#show running-config
interface Ethernet3/28
  switchport
  switchport mode trunk
```

6. For the exam objectives, you need to use the show int *int* switchport command and understand the output. Let's take a look.

```
Nexus7k(config-if)#sh int e3/28 switchport
Name: Ethernet3/28
  Switchport: Enabled
  Switchport Monitor: Not enabled
  Operational Mode: trunk
  Access Mode VLAN: 1 (default)
  Trunking Native Mode VLAN: 1
  Trunking VLANs Enabled: 1-4093
  Administrative private-vlan primary host-association: none
  Administrative private-vlan secondary host-association: none
  Administrative private-vlan primary mapping: none
  Administrative private-vlan secondary mapping: none
  Administrative private-vlan trunk native VLAN: none
  Administrative private-vlan trunk encapsulation: dot1q
  Administrative private-vlan trunk normal VLANs: none
  Administrative private-vlan trunk private VLANs: none
  Operational private-vlan: none
```

Notice the Operation Mode, Access Mode VLAN, Trunking Native Mode and Trunking VLANs enabled.

Review Questions

You can find the answers in Appendix B.

The following questions are designed to test your understanding of this chapter's material. For more information on how to get additional questions, please see this book's introduction.

1. Which of the following is true regarding VLANs?

   A. You must have at least two VLANs defined in every Cisco switched network.

   B. All VLANs are configured at the fastest switch and, by default, propagate this information to all other switches.

   C. You should not have more than 10 switches in the same VTP domain.

   D. VTP is used to send VLAN information to switches in a configured VTP domain.

2. According to the following diagram, which of the following describes the router port configuration and the switch port configuration as shown in the topology? (Choose three.)

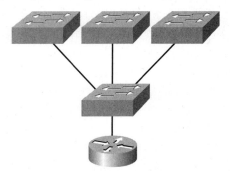

Router connecting all VLANs together
allowing for inter-VLAN communication,
using only one router interface
(router on a stick).

   A. The router WAN port is configured as a trunk port.

   B. The router port connected to the switch is configured using subinterfaces.

   C. The router port connected to the switch is configured at 10Mbps.

   D. The switch port connected to the hub is configured as full duplex.

   E. The switch port connected to the router is configured as a trunking port.

   F. The switch ports connected to the hosts are configured as access ports.

3. A switch has been configured for three different VLANs: VLAN2, VLAN3, and VLAN4. No router has been added to provide communication between the VLANs. What is the command to enable SVI routing on a Nexus switch?

    A. `feature svi`

    B. `feature interface-vlan`

    C. `ip routing`

    D. `interface vlan vlan_number`

4. You want to improve network performance by increasing the bandwidth available to hosts and limit the size of the broadcast domains. Which of the following options will achieve this goal?

    A. Managed hubs

    B. Bridges

    C. Switches

    D. Switches configured with VLANs

5. Which VTP mode disallows the creation of local VLANs? (Choose two.)

    A. Transparent

    B. Native

    C. Client

    D. Off

    E. Server

6. When a new trunk link is configured on an IOS-based switch, which VLANs are allowed over the link?

    A. By default, all VLANs are allowed on the trunk.

    B. No VLANs are allowed; you must configure each VLAN by hand.

    C. Only configured VLANs are allowed on the link.

    D. Only extended VLANs are allowed by default.

7. Which switching technology reduces the size of a broadcast domain?

    A. ISL

    B. 802.1q

    C. VLANs

    D. STP

8. What VTP mode allows you to change VLAN information on the switch?

   A. Client

   B. STP

   C. Server

   D. 802.1q

9. Which command displays the trunking native mode VLAN on part Ethernet 3/28?

   A. `show running-config switchport e3/28`

   B. `show running-config e3/28switchport`

   C. `show interface e3/28`

   D. `show interface e3/28 switchport`

   E. `show interface e3/28 native`

10. Which of the following is true regarding VTP?

   A. All switches are VTP servers by default.

   B. All switches are VTP transparent by default.

   C. VTP is on by default with a domain name of Cisco on all Cisco switches.

   D. All switches are VTP clients by default.

   E. The domain name must be the same on all switches.

11. Which protocol reduces administrative overhead in a switched network by allowing the configuration of a new VLAN to be distributed to all the switches in a domain?

   A. STP

   B. VTP

   C. DHCP

   D. ISL

12. Which statement correctly describes an SVI?

   A. An SVI is a layer 2 interface and uses a dynamic MAC address.

   B. An SVI cannot have an IP address assigned to it.

   C. An SVI provides layer 3 routing between VLANs.

   D. Each switch port requires an SVI assignment.

13. Which of the following is an IEEE standard for frame tagging?

   A. ISL

   B. 802.3Z

   C. 802.1q

   D. 802.3U

14. You connect a host to a switch port, but the new host cannot log into the server that is plugged into the same switch. What could the problem be? (Choose the most likely answer.)

    A. The router is not configured for the new host.

    B. The VTP configuration on the switch is not updated for the new host.

    C. The host has an invalid MAC address.

    D. The switch port the host is connected to is not configured with the correct VLAN membership.

15. New VLANs have just been configured on a Nexus switch; however, a directly connected switch is not receiving the VLAN via a summary update. What two reasons could cause this problem?

    A. The VTP passwords are set incorrectly.

    B. The VTP feature has not been enabled.

    C. The VTP domain names do not match.

    D. VTP is not supported on Nexus switches.

16. These two switches are not sharing VLAN information. From the following output, what is the reason these switches are not sharing VTP messages?

```
SwitchA#sh vtp status
VTP Version                      : 2
Configuration Revision           : 0
Maximum VLANs supported locally  : 64
Number of existing VLANs         : 7
VTP Operating Mode               : Server
VTP Domain Name                  : Lammle
VTP Pruning Mode                 : Disabled


SwitchB#sh vtp status
VTP Version                      : 2
Configuration Revision           : 1
Maximum VLANs supported locally  : 64
Number of existing VLANs         : 7
VTP Operating Mode               : Server
VTP Domain Name                  : GlobalNet
VTP Pruning Mode                 : Disabled
```

    A. One of the switches needs to be set to VTP version 1.

    B. Both switches are set to VTP server and one must be set to client.

    C. The VTP domain names are not configured correctly.

    D. VTP pruning is disabled.

17. Which command will you use to find how many extended VLANs are on your Nexus switch? (Choose two.)

   A. `show running-config`

   B. `show startup-config`

   C. `show vlan summary`

   D. `show vlan extended`

   E. `show vlan`

18. To configure the VLAN Trunking Protocol to communicate VLAN information between two switches, what requirements must be met? (Choose two.)

   A. Each end of the trunk link must be set to the IEEE 802.1e encapsulation.

   B. The VTP management domain name of both switches must be set the same.

   C. All ports on both the switches must be set as access ports.

   D. One of the two switches must be configured as a VTP server.

   E. A rollover cable is required to connect the two switches together.

   F. A router must be used to forward VTP traffic between VLANs.

19. These two switches are not sharing VLAN information. From the following output, what is the reason these switches are not sharing VTP messages?

```
SwitchA#sh vtp status
VTP Version                       : 2
Configuration Revision            : 0
Maximum VLANs supported locally : 64
Number of existing VLANs          : 7
VTP Operating Mode                : Server
VTP Domain Name                   : Lammle
VTP Pruning Mode                  : Disabled
MD5 Digest                        : 0x2C 0x00 0xCD 0xAE 0x1E 0x08 0xF4 0xE4


SwitchB#sh vtp status
VTP Version                       : 2
Configuration Revision            : 1
Maximum VLANs supported locally : 64
Number of existing VLANs          : 7
VTP Operating Mode                : Server
VTP Domain Name                   : Lammle
VTP Pruning Mode                  : Disabled
MD5 Digest                        : 0x2C 0x00 0xCD 0xAE 0x1E 0xCD 0x99 0x54
```

    A. One of the switches needs to be set to VTP version 1.

    B. Both switches are set to VTP server and one must be set to client.

    C. The VTP domain names are not configured correctly.

    D. VTP pruning is disabled.

    E. The VTP passwords do not match.

20. Devices on a directly connected switch are not able to communicate on VLANs 800 through 810 connected to your interface e3/28, but all other VLANs are fine. Which of the following reasons might explain the problem?

    A. Spanning tree is not enabled.

    B. The VTP feature is not enabled on the directly connected switch.

    C. The VLAN range is not allowed on your interface e3/28.

    D. The interface is not trunking.

Chapter

12

Redundant Switched Technologies

THE FOLLOWING TOPICS ARE COVERED IN THIS CHAPTER:

✓ **Building a Redundant Switched Topology**

- Recognizing Issues Associated with a Redundant Switched Topology

- Resolving Redundant Switched Issues with STP

- Describing 802.1w RSTP

- Describing 802.1s MSTP

- Describing LAN Port Channels

- Verifying LAN Port Channels

Long ago, a company called Digital Equipment Corporation (DEC) was purchased and renamed Compaq. But 30 years before that happened, DEC created the original version of *Spanning Tree Protocol*, or *STP*. The IEEE later created its own version of STP called 802.1D. Cisco has moved toward another industry standard in its newer switches called 802.1w, which NX-OS runs by default. It actually can't even run the older 802.1d legacy protocols, though the new 802.1w RSTP is backward compatible.

We'll explore both the old and new versions of STP in this chapter, but first, I'd like to define some important STP basics.

Routing protocols like RIP and OSPF have processes for preventing network loops from occurring at the Network layer, but if you have redundant physical links between your switches, these protocols won't do a thing to stop loops from occurring at the Data Link layer. That's exactly why Spanning Tree Protocol (STP) was developed—to put an end to loop issues in a layer 2 switched network. It's also why we'll be thoroughly exploring the key features of this vital protocol as well as how it works within a switched network in this chapter.

Spanning Tree Protocol

Spanning Tree Protocol (STP) achieves its primary objective of preventing network loops on layer 2 network bridges or switches by monitoring the network to track all links and shut down the redundant ones. STP uses the spanning-tree algorithm (STA) to first create a topology database and then search out and disable redundant links. With STP running, frames will be forwarded on only premium, STP-chosen links.

Let's take a minute to discuss why we really need STP in more detail.

Loop Avoidance

Redundant links between switches are good because they help prevent serious network failures if a link stops working. This sounds great, but even though redundant links can be extremely helpful, they often cause more problems than they solve. This is because frames can be flooded down all redundant links simultaneously, creating network loops as well as other evils. Here are the more vile issues redundant links can cause:

- If there are no loop avoidance strategies in place, the switches will flood broadcasts endlessly throughout the internetwork. This is sometimes referred to as a *broadcast storm*, but most of the time it's referred to in less printable ways! Figure 12.1 illustrates how a broadcast storm quickly propagates throughout the physical network media.

FIGURE 12.1   Broadcast storm

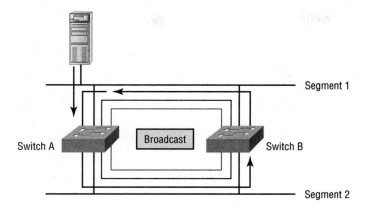

Because a frame can arrive from different segments simultaneously, a device can receive multiple copies of the same frame. Figure 12.2 demonstrates how a whole bunch of frames can arrive from multiple segments at the same time. In the figure, we see the server sending a unicast frame to Router C. Since it's a unicast frame, Switch A forwards the frame and Switch B follows suit. This is bad because it means that Router C receives that unicast frame twice, causing unnecessary overhead on the network.

FIGURE 12.2   Multiple frame copies

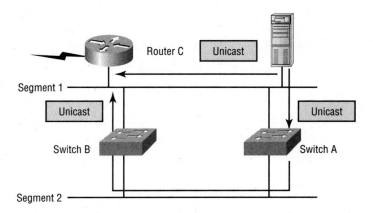

- You may have thought of this one: the MAC address filter table could become totally confused about the source device's location because the switch can receive the frame from more than one link. Worse, the then muddled switch could get so caught up in constantly updating the MAC filter table with source hardware address locations that it will fail to forward a frame. This is called thrashing the MAC table.

- One of the nastiest things that can happen is when multiple loops spread throughout a network. Loops occur within other loops, and if a broadcast storm happens on top of it all, the network hoses up and can't perform frame switching at all!

All of these problems must clearly be avoided or at least fixed, and the Spanning Tree Protocol was developed to solve each and every one of them.

 STP is a layer 2 protocol employed to maintain a loop-free switched network.

The Spanning Tree Protocol is key for use in networks like the one shown in Figure 12.3.

FIGURE 12.3 A switched network with switching loops

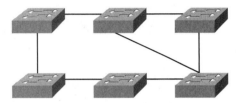

Here you see a switched network with a redundant topology that includes switching loops. Without some type of layer 2 mechanism in place to prevent a network loop, the network could be plagued by any of the problems I just talked about: broadcast storms, multiple frame copies, and MAC table thrashing.

 Understand that the network in Figure 12.3 without STP enabled would actually work, albeit slowly. This clearly demonstrates the danger of switching loops. And be warned—it can be really hard to find the source of this problem once it starts!

Spanning Tree Terms

Before I get into describing the details of how STP works within a network, it would be good for you to have some basic ideas and terms down:

Root bridge The *root bridge* is the bridge with the lowest and therefore, best bridge ID. The switches within the STP network elect a root bridge, which becomes the focal point in the network. All other decisions in the network, like which ports should be blocked or put in forwarding mode, are made from the perspective of the root bridge, and once it has been elected, all other bridges must create a single path to it. The port with the best path to the root bridge is called the root port.

Non-root bridges   Non-root bridges exchange BPDUs with all the other bridges and update the STP topology database on all switches. This prevents loops and helps defend against link failures.

BPDU   All switches exchange information to use for the subsequent configuration of the network. Each switch compares the parameters in the *Bridge Protocol Data Unit (BPDU)* that it sends to one neighbor with the parameters in the BPDU that it receives from other neighbors.

Bridge ID   The *bridge ID* is how STP keeps track of all the switches in the network and is determined by a combination of the bridge priority, which is 32,768 by default on all Cisco switches, plus the base MAC address. The bridge with the lowest bridge ID becomes the root bridge in the network.

Port cost   *Port cost* determines the best path when multiple links are used between two switches. The cost of a link is determined by the link's bandwidth.

Root port   Cost is king when it comes to the *root port*—it's always the link with the lowest-cost path to the root bridge. And do not assume that it will be a directly connected link between switches because a gigabit link that passes through two switches to get to the root bridge will be used over a directly connected Fast Ethernet link. When non-root switches start up, they must each determine a single path to the root bridge with the lowest-cost port becoming the root port. When multiple links connect to the same device and they have the same cost, the port connected to the lowest port number on the upstream switch will be used. The higher port number will have the discarding role.

Designated port   A *designated port* is one determined as having the lowest cost to the root bridge via its root port. A designated port will be marked as a forwarding port. All ports on a root bridge are designated ports.

Non-designated port   A *non-designated port* is one with a higher cost than the designated port. These are the leftovers after the root and designated ports have been determined. Non-designated ports are put in blocking mode—they're not forwarding ports.

Forwarding port   A *forwarding port* forwards frames and can be either a root or a designated port.

Blocked/Discarding port   A *blocked port* exists to prevent loops, so it will not forward frames. These ports always listen to BPDU frames but drop any and all other frames. To prevent confusion, make note of the fact that IEEE 802.1d uses blocked ports, whereas 802.1w (RSTP) uses the discarding role.

Spanning Tree Operations

Let me summarize here in order to tie the descriptions in the previous list together. Basically, STP's job is to find all links in the network and shut down any redundant ones, thereby preventing network loops from occurring. It achieves this by first electing a root bridge that will forward through all ports and act as a point of reference for all other devices within the STP domain. Once all switches agree on who the root bridge is, they must then find their one and only root port. Each and every link between two switches must have only one designated port—the port on that link that provides the highest bandwidth toward the root. It's really important to remember that a bridge can go through many other bridges to get to the root, but it's not always the shortest path that will be chosen. Whichever port happens to offer the fastest, highest bandwidth will be given that role.

Every port on the root bridge is a designated, or forwarding, port for a segment because you just can't get any closer to the root without actually being the root. And after the dust settles, any port that isn't either a root or a designated port will predictably become a non-designated port and put into the blocking state to prevent switching loops. Finally, there can be only one root bridge within any given network. I'll discuss the root bridge election process more completely in the next section.

Selecting the Root Bridge

The bridge ID is used to elect the root bridge in the STP domain and to determine the root port for each of the remaining devices when there's more than one potential root port available with equal-cost paths. This ID is 8 bytes long and includes both the priority and the MAC address of the device. The default priority on all devices running the IEEE STP version is 32,768.

To determine the root bridge, the priority of each bridge is combined with its MAC address. If two switches or bridges happen to have the same priority value, the MAC address becomes the tiebreaker for figuring out which one has the lowest and therefore the best ID. So basically, if two switches—I'll name them A and B—both use the default priority of 32,768, then the MAC address will be used instead. If Switch A's MAC address is 0000.0c00.1111 and Switch B's MAC address is 0000.0c00.2222, then Switch A would become the root bridge. Just remember that the lower value is always the better one when it comes to electing a root bridge.

Prior to the election of the root bridge, BPDUs are sent every 2 seconds out all active ports on a bridge/switch by default, and they are received and processed by all bridges. The root bridge is elected based on this information. You can change the bridge's ID by lowering its priority so that it will become a root bridge automatically. Being able to do that is important in a large switched network because it ensures that the best paths are chosen. Efficiency is always good!

Figure 12.4 illustrates a typical switched network with redundant switched paths. We'll determine which switch is the root and then make the non-root bridge become the root by changing the switch's priority.

By looking at Figure 12.4, you can tell that Switch A is the root bridge because it's the one with the lowest bridge ID. Switch B must shut down one of its ports connected to Switch A to prevent a switching loop from occurring. Remember that even though Switch B won't transmit out the blocked port, it will still receive BPDUs.

To determine which port STP will shut down on Switch B, it will first check each link's bandwidth and then shut down the link with the lowest value. Since both links between Switch A and Switch B are 100Mbps, STP will typically shut down the higher of the port numbers. In this example, 12 is higher than 11, so port 12 would be put into blocking mode.

FIGURE 12.4   A switched network with redundant switched paths

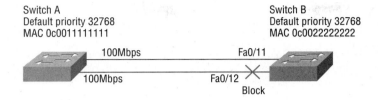

Changing the default priority is the best way to choose a root bridge. This is important because you want the switch closest to the center of your network to be the root bridge so STP will converge quickly.

Okay, now let's make Switch B the root in our network via the show spanning-tree command. The output from Switch B shows the default priority:

```
Switch B(config)# show spanning-tree
VLAN0001
  Spanning tree enabled protocol rstp
  Root ID    Priority    32769
             Address     0005.74ae.aa40
             Cost        19
             Port        1 (Ethernet3/9)
             Hello Time    2 sec  Max Age 20 sec  Forward Delay 15 sec


  Bridge ID  Priority    32769  (priority 32768 sys-id-ext 1)
             Address     0012.7f52.0280
             Hello Time    2 sec  Max Age 20 sec  Forward Delay 15 sec
             Aging Time 300
[output cut]
```

There are two things to notice here: Switch B is running the IEEE RSTP protocol—the older STP version would read "ieee." Also, the first output, or Root ID, is the root bridge information for the switched network. But it's not Switch B. Switch B's port, the root port to the root bridge, is port 1. The Bridge ID is the actual spanning tree Bridge ID information for Switch B and for VLAN 1. It's listed as VLAN0001. Note that each VLAN can have a different root bridge. Switch B's MAC address is listed as well, and you can see that it's different than the root bridge's MAC address.

Switch B's priority is 32,768—the default for every switch. You see it listed here as 32769, but the actual VLAN ID is added and called the sys-id-ext. So in this case, it shows up as 32769 for VLAN 1. VLAN 2 would be 32770, and so on.

Now let's move on and change Switch B's priority using the command shown in bold to change bridge priority on a Nexus switch:

```
Switch B(config)# spanning-tree vlan ?
  <1-3967,4048-4093>  Vlan range, Example: 1,3-5,7,9-11
Switch B(config)# spanning-tree vlan 1 priority ?
  <0-61440>  bridge priority in increments of 4096
Switch B(config)# spanning-tree vlan 1 priority 4096
```

You can set the priority to any value from 0 through 61440 in increments of 4096. Setting it to zero (0) means that the switch will always be a root as long as it has a lower MAC than another switch with its bridge ID also set to 0. If you want to set a switch to be the root bridge for every VLAN in your network, then you have to change the priority for each VLAN, with 0 being the lowest priority you can use. It's never a good idea to set all switches to a priority of 0!

Now that we've changed the priority of Switch B for VLAN 1 to 4096, we've successfully forced this switch to become the root. Check out the output:

```
Switch B(config)# show spanning-tree
VLAN0001
  Spanning tree enabled protocol rstp
  Root ID    Priority    4097
             Address     0012.7f52.0280
             This bridge is the root
             Hello Time   2 sec  Max Age 20 sec  Forward Delay 15 sec


  Bridge ID  Priority    4097    (priority 4096 sys-id-ext 1)
             Address     0012.7f52.0280
             Hello Time   2 sec  Max Age 20 sec  Forward Delay 15 sec
             Aging Time 15
[output cut]
```

Both the root's MAC address and the bridge priority of Switch B are now the same, meaning that Switch B is now the root bridge. Knowing the show spanning-tree command is very important, and we'll use it again toward the end of this chapter.

There's yet another command that you can use to set your root bridge, which I'll tell you about soon when I show you my switch configuration examples later in this chapter.

As you know, you can verify your root bridge with the show spanning-tree command, and it is important that you practice and understand the output from this command. However, if you quickly want to find all the VLANs for which your switch is the root bridge, you can use the show spanning-tree summary command and get a nice output:

```
Nexus7k# sh spanning-tree summary
Switch is in rapid-pvst mode
Root bridge for: VLAN0010, VLAN0020, VLAN0030
Port Type Default                       is disabled
Edge Port [PortFast] BPDU Guard Default  is disabled
Edge Port [PortFast] BPDU Filter Default is disabled
Bridge Assurance                        is enabled
Loopguard Default                       is disabled
Pathcost method used                    is short
STP-Lite                                is enabled


Name             Blocking Listening Learning Forwarding STP Active
---------------- -------- --------- -------- ---------- ----------
VLAN0001                7         0        0          1          8
VLAN0010                8         0        0          0          8
VLAN0020                8         0        0          0          8
VLAN0030                8         0        0          0          8
---------------- -------- --------- -------- ---------- ----------
4 vlans                31         0        0          1         32
Nexus7k#
```

By using this command, you can quickly see that this Nexus switch is the root bridge for VLANs 10, 20 and 30.

Per-VLAN Spanning-Tree+

So, if you're running Common Spanning-Tree (CST), which means you're running only one instance of STP, in your switched network with redundant links, there will be an election to choose what STP considers the best root bridge for your network. That switch will also become the root for all VLANs in your network, and all bridges in your network will create a single path to it. And as you now know, you can manually override this selection and pick whichever one you want that makes sense for you regarding your particular network.

Figure 12.5 shows how a typical root bridge would look on your switched network when running CST.

Notice that Switch A is the root bridge for all VLANs even though it's really not the best path for some VLANs because all switches must make a single path to it! This is where Per-VLAN Spanning-Tree+ (PVST+) comes into play. Because it allows for a separate instance of STP for each VLAN, it frees up the individual selection of the most optimal path.

FIGURE 12.5   STP single root bridge for all VLANs

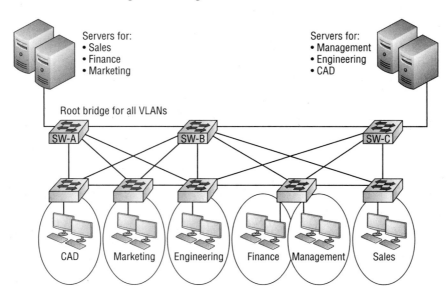

PVST+ is a Cisco proprietary extension to 802.1D STP that provides a separate 802.1 spanning-tree instance for each VLAN configured on your switches. All Cisco proprietary extensions were created to improve convergence time, which is 50 seconds by default. Cisco IOS switches run 802.1d PVST+ by default, but the NX-OS runs RSTP PVST+ by default. It's a newer, faster protocol that's also backward compatible if you happen to connect a switch running STP to a Nexus. No worries—I'll talk more about RSTP really soon!

Creating a Per-VLAN STP instance for each VLAN is worth the increased CPU and memory requirements because it allows for Per-VLAN root bridges. This feature allows the STP tree to be optimized for the traffic of each VLAN by allowing you to configure the root bridge in the center of each of them. Figure 12.6 shows how PVST+ would look in a switched network with multiple redundant links.

This root bridge placement clearly enables faster convergence as well as optimal path determination. The convergence of this version is really similar to that of 802.1 CST, which has one instance of STP no matter how many VLANs you have configured on your network, but with PVST+, convergence is on a Per-VLAN basis. Figure 12.6 also illustrates that we now have a nice, efficient root bridge selection for each VLAN.

Rapid Spanning Tree Protocol 802.1w

Wouldn't it be wonderful to have a solid STP configuration running on your switched network, regardless of switch type, and still have all the features we just discussed built in and enabled on every one of your switches too? Rapid Spanning Tree Protocol, or RSTP, brings that amazing capacity right to us!

FIGURE 12.6   PVST+ provides efficient root bridge selection.

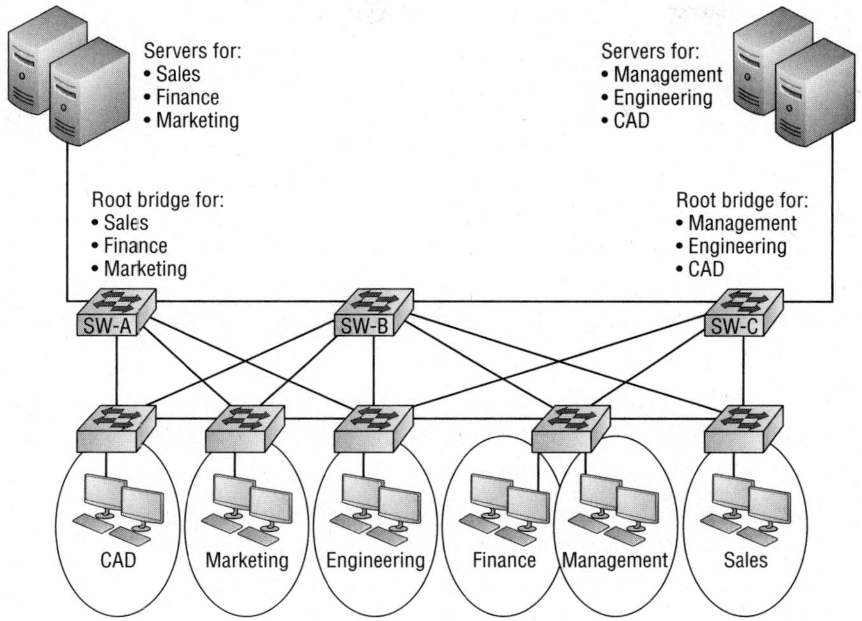

Cisco created proprietary extensions to "fix" all the sinkholes and liabilities the IEEE 802.1d standard threw at us, with the main drawback to them being that because they're Cisco proprietary, they need additional configuration. But RSTP, the new 802.1w standard, brings us most of the patches in one concise solution! The only prerequisite is that you've got to make sure all the switches in your network are running the 802.1w protocol first.

RSTP, or IEEE 802.1w, is essentially an evolution of STP that allows for much faster convergence. But even though it does address all the convergence issues, it still only permits a single instance of STP, so it doesn't help to take the edge off suboptimal traffic flow issues. And as I mentioned, to support that faster convergence, the CPU usage and memory demands are slightly higher than those of CST. The good news is that Cisco NX-OS runs the Rapid PVST+ by default—a Cisco enhancement of RSTP that provides a separate 802.1w spanning-tree instance for each VLAN configured within the network. But all that power needs fuel, and though this version addresses both convergence and traffic flow issues, it also demands the most CPU and memory of all solutions!

RSTP wasn't meant to be something completely new and different. The protocol is more of an evolution than an innovation of the 802.1d standard, which offers faster convergence whenever a topology change occurs. Backward compatibility was a must when 802.1w was created.

So, RSTP helps with convergence issues that were the bane of traditional STP, and Rapid PVST+ is based on the 802.1w standard in the same way that PVST+ is based on 802.1d.

The operation of Rapid PVST+ is simply a separate instance of 802.1w for each VLAN, and here's how this all breaks down:

- RSTP speeds the recalculation of the spanning tree when the layer 2 network topology changes.
- It's an IEEE standard that redefines STP port roles, states, and BPDUs.
- RSTP is extremely proactive and very quick, so it doesn't need the 802.1 delay timers.
- RSTP (802.1w) supersedes 802.1 while remaining backward compatible.
- Much of the 802.1d terminology and most parameters remain unchanged.
- 802.1w is capable of reverting to 802.1 to interoperate with traditional switches on a per-port basis.

And to clear up confusion, there are also five terminology adjustments between 802.1d's five port states and 802.1w's, compared here, respectively.

- Disabled = discarding
- Blocking = discarding
- Listening = discarding
- Learning = learning
- Forwarding = forwarding

Make note of the fact that RSTP basically just goes from discarding to learning to forwarding, whereas 802.1d requires five states to transition.

The task of determining the root bridge, root ports, and designated ports hasn't changed from 802.1d to RSTP, and understanding the cost of each link is still key to making these decisions well. Table 12.1 shows the IEEE costs based on bandwidth that STP and RSTP use in comparison to determine the best path to the root bridge.

TABLE 12.1 IEEE costs

Link Speed	Cost (Revised IEEE Specification)	Cost (Previous IEEE Specification)
10Gb/s	2	1
1Gb/s	4	1
100Mb/s	19	10
10Mb/s	100	100

Let's take a look at an example of how to determine ports using the revised IEEE cost specifications in Figure 12.7.

FIGURE 12.7   RSTP example 1

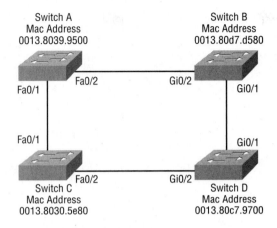

Switch A
Mac Address
0013.8039.9500

Switch B
Mac Address
0013.80d7.d580

Fa0/1   Fa0/2   Gi0/2   Gi0/1

Fa0/1   Gi0/1

Fa0/2   Gi0/2
Switch C   Switch D
Mac Address   Mac Address
0013.8030.5e80   0013.80c7.9700

Which is the root?
Which are the root ports?
Which ports are designated (F)?

Can you figure out which is the root bridge and, alternately, which are the root and designated ports here? Well, because Switch C has the lowest MAC address, it becomes the root bridge, and since all ports on a root bridge are forwarding designated ports, well, that's the easy part, right? But which would be the root port for Switch A? If the paths between Switch A and Switch B were both gigabit, their cost would only be 4, but since they are Fast Ethernet links instead, the cost is a whopping 19. A quick glance at the link between Switch B and Switch D tells us that's a gigabit link with a cost of 4. The cost of the link between Switch D and Switch C is 19 because that's also Fast Ethernet link, bringing the full cost from Switch A to Switch C through Switch B and D to total of 19+4+19, which equals 42. The alternate route through Switch A directly to Switch C, with a total cost of 19, is actually the lowest, making Fa0/1 on Switch A the root port. For Switch B, the best path is through Switch D with a cost of 4+19 = 23. This means Gi0/1 would be the root port for Switch B and Gi0/2 the root port for Switch D. Now, all that's needed is a forwarding port on the link between Switch A and Switch B. Because Switch A has the lowest bridge ID, Fa0/2 on Switch A wins that role. Any port not mentioned here would go into blocking mode (non-designated) to prevent loops.

If this seems confusing, remember that this process always unfolds in the following order: first, find your root bridge then determine your root ports, and then your designated ports. The best way to get it down, is always to practice, so let's take a look at another example shown in Figure 12.8.

Now tell me which bridge is your root bridge? Since all priorities are assumed default, SW-C would be the root bridge because it has the lowest MAC address. We can quickly see that SW-D has a direct gigabit port to SW-C, so that would be the root port for SW-D with a cost of 4. SW-B's best path would also be the direct gigabit port to SW-C with a cost of 4, but what about SW-A? The root port for SW-A can't be the direct 100Mbps port with a cost of 19, but the Gigabit port to SW-D and then the gigabit port to SW-C can with a total cost of only 8—not so hard!

FIGURE 12.8   RSTP example 2

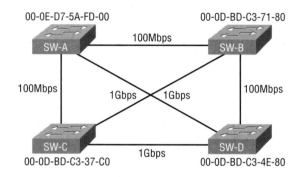

 It might come as a surprise, but RSTP actually can interoperate with legacy STP protocols. Just remember that famously fast 802.1w convergence time is lost when it interacts with legacy bridges!

Multiple Spanning Tree Protocol 802.1s

Multiple Spanning Tree Protocol (MSTP), also known as IEEE 802.ls, gives us the same fast convergence as RSTP but reduces the number of required STP instances by allowing us to map multiple VLANs with the same traffic flow requirements into the same spanning-tree instance. It essentially allows us to create VLAN sets.

So clearly, you would opt to use MSTP over RSTP when you've got a configuration involving lots of VLANs, resulting in CPU and memory requirements that would be too high otherwise. But there's no free lunch—though MSTP reduces the demands of Rapid PVST+, you've got to configure it correctly because MSTP does nothing by itself!

This brings us to Figure 12.9, which shows how we can configure MSTP to allow optimal path determination for each VLAN without the overhead of PVST+.

Figure 12.9 shows how SW-A provides root bridge services for the Sales, Finance, and Marketing VLANs in a single VLAN instance and how SW-B does the same for the Management, Engineering, and CAD VLANs. This shows each switch capitalizing on the benefits of PVST+ without the overhead drag on their CPUs.

FIGURE 12.9   MSTP 802.1s

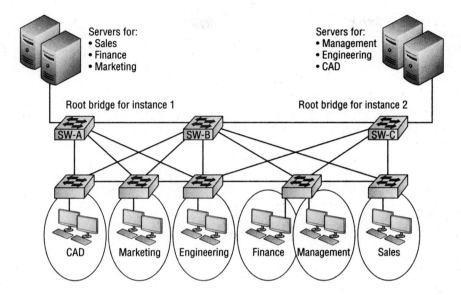

Servers for:
• Sales
• Finance
• Marketing

Servers for:
• Management
• Engineering
• CAD

Root bridge for instance 1   Root bridge for instance 2

SW-A   SW-B   SW-C

CAD   Marketing   Engineering   Finance   Management   Sales

Convergence

Convergence occurs when all ports on bridges and switches have transitioned to either forwarding or blocking modes. No data will be forwarded until convergence is complete. And
yes, that means that while STP is converging within a given VLAN, all host data will cease
to transmit until that process has concluded. If you want to remain gainfully employed,
it's a good idea to make sure your switched network is designed to ensure that whichever
version of STP running on it converges quickly! Toward that goal, Figure 12.10 shows you
some great network design samples for implementing STP on your switched network so
that it will converge efficiently.

FIGURE 12.10   An optimal hierarchical switch design

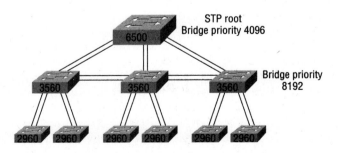

STP root
Bridge priority 4096

6500

Bridge priority
8192

3560   3560   3560

2960 2960   2960 2960   2960 2960

Create core switch as STP root for fastest STP convergence

Convergence is vital because it ensures that all devices have a coherent database, and it will require your time and attention to make that happen painlessly. The original STP (802.1d) takes 50 seconds to go from blocking to forwarding mode, and I don't recommend changing the default STP timers. You can adjust those timers for a large network, but the better solution is to not use 802.1d at all! By creating your physical switch design in a hierarchical manner, as shown in Figure 12.10, you can make your core switch the STP root, which will shorten your network's STP convergence time nicely.

Another reason that typical 50-second convergence time can be a bad thing is because it's long enough to cause time-out problems affecting your servers or hosts, especially when you've got to reboot them as a result. To address this hitch, you can disable spanning tree **services** on individual ports with the Catalyst IOS using Cisco's PortFast. Nexus, which runs RSTP by default, takes convenience a step further by allowing us to configure the ports to be either Edge ports or Network ports. This capability speeds up convergence time even more! Figure 12.11 illustrates how a switched network would look with the ports configured as I just described.

FIGURE 12.11   RSTP port types

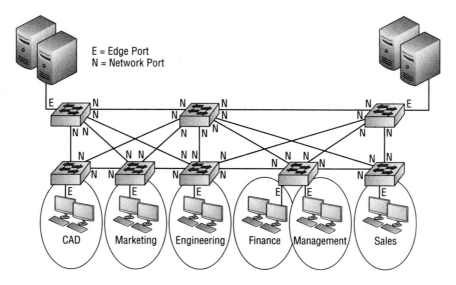

If hosts are connected to a port, you would individually configure it as an Edge port with no worries because if it ever receives a BPDU, it can immediately change into a switch port. But if you're connecting switches together, you've got to configure these ports as switch ports, which will start out in the discarding role in order to make sure no loops exist. Once a BPDU is received, the switch determines if it can be the root bridge, if it already is the root bridge, or if it should remain in its discarding role to prevent loops. If a network or switch port doesn't receive any BPDUs, it will place itself in a designated role instead.

Configuring Spanning Tree on Nexus

Spanning tree is actually configured pretty much the same way on Nexus as it is on an IOS switch, and it's verified with the same commands, but I'm still going to demonstrate how to configure the port types I just described on a Nexus switch.

You set ports to Edge only when connecting a host, printer, server, and so on to them and only if that port doesn't connect to another switch. Remember, if a port in Edge configuration receives a BPDU, it will turn into a Network port thinking it's connected to another switch. The port will then automatically become part of the STP process. So, here's how you'd configure a port to operate in Edge and Network modes:

```
nexus7k(config)# int e3/40-44
nexus7k(config-if-range)# spanning-tree port type ?
  edge     Consider the interface as edge port (enable portfast)
  network  Consider the interface as inter-switch link
  normal   Consider the interface as normal spanning tree port


nexus7k(config-if-range)# spanning-tree port type edge
Warning: edge port type (portfast) should only be enabled on ports connected
To a single host. Connecting hubs, concentrators, switches, bridges, etc...
to this interface when edge port type (portfast) is enabled, can cause temporary
bridging loops.
 Use with CAUTION
Edge Port Type (Portfast) will be configured in 5 interfaces due to the range
 Command but will only have effect when the interfaces are in a non-trunking
mode.


nexus7k(config-if-range)# int e3/45-48
nexus7k(config-if-range)# spanning-tree port type network
```

Notice that we can configure our switch ports as Edge, Network, or Normal, which is the default and is always part of all STP instances. Setting the port to Edge enables PortFast on it, meaning that port is not part of any STP instance. It will immediately go into forwarding mode when a host is connected. Pay attention to that warning I received when I set some ports into Edge mode. Plugging a switch into an Edge port would cause temporary bridging loops in NX-OS! In IOS switches, this would cause a major bridging loop unless you set up BPDU filters, but with NX-OS, the port will automatically convert to Network mode when it gets a BPDU.

Let's take a look at configuring and verifying spanning tree on NX-OS. Make a note to self that you can only configure either Rapid PVST+ or MST:

```
nexus7k(config)# spanning-tree mode ?
  mst          Multiple spanning tree mode
```

```
  rapid-pvst  Per-Vlan spanning tree mode
Nexus7k(config-if)# spanning-tree ?
  bpdufilter    Don't send or receive BPDUs on this interface
  bpduguard     Don't accept BPDUs on this interface
  cost          Change an interface's spanning tree port path cost
  guard         Change an interface's spanning tree guard mode
  lc-issu       Configure Linecard ISSU type
  link-type     Specify a link type for spanning tree tree protocol use
  mst           Multiple spanning tree
  port          Spanning tree port options
  port-priority Change an interface's spanning tree port priority
  vlan          VLAN Switch Spanning Trees
nexus7k(config-if)# sh spanning-tree
VLAN0001
  Spanning tree enabled protocol rstp
  Root ID    Priority    32769
             Address     0012.4362.a280
             Cost        57
             Port        393 (Ethernet3/9)
             Hello Time  2  sec  Max Age 20 sec  Forward Delay 15 sec


  Bridge ID  Priority    32769  (priority 32768 sys-id-ext 1)
             Address     0026.9823.7c41
             Hello Time  2  sec  Max Age 20 sec  Forward Delay 15 sec
Interface         Role Sts Cost      Prio.Nbr Type
---------------- ---- --- --------- -------- -------------------------
Eth3/1            Desg FWD 19        128.385  P2p
Eth3/9            Root FWD 19        128.393  P2p Peer(STP)
```

As you can readily see in the preceding output, there are lots of commands we can use to configure STP on NX-OS! I'm not going into all of them here because, again, that would be going outside of this book's purpose.

Back to the output—when verifying STP, we can see that this bridge isn't the root bridge for VLAN 1, but look at the cost to the root—a whopping 57! That's a huge amount of links between our switch and root bridge, which is off interface e3/9. If this were a production network, we'd definitely want to reconfigure our root bridge to be way more efficient for each of our VLANs.

There's one last command I want to tell you about, if you want to skip all this verification and configuration of the root bridge stuff—and no, you don't get to skip all that if you want to pass the Cisco exams! You don't get to skip this either, so here's the command you can run on a switch to set it as a root bridge:

```
nexus7k(config)#spanning-tree vlan 1 root ?
  primary    Configure this switch as primary root for this spanning tree
  secondary  Configure switch as secondary root
nexus7k(config)#spanning-tree vlan 1 root primary
```

Did I mention that you've got to configure this on a per-VLAN basis and that you can also set a primary and secondary switch as roots? Yep, you can, and it's certainly a whole lot easier than how we've done it in this chapter. But this is, first and foremost, a guide to prepare you for the CCNA DC exam—something you definitely want to pass. So make sure you know how to do it as we did even though it really is the hard way!

LAN Port Channels

Know that most medium- to larger-scale Ethernet networks will typically have multiple links between switches because this provides redundancy and resiliency. Even so, we can also bundle these links to gain more bandwidth between switches. It's good to watch for when you've got an improperly configured, multilink-switched network because you could very well end up with blocked ports! This is actually the result of STP just doing its job. In addition to that, routing protocols like OSPF and EIGRP will likely see all these redundant links as individual ones, which will only increase routing overhead.

Cisco PortChannel to the rescue! Cisco PortChannel allows us to bundle up to 16 ports between switches, but some Nexus switches allow only eight ports active between switches. The other eight are just standby links, depending on your hardware and software. But I really don't think having eight 10Gbps or higher links between switches is anything to complain about!

Figure 12.12 shows how our network would look if we had four connections between switches, before and after configuring PortChannel.

FIGURE 12.12 Before and after PortChannel

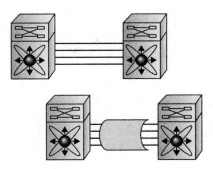

Okay, once your port channels are configured correctly, the Nexus switches can then load-balance across all links by hashing the various header fields in a frame into a numerical value to select each link. These links operate via hardware-based load balancing. Important to note is that once your port channel is up and working, layer 2 STP and layer 3 routing protocols will treat those bundled links as a single one, which would stop STP from performing blocking. The result is that because the routing protocols now only see this as a single link, a single adjacency across the link can be formed.

You can configure port channels as either layer 2 interfaces or layer 3 interfaces, and it's important to remember that when *virtual device contexts*, or VDCs, are used, all ports in a port channel must be in the same VDC. If you do make the mistake of trying to configure ports from various VDCs together, your trunks would never come up between VDCs, meaning no worries—this is a mistake you're not likely to make twice!

Another important factor you'll come across when trying to configure a port channel is that all ports you use must be configured identically. This is because the NX-OS performs a compatibility check before adding ports to a port channel, and if the ports aren't configured identically, you'll get this error:

```
command failed: port not compatible [port access VLAN]


 ** You can use force option to override the port's parameters
 ** (e.g. "channel-group X force")
```

As the error output shows, one of the ports I tried to tweak was configured to be in an access VLAN, but it wasn't configured identically to the other ports. This can be overwritten with the force command, but it's always better to actually fix your issues instead of trying to force a port channel. Moreover, using the force command will not override any QoS mismatched configuration, so trying to get around that would fail regardless.

You can configure port channels on a Nexus switch statically, or dynamically via the Link Aggregation Control Protocol (LACP), which can bundle multiple links into a single port channel as well as help to detect link failures. LACP is a non-proprietary IEEE 802.1AX port channel negotiation standard. After enabling it globally on the device, you can then enable LACP for each channel by setting the channel mode for each interface to either active or passive. When a port is configured for passive mode, it will respond to the LACP packets it receives, but it won't initiate an LACP negotiation. When a port is configured for active mode, the port initiates negotiations with other ports by sending LACP packets.

Configuring and Verifying Port Channels

Let's take a look at a simple example of configuring port channels and then verifying them. First I'll go to global configuration mode and create a port channel interface, and then we'll add this port channel to the physical interfaces. I'll start with the interface port-channel command, and then apply the port channel to the interfaces with the channel-group command. Let's take a look:

```
Nexus7k(config)# interface port-channel ?
  <1-4096>  Port Channel number
```

Notice that we can use the number up to 4096 on our port channel, but you can only create up to 256 across all VDCs. I'll just use port channel 1 for our example:

```
Nexus7k(config)# interface port-channel 1
Nexus7k(config-if)# int e3/31-38
Nexus7k(config-if-range)# switchport
Nexus7k(config-if-range)# switchport mode trunk
Nexus7k(config-if-range)# channel-group 1 ?
  <CR>
  force  Forcefully add a port
  mode   Specify channeling mode


Nexus7k(config-if-range)# channel-group 1 mode ?
  active   Set channeling mode to ACTIVE
  on       Set channeling mode to ON
  passive  Set channeling mode to PASSIVE


Nexus7k(config-if-range)# channel-group 1 mode on


 ** You can use force option to override the port's parameters
 ** (e.g. "channel-group X force")
 ** Use "show port-channel compatibility-parameters" to get more
 Information on failure
nexus7k(config-if-range)# show port-channel compatibility-parameters
* port mode


Members must have the same port mode configured, either E,F or AUTO. If
they are configured in AUTO port mode, they have to negotiate E or F mode
when they come up. If a member negotiates a different mode, it will be
suspended.


* speed


Members must have the same speed configured. If they are configured in AUTO
speed, they have to negotiate the same speed when they come up. If a member
negotiates a different speed, it will be suspended.
nexus7k(config-if-range)# channel-group 1 force mode on
```

As this output demonstrates, after I created the logical interface, I applied it to the group of interfaces I wanted to EtherChannel using the channel-group command (Cisco can and will use EtherChannel and PortChannel terms interchangeably! Please remember this is a book about the exam objectives!). Notice that I chose to force the ports instead of spending the time to make them all compatible. I decided to save some time and let the NX-OS do that for me. But I still made sure to verify the ports' compatibility with the show port-channel compatibility parameters command first, and I didn't skip this critical step before forcing!

Okay, now after creating the interface port channel, I chose the mode I wanted to use. Don't forget that interfaces can be configured individually as active or passive, which allows the link to operate with LACP. If you choose the default, on mode, the port channel must be created statically without LACP.

To verify the port channel, I'm going to use the show running-config command plus the show interface command:

```
nexus7k(config-if-range)# sh run int port-channel 1


!Command: show running-config interface port-channel1
!Time: Thu Feb 28 20:25:12 2013


version 6.1(3)


interface port-channel1
  switchport
  switchport mode trunk


nexus7k(config-if-range)# sh int port-channel 1
port-channel1 is up
admin state is up,
  Hardware: Port-Channel, address: 0026.9823.7c41 (bia f866.f23e.0ff1)
  MTU 1500 bytes, BW 8000000 Kbit, DLY 10 usec
  reliability 255/255, txload 1/255, rxload 1/255
  Encapsulation ARPA, medium is broadcast
  full-duplex, 1000 Mb/s
  Input flow-control is off, output flow-control is off
  Auto-mdix is turned off
  Switchport monitor is off
  EtherType is 0x8100
  Members in this channel: Eth3/41, Eth3/42, Eth3/43, Eth3/44, Eth3/45, Eth3/46,
Eth3/47, Eth3/48
  Last clearing of "show interface" counters never
  2 interface resets
```

```
  30 seconds input rate 0 bits/sec, 0 packets/sec
  30 seconds output rate 0 bits/sec, 0 packets/sec
  Load-Interval #2: 5 minute (300 seconds)
    input rate 528 bps, 0 pps; output rate 3.78 Kbps, 0 pps
  L3 in Switched:
    ucast: 0 pkts, 0 bytes - mcast: 0 pkts, 0 bytes
  L3 out Switched:
    ucast: 0 pkts, 0 bytes - mcast: 0 pkts, 0 bytes
  RX
    18 unicast packets  38 multicast packets  0 broadcast packets
    56 input packets  10416 bytes
    0 jumbo packets  0 storm suppression packets
    0 runts  0 giants  0 CRC  0 no buffer
    0 input error  0 short frame  0 overrun   0 underrun  0 ignored
    0 watchdog  0 bad etype drop  0 bad proto drop  0 if down drop
    0 input with dribble  0 input discard
    0 Rx pause
  TX
    0 unicast packets  48 multicast packets  0 broadcast packets
    48 output packets  11136 bytes
    0 jumbo packets
    0 output error  0 collision  0 deferred  0 late collision
    0 lost carrier  0 no carrier  0 babble  0 output discard
    0 Tx pause


nexus7k-30# sh port-channel summ
Flags:  D - Down       P - Up in port-channel (members)
        I - Individual H - Hot-standby (LACP only)
        s - Suspended  r - Module-removed
        S - Switched   R - Routed
        U - Up (port-channel)
        M - Not in use. Min-links not met
--------------------------------------------------------------------------------
Group Port-        Type    Protocol  Member Ports
      Channel
--------------------------------------------------------------------------------
1     Po1(RU)      Eth     NONE      Eth3/31(P)   Eth3/32(P)   Eth3/33(P)
                                     Eth3/34(P)   Eth3/35(P)   Eth3/36(P)
                                     Eth3/37(P)   Eth3/38(P)
```

The command show running-config provides the configuration for the logical port channel interfaces I'm using, and show interface port-channel *number* tells me that the interface is up if it's working, down if not. The resulting output also tells me all the ports that are members of this particular port channel. Last, the show port-channel summary provides a quick overview of interfaces that are members of the configured port channels.

Summary

This chapter was all about switching technologies, with particular focus on the Spanning Tree Protocol (STP) and its evolution to newer versions like RSTP and MSTP in addition to their individual degree of compatibility with 802.1d. You also learned about the problems that can occur if you have multiple links between bridges (switches) and the solutions attained with STP.

Finally, I covered configuring and monitoring of port channels with Cisco NX-OS.

Exam Essentials

Understand the main purpose of the Spanning Tree Protocol in a switched LAN.   The main purpose of STP is to prevent switching loops in a network with redundant switched paths.

Remember the states of STP.   The purpose of the blocking state is to prevent the use of looped paths. A port in listening state prepares to forward data frames without populating the MAC address table. A port in learning state populates the MAC address table but doesn't forward data frames. A port in forwarding state sends and receives all data frames on the bridged port. Last, a port in the disabled state is virtually non-operational.

Remember the command show spanning-tree.   You must be familiar with the command show spanning-tree and how to determine who the root bridge is of each VLAN; also, use the show spanning-tree summary command to help you.

Written Lab 12

You can find the answers in Appendix A. Write the answers to the following questions:

1. What command will show you the forward/filter table?
2. What command will show you the STP root bridge for a VLAN?
3. What standard is RSTP PVST+ based on?
4. Which protocol is used in a layer 2 network to maintain a loop-free network?

5. What protocol is used to prevent switching loops in a network with redundant switched paths?

6. You want to configure a switch port to not transition through the STP port states but to go immediately to forwarding mode. What command will you use on a per-port basis?

7. To see the status of an EtherChannel bundle, what command will you use?

8. You want to configure a switch port to connect to other switches and make sure that it transitions through the STP port states. What command will you use on a per-port basis?

9. You need to find out which VLANs your switch is the root bridge for. What two commands can you use?

10. What two versions of STP does NX-OS support?

Hands-On Lab 12

This lab will have you verify spanning-tree running on your Nexus switch.

Log in to the console of your switch or Nexus simulator.

Use the command show spanning-tree to verify that spanning-tree is running. Unlike IOS switches, if there are no ports between switches, spanning-tree doesn't display output on NX-OS. You need to press space bar to display multiple pages of output:

```
Nexus7k# sh spanning-tree


VLAN0001
  Spanning tree enabled protocol rstp
  Root ID    Priority    32769
             Address     0026.9823.7c41
             Cost        4
             Port        415 (Ethernet3/31)
             Hello Time  2  sec  Max Age 20 sec  Forward Delay 15 sec


  Bridge ID  Priority    32769  (priority 32768 sys-id-ext 1)
             Address     0026.9823.7c44
             Hello Time  2  sec  Max Age 20 sec  Forward Delay 15 sec


Interface          Role Sts Cost      Prio.Nbr Type
---------------- ---- --- --------- -------- --------------------------------
Eth3/31            Root FWD 4         128.415  P2p
Eth3/32            Altn BLK 4         128.416  P2p
Eth3/33            Altn BLK 4         128.417  P2p
```

```
Eth3/34          Altn BLK 4          128.418  P2p
Eth3/35          Altn BLK 4          128.419  P2p
Eth3/36          Altn BLK 4          128.420  P2p
Eth3/37          Altn BLK 4          128.421  P2p
Eth3/38          Altn BLK 4          128.422  P2p


VLAN0010
  Spanning tree enabled protocol rstp
  Root ID    Priority    32778
             Address     0026.9823.7c44
             This bridge is the root
             Hello Time  2  sec  Max Age 20 sec  Forward Delay 15 sec


  Bridge ID  Priority    32778  (priority 32768 sys-id-ext 10)
             Address     0026.9823.7c44
             Hello Time  2  sec  Max Age 20 sec  Forward Delay 15 sec


Interface        Role Sts Cost       Prio.Nbr Type
---------------- ---- --- ---------- -------- --------------------------------
Eth3/31          Desg FWD 4          128.415  P2p
Eth3/32          Desg FWD 4          128.416  P2p
Eth3/33          Desg FWD 4          128.417  P2p
Eth3/34          Desg FWD 4          128.418  P2p
Eth3/35          Desg FWD 4          128.419  P2p
Eth3/36          Desg FWD 4          128.420  P2p
Eth3/37          Desg FWD 4          128.421  P2p
Eth3/38          Desg FWD 4          128.422  P2p


VLAN0020
  Spanning tree enabled protocol rstp
  Root ID    Priority    32788
             Address     0026.9823.7c44
             This bridge is the root
             Hello Time  2  sec  Max Age 20 sec  Forward Delay 15 sec
```

```
     Bridge ID  Priority    32788  (priority 32768 sys-id-ext 20)
                Address     0026.9823.7c44
                Hello Time  2  sec  Max Age 20 sec  Forward Delay 15 sec


Interface          Role Sts Cost      Prio.Nbr Type
---------------    ---- --- --------- -------- --------------------------------
Eth3/31            Desg FWD 4         128.415  P2p
Eth3/32            Desg FWD 4         128.416  P2p
Eth3/33            Desg FWD 4         128.417  P2p
Eth3/34            Desg FWD 4         128.418  P2p
Eth3/35            Desg FWD 4         128.419  P2p
Eth3/36            Desg FWD 4         128.420  P2p
Eth3/37            Desg FWD 4         128.421  P2p
Eth3/38            Desg FWD 4         128.422  P2p



VLAN0030
  Spanning tree enabled protocol rstp
  Root ID    Priority    32798
             Address     0026.9823.7c44
             This bridge is the root
             Hello Time  2  sec  Max Age 20 sec  Forward Delay 15 sec


     Bridge ID  Priority    32798  (priority 32768 sys-id-ext 30)
                Address     0026.9823.7c44
                Hello Time  2  sec  Max Age 20 sec  Forward Delay 15 sec


Interface          Role Sts Cost      Prio.Nbr Type
---------------    ---- --- --------- -------- --------------------------------
Eth3/31            Desg FWD 4         128.415  P2p
Eth3/32            Desg FWD 4         128.416  P2p
Eth3/33            Desg FWD 4         128.417  P2p
Eth3/34            Desg FWD 4         128.418  P2p
Eth3/35            Desg FWD 4         128.419  P2p
Eth3/36            Desg FWD 4         128.420  P2p
Eth3/37            Desg FWD 4         128.421  P2p
Eth3/38            Desg FWD 4         128.422  P2p


Nexus7k0#
```

Notice that this switch has VLANs 1 (default), 10, and 30. It is extremely important to notice that this switch is the root bridge for VLANs 10, 20 and 30.

Use the command show spanning-tree summary to get quick information on which VLANs your switch is the root bridge for.

```
Nexus7k# sh spanning-tree summary
Switch is in rapid-pvst mode
Root bridge for: VLAN0010, VLAN0020, VLAN0030
Port Type Default                            is disable
Edge Port [PortFast] BPDU Guard Default  is disabled
Edge Port [PortFast] BPDU Filter Default is disabled
Bridge Assurance                         is enabled
Loopguard Default                        is disabled
Pathcost method used                     is short
STP-Lite                                 is enabled


Name              Blocking Listening Learning Forwarding STP Active
---------------- -------- --------- -------- ---------- ----------
VLAN0001              7         0        0         1          8
VLAN0010              0         0        0         8          8
VLAN0020              0         0        0         8          8
VLAN0030              0         0        0         8          8
---------------- -------- --------- -------- ---------- ----------
4 vlans              7         0        0        25         32
Nexus7k#
```

Notice that you can quickly and easily see that your switch is the root bridge for VLAN's 10, 20 and 30.

Review Questions

You can find the answers in Appendix B.

The following questions are designed to test your understanding of this chapter's material. For more information on how to get additional questions, please see this book's introduction.

1. Which of the following is a layer 2 protocol used to maintain a loop-free network?

   A. VTP

   B. STP

   C. RIP

   D. CDP

2. What is wrong with port-channel 1 on nexus7k?

```
nexus7k# sh int port-channel 1
port-channel1 is up
admin state is up,
  Hardware: Port-Channel, address: 0026.9823.7c41 (bia f866.f23e.0ff1)
  MTU 1500 bytes, BW 8000000 Kbit, DLY 10 usec
  reliability 255/255, txload 1/255, rxload 1/255
  Encapsulation ARPA, medium is broadcast
  full-duplex, 1000 Mb/s
  Input flow-control is off, output flow-control is off
  Auto-mdix is turned off
  Switchport monitor is off
  EtherType is 0x8100
  Members in this channel: Eth3/41, Eth3/42, Eth3/43, Eth3/44,
Eth3/45, Eth3/46, Eth3/47, Eth3/48
```

   A. Port-channel 1 is operating normally.

   B. LACP is not enabled on port-channel 1.

   C. Port-channel 1 requires at least two members for load-balancing purposes before it comes active.

   D. Rapid-PVST is not running on port-channel 1.

3. Which statement describes a spanning-tree network that has converged?

    A. All switch and bridge ports are in the forwarding state.

    B. All switch and bridge ports are assigned as either root or designated ports.

    C. All switch and bridge ports are in either the forwarding or blocking state.

    D. All switch and bridge ports are either blocking or looping.

4. What is the purpose of Spanning Tree Protocol in a switched LAN?

    A. To provide a mechanism for network monitoring in switched environments

    B. To prevent routing loops in networks with redundant paths

    C. To prevent switching loops in networks with redundant switched paths

    D. To manage the VLAN database across multiple switches

    E. To create collision domains

5. Which of the following is true regarding RSTP? (Choose 3.)

    A. RSTP speeds the recalculation of the spanning tree when the layer 2 network topology changes.

    B. RSTP is an IEEE standard that redefines STP port roles, states, and BPDUs.

    C. RSTP is extremely proactive and very quick, and therefore it absolutely needs the 802.1 delay timers.

    D. RSTP (802.1w) supersedes 802.1d while remaining proprietary.

    E. All of the 802.1d terminology and most parameters have been changed.

    F. 802.1w is capable of reverting to 802.1 to interoperate with traditional switches on a per-port basis.

6. In which circumstance are multiple copies of the same unicast frame likely to be transmitted in a switched LAN?

    A. During high-traffic periods

    B. After broken links are reestablished

    C. When upper-layer protocols require high reliability

    D. In an improperly implemented redundant topology

7. If you want to effectively disable STP on a port connected to a server, which command would you use?

    A. `disable spanning-tree`

    B. `spanning-tree off`

    C. `spanning-tree port type network`

    D. `spanning-tree port type edge`

    E. `spanning-tree enable portfast`

8. You have two switches connected together with two crossover cables for redundancy, and STP is disabled. Which of the following will happen between the switches?

   A. The routing tables on the switches will not update.

   B. The MAC forward/filter table will not update on the switch.

   C. Broadcast storms will occur on the switched network.

   D. The switches will automatically load-balance between the two links.

9. Which of the following would you use to find out which VLANs your switch is the root bridge for? (Choose 2.)

   A. `show spanning-tree`

   B. `show root all`

   C. `spanning-tree port root VLAN`

   D. `spanning-tree summary`

10. What command at interface level bundles your interfaces together into a single LAN channel?

    A. `interface port-channel`

    B. `channel-group`

    C. `switchport`

    D. `switchport mode trunk`

Chapter

13

Security

THE FOLLOWING TOPICS ARE COVERED IN THIS CHAPTER:

✓ Configure, verify, and troubleshoot basic router operation and routing on Cisco devices using Nexus

If you're a sys admin, I'm guessing that shielding sensitive, critical data and your network's resources from every evil exploit and intrusion is a top priority of yours. If so, it's good to know you're on the right page. You'll be happy to know that Cisco has some solid security solutions to equip you with the tools you need to make your network as secure as you want it!

Access control lists, (ACLs), also referred to as access lists, are an integral part of Cisco's security solution. In this chapter, I'll demonstrate the keys to creating simple and advanced access lists, which are vital to an internetwork's security. I'll also show you how to effectively mitigate some common security-oriented network threats.

In addition to fortifying security, creating and using access lists wisely is a critical part of router configuration because they're such versatile networking accessories. Contributing mightily to the efficiency and operation of your network, access lists give network managers a huge amount of control over traffic flow throughout the enterprise. With access lists, managers can gather basic statistics on packet flow and security policies can be implemented. Sensitive devices can also be protected from unauthorized access.

We'll cover the important topic of access lists for TCP/IP as well as explore some of the tools available to test and monitor the functionality of applied access lists using NX-OS.

For up-to-the minute updates for this chapter, please see www.lammle.com/forum.

Introduction to Access Lists

At the most basic level, an *access list* is a list of conditions that categorize packets and because of this, they can be really helpful when you need to exercise control over network traffic. An access list is actually so effective in this kind of situation, it would be your go-to tool of choice for decision making!

One of the most common and easiest-to-understand uses of access lists is filtering unwanted packets when implementing security policies. For example, you can set ACLs up to make very specific decisions for regulating traffic patterns so that they'll allow only certain hosts to access web resources on the Internet while restricting others. With the right combination of access lists, network managers give themselves the power to enforce nearly any security policy they can invent.

Creating access control lists (ACLs) is really a lot like programming a series of if-then-else statements—if a given condition is met, then a given action is taken. If the specific condition isn't met, nothing happens and the next statement is evaluated. Access list statements are basically packet filters that packets are compared against, categorized by, and acted upon accordingly. Once the lists are built, they can be applied to either inbound or outbound traffic on any interface. Applying an access list causes the router to analyze every packet crossing that interface in the specified direction and take the appropriate action.

There are a few important rules that a packet follows when it's being compared with an access list:

- It's always compared with each line of the ACL in sequential order and progress in that way, beginning with the first line of the ACL, moving to line 2, then line 3, and so on.

- Packets are compared with lines of the ACL only until a match is made. Once the packet matches the specified condition delimited on a line of the ACL, the packet is acted upon and no further comparisons take place.

- There is an implicit "deny" at the end of each ACL, which means that if a packet doesn't match the condition on any of the lines in it, the packet will be discarded.

Each of these rules has powerful implications when filtering IP packets so keep in mind that creating effective access lists will take some time and practice.

There are two main types of access lists for the objectives:

Standard access lists   These use only the source IP address in an IP packet as the condition test. All decisions are made based on the source IP address. This means that standard access lists basically permit or deny an entire suite of protocols. They don't distinguish between any of the many types of IP traffic such as Web, Telnet, UDP, and so on. Standard ACLs are old and not used any longer in production networks.

Extended access lists   Extended access lists can evaluate many of the other fields in the layer 3 and layer 4 headers of an IP packet. They can evaluate source and destination IP addresses, the Protocol field in the Network layer header, and the port number at the Transport layer header. This gives extended access lists the ability to make much more granular decisions when controlling traffic.

Named access lists   Hey, wait a minute—I said there were two types of access lists but listed three! Well, technically there really are only two since named access lists are either standard or extended and not actually a separate type. I'm just distinguishing them because they're created and referred to differently than standard and extended access lists, but they're functionally the same.

We will look at these types of ACLs more in depth, later in the chapter.

Okay, so once you've created an access list, understand that it's not really going to do anything until you apply it. Yes, they're there on the router, but they're also inactive until you tell that router what to do with them. To use an access list as a packet filter, you must apply it to an interface on the router where you want the traffic filtered. And you've got to specify which direction of traffic you want the access list applied to. There's a good reason for this—you may want different controls in place for traffic leaving your enterprise destined for the Internet than you want in place for traffic coming into your enterprise from the Internet. So, by specifying the direction of traffic, you can—and frequently you'll need to—use different access lists for inbound and outbound traffic on a single interface:

Inbound access lists   When an ACL is applied to inbound packets on an interface, those packets are processed through it before being routed to the outbound interface. Any packets that are denied won't be routed because they're discarded before the routing process is invoked.

Outbound access lists   When an ACL is applied to outbound packets on an interface, packets are routed to the outbound interface and then processed through the access list before being queued.

Here are some general guidelines to follow when creating and implementing access lists on a router:

- You can only assign one access list per interface, per protocol and, per direction; meaning you can have only one inbound access list and one outbound access list per interface.

NOTE   When you consider the implications of the implicit deny at the end of any access list, it makes sense that you can't have multiple access lists applied on the same interface in the same direction for the same protocol. That's because any packets that don't match some condition in the first access list would be denied and there wouldn't be any packets left over to compare against a second access list.

- Organize your access lists so that the more specific tests are at the top.
- Anytime you add a new entry to the ACL, it will be placed at the bottom of the list, so using a text editor for access lists is highly recommended.
- You cannot simply remove one line from a numbered access list. If you try to do this, you will remove the entire list, which is why it's best to copy the ACL to a text editor before trying to edit it. The only exception is when using named access lists.
- Unless your access list ends with a permit ip any any command, all packets will be discarded if they do not meet any one of the list's tests. This means that every list should have at least one permit statement or it will deny all traffic.
- Create ACLs and then apply them to an interface because any access list applied to an interface without access-list test statements present will not filter traffic.
- Access lists are designed to filter traffic going through the router. They will not filter traffic that has originated from the router.
- Place IP standard access lists as close to the destination as possible. The big reason we don't use standard ACLs in our networks is that you can't place one close to the source

host or network because you can only filter based on source address. This would mean that any and all destinations would be affected and it's why standard access lists aren't typically used in today's networks.

- Place IP extended access lists as close to the source as possible. Since extended access lists can filter on very specific addresses and protocols, you don't want your traffic to traverse the entire network only to be denied. So placing this list as close to the source address as possible will ensure that it filters network traffic before unnecessarily using up precious bandwidth.

Before we move on to how to configure access lists, let's discuss how ACLs can be used to mitigate the security threats discussed earlier in this chapter.

Mitigating Security Issues with ACLs

Here's a list of the many security threats you can mitigate with ACLs:

- IP address spoofing, inbound
- IP address spoofing, outbound
- Denial of service (DoS) TCP SYN attacks, blocking external attacks
- DoS TCP SYN attacks, using TCP Intercept
- DoS smurf attacks
- Denying/filtering ICMP messages, inbound
- Denying/filtering ICMP messages, outbound
- Denying/filtering traceroute

 This book is not an introduction to security, so you may have to research some of the preceding terms if you're not already familiar with them.

It's generally wise not to allow any external IP packets that contain the source address of any internal hosts or networks into a private network—just don't do it!

Here's a list of rules to live by when configuring ACLs from the Internet to your production network to mitigate security problems:

- Deny any source addresses from your internal networks.
- Deny any local host addresses (127.0.0.0/8).
- Deny any reserved private addresses (RFC 1918).
- Deny any addresses in the IP multicast address range (224.0.0.0/4).

None of these source addresses should ever be allowed to enter your internetwork!

Before we get to work on configuring some advanced access lists, I need to cover the inverse masking that can be used with ACLs with some simple examples to get us started. I'll start off with simple examples, and then after we understand the basics we'll move into the NX-OS access-list configuration.

Wildcard Masking

Wildcards are used with access lists to specify an individual host, a network, or a certain range of a network or networks. To understand a *wildcard*, you need to know that a *block size* is used to specify a range of addresses. Some of the different block sizes available are 64, 32, 16, 8, and 4.

When specifying a range of addresses, you choose the next-largest block size up that's required to meet your needs. This means that if you need to specify 34 networks, you would specify a block size of 64, for 18 hosts, you need a block size of 32, and for 2 networks, you would go with a block size of 4.

Wildcards are used with the host or network address to tell the router a range of available addresses to filter, and to specify a host, the address would look like this:

```
172.16.30.5 0.0.0.0
```

The four zeros represent each octet of the address. Whenever a zero is present, it means that specific octet in the address must match the corresponding reference octet exactly. Another command you can use to match an exact IP address is this:

```
host 172.16.30.5
```

There's no difference between using the host command and the 0.0.0.0 wildcard option. To state that an octet can be any value, 255 is used. As an example, here's how a /24 subnet is specified with a wildcard mask:

```
172.16.30.0 0.0.0.255
```

This tells the router to match up the first three octets exactly, but the fourth octet can be any value.

That was pretty easy, but let's say you want to specify only a small range of subnets? This is where block sizes come in—you have to specify the range of values to be compatible with your chosen block size. You can't choose to specify 20 networks because there is no "size 20" block size, so your choices are limited to either 16 or 32. And as I said, you need to go with the next block size up not down, meaning you would go with 32.

Let's say that you want to block access to part of the network that is in the range from 172.16.8.0 through 172.16.15.0. That's a block size of 8, so your network number would be 172.16.8.0, and the wildcard would be 0.0.7.255. Whoa! What is that? The 7.255 is what the router uses to determine the block size. The network and wildcard tell the router to start at 172.16.8.0 and go up a block size of eight addresses to network 172.16.15.0.

Seriously—it really is easier than it looks—really! I could certainly go through the binary math for you, but no one needs that. Actually, all you have to do is remember that the wildcard is always one number less than the block size. So, in my example, the wildcard would be 7 since my block size is 8. If you used a block size of 16, the wildcard would be 15. Easy, huh?

But just to be sure you've got this, I'll guide you through a few more examples. The following example tells the router to match the first three octets exactly, but that the fourth octet can be anything:

```
Corp(config)#access-list 10 deny 172.16.10.0 0.0.0.255
```

The next example tells the router to match the first two octets, but that the last two octets can be any value:

```
Corp(config)#access-list 10 deny 172.16.0.0 0.0.255.255
```

Hopefully this is getting crystal clear! Try to figure out what this next line is specifying:

```
Corp(config)#access-list 10 deny 172.16.16.0 0.0.3.255
```

This configuration tells the router to start at network 172.16.16.0 and use a block size of 4, making your range, 172.16.16.0 through 172.16.19.255. Oh, and to give you a "heads-up", this particular example just happens to be a favorite Cisco objective!

Okay, so keep practicing and take a shot at this next one:

```
Corp(config)#access-list 10 deny 172.16.16.0 0.0.7.255
```

This example describes an access list starting at 172.16.16.0 and going up a block size of 8 to 172.16.23.255.

And can you determine the range of this one?

```
Corp(config)#access-list 10 deny 172.16.32.0 0.0.15.255
```

This example starts at network 172.16.32.0 and goes up a block size of 16 to 172.16.47.255.

Okay, you're almost done... Just a couple more examples before moving on to extended ACLs! Take a look at this configuration and determine the range:

```
Corp(config)#access-list 10 deny 172.16.64.0 0.0.63.255
```

This example starts at network 172.16.64.0 and goes up a block size of 64 to 172.16.127.255.

One last example:

```
Corp(config)#access-list 10 deny 192.168.160.0 0.0.31.255
```

If you answered that it starts at network 192.168.160.0 and goes up a block size of 32 to 192.168.191.255, you've nailed this! If not, just run through the examples another time and I'm sure you'll get it down.

Here are two more things to keep in mind when working with block sizes and wildcards:

- Each block size must start at 0 or a multiple of the block size. For example, you can't say that you want a block size of 8 and then start at 12. You must use 0–7, 8–15, 16–23, and so on. For a block size of 32, the ranges are 0–31, 32–63, 64–95, and so on.

- The command any is the same thing as writing out the wildcard 0.0.0.0 255.255.255.255.

Wildcard masking is a crucial skill to master when creating IP access lists, so keep at it until you're confident in yourself. Also, keep in mind that it's used identically whether you're creating standard or extended IP access lists.

Extended Access Lists

Standard access lists have simply become too limiting for use in our enterprise networks today because you can't allow users to get to one network service but not another. It's all or nothing with standard lists—they won't allow you key options like making decisions based on both source and destination addresses, protocols, and port numbers, and the ability to restrict or allow based only on the source address just doesn't cut it anymore.

On the other hand, an *extended access list* will really brighten your day! These beauties will allow you to specify source and destination addresses as well as the protocol and port number, which will even identify the upper-layer protocol or application. By using extended access lists, you get lots of levels of control and can affectively allow users access to a physical LAN, yet still completely prevent them from accessing specific hosts—even specific services on specific hosts!

To let you begin at the basics while learning ACL configuration, here's an example of an extended IP access list on IOS:

```
Corp(config)#access-list ?
  <1-99>           IP standard access list
  <100-199>        IP extended access list
  <1100-1199>      Extended 48-bit MAC address access list
  <1300-1999>      IP standard access list (expanded range)
  <200-299>        Protocol type-code access list
  <2000-2699>      IP extended access list (expanded range)
  <700-799>        48-bit MAC address access list
  compiled         Enable IP access-list compilation
  dynamic-extended Extend the dynamic ACL absolute timer
  rate-limit       Simple rate-limit specific access list
```

The first command shows the access list numbers available. I'll use the extended access list range from 100 to 199, but still make sure to note that the range 2000–2699 is also available for extended IP access lists.

At this point, I need to decide what type of list entry to make. For this example, I'll choose a deny list entry:

```
Corp(config)#access-list 110 ?
  deny     Specify packets to reject
  dynamic  Specify a DYNAMIC list of PERMITs or DENYs
```

```
permit   Specify packets to forward
remark   Access list entry comment
```

Once I've chosen the ACL type, I need to select a protocol field entry:

```
Corp(config)#access-list 110 deny ?
  <0-255>  An IP protocol number
  ahp      Authentication Header Protocol
  eigrp    Cisco's EIGRP routing protocol
  esp      Encapsulation Security Payload
  gre      Cisco's GRE tunneling
  icmp     Internet Control Message Protocol
  igmp     Internet Gateway Message Protocol
  ip       Any Internet Protocol
  ipinip   IP in IP tunneling
  nos      KA9Q NOS compatible IP over IP tunneling
  ospf     OSPF routing protocol
  pcp      Payload Compression Protocol
  pim      Protocol Independent Multicast
  tcp      Transmission Control Protocol
  udp      User Datagram Protocol
```

If you want to filter by Application layer protocol, you have to choose the appropriate layer 4 transport protocol after the permit or deny statement. For example, to filter Telnet or FTP, you choose TCP since both Telnet and FTP use TCP at the Transport layer. If you were to choose IP, you wouldn't be allowed to specify a specific application protocol later and could only filter on source and destination address.

Here, you'll choose to filter an Application layer protocol that uses TCP by selecting TCP as the protocol. You'll specify the specific TCP port later. Next, you will be prompted for the source IP address of the host or network. Choose the any command to allow any source address:

```
Corp(config)#access-list 110 deny tcp ?
  A.B.C.D  Source address
  any      Any source host
  host     A single source host
```

After you've selected the source address, you then get to select the destination address:

```
Corp(config)#access-list 110 deny tcp any ?
  A.B.C.D  Destination address
  any      Any destination host
  eq       Match only packets on a given port number
```

```
gt       Match only packets with a greater port number
host     A single destination host
lt       Match only packets with a lower port number
neq      Match only packets not on a given port number
range    Match only packets in the range of port numbers
```

In the following example, any source IP address that has a destination IP address of 172.16.30.2 has been denied:

```
Corp(config)#access-list 110 deny tcp any host 172.16.30.2 ?
  ack          Match on the ACK bit
  dscp         Match packets with given dscp value
  eq           Match only packets on a given port number
  established  Match established connections
  fin          Match on the FIN bit
  fragments    Check non-initial fragments
  gt           Match only packets with a greater port number
  log          Log matches against this entry
  log-input    Log matches against this entry, including input interface
  lt           Match only packets with a lower port number
  neq          Match only packets not on a given port number
  precedence   Match packets with given precedence value
  psh          Match on the PSH bit
  range        Match only packets in the range of port numbers
  rst          Match on the RST bit
  syn          Match on the SYN bit
  time-range   Specify a time-range
  tos          Match packets with given TOS value
  urg          Match on the URG bit
  <cr>
```

Once you have the destination host addresses in place, just specify the type of service you want to deny using the equal to command, which you would just type in as eq. The following help screen shows you the available options. You can choose a port number or use the application name:

```
Corp(config)#access-list 110 deny tcp any host 172.16.30.2 eq ?
  <0-65535>   Port number
  bgp         Border Gateway Protocol (179)
  chargen     Character generator (19)
  cmd         Remote commands (rcmd, 514)
  daytime     Daytime (13)
  discard     Discard (9)
  domain      Domain Name Service (53)
```

```
drip          Dynamic Routing Information Protocol (3949)
echo          Echo (7)
exec          Exec (rsh, 512)
finger        Finger (79)
ftp           File Transfer Protocol (21)
ftp-data      FTP data connections (20)
gopher        Gopher (70)
hostname      NIC hostname server (101)
ident         Ident Protocol (113)
irc           Internet Relay Chat (194)
klogin        Kerberos login (543)
kshell        Kerberos shell (544)
login         Login (rlogin, 513)
lpd           Printer service (515)
nntp          Network News Transport Protocol (119)
pim-auto-rp   PIM Auto-RP (496)
pop2          Post Office Protocol v2 (109)
pop3          Post Office Protocol v3 (110)
smtp          Simple Mail Transport Protocol (25)
sunrpc        Sun Remote Procedure Call (111)
syslog        Syslog (514)
tacacs        TAC Access Control System (49)
talk          Talk (517)
telnet        Telnet (23)
time          Time (37)
uucp          Unix-to-Unix Copy Program (540)
whois         Nicname (43)
www           World Wide Web (HTTP, 80)
```

Okay now let's block Telnet (port 23) to host 172.16.30.2 only. If the users want to use ftp, fine—that's allowed. The log command is used to log messages every time the access list entry is hit. Be careful when you use this because it could overload your console with an enormous amount of messages.

Here's our config result:

```
Corp(config)#access-list 110 deny tcp any host 172.16.30.2 eq 23 log
```

You need to keep in mind that the next line is an implicit deny ip any any by default. If you apply this access list to an interface, you might as well just shut it down since there's an implicit deny all at the end of every access list by default! Instead, you've got to follow up the access list with the following command:

```
Corp(config)#access-list 110 permit ip any any
```

Remember, the 0.0.0.0 255.255.255.255 is the same command as any, so this command could also look like this:

```
Corp(config)#access-list 110 permit ip 0.0.0.0 255.255.255.255
0.0.0.0 255.255.255.255
```

But if we left it like this, the commands would be replaced with any any when you looked at the running-config so we'll use the any command because less typing is always nice.

Okay, once we've created our ACL, we need to apply it to an interface using the same command as the IP standard list:

```
Corp(config-if)#ip access-group 110 in
```

Doing this is your other option:

```
Corp(config-if)#ip access-group 110 out
```

Now that you've run through the basics, it's time to advance with some examples of how to use an extended access list.

Extended Access List Example

Referring to Figure 13.1 below, let's deny access to a host at 172.16.50.5 on the Finance department LAN for both Telnet and FTP services. All other services on this and all other hosts are acceptable for the Sales and Marketing departments to access.

FIGURE 13.1   IOS ACL example

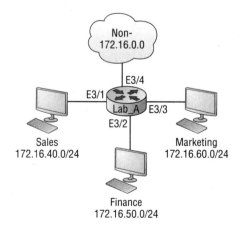

The following access list should be created:

```
Lab_A#config t
Lab_A(config)#access-list 110 deny tcp any host 172.16.50.5 eq 21
```

```
Lab_A(config)#access-list 110 deny tcp any host 172.16.50.5 eq 23
Lab_A(config)#access-list 110 permit ip any any
```

The access-list 110 tells the router we are creating an extended IP access list on an IOS device. The tcp is the protocol field in the Network layer header. If the list doesn't say tcp here, we can't filter by TCP port numbers 21 and 23, which is what we need to do. Remember, FTP and Telnet, both use TCP for connection-oriented services. The any command is the source, which means any source IP address, and the host is the destination IP address. This ACL specifically states that all IP traffic except FTP and Telnet is permitted to host 172.16.50.5 from any source.

Remember that instead of using the host 172.16.50.5 command when we created the extended access list, we could have entered 172.16.50.5 0.0.0.0 and there would technically be no difference in the result. The only change that would occur is that the router would modify the command to host 172.16.50.5 in the running-config.

After we've created the list, we'll need to apply it to the Ethernet 3/2 interface outbound because we want to block all traffic from getting to host 172.16.50.5 and performing FTP and telnet. But remember, if this list was created to block access only from the Sales LAN to host 172.16.50.5, then we'd want to either place it closer to the source, or put it on Ethernet 3/1. In this situation, it is best to apply the list to inbound traffic in order to prevent extra overhead on the network before the packets are dropped. This is a great example of why it's important to examine each situation individually and carefully before creating and applying ACLs!

Let's go ahead and apply our list to interface E3/1 and block all outside FTP and Telnet access to the host 172.16.50.5:

```
Lab_A(config)#int e3/1
Lab_A(config-if)#ip access-group 110 out
```

Done! Now it's time to move on and create extended ACLs using names on NX-OS.

You can only use named extended ACLs on Nexus switches because standard ACLs and numbered lists are not supported.

Named ACLs

As I said earlier, named access lists are really just another way to create standard and extended access lists. In medium to large enterprises, managing access lists can become an ugly, labor intensive hassle over time. Instead of mindlessly retyping the bulk of the old ACL with an added change or two, a common way to deal with the messy editing issue is to simply copy the ACL to a text editor, make your changes, and then paste the new list back into the router.

This would work pretty well if it weren't for human nature and our all too common pack rat problem. Sys admins everywhere, faced with tossing out (deleting) the old access list after pasting in the new one ask themselves, "What do I do with the old access list? Delete it? Maybe I should I just save it in case I find a problem with the new list and need to back out of the change?" So people usually save the old one and what happens over time, through this and countless other scenarios, is that mountains of unapplied access lists begin forming on a router like stacks of old magazines in a hoarders house. What were they for? Are they important? Do you still need them? All good questions, and named access lists are the solution to this dilemma!

This also applies to access lists that are currently up and running. Let's say you're called into an existing network and when looking into access lists on a router, you find one named 177 that's 33 lines long. This could either set you back to answering a whole bunch of existential questions—What is it for? Why is it here…? Or instead, the ACL could be clearly identified by a sensible name like, "Finance LAN", instead of the blank and obscure, "177"!

Access lists on NX-OS allow you to use *only* names to create and apply extended access lists. There's nothing new or different about these access lists aside from being able to only refer to them in a singularly human way—by naming them. Also, don't forget that you can only create extended ACLs on NX-OS because the OS doesn't even provide the option to create the outmoded, standard flavor. But there are some subtle changes to the syntax, so let's take a look at another business requirement and use the NX-OS to create the named ACL.

Figure 13.2 shows a Nexus switch with three LANs attached.

FIGURE 13.2   NX-OS ACL example

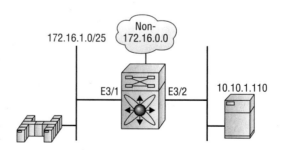

By looking at Figure 13.2, how would you configure an ACL on the Nexus switch to deny FTP traffic from any source to destination host 10.10.1.110?

This is a pretty simple ACL; here's what I came up with:

```
nexus7k(config)# ip access-list Deny_FTP
nexus7k(config-acl)# deny tcp any host 10.10.1.110 eq ftp
nexus7k(config-acl)# permit ip any any
nexus7k(config-acl)# int e3/2
nexus7k(config-if)# ip access-group Deny_FTP out
```

Notice that I started by typing ip access-list, not access-list. This allows me to enter a named access list. Next, I'll need to specify the name of the list, which I just made up as Deny_FTP. Be careful not to get confused on the exam objectives regarding named access lists because you can just as easily use numbers as letters to name your ACL. So just trust me and use a clearly descriptive name like "Deny_FTP!" That said, notice that after entering the name, I pressed Enter and the switch prompt changed to (config-acl).

I'm now in named access list configuration mode and entering the named access list. My first line is a deny to any source with a destination host of 10.10.1.110, using port 21, or FTP.

I then permitted all other traffic with the permit ip any any command. Remember, you can't just create an ACL with deny statements because you might as well unplug the interface if you do that! You have to have at least one permit statement in every list. The last thing I did was to apply the list to the interface with the ip access-group command.

Next, we'll take a look at the running configuration to verify that the access list is indeed in the router:

```
nexus7k(config-if)# sh run | begin access-list
ip access-list Deny_FTP
      10 deny tcp any 10.10.1.110/32 eq ftp
      20 permit ip any any
```

We can also verify the configuration with the show access-list command:

```
nexus7k(config-if)# sh access-lists
IP access list Deny_FTP
      10 deny tcp any 10.10.1.110/32 eq ftp
      20 permit ip any any
```

In an IOS router, you could use the show ip interface command to see if an ACL is set on an interface. At this point, with the NX-OS, we can see this with the show run command. We can also verify the ACL with two new commands, the show run aclmgr, and show access-list summary, the latter of which is now my favorite ACL verification command:

```
nexus7k(config-if)# sh run int e3/2


!Command: show running-config interface Ethernet3/2
!Time: Wed Feb 27 23:52:38 2013


version 5.0(2a)


interface Ethernet3/2
  ip access-group Deny_FTP out
  ip address 10.10.1.1/16
  no shutdown
```

Let's take a look at the new commands:

```
nexus7k(config-if)# sh running-config aclmgr


!Command: show running-config aclmgr
!Time: Wed Mar 20 17:43:25 2013


version 6.1(3)
ip access-list Deny_FTP
  10 deny tcp any 10.10.1.110/32 eq ftp
  20 permit ip any any


interface Ethernet3/2
  ip access-group Deny_FTP out
```

And by checking out this output, you can probably see why it's now my favorite ACL verification command! Using it reveals the list plus the interface configuration neatly and cleanly in a single output. But wait, there's another one that is just as good— take a look:

```
nexus7k(config-if)# sh access-list summary
IPV4 ACL Deny_FTP
        Total ACEs Configured: 1
        Configured on interfaces:
                Ethernet3/2 - egress (Router ACL)
        Active on interfaces:
Ethernet3/2 - egress (Router ACL)
```

Nice! At this point, I've re-created the work done earlier using a named access list on NX-OS. Let me give you another challenge: Looking at Figure 13.2 again, try to configure an ACL to use on a Cisco Nexus switch that would permit only unencrypted web traffic from the 172.16.1.0/25 network to destination host 10.10.1.110.

If you've read the requirements well, you can see that you can achieve this goal by creating this list with one line, plus the interface configuration.

Check it out:

```
nexus7k(config)# ip access-list 101
nexus7k(config-acl)# permit tcp 172.16.1.0/25 any eq 80
nexus7k(config-acl)# int e3/2
nexus7k(config-if)# ip access-group 101 out
```

A very elegant solution! By using the implicit deny ip any any that's at the end of every ACL by default, you can create this list easily and simply to meet the business requirements. Also, notice that the name of the list is a number! Yes you can do this, and so can the exam objectives, which you're likely to be confronted with when you take the test!

Let's do one more example, using the same list that we used earlier only we'll use a deny statement instead of a permit. What ACL would you use to deny unencrypted web traffic from any source to destination host 10.10.1.110?

```
nexus7k(config)# ip access-list 102
nexus7k(config-acl)# deny tcp any host 10.10.1.110 any eq 80
nexus7k(config-acl)# int e3/2
nexus7k(config-if)# ip access-group 102 out
```

Be sure to go through these NX-OS examples over and over until you're sure that you really understand them. And while you're prepping, please go through the hands-on lab at the end of this chapter with your NX-OS switch or simulator before attempting your exam. You'll be very glad you did!

Configure Session

Okay, so no one's doubting that the NX-OS has some great features, right? Well here's another one that I really like and want to share with you. This is called configure session and it allows you to create an ACL but withhold it so it doesn't yet actually exist in the running-config. Doing this allows you to verify the list against system resources before actually applying it to the configuration! Here's how you would configure this:

```
Nexus7(config)# config session Todd_Example
Config Session started, Session ID is 1
Nexus7(config-s)# ip access-list Verify_Me
Nexus7(config-s-acl)# deny tcp 10.0.0.0/8 any
Nexus7(config-s-acl)# deny tcp 192.168.10.0/24 any
Nexus7(config-s-acl)# deny tcp 172.16.0.0/12 any
Nexus7(config-s-acl)# permit ip any any
Nexus7(config-s-acl)# int e3/1
Nexus7(config-s-if)# ip access-group Verify_Me in
```

Pretty straightforward, with the only difference between this process and a regular list being that you just need to start the session with a unique name. But still, there are two more steps. First, we need to verify the list:

```
Nexus7(config-s)# verify
Verification Successful
```

For the system to validate the list, it first must be established that there's enough resources to run it, and also that the configuration is correct. Now we can commit the ACL to the active configuration and interface like this:

```
Nexus7(config-s)# commit
Commit Successful
```

With this new command, I'll never apply an ACL without verifying it first!

Object Groups

Object groups are a nice way to create what is basically a list of test statements that can then be easily applied to an access list as one line. We use object groups to simplify creation and maintenance.

We can create the object groups as either IP address or TCP and UDP port numbers. Let's take a look at some output which demonstrates this in real time:

```
Nexus7(config)# object-group ?
  ip    IP Object groups
  ipv6  IPv6 Object groups


Nexus7(config)# object-group ip ?
  address  Address object group
  port     IP port object group (can be used in IPv4 and IPv6 access-lists)


Nexus7(config)# object-group ip address Todd_Deny
Nexus7(config-ipaddr-ogroup)# 10.0.0.0/8
Nexus7(config-ipaddr-ogroup)# 172.16.0.0/12
Nexus7(config-ipaddr-ogroup)# 192.168.0.0/24
Nexus7(config-ipaddr-ogroup)# show object-group Todd_Deny


IPv4 address object-group Todd_Deny
        10 10.0.0.0/8
        20 172.16.0.0/12
        30 192.168.0.0/24
Nexus7(config-ipaddr-ogroup)#
```

The preceding object group denied all private IP addresses, but what exactly are we denying them? We'll get to that in a minute, but first I'll create an object group using TCP and UDP port numbers:

```
Nexus7(config)# object-group ip port Permit_Ports
Nexus7(config-port-ogroup)# range 2011 2099
```

```
Nexus7(config-port-ogroup)# eq 31156
Nexus7(config-port-ogroup)# gt 32655
Nexus7(config-port-ogroup)# show object-group Permit_Ports


Protocol port object-group Permit_Ports
        10 range 2011 - 2099
        20 eq 31156
        30 gt 32655
Nexus7(config-port-ogroup)#
```

In this object-group, I created an object group that contains TCP or UDP port numbers. First, I started with a range of ports from 2011 to 2099, then added an entry of equal to (eq) port 31156, then finished with a greater than (gt) port number 32655.

As I said, at this point we'd simply just apply these lists to an access list, but we'll use special commands. Let's take a look:

```
Nexus7(config)# ip access-list Summary_ACL
Nexus7(config-acl)# deny ip addrgroup Todd_Deny any
Nexus7(config-acl)# permit tcp any any portgroup Permit_ports
```

I used the command addrgroup for the IP object group and the command portgroup to apply the port object groups. To verify our object-groups, we'd simply use the following commands:

```
Nexus7(config-acl)# sh object-group


Protocol port object-group Permit_Ports
        10 range 2011 - 2099
        20 eq 31156
        30 gt 32655
IPv4 address object-group Todd_Deny
        10 10.0.0.0/8
        20 172.16.0.0/12
        30 192.168.0.0/24
Nexus7(config-acl)#
```

The show object-group command provides a nice output revealing my configured object groups. Let's just see what the show access-list provides:

```
Nexus7(config-acl)# sh access-lists
```

```
IP access list Summary_ACL
        10 deny ip addrgroup Todd_Deny any
        20 permit tcp any any portgroup Permit_ports
```

This reveals to us which object groups are applied, with what protocol, and if they're applied as source or destination limitations. Let's take a look at the last command that provides an output of what these groups actually provide for us:

```
Nexus7(config-acl)# sh access-lists expanded
IP access list Summary_ACL
        10 deny ip 10.0.0.0/8 any
        10 deny ip 172.16.0.0/12 any
        10 deny ip 192.168.0.0/24 any
IP access list Verify_Me
        10 deny tcp 10.0.0.0/8 any
        20 deny tcp 192.168.10.0/24 any
        30 deny tcp 172.16.0.0/12 any
        40 permit ip any any
```

The show access-list expanded provides all the test statements that the object group applies to the ACL.

Summary

This chapter covered how to configure access lists to properly filter IP traffic. You learned what an access list is and how to apply it to a Cisco router to add security to your network. You also learned how to configure named-extended access lists on NX-OS to further filter IP traffic.

I then went through some examples on both IOS routers and NX-OS by using business requirements as goals, then solving and meeting them with the operating system. I then applied them to an interface.

Last, I covered how to configure ACLs and verify them before you apply them to the active configuration file and then finished with how to configure and verify object groups.

Exam Essentials

Understand the term implicit deny.   At the end of every access list is an implicit deny. What this means is that if a packet does not match any of the lines in the access list, it will be discarded. Also, if you have nothing but deny statements in your list, the list will not permit any packets.

Understand the NX-Os extended IP access list configuration command.   To configure an extended IP access list with NX-OS, use the `ip access-list` command followed by a name in global configuration mode. Remember that this name can be a number! Choose your permit or deny statements, the Network layer protocol field, the source IP address you want to filter on, the destination address you want to filter on, the Transport layer port number if TCP or UDP has been specified as the protocol, and finally, the port number or application.

Remember the command to verify the access list configuration.   To see the configured access lists on your router, use the `show access-list` command. This command will not show you which interfaces have an access list set. To see your interface configuration, you need to use the show `running-config aclmgr` and/or show `access-list summary` command.

Written Lab 13

You can find the answers in Appendix A.

In this section, write the answers to the following questions:

1. What commands would you use to configure an access list to prevent all machines on network 172.16.0.0 from accessing your Ethernet network?

2. What command would you use to apply the access list you created in question 1 to an outbound Ethernet interface?

3. What command would you use to create an access list that denies host 192.168.15.5 access to an Ethernet network?

4. Which command verifies that you've entered the access list correctly?

5. What commands would you use to create a named access list that stops host 172.16.10.1 from telnetting to host 172.16.30.5?

Hands-on Lab

In this section, you will complete a simple ACL lab in NX-OS. To complete this lab, you will need only one Nexus switch.

Hands-on Lab 13.1: NX-OS IP Access Lists

In this lab, you will use the following diagram for configuring the ACL.

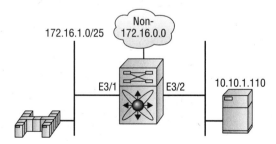

Hands-on Lab 13.1: NX-OS IP Access Lists

Follow these steps to configure an access control list on a Cisco Nexus switch to deny hosts on the 172.16.1.0/21 network from accessing HTTP proxy servers listening on port 8080:

1. Remove any access lists on your Nexus switch or simulator and add an extended named list to your switch.

2. Choose a name to create an extended IP list. Remember, your name could be a number. Here is an example:

```
nexus7k(config)# ip access-list Todd_Lab
```

Remember that named lists start with the command IP.

3. Use a deny statement. (You'll add a permit statement in step 8 to allow other traffic to still work.)

```
nexus7k(config-acl)# deny ?
  <0-255>  A protocol number
  ahp      Authentication header protocol
  eigrp    Cisco's EIGRP routing protocol
  esp      Encapsulation security payload
  gre      Cisco's GRE tunneling
  icmp     Internet Control Message Protocol
  igmp     Internet Group Management Protocol
  ip       Any IP protocol
  nos      KA9Q NOS compatible IP over IP tunneling
  ospf     OSPF routing protocol
  pcp      Payload compression protocol
  pim      Protocol independent multicast
  tcp      Transmission Control Protocol
  udp      User Datagram Protocol
```

4. Since you are going to deny port 8080 (HTTP), you must choose TCP as a Transport layer protocol:

```
nexus7k(config-acl)# deny tcp ?
  A.B.C.D      Source network address
  A.B.C.D/LEN  Source network prefix
  addrgroup    Source address group
  any          Any source address
  host         A single source host
```

5. Add the source network address you want to filter on. You need to use the wildcards for a /21 network in the source:

```
nexus7k(config-acl)# deny tcp 172.16.1.0 0.0.0.7 ?
  A.B.C.D      Destination network address
  A.B.C.D/LEN  Destination network prefix
  addrgroup    Destination address group
  any          Any destination address
```

```
eq            Match only packets on a given port number
gt            Match only packets with a greater port number
host          A single destination host
lt            Match only packets with a lower port number
neq           Match only packets not on a given port number
portgroup     Src port group
range         Match only packets in the range of port numbers
```

I used the wildcards 0.0.0.7, meaning the first three octets match exactly but the fourth octet is a block size of 7 (/21 is a 248 mask).

6. Now you need to add the destination address:

```
nexus7k(config-acl)# deny tcp 172.16.1.0 0.0.0.7 any ?
  <CR>
  ack             Match on the ACK bit
  capture         Enable packet capture on this filter for session
  dscp            Match packets with given dscp value
  eq              Match only packets on a given port number
  established     Match established connections
  fin             Match on the FIN bit
  fragments       Check non-initial fragments
  gt              Match only packets with a greater port number
  log             Log matches against this entry
  lt              Match only packets with a lower port number
  neq             Match only packets not on a given port number
  packet-length   Match packets based on layer 3 packet length
  portgroup       Dst port group
  precedence      Match packets with given precedence value
  psh             Match on the PSH bit
  range           Match only packets in the range of port numbers
  rst             Match on the RST bit
  syn             Match on the SYN bit
  time-range      Specify a time range
  urg             Match on the URG bit
```

7. At this point, you can add the eq 8080 command to filter hosts from the 172.16.10.0/21 network from using HTTP with destination port 8080 to any destination:

```
nexus7k(config-acl)# deny tcp 172.16.1.0 0.0.0.7 any eq 8080
```

Alternately you can type the following line to get the same results:

```
nexus7k(config-acl)# deny tcp 172.16.1.0/29 any eq 8080
```

8. It is important to add this line next to create a `permit` statement:

```
nexus7k(config-acl)# permit ip any any
```

You must create a `permit` statement and in this example, any source and any destination is permitted. If you just add a deny statement, nothing will be permitted at all. Please see the section, "Named ACLs," earlier in this chapter for more detailed information on the `deny ip any any` command implied at the end of every ACL.

9. Apply the access list to the interface Ethernet3/1 to stop the HTTP port 8080 traffic as soon as it hits the first inbound interface:

```
nexus7k(config-acl)# int e3/1
nexus7k(config-if)# ip access-group Todd_Lab in
```

10. Verify your list with the `show running-config` command:

```
nexus7k(config-if)# sh run | begin Todd_Lab
ip access-list Todd_Lab
  10 deny tcp 172.16.1.0/29 any eq 8080
  20 permit ip any any
[output cut]
!
interface Ethernet3/1
  ip access-group Todd_Lab in
```

11. Verify your list with the following command:

```
Nexus7k# sh running-config aclmgr


!Command: show running-config aclmgr
!Time: Wed Mar 20 17:43:25 2013


version 6.1(3)
ip access-list Todd_Lab
  10 deny tcp 172.16.1.0/29 any eq 8080
  20 permit ip any any


interface Ethernet3/1
  ip access-group Todd_Lab in
```

Review Questions

You can find the answers in Appendix B.

 The following questions are designed to test your understanding of this chapter's material. For more information on how to get additional questions, please see this book's introduction.

1. Which of the following is an example of a NX-OS IP access list?

    A. access-list 110, permit ip host 1.1.1.1 any

    B. ip access-list 1, deny ip 172.16.10.1 0.0.0.0 any

    C. access-list 1 permit 172.16.10.1 255.255.0.0

    D. ip access-list extended, permit ip host 1.1.1.1

2. You need to create an access list that will prevent hosts in the network range of 192.168.160.0 to 192.168.191.255. Which of the following lists will you use?

    A. deny ip 192.168.160.0 255.255.224.0 any

    B. deny ip 192.168.160.0 0.0.191.255 any

    C. deny ip 192.168.160.0 0.0.31.255 any

    D. deny tcp 192.168.0.0 0.0.31.255 any

3. You have created a named access list called Blocksales. Which of the following is a valid command for applying this to packets trying to enter interface e1/0 of your router?

    A. (config)#ip access-group 110 in

    B. (config-if)#ip access-group NX-OS in

    C. (config-if)#ip access-group Blocksales in

    D. (config-if)#Blocksales ip access-list in

4. Which of the following are valid ways to refer only to host 172.16.30.55 in an IP access list? (Choose two.)

    A. 172.16.30.55 0.0.0.255

    B. 172.16.30.55 0.0.0.0

    C. any 172.16.30.55

    D. host 172.16.30.55

    E. 0.0.0.0 172.16.30.55

    F. ip any 172.16.30.55

5. Which of the following access lists will allow only HTTP traffic into network 196.15.7.0?

   A. `permit tcp any 196.15.7.0 0.0.0.255 eq www`

   B. `deny tcp any 196.15.7.0 eq www`

   C. `permit 196.15.7.0 0.0.0.255 eq www`

   D. `permit ip any 196.15.7.0 0.0.0.255`

   E. `permit www 196.15.7.0 0.0.0.255`

6. What is the correct format of an access control list on a Cisco Nexus switch to deny hosts on the 172.16.1.0/21 network from accessing HTTP proxy servers listening on port 8080? (Choose two.)

   A. `IP access-list 101, deny ip 172.16.1.0 0.0.0.255 any eq 8080`

   B. `IP access-list 101, deny tcp 172.16.1.0 0.0.7.255 any eq 8080`

   C. `permit tcp any any`

   D. `permit ip any any`

7. Which router command allows you to view the entire contents of all access lists?

   A. `show interface`

   B. `show ip interface`

   C. `show access-lists`

   D. `show all access-lists`

8. If you wanted to deny all Telnet connections to only network 192.168.10.0, which command could you use?

   A. `deny tcp 192.168.10.0 255.255.255.0 eq telnet`

   B. `deny tcp 192.168.10.0 0.255.255.255 eq telnet`

   C. `deny tcp any 192.168.10.0 0.0.0.255 eq 23`

   D. `deny 192.168.10.0 0.0.0.255 any eq 23`

9. If you wanted to deny FTP access from network 200.200.10.0 to network 200.199.11.0 but allow everything else, which of the following command strings is valid?

   A. `deny 200.200.10.0 to network 200.199.11.0 eq ftp`

   `permit ip any 0.0.0.0 255.255.255.255`

   B. `deny ftp 200.200.10.0 200.199.11.0 any any`

   C. `deny tcp 200.200.10.0 0.0.0.255 200.199.11.0 0.0.0.255 eq ftp`

   D. `deny tcp 200.200.10.0 0.0.0.255 200.199.11.0 0.0.0.255 eq ftp`

   `permit ip any any`

10. You want to create a standard access list that denies the subnet of the following host: 172.16.50.172/20. Which of the following would you start your list with?

    A. deny ip 172.16.48.0 255.255.240.0 any

    B. deny ip 172.16.0.0 0.0.255.255 any

    C. deny ip 172.16.64.0 0.0.31.255 any

    D. deny ip 172.16.48.0 0.0.15.255 any

11. Which command would you use to apply an access list to a router interface?

    A. ip access-list 101 out

    B. access-list ip 101 in

    C. ip access-group 101 in

    D. access-group ip 101 in

12. You want to create an access list that denies the subnet of the following host: 172.16.198.94/19. Which of the following would you start your list with?

    A. deny ip 172.16.192.0 0.0.31.255 any

    B. deny ip 172.16.0.0 0.0.255.255 any

    C. deny ip 172.16.172.0 0.0.31.255 any

    D. deny ip 172.16.188.0 0.0.15.255 any

13. You want to create a standard access list that denies the subnet of the following host: 172.16.144.17/21. Which of the following would you start your list with?

    A. deny ip 172.16.48.0 255.255.240.0 any

    B. deny ip 172.16.144.0 0.0.7.255 any

    C. deny ip 172.16.64.0 0.0.31.255 any

    D. deny ip 172.16.136.0 0.0.15.255 any

14. What ACL would you use on a Cisco Nexus switch to deny unencrypted web traffic from any source to destination host 10.10.1.110? (Choose two.)

    A. ip access-list 101, deny tcp any host 10.10.1.110 eq 80

    B. ip access-list 101, deny ip any host 10.10.1.110 eq 80

    C. permit tcp any any

    D. permit ip any any

15. What command will permit SMTP mail to only host 1.1.1.1?

    A. `permit smtp host 1.1.1.1`

    B. `permit ip smtp host 1.1.1.1`

    C. `permit tcp any host 1.1.1.1 eq smtp`

    D. `permit tcp any host 1.1.1.1 eq smtp`

16. You configure the following access list:

```
ip access-list 110
deny tcp 10.1.1.128 0.0.0.63 any eq smtp
deny tcp any any eq 23
int ethernet 3/1
ip access-group 110 out
```

What will the result of this access list be?

    A. E-mail and Telnet will be allowed out E3/1.

    B. E-mail and Telnet will be allowed in E3/1.

    C. Everything but e-mail and Telnet will be allowed out E3/1.

    D. No IP traffic will be allowed out E3/1.

17. What ACL would you configure on the Nexus switch to deny FTP traffic from any source to destination host 10.10.1.110?

    A. `(config)#ip access-list 101`

        `(config-acl)#deny tcp any host 10.10.1.110 eq ftp`

        `(config-acl)#permit ip any any`

    B. `(config)#access-list 101`

        `(config-acl)#deny tcp any host 10.10.1.110 eq ftp`

        `(config-acl)#permit ip any any`

    C. `(config)#ip access-list 101 deny any host 10.10.1.110 eq 21`

        `(config)#permit ip any any`

    D. `(config)#ip access-list 101`

        `(config-acl)#deny tcp any host 10.10.1.110 eq ftp`

18. Which of the following is true regarding access lists applied to an interface?

    A. You can place as many access lists as you want on any interface until you run out of memory.

    B. You can apply only one access list on any interface.

    C. One access list may be configured, per direction, for each layer 3 protocol configured on an interface.

    D. You can apply two access lists to any interface.

19. What are the types of ACLs available with IOS? (Choose 3.)

    A. Standard

    B. Basic

    C. Extended

    D. Numbered

    E. Named

20. What is the only type of ACL you can create with NX-OS?

    A. Standard numbered

    B. Basic named

    C. Extended named

    D. Standard named

    E. Extended numbered

Appendix A

Answers to Written Labs

Chapter 1: Understanding Basic Networking

Answers to Written Lab 1

1. Bus, ring, and star
2. Ring
3. Server
4. Client/server
5. Point-to-point
6. Switch
7. Star and extended star
8. Virtual LAN
9. A segment
10. Bus

Chapter 2: Internetworking

Answers to Written Lab 2.1

1. The Application layer is responsible for finding the network resources broadcast from a server and adding flow control and error control (if the application developer chooses).
2. The Physical layer takes frames from the Data Link layer and encodes the 1s and 0s into a digital signal for transmission on the network medium.
3. The Network layer provides routing through an internetwork and logical addressing.
4. The Presentation layer makes sure that data is in a readable format for the Application layer.
5. The Session layer sets up, maintains, and terminates sessions between applications.
6. PDUs at the Data Link layer are called frames and provide physical addressing plus other options to place packets on the network medium.
7. The Transport layer uses virtual circuits to create a reliable connection between two hosts.
8. The Network layer provides logical addressing, typically IP addressing and routing.

9. The Physical layer is responsible for the electrical and mechanical connections between devices.

10. The Data Link layer is responsible for the framing of data packets.

11. The Session layer creates sessions between different hosts' applications.

12. The Data Link layer frames packets received from the Network layer.

13. The Transport layer segments user data.

14. The Network layer creates packets out of segments handed down from the Transport layer.

15. The Physical layer is responsible for transporting 1s and 0s (bits) in a digital signal.

16. Transport

17. Transport

18. Data Link

19. Network

20. 48 bits (6 bytes) expressed as a hexadecimal number

Answers to Written Lab 2.2

Description	Device or OSI Layer
This device sends and receives information about the Network layer.	Router
This layer creates a virtual circuit before transmitting between two end stations.	Transport
This device uses hardware addresses to filter a network.	Bridge or switch
Ethernet is defined at these layers.	Data Link and Physical
This layer supports flow control, sequencing and acknowledgments.	Transport
This device can measure the distance to a remote network.	Router
Logical addressing is used at this layer.	Network
Hardware addresses are defined at this layer.	Data Link (MAC sublayer)
This device creates one big collision domain and one large broadcast domain.	Hub
This device creates many smaller collision domains, but the network is still one large broadcast domain.	Switch or bridge

(continued)

Description	Device or OSI Layer
This device can never run full duplex.	Hub
This device breaks up collision domains and broadcast domains.	Router

Answers to Written Lab 2.3

1. Hub: One collision domain, one broadcast domain
2. Bridge: Two collision domains, one broadcast domain
3. Switch: Four collision domains, one broadcast domain
4. Router: Three collision domains, three broadcast domains

Chapter 3: Ethernet Technologies

Answers to Written Lab 3.1

1. Convert from decimal IP address to binary format.

   Complete the following table to express 192.168.10.15 in binary format.

Decimal	128	64	32	16	8	4	2	1	Binary
192	1	1	0	0	0	0	0	0	11000000
168	1	0	1	0	1	0	0	0	10101000
10	0	0	0	0	1	0	1	0	00001010
15	0	0	0	0	1	1	1	1	00001111

Complete the following table to express 172.16.20.55 in binary format.

Decimal	128	64	32	16	8	4	2	1	Binary
172	1	0	1	0	1	1	0	0	10101100
16	0	0	0	1	0	0	0	0	00010000
20	0	0	0	1	0	1	0	0	00010100
55	0	0	1	1	0	1	1	1	00110111

Complete the following table to express 10.11.12.99 in binary format.

Decimal	128	64	32	16	8	4	2	1	Binary
10	0	0	0	0	1	0	1	0	00001010
11	0	0	0	0	1	0	1	1	00001011
12	0	0	0	0	1	1	0	0	00001100
99	0	1	1	0	0	0	1	1	01100011

2. Convert the following from binary format to decimal IP address.

Complete the following table to express 11001100.00110011.10101010.01010101 in decimal IP address format.

Binary	128	64	32	16	8	4	2	1	Decimal
11001100	1	1	0	0	1	1	0	0	204
00110011	0	0	1	1	0	0	1	1	51
10101010	1	0	1	0	1	0	1	0	170
01010101	0	1	0	1	0	1	0	1	85

Complete the following table to express 11000110.11010011.00111001.11010001 in decimal IP address format.

Binary	128	64	32	16	8	4	2	1	Decimal
11000110	1	1	0	0	0	1	1	0	198
11010011	1	1	0	1	0	0	1	1	211
00111001	0	0	1	1	1	0	0	1	57
11010001	1	1	0	1	0	0	0	1	209

Complete the following table to express 10000100.11010010.10111000.10100110 in decimal IP address format.

Binary	128	64	32	16	8	4	2	1	Decimal
10000100	1	0	0	0	0	1	0	0	132
11010010	1	1	0	1	0	0	1	0	210
10111000	1	0	1	1	1	0	0	0	184
10100110	1	0	1	0	0	1	1	0	166

3. Convert the following from binary format to hexadecimal.

Complete the following table to express 11011000.00011011.00111101.01110110 in hexadecimal.

Binary	128	64	32	16	8	4	2	1	Hexadecimal
11011000	1	1	0	1	1	0	0	0	D8
00011011	0	0	0	1	1	0	1	1	1B
00111101	0	0	1	1	1	1	0	1	3D
01110110	0	1	1	1	0	1	1	0	76

Complete the following table to express 11001010.11110101.10000011.11101011 in hexadecimal.

Binary	128	64	32	16	8	4	2	1	Hexadecimal
11001010	1	1	0	0	1	0	1	0	CA
11110101	1	1	1	1	0	1	0	1	F5
10000011	1	0	0	0	0	0	1	1	83
11101011	1	1	1	0	1	0	1	1	EB

Complete the following table to express 10000100.11010010.01000011.10110011 in hexadecimal.

Binary	128	64	32	16	8	4	2	1	Hexadecimal
10000100	1	0	0	0	0	1	0	0	84
11010010	1	1	0	1	0	0	1	0	D2
01000011	0	1	0	0	0	0	1	1	43
10110011	1	0	1	1	0	0	1	1	B3

Answers to Written Lab 3.2

When a collision occurs on an Ethernet LAN, the following happens:

1. A jam signal informs all devices that a collision occurred.
2. The collision invokes a random backoff algorithm.
3. Each device on the Ethernet segment stops transmitting for a short time until the timers expire.
4. All hosts have equal priority to transmit after the timers have expired.

Answers to Written Lab 3.3

1. Crossover
2. Straight-through
3. Crossover

4. Crossover

5. Straight-through

6. Crossover

7. Crossover

8. Rolled

Answers to Written Lab 3.4

At a transmitting device, the data encapsulation method works like this:

1. User information is converted to data for transmission on the network.

2. Data is converted to segments, and a reliable connection is set up between the transmitting and receiving hosts.

3. Segments are converted to packets or datagrams, and a logical address is placed in the header so each packet can be routed through an internetwork.

4. Packets or datagrams are converted to frames for transmission on the local network. Hardware (Ethernet) addresses are used to uniquely identify hosts on a local network segment.

5. Frames are converted to bits, and a digital encoding and clocking scheme is used.

Chapter 4: TCP/IP DoD Model

1. TCP

2. Host-to-Host

3. UDP

4. TCP

5. ICMP

6. Frames

7. Segment

8. Port numbers

9. IP addresses

10. 1, 2

Chapter 5: IP Adressing

1. 4 billion
2. NAT
3. 1 through 126
4. Loopback or diagnostics
5. Turn all host bits off.
6. Turn all host bits on.
7. 10.0.0.0 through 10.255.255.255
8. 172.16.0.0 through 172.31.255.255
9. 192.168.0.0 through 192.168.255.255
10. 128-bit colon-delimited hexadecimal

Chapter 6: Easy Subnetting

Answers to Written Lab 6.1

1. 192.168.100.25/30. A /30 is 255.255.255.252. The valid subnet is 192.168.100.24, broadcast is 192.168.100.27, and valid hosts are 192.168.100.25 and 26.

2. 192.168.100.37/28. A /28 is 255.255.255.240. The fourth octet is a block size of 16. Just count by 16s until you pass 37. 0, 16, 32, 48. The host is in the 32 subnet, with a broadcast address of 47. Valid hosts 33–46.

3. 192.168.100.66/27. A /27 is 255.255.255.224. The fourth octet is a block size of 32. Count by 32s until you pass the host address of 66. 0, 32, 64. The host is in the 32 subnet, broadcast address of 63. Valid host range of 33–62.

4. 192.168.100.17/29. A /29 is 255.255.255.248. The fourth octet is a block size of 8. 0, 8, 16, 24. The host is in the 16 subnet, broadcast of 23. Valid hosts 17–22.

5. 192.168.100.99/26. A /26 is 255.255.255.192. The fourth octet has a block size of 64. 0, 64, 128. The host is in the 64 subnet, broadcast of 127. Valid hosts 65–126.

6. 192.168.100.99/25. A /25 is 255.255.255.128. The fourth octet is a block size of 128. 0, 128. The host is in the 0 subnet, broadcast of 127. Valid hosts 1–126.

7. A default Class B is 255.255.0.0. A Class B 255.255.255.0 mask is 256 subnets, each with 254 hosts. We need fewer subnets. If we used 255.255.240.0, this provides 16 subnets. Let's add one more subnet bit. 255.255.248.0. This is 5 bits of subnetting, which provides 32 subnets. This is our best answer, a /21.

8. A /29 is 255.255.255.248. This is a block size of 8 in the fourth octet. 0, 8, 16. The host is in the 8 subnet, broadcast is 15.

9. A /29 is 255.255.255.248, which is 5 subnet bits and 3 host bits. This is only 6 hosts per subnet.

10. A /23 is 255.255.254.0. The third octet is a block size of 2. 0, 2, 4. The subnet is in the 16.2.0 subnet; the broadcast address is 16.3.255.

Answers to Written Lab 6.2

Classful Address	Subnet Mask	Number of Hosts per Subnet ($2^n - 2$)
/16	255.255.0.0	65,534
/17	255.255.128.0	32,766
/18	255.255.192.0	16,382
/19	255.255.224.0	8,190
/20	255.255.240.0	4,094
/21	255.255.248.0	2,046
/22	255.255.252.0	1,022
/23	255.255.254.0	510
/24	255.255.255.0	254
/25	255.255.255.128	126
/26	255.255.255.192	62
/27	255.255.255.224	30
/28	255.255.255.240	14
/29	255.255.255.248	6
/30	255.255.255.252	2

Answers to Written Lab 6.3

Decimal IP Address	Address Class	Number of Subnet and Host Bits	Number of Subnets (2x)	Number of Hosts (2x – 2)
10.25.66.154/23	A	15/9	32,768	510
172.31.254.12/24	B	8/8	256	254
192.168.20.123/28	C	4/4	16	14
63.24.89.21/18	A	10/14	1,024	16,384
128.1.1.254/20	B	4/12	16	4,094
208.100.54.209/30	C	6/2	64	2

Chapter 7: Introduction to Nexus

Answers to Written Lab 7.1

1. The console port is a serial port used for out-of-band configuration.
2. The management port is a dedicated Ethernet port that allows for remote out-of-band configuration.
3. L1/L2 ports are not used.

Answers to Written Lab 7.2

Each of these are virtualized with a different technology.

1. VLAN
2. Trunking
3. Switch virtual interfaces (SVIs)
4. Virtual Routing and Forwarding (VRF)
5. Virtual Device Context (VDC)

Answers to Written Lab 7.3

At a transmitting device, the data encapsulation method works like this:

1. HSRP is a layer 3 process.
2. STP is a layer 2 process.
3. Pim is a layer 2 process.
4. Cisco Discovery Protocol is a layer 2 process.
5. OSPF is a layer 3 process.
6. UDLD is a layer 2 process.

Answers to Written Lab 7.4

Remember, these are purely virtual devices and only software. There is no hardware.

1. Zero
2. None
3. None
4. None

Answers to Written Lab 7.5

VRF allows for multiple routing tables on a single device. This is useful because you may wish for a different interface to treat layer 3 traffic differently. VDC effectively creates another switch with its own administration and configuration. This is very useful in a multi-tenant environment or anywhere you want to have administration separated.

Chapter 8: Configuring Nexus

1. no shutdown
2. write erase boot
3. username todd role network-admin password todd
4. username todd role network-operator password cisco
5. reload
6. switchname Chicago, or hostname Chicago

Chapter 9: IP Routing

Answers to Written Lab 9

1. False. The MAC address would be the router interface, not the remote host.
2. It will use the gateway interface MAC at layer 2 (L2) and the actual destination IP at layer 3 (L3).
3. True.
4. None; not on this planet.
5. IP will discard the packet, and ICMP will send a destination unreachable packet out the interface on which the packet was received.

Chapter 10: Routing Protocols

1. EIGRP
2. 15
3. 30 seconds
4. RIP
5. Address-family

Chapter 11: Layer 2 Switching Technologies

1. Client
2. show vtp status
3. Broadcast
4. Collision
5. Transparent
6. Trunking allows you to make a single port part of multiple VLANs at the same time.
7. Frame identification (frame tagging) uniquely assigns a user-defined ID to each frame. This is sometimes referred to as a VLAN ID or color.

8. True

9. Access link

10. interface-vlan

Chapter 12: Redundant Switched Technologies

1. show mac address-table

2. show spanning-tree or show spanning-tree vlan vlan#

3. 802.1w

4. STP, or RSTP in NX-OS

5. Rapid-PVST+

6. spanning-tree port type edge

7. show interface port-channel number

8. spanning-tree port type switch

9. show spanning-tree and show spanning-tree summary

10. RSTP and MSTP

Chapter 13: Security

1. ip access-list 101, deny ip 172.16.0.0 0.0.255.255 any, permit ip any any

2. ip access-group 101 out

3. ip access-list 101, deny ip host 192.168.15.5 any, permit ip any any

4. show access-lists

5. ip access-list 110

Deny tcp host 172.16.10.1 host 172.16.30.5 eq 23

permit ip any any

Appendix B

Answers to Review Questions

Chapter 1: Understanding Basic Networking

1. **B, D.** Physical star and physical extended-star are the most popular physical LAN networks today.

2. **B.** FDDI and Token Ring are no longer used, but they used a physical ring topology.

3. **D.** Only a mesh physical topology has point-to-point connections to every device, so it has more connections, and is not a popular LAN technology.

4. **B.** In a star topology, each workstation connects to a hub, switch, or similar central device, but not to other workstations. The benefit is that when connectivity to the central device is lost, the rest of the network lives on.

5. **A.** In Chapter 3, we'll cover Ethernet and the standards, but you need to know that the original Ethernet used a classical CSMA/CD as its physical and logical topology.

6. **B.** A logical grouping of hosts is called a LAN, and they are typically grouped by connecting them to a switch.

7. **C.** Security is easy to relax in a peer-to-peer environment. Because of the trouble it takes to standardize authentication, a piecemeal approach involving users' personal preferences develops. There are no dedicated servers in a peer-to-peer network, and such a network can be created with as few as two computers.

8. **A.** When a central office, such as a headquarters, needs to communicate directly with its branch offices, but the branches do not require direct communication with one another, the point-to-multipoint model is applicable. The other scenarios tend to indicate the use of a point-to-point link between sites.

9. **D.** LANs generally have a geographic scope of a single building or smaller. They can range from simple (two hosts) to complex (with thousands of hosts).

10. **B.** The only disadvantage mentioned is the fact that there is a single point of failure in the network. However, this topology makes troubleshooting easier; if the entire network fails, you know where to look first. The central device also ensures that the loss of a single port and the addition of a new device to an available port do not disrupt the network for other stations attached to such a device.

11. **D.** A typical WAN connects two or more remote LANs together using someone else's network (your ISP's) and a router. Local host and router see these networks as remote networks and not as local networks or local resources.

12. **C.** *Hybrid topology* means just that—a combination of two or more types of physical or logical network topologies working together within the same network.

13. D. In a star topology, if a cable fails, it brings down only particular machine or network segment it's connected to and makes it easier to troubleshoot.

14. D. In client/server networks, requests for resources go to a main server that responds by handling security and directing the client to the resource it wants instead of the request going directly to the machine with the desired resource (as in peer-to-peer).

15. A. The best answer to this question is an Ethernet switch, which uses a star physical topology with a logical bus technology.

16. D. Routers break up broadcast domains and are used to connect different networks together.

17. D. In the mesh topology, there is a path from every machine to every other one in the network. A mesh topology is used mainly because of the robust fault tolerance it offers—if one connection goes on the blink, computers and other network devices can simply switch to one of the many redundant connections that are up and running.

18. A. As its name implies, in a point-to-point topology you have a direct connection between two routers, giving you one communication path. The routers in a point-to-point topology can either be linked by a serial cable, making it a physical network, or be far away and only connected by a circuit within a Frame Relay network, making it a logical network.

19. B. A hybrid topology is a combination of two or more types of physical or logical network topologies working together within the same network.

20. A, B, C, D. Each topology has its own set of pros and cons regarding implementation, so in addition to asking the right questions, cost, ease of installation, maintenance, and fault tolerance are all important factors to be considered.

Chapter 2: Internetworking

1. D. A receiving host can control the transmitter by using flow control (TCP uses windowing by default). By decreasing the window size, the receiving host can slow down the transmitting host so the receiving host does not overflow its buffers.

2. A. The only reliable protocol in the IP stack is TCP, which is found at the Transport layer, layer 4.

3. C, D. Not that you really want to enlarge a single collision domain, but a hub (multiport repeater) will provide this for you.

4. D. The Transport layer receives large data streams from the upper layers and breaks them up into smaller pieces called segments.

5. A, C, E, G. Routers provide packet switching, packet filtering, internetwork communication, and path selection. Although routers do create or terminate collision domains, this is not the main purpose of a router, so option B is not a correct answer to this question.

6. B. Routers operate at layer 3. LAN switches operate at layer 2. Ethernet hubs operate at layer 1. Word processing applications communicate to the Application layer interface but do not operate at layer 7, so the answer would be none.

7. D. The Transport layer is responsible for segmenting data and then reassembling the data on the receiving host.

8. A, D. The main advantage of a layered model is that it can allow application developers to change aspects of a program in just one layer of the layer model's specifications. Advantages of using the OSI layered model include, but are not limited to, the following: It divides the network communication process into smaller and simpler components, thus aiding component development and design and troubleshooting; it allows multiple-vendor development through standardization of network components; it encourages industry standardization by defining what functions occur at each layer of the model; it allows various types of network hardware and software to communicate; and it prevents changes in one layer from affecting other layers, so it does not hamper development.

9. B, C. Bridges and switches break up collision domains, which Cisco calls microsegmentation. This will add more bandwidth for users.

10. B. Adding switches for connectivity to the network would reduce LAN congestion rather than cause LAN congestion.

11. C. If a switch has three computers connected to it, with no VLANs present, one broadcast and three collision domains are created.

12. B, D. Layer 3, the Network layer, uses routers and IP addresses to do packet forwarding, and layer 1, the Physical layer, provides transmission of bits over a wire.

13. A, C, D. The common types of flow control are buffering, windowing, and congestion avoidance.

14. D. If a hub has three computers connected to it, one broadcast and one collision domain are created.

15. C. Flow control allows the receiving device to control the transmitter so the receiving device's buffer does not overflow.

16. C, D, E. Layer 4 (Transport) data is referred to as Segments, layer 2 is Frames, and layer 1 is bits.

17. A. Reference models prevent rather than allow changes on one layer to affect operations on other layers as well, so the model doesn't hamper development.

18. B. Routers operate no higher than layer 3 of the OSI model.

19. C. When an HTTP document must be retrieved from a location other than the local machine, the Application layer must be accessed first.

20. D. The Session layer of the OSI model offers three different modes of communication: *simplex*, *half duplex*, and *full duplex*.

Chapter 3: Ethernet Technologies

1. A, D. An Ethernet frame has source and destination MAC addresses, an Ether-Type field to identify the Network layer protocol, the data, and the FCS field that holds the answer to the CRC.

2. A, D. Half-duplex Ethernet works in a shared medium or collision domain. Half duplex provides a lower effective throughput than full duplex.

3. D. Fiber-optic cable provides a more secure, long-distance cable that is not susceptible to EMI interference at high speeds.

4. C. The old Source and Destination Service Access Point fields in a SNAP frame defined the Network layer protocol that the packet uses.

5. B. To connect two switches together, you would use an RJ45 UTP crossover cable.

6. B, E. Once transmitting stations on an Ethernet segment hear a collision, they send an extended jam signal to ensure that all stations recognize the collision. After the jamming is complete, each sender waits a predetermined amount of time, plus a random time. After both timers expire, they are free to transmit, but they must make sure the media is clear before transmitting and that they all have equal priority.

7. D. To connect to a router or switch console port, you would use an RJ45 UTP rolled cable.

8. B. You must be able to take a binary number and convert it into both decimal and hexadecimal. To convert to decimal, just add up the 1s using their values. The values that are turned on with the binary number of 10110111 are 128 + 32 + 16 + 4 + 2 + 1 = 183. To get the hexadecimal equivalent, you need to break the eight binary digits into nibbles (4 bits), 1011 and 0111. By adding up these values, you get 11 and 7. In hexadecimal, 11 is B, so the answer is 0xB7.

9. B. Ethernet networking uses Carrier Sense Multiple Access with Collision Detection (CSMA/CD), a protocol that helps devices share the bandwidth evenly without having two devices transmit at the same time on the network medium.

10. A. After the expiration of the backoff algorithm, all hosts have equal priority.

11. D. I always say the 2 in the 10Base2 name means "almost 200 meters" because the specification runs only to 185 meters, although way back in the mid 1980s there were many networks that went further distances. I'm giving away my age here, which also shows you how old this specification is.

12. C. There are no collisions in full-duplex mode.

13. D. A MAC, or hardware, address is a 48-bit (6-byte) address written in a hexadecimal format.

14. A. The first 24 bits, or 3 bytes, of a MAC address is called the organizationally unique identifier (OUI).

15. B. The Data Link layer of the OSI model is responsible for combining bits into bytes and bytes into frames.

16. C. The term for the unwanted signal interference from adjacent pairs in the cable is crosstalk.

17. C. Starting with our leftmost bit, which has a 1024 value, we then have bits valued at 128, 62, 32, 8, 4, 2, 1, which makes the binary number 1011101111.

18. B. To answer this, we must first put the IP address into binary. 172.13.99.225 is 1010 1100.00001101.01100011.11100001. This now needs to be made into nibbles of four bits each: 1010 1100.0000 1101.0110 0011.1110 0001. Each nibble can then represent a hexadecimal number from 0 to 15 (F). 1010 is A, 1100 is C, 0000 is 0, 1101 is D, 0110 is 6, 0011 is 3, 1110 is E, and 0001 is 1.

19. C. Hexadecimal values 0x718 in binary is 11100011000. The 0x just means the following characters are in hexadecimal, not binary. In decimal that would be 1318 because the valid bits on are 8, 16, 256, 512, and 1024, which adds up to 1318.

20. D. Explanation: The Ether-Type field found in an Ethernet_II frame defines the Network layer protocol, which is the same function as the SAP fields in an 802.3 Ethernet SNAP frame.

Chapter 4: TCP/IP DoD Model

1. C. If a DHCP conflict is detected, either by the server sending a ping and getting a response or by a host using a gratuitous ARP (arp'ing for its own IP address and seeing if a host responds), then the server will hold that address and not use it again until it is fixed by an administrator.

2. A, D. Both TCP and UDP provide session multiplexing, but only TCP is connection oriented, so UDP is considered best effort packet delivery.

3. C. Dynamic Host Configuration Protocol (DHCP) is used to provide IP information to hosts on your network. DHCP can provide a lot of information, but the most common is IP address, subnet mask, default gateway, and DNS information.

4. B. Address Resolution Protocol (ARP) is used to find the hardware address from a known IP address.

5. A, C, D. This seems like a hard question at first because it doesn't make sense. The listed answers are from the OSI model and the question asked about the TCP/IP protocol stack (DoD model). However, let's just look for what is wrong. First, the Session layer is not in the TCP/IP model; neither are the Data Link and Physical layers. This leaves us with the Transport layer (Host-to-Host in the DoD model), Internet layer (Network layer in the OSI), and Application layer (Application/Process in the DoD).

6. A, B. The OSI Data Link (layer 2) and the OSI Physical layer (layer 1) are combined into the Network Access layer of the Internet Protocol suite.

7. A, B. A client that sends out a DHCP Discover message in order to receive an IP address sends out a broadcast at both layer 2 and layer 3. The layer 2 broadcast is all Fs in hex, or FF:FF:FF:FF:FF:FF. The layer 3 broadcast is 255.255.255.255, which means any networks and all hosts. DHCP is connectionless, which means it uses User Datagram Protocol (UDP) at the Transport layer, also called the Host-to-Host layer.

8. B. Although Telnet does use TCP and IP (TCP/IP), the question specifically asks about layer 4, and IP works at layer 3. Telnet uses TCP at layer 4.

9. D. To stop possible address conflicts, a DHCP client will use gratuitous ARP (broadcast an ARP request for its own IP address) to see if another host responds.

10. B, D, E. SMTP, FTP, and HTTP use TCP.

11. A, C, F. DHCP, SNMP, and TFTP use UDP. SMTP, FTP, and HTTP use TCP.

12. C, D, E. Telnet, File Transfer Protocol (FTP), and Trivial FTP (TFTP) are all Application layer protocols. IP is a Network layer protocol. Transmission Control Protocol (TCP) is a Transport layer protocol.

13. C. First, you should know easily that only TCP and UDP work at the Transport layer, so now you have a 50/50 shot. However, since the header has sequencing, acknowledgment, and window numbers, the answer can only be TCP.

14. A. Both FTP and Telnet use TCP at the Transport layer; however, they both are Application layer protocols, so the Application layer is the best answer for this question.

15. C. The four layers of the DoD model are Application/Process, Host-to-Host, Internet, and Network Access. The Internet layer is equivalent to the Network layer of the OSI model.

16. C, D. The real answer is 5, 6, and 7, but we only get to choose two on this question and Cisco's answer in their curriculum is the Session layer and the Presentation layer. This is the best answer.

17. B. The four layers of the TCP/IP stack (also called the DoD model) are Application/ Process, Host-to-Host, Internet, and Network Access. The Host-to-Host layer is equivalent to the Transport layer of the OSI model.

18. B, C. ICMP is used for diagnostics and destination unreachable messages. ICMP is encapsulated within IP datagrams, and because it is used for diagnostics, it will provide hosts with information about network problems.

19. C. All LAN protocols, and WAN protocols, work at the Data Link layer (layer 2).

20. D. DNS uses TCP for zone exchanges between servers and UDP when a client is trying to resolve a hostname to an IP address.

Chapter 5: IP Addressing

1. A. RFC 1918 specifies that only 1 network is reserved in the Class A range (10.0.0.0/8), 16 with Class B (172.16.0.0/28), and 256 with Class C (192.168.0.0/24).

2. B, C. RFC 1918 specifies that 1 network in Class A, 16 networks in Class B, and 256 in Class C are reserved and cannot be routed on the global Internet.

3. B. RFC 1918 specifies that only 1 network is reserved in the Class A range (10.0.0.0/8), 16 with Class B (172.16.0.0/28), and 256 with Class C (192.168.0.0/24).

4. C. Broadcasts have been eliminated, and the need for NAT and DHCP is not needed in IPv6.

5. C. RFC 1918 specifies that only 1 network is reserved in the Class A range (10.0.0.0/8), 16 with Class B (172.16.0.0/28), and 256 with Class C (192.168.0.0/24).

6. C. A Class C network address has only 8 bits for defining hosts: $2^8 - 2 = 254$.

7. A. Private addresses from RFC 1918 cannot be placed on an interface going to the public Internet. You must use NAT.

8. B, C. RFC 1918 describes the private addresses used in IPv6 and RFC 4193 describes the Unique Local Addresses (ULA's) used in IPv6, which is equivalent to private address. Neither RFC 1918 or 4193 addresses are routable on the Internet.

9. D. An anycast address identifies a single unicast address on multiple interfaces, on multiple hosts. Hosts actually use the same unicast address for load-sharing possibilities. Anycast is referred to as "one-to-nearest."

10. A. Link-local addresses are the APIPA of the IPv6 world and start with FE80.

11. A, D, F. RFC 1918 specifies that only one network is reserved in the Class A range (10.0.0.0/8), 16 with Class B (172.16.0.0/20), and 256 with Class C (192.168.0.0/24).

12. C. To implement RFC 1918 on your private network, you need to implement Network Address Translation (NAT) on the border router.

13. A, B, D. With IPv6, we no longer need NAT or DHCP, and we no longer use broadcasts. There are plenty of addresses.

14. C, E. Class A private address range is 10.0.0.0 through 10.255.255.255. Class B private address range is 172.16.0.0 through 172.31.255.255, and Class C private address range is 192.168.0.0 through 192.168.255.255.

15. C. The range of a Class B network address is 128–191. This makes our binary range 10*xxxxxx*.

16. C. IPv6 uses 128 bits, and it is displayed in colon-delimited hexadecimal in eight, 16-bit fields.

17. D. The class A address 127.0.0.0 is reserved for diagnostics. Typically people use 127.0.0.1 to test their local IP stack, but the address can be used by applications as well to communicate within the system.

18. C. By finding the host bits of an IP address and turning them all off, you'll find your network address; by turning them all on, you'll find your broadcast address.

19. D. By finding the host bits of an IP address and turning them all off, you'll find your network address; by turning them all on, you'll find your broadcast address.

20. B. You cannot assign an address from RFC 1918 to an interface of a router connecting to the global Internet.

Chapter 6: Easy Subnetting

1. D. A /27 (255.255.255.224) is 3 bits on and 5 bits off. This provides 8 subnets, each with 30 hosts. Does it matter if this mask is used with a Class A, B, or C network address? Not at all. The number of host bits would never change.

2. D. A 240 mask is 4 subnet bits and provides 16 subnets, each with 14 hosts. We need more subnets, so let's add subnet bits. One more subnet bit would be a 248 mask. This provides 5 subnet bits (32 subnets) with 3 host bits (6 hosts per subnet). This is the best answer.

3. C. This is a pretty simple question. A /28 is 255.255.255.240, which means that our block size is 16 in the fourth octet. 0, 16, 32, 48, 64, 80, etc. The host is in the 64 subnet.

4. F. A CIDR address of /19 is 255.255.224.0. This is a Class B address, so that is only 3 subnet bits, but it provides 13 host bits, or 8 subnets, each with 8,190 hosts.

5. B, D. The mask 255.255.254.0 (/23) used with a Class A address means that there are 15 subnet bits and 9 host bits. The block size in the third octet is 2 (256 − 254). So this makes the subnets in the interesting octet 0, 2, 4, 6, etc., all the way to 254. The host 10.16.3.65 is in the 2.0 subnet. The next subnet is 4.0, so the broadcast address for the 2.0 subnet is 3.255. The valid host addresses are 2.1 through 3.254.

6. D. A /30, regardless of the class of address, has a 252 in the fourth octet. This means we have a block size of 4 and our subnets are 0, 4, 8, 12, 16, etc. Address 14 is obviously in the 12 subnet.

7. D. A point-to-point link uses only two hosts. A /30, or 255.255.255.252, mask provides two hosts per subnet.

8. C. A /21 is 255.255.248.0, which means we have a block size of 8 in the third octet, so we just count by 8 until we reach 66. The subnet in this question is 64.0. The next subnet is 72.0, so the broadcast address of the 64 subnet is 71.255.

9. A. A /29 (255.255.255.248), regardless of the class of address, has only 3 host bits. Six hosts is the maximum number of hosts on this LAN, including the router interface.

10. C. A /29 is 255.255.255.248, which is a block size of 8 in the fourth octet. The subnets are 0, 8, 16, 24, 32, 40, etc. 192.168.19.24 is the 24 subnet, and since 32 is the next subnet, the broadcast address for the 24 subnet is 31. 192.168.19.26 is the only correct answer.

11. A. A /29 (255.255.255.248) has a block size of 8 in the fourth octet. This means the subnets are 0, 8, 16, 24, etc. 10 is in the 8 subnet. The next subnet is 16, so 15 is the broadcast address.

12. B. You need 5 subnets, each with at least 16 hosts. The mask 255.255.255.240 provides 16 subnets with 14 hosts—this will not work. The mask 255.255.255.224 provides 8 subnets, each with 30 hosts. This is the best answer.

13. C. First, you cannot answer this question if you can't subnet. The 192.168.10.62 with a mask of 255.255.255.192 is a block size of 64 in the fourth octet. The host 192.168.10.62 is in the zero subnet, and the error occurred because `ip subnet-zero` is not enabled on the router.

14. A. A /25 mask is 255.255.255.128. Used with a Class B network, the third and fourth octets are used for subnetting with a total of 9 subnet bits, 8 bits in the third octet and 1 bit in the fourth octet. Since there is only 1 bit in the fourth octet, the bit is either off or on—which is a value of 0 or 128. The host in the question is in the 0 subnet, which has a broadcast address of 127 since 112.128 is the next subnet.

15. A. A /28 is a 255.255.255.240 mask. Let's count to the ninth subnet (we need to find the broadcast address of the eighth subnet, so we need to count to the ninth subnet). Starting at 16 (remember, the question stated that we will not use subnet zero, so we start at 16, not 0), 16, 32, 48, 64, 80, 96, 112, 128, 144. The eighth subnet is 128 and the next subnet is 144, so our broadcast address of the 128 subnet is 143. This makes the host range 129–142. 142 is the last valid host.

16. C. A /28 is a 255.255.255.240 mask. The first subnet is 16 (remember that the question stated not to use subnet zero) and the next subnet is 32, so our broadcast address is 31. This makes our host range 17–30. 30 is the last valid host.

17. E. A Class C subnet mask of 255.255.255.224 is 3 bits on and 5 bits off (11100000) and provides eight subnets, each with 30 hosts. However, if the command ip subnet-zero is not used, then only six subnets would be available for use.

18. E. A Class B network ID with a /22 mask is 255.255.252.0, with a block size of 4 in the third octet. The network address in the question is in subnet 172.16.16.0 with a broadcast address of 172.16.19.255. Only option E has the correct subnet mask listed, and 172.16.18.255 is a valid host.

19. D, E. The router's IP address on the E0 interface is 172.16.2.1/23, which is 255.255.254.0. This makes the third octet a block size of 2. The router's interface is in the 2.0 subnet, and the broadcast address is 3.255 because the next subnet is 4.0. The valid host range is 2.1 through 3.254. The router is using the first valid host address in the range.

20. C. To test the local stack on your host, ping the loopback interface of 127.0.0.1.

Chapter 7: Introduction to Nexus

1. D. The last version of the MDS SAN-OS was version 3.2. As of version 4.1, both MDS and Nexus devices run NX-OS.

2. A, D, E. Spanning Tree Protocol (STP), UniDirectional Link Detection (UDLD), and Cisco Discovery Protocol (CDP) are layer 2 technologies.

3. B, C, F. Protocol Independent Multicast (PIM), Hot Standby Routing Protocol (HSRP), and Open Shortest Path First (OSPF) are layer 3 technologies.

4. D. UniDirectional Link Detection (UDLD) is a Data Link layer protocol used to monitor the physical configuration of the cables and detect when communication is occurring in only one-direction links.

5. A. An SVI is a layer 3 interface that represents a VLAN and can have an IP address and other layer 3 properties. The SVI is created with the `interface VLAN` command.

6. B. Virtual device contexts can logically separate a switch into two administrative domains. In this case, one VDC would be assigned all of the Ethernet ports and the other VDC would be assigned all of the storage ports.

7. A, B. Small form-factor pluggable modules give you flexibility in selecting what type of cable that you want to use. TwinAx is a copper cable with SFPs embedded in the end and is cost effective.

8. D. L1 and L2 are not implemented on the Nexus 5010.

9. C. Ethernet interfaces are always referenced as "Ethernet" on a Nexus device regardless of the speed at which they are operating.

10. B. Virtual device contexts can logically separate a switch into two administrative domains. In this case, one VDC would be assigned all of the Ethernet ports and the other VDC would be assigned all of the storage ports.

11. A. Virtual Routing and Forwarding and virtual device contexts could both accomplish this task, but VRF would be less disruptive.

12. D. Not all features are enabled by default. The RIP feature needs to be enabled before any command will work.

13. D. Unified ports can support either Fibre Channel or Ethernet, but not both at the same time.

14. B. The console port on an NX-OS device is almost identical to one on a Cisco IOS device. It is a serial port, which is typically used for initial configuration.

15. A. Persistent Storage Service (PSS) allows services to periodically save their state by making a checkpoint.

Chapter 8: Configuring Nexus

1. A. There are two commands that start with *co*, configure and copy:

```
switch# co?
  configure  Enter configuration mode
  copy       Copy from one file to another
switch# con
Enter configuration commands, one per line.  End with CNTL/Z.
nexus(config)#
```

So the shortest command you can type is con.

2. B. The END command or Ctrl-Z will exit any configuration mode and place you back into user-exec mode.

3. A, F. The two-step process to reset a device is to erase the configuration and the reboot the device. To accomplish this, we do the following:

```
switch# write erase boot
Warning: This command will erase the startup-configuration.
Do you wish to proceed anyway? (y/n)  [n] y
switch# reload
WARNING: This command will reboot the system
Do you want to continue? (y/n) [n] y
```

4. C. The feature command turns on a feature and enables the commands for that feature. The command will not be visible until enabled.

5. C. The switchport command enables the configuration of layer 2 properties like VLAN, trunking, and access mode.

```
nexus(config-if)# switchport ?
  <CR>
  access      Set access mode characteristics of the interface
  autostate   Include or exclude this port from vlan link up calculation
  block       Block specified outbound traffic for all VLANs
  description Enter description of maximum 80 characters
  host        Set port host
  mode        Enter the port mode
  monitor     Monitor session related traffic
  monitor     Configures an interface as span-destination
```

```
priority      CoS Priority parameter
trunk         Configure trunking parameters on an interface
voice         Set voice mode characterestics of the interface
```

6. B. The switchport command is used to switch between a port being used for layer 2 and layer 3.

```
core(config-if)# ip add 1.1.1.1 255.255.255.0
                       ^

% Invalid command at '^' marker.
core(config-if)# no switchport
core(config-if)# ip add 1.1.1.1 255.255.255.0
core(config-if)#
```

7. A, B. Network-Admin (sometimes just called Admin) and Network-Operator are the two most commonly used roles.

```
nexus(config)# user John role ?
  network-admin      System configured role
  network-operator   System configured role
  priv-0             Privilege role
  priv-1             Privilege role
  priv-10            Privilege role
  priv-11            Privilege role
  priv-12            Privilege role
  priv-13            Privilege role
  priv-14            Privilege role
  priv-15            Privilege role
  priv-2             Privilege role
  priv-3             Privilege role
  priv-4             Privilege role
  priv-5             Privilege role
  priv-6             Privilege role
  priv-7             Privilege role
  priv-8             Privilege role
  priv-9             Privilege role
  vdc-admin          System configured role
  vdc-operator       System configured role
```

8. D. The Tab key enables auto-completion on Nexus and other Cisco devices.

9. A. An SVI is a layer 3 interface that represents a VLAN and can have an IP address and other layer 3 properties. The SVI interface is created with the `interface vlan` command.

10. C. The `switchport` option is added to the end of the `show interface` command to display all of the layer 2 details about a port.

```
nexus(config)# show int e1/1 switchport
Name: Ethernet1/1
   Switchport: Enabled
   Switchport Monitor: Not enabled
   Operational Mode: trunk
   Access Mode VLAN: 1 (default)
   Trunking Native Mode VLAN: 1 (default)
   Trunking VLANs Enabled: 1,10
```

11. E. One of my favorite features of NX-OS is not having to type in subnet masks, and creating a default route is no exception. There is nothing new with static or default routing with NX-OS except we can use the slash notation for the mask (/). Only answer E has the correct syntax.

12. E. The running configuration (active configuration file) is store, in RAM. In the event of a power failure or reload, any changes made to the running configuration that have not been saved to the startup configuration are lost.

13. D. The erase `startup-config` command erases the contents of NVRAM and will put you in setup mode if the router is restarted.

14. B. On the third line, the `admin-down` indicates that the interface is shut down. The command `no shutdown` would enable the interface.

15. D. NX-OS uses locally created usernames and passwords by default; there is no user mode and privileged mode as in the IOS.

16. C. The `interface VLAN 30` creates a switched virtual interface only if the feature has been previously enabled.

17. D. You can view the interface statistics from user mode, but the command is `show interface Ethernet 1/1`.

18. B. The `%` `ambiguous command` error means that there is more than one possible show command that starts with *r*. Use a question mark to find the correct command.

19. B, D. The commands `show interfaces` and `show ip interface` will show you the layer 1 and 2 status and the IP addresses of your router's interfaces.

20. A. If you see that an Ethernet interface and `Link not connected`, then you have a Physical layer problem.

Chapter 9: IP Routing

1. C, F. The switches are not used as either a default gateway or other destination. Switches have nothing to do with routing. It is very important to remember that the destination MAC address will always be the router's interface. The destination address of a frame, from HostA, will be the MAC address of the Fa0/0 interface of RouterA. The destination address of a packet will be the IP address of the network interface card (NIC) of the HTTPS server. The destination port number in the segment header will have a value of 443 (HTTPS).

2. A, D. RouterC will use ICMP to inform HostA that HostB cannot be reached. It will perform this by sending a destination unreachable ICMP message type.

3. C. Frames are discarded as they reach a router, so MAC addresses change at every hop—no exception! The packet is removed from the frame, and the packet is packet-switched.

4. C. Frames are discarded as they reach a router. The packet is removed from the frame, and the packet is packet-switched.

5. D. Frames are discarded as they reach a router, so MAC addresses change at every hop—no exception! The packet is removed from the frame, and the packet is packet-switched.

6. C, D. IP will encapsulate an ICMP packet with an ICMP echo request, echo reply pair, but first will use ARP to resolve the IP destination address to a hardware address.

7. A, C. To be able to route packets, a router must know, at a minimum, the destination address, the location of neighboring routers through which it can reach remote networks, possible routes to all remote networks, the best route to each remote network, and how to maintain and verify routing information.

8. D. IP uses the ARP protocol to find the destination hardware address of the host on the local LAN. If the destination is a remote host, IP will ARP for the default gateway hardware address.

9. C. Internet Control Message Protocol (ICMP) is used by IP to send error messages through the internetwork.

10. A, C. To be able to route packets, a router must know, at a minimum, the destination address, the location of neighboring routers through which it can reach remote networks, possible routes to all remote networks, the best route to each remote network, and how to maintain and verify routing information.

Chapter 10: Routing Protocols

1. B. Only the EIGRP routes will be placed in the routing table because EIGRP has the lowest administrative distance (AD), and AD is always used before metrics.

2. D. Cisco considers EIGRP an advance distance-vector routing protocol because it has more distance-vector qualities than link state.

3. A, C. Each routing protocol on Nexus can have many processes running, so it is mandatory that when you configure a routing protocol, you configure the instance ID.

4. C. The maximum hop count a route update packet can traverse before considering the route invalid is 15, for both RIPv1 and RIPv2.

5. B, E. Classful routing means that all hosts in the internetwork use the same mask and that only default masks are in use. Classless routing means that you can use Variable Length Subnet Masks (VLSMs) and can also support discontiguous networking.

6. B, C. The distance-vector routing protocol sends its complete routing table out all active interfaces at periodic time intervals. Link-state routing protocols send updates containing the state of its own links to all routers in the internetwork.

7. B. RIP has an administrative distance (AD) of 120, while EIGRP has an administrative distance of 90, so the router will discard any route with an AD higher than 90 to that same network.

8. A. RIPv1 and RIPv2 use only the lowest hop count to determine the best path to a remote network.

9. C. Static routes have an administrative distance of 1 by default. Unless you change this, a static route will always be used over any other dynamically-learned route. EIGRP has an administrative distance of 90, RIP is 120.

10. B. When a routing update is received by a router, the router first checks the administrative distance (AD) and always chooses the route with the lowest AD. However, if two routes are received and they both have the same AD and differing metrics, then the router will choose the one route with the lowest metrics or, in RIP's case, hop count.

11. C. RIPv2 is pretty much just like RIPv1. It has the same administrative distance and timers and is configured similarly.

12. C, D, E. RIPv1 and IGRP are true distance-vector routing protocols and can't do much, really—except build and maintain routing tables and use a lot of bandwidth! RIPv2, EIGRP, and OSPF build and maintain routing tables, but they also provide classless routing, which allows for VLSM, summarization, and discontiguous networking.

13. C, D, E. Loopback interfaces are created on a router, and the highest IP address on a loopback (logical) interface becomes the RID of the router but has nothing to do with areas and is optional, so option A is wrong. The numbers you can create an area with are from 0 to 4,294,967,295—option B is wrong. The backbone area is called area 0, so option C is correct. All areas must connect to area 0, so option E is correct. If you have only one area, it must be called area 0, so option F is incorrect. This leaves option D, which must be correct; it doesn't make much sense, but it is the best answer.

14. D. In this question, I'm calling EIGRP just plain old distance vector. EIGRP is an advanced distance-vector routing protocol, sometimes called a hybrid routing protocol because it uses the characteristics of both distance-vector and link-state routing protocols.

15. A, B, C. OSPF is created in a hierarchical design, not a flat design like RIP. This decreases routing overhead, speeds up convergence, and confines network instability to a single area of the network.

16. C. The administrative distance (AD) is a very important parameter in a routing protocol. The lower the AD, the more trusted the route. If you have IGRP and OSPF running, by default IGRP routes would be placed in the routing table because IGRP has a lower AD of 100. OSPF has an AD of 110. RIPv1 and RIPv2 both have an AD of 120, and EIGRP is the lowest, at 90.

17. C. RIP and RIPv2 are examples of distance-vector routing protocols.

18. B. RIP uses periodic timers, which means it sends updates on predetermined times, which is 30 seconds by default.

19. E. EIGRP sends incremental updates, not periodic like RIP, meaning that updates are only sent when a change occurs.

20. A. The administrative distance (AD) is a very important parameter in a routing protocol. The lower the AD, the more trusted the route. If you have IGRP and OSPF running, by default IGRP routes would be placed in the routing table because IGRP has a lower AD of 100. OSPF has an AD of 110. RIPv1 and RIPv2 both have an AD of 120, and EIGRP is the lowest, at 90.

Chapter 11: Layer 2 Switching Technologies

1. D. VLAN Trunk Protocol (VTP) is used to propagate and synchronize VLAN information across a trunked link.

2. B, E, F. A router connected to a switch that provides inter-VLAN communication is configured using subinterfaces. The switch port connected to the router must be using

either ISL or 802.1Q trunking protocol, and the hosts are all connected as access ports, which is the default on all switch ports.

3. B. To enable inter-VLAN routing on a Nexus switch you need to start the `feature interface-vlan`, which allows the creation of SVIs.

4. D. By creating and implementing VLANs in your switched network, you can break up broadcast domains at layer 2. For hosts on different VLANs to communicate, you must have a router or layer 3 switch.

5. C, D. You can create local VLANs in both VTP server mode and transparent mode. Clients can receive a VLAN database only from a server.

6. A. By default, all VLANs are allowed on the trunk link and you must remove by hand each VLAN that you don't want traversing the trunked link.

7. C. Virtual LANs break up broadcast domains in layer 2 switched internetworks.

8. C. Only in server and transparent mode can you change VLAN information on a switch.

9. D. The `show interface` *interface* `switchport` command shows the native VLAN for that interface, but so does the `show interface trunk` command. You need to know both commands!

10. E. All Cisco switches are *not* VTP servers by default. I have Nexus switches that default to transparent. You must set the VTP domain name on all switches to be the same domain name or they will not share the VTP database.

11. B. Virtual Trunk Protocol (VTP) is used to pass a VLAN database to any or all switches in the switched network. The three VTP modes are server, client, and transparent.

12. C. Switched virtual interfaces are created by the administrator for each VLAN to provide IVR.

13. C. 802.1Q was created to allow trunked links between disparate switches.

14. D. This question is a little vague, but the best answer is that the VLAN membership for the port is not configured.

15. A, C. To troubleshoot VTP, you first need to verify that the domain names match and that they are case sensitive as well. You should also check that the server has a higher revision number than the client or the client won't update the database. Also, if the passwords are set and do not match, the client will reject the update. Type `show vtp status` and check the MD5 checksum and make sure the values are the same, or type `show vtp password` to verify the match.

16. C. Although one of the switches can be set to client, that would not stop them from sharing VLAN information through VTP. However, they will not share VLAN information through VTP if the domain names are not set the same.

17. C, E. The command show vlan will provide you all your VLANs; you'd just have to count all the VLANs configured from 1006 to 4094. You can more easily type the command show vlan summary to get your information.

18. B, D. You must have the same VTP domain name on all switches in order to share VLAN information between the switches. At least one of the switches must be a VTP server; the other switches should be set to VTP client mode.

19. E. It is not easy to see the problem at first look. However, check out the MD5 digest. The MD5 digest does not match between switches, which means the VTP passwords do not match!

20. C. To find this problem on your local switch, you'd have to verify with the command show interface trunk or show interface e3/28 switchport in order to see the VLANs allowed across the trunk link.

Chapter 12: Redundant Switched Technologies

1. B. The Spanning Tree Protocol is used to stop switching loops in a layer 2 switched network with redundant paths.

2. A. Notice the port-channel 1 is up, admin state is up. This is a working port-channel.

3. C. Convergence occurs when all ports on bridges and switches have transitioned to either the forwarding or blocking state. No data is forwarded until convergence is complete. Before data can be forwarded again, all devices must be updated.

4. C. The Spanning Tree Protocol (STP) was designed to stop layer 2 loops. All Cisco switches have the STP on by default.

5. A, B, F. RSTP helps with convergence issues that plague traditional STP. Rapid PVST+ is based on the 802.1w standard in the same way that PVST+ is based on 802.1d. The operation of Rapid PVST+ is simply a separate instance of 802.1w for each VLAN.

6. D. If the Spanning Tree Protocol is not running on your switches and you connect them together with redundant links, you will have broadcast storms and multiple frame copies.

7. D. If you have a server or other devices connected into your switch that you're totally sure won't create a switching loop if STP is disabled, you can use something called port type edge on these ports. Using it means the port won't spend the usual time to come up while STP is converging.

8. C. If spanning tree is disabled on a switch and you have redundant links to another switch, broadcast storms will occur, among other possible problems.

9. A, D. It is important that you can find your root bridge, and the show spanning-tree command will help you do this. To quickly find out which VLANs your switch is the root bridge for, use the show spanning-tree summary command.

10. B. To bundle your interfaces together, use the channel-group number command at interface level. From global configuration mode, you need to create the bundle interface with the interface port-channel command.

Chapter 13: Security

1. B. You can name your ACLs with a number, no problem, so that isn't the problem with any of the options. First, remember that Nexus allows only extended named lists, and the command to name the list starts with ip. Then you need to add the protocol and then at a minimum the source and destination addresses. Only option B provides the minimum correct commands and syntax needed to create an ACL on NX-OS.

2. C. The range of 192.168.160.0 to 192.168.191.255 is a block size of 32. The network address is 192.168.160.0 and the mask would be 255.255.224.0, which for an access list must be a wildcard format of 0.0.31.255. The 31 is used for a block size of 32. The wildcard is always one less than the block size.

3. C. Using a named access list just replaces the number used when applying the list to the router's interface. ip access-group Blocksales in is correct.

4. B, D. The wildcard 0.0.0.0 tells the router to match all four octets. This wildcard format alone can be replaced with the host command.

5. A. The first thing to check is the protocol. If you are filtering by upper-layer protocol, then you must be using either UDP or TCP; this eliminates the fourth option. The second, third, and last options have the wrong syntax.

6. B, D. In solving this business requirement, we first need to create a deny statement to any destination using HTTP with destination port 8080. The source is network 172.16.1.0/21. The second line is permit all other traffic. See Hands-on Lab 13.1 for more detailed information regarding the answer to this question.

7. C. The show access-lists command will allow you to view the entire contents of all access lists, but it will not show you the interfaces to which the access lists are applied.

8. C. Telnet uses TCP, so the protocol TCP is valid. Now you just need to look for the source and destination address. Only the third option has the correct sequence of parameters. Option B may work, but the question specifically states "only" to network 192.168.10.0, and the wildcard in option B makes it too broad.

9. D. Extended IP access lists filter based on source and destination IP address, protocol number, and port number. The last option is correct because of the second line that specifies `permit ip any any`. The third option does not have this, so it would deny access but not allow everything else.

10. D. First, you must know that a /20 is 255.255.240.0, which is a block size of 16 in the third octet. Counting by 16s, this makes our subnet 48 in the third octet, and the wildcard for the third octet would be 15 since the wildcard is always one less than the block size.

11. C. To apply an access list inbound named 101, the proper command is `ip access-group 101 in`.

12. A. First, you must know that a /19 is 255.255.224.0, which is a block size of 32 in the third octet. Counting by 32, this makes our subnet 192 in the third octet, and the wildcard for the third octet would be 31 since the wildcard is always one less than the block size.

13. B. First, you must know that a /21 is 255.255.248.0, which is a block size of 8 in the third octet. Counting by eight, this makes our subnet 144 in the third octet, and the wildcard for the third octet would be 7 since the wildcard is always one less than the block size.

14. A, D. In solving this business requirement, we first need to create a `deny statement from any source` to destination host 10.10.1.110 using HTTP with destination port 80. The second line is `permit all other traffic`.

15. D. When trying to find the best answer to an access list question, always check the access list number and then the protocol. When you filter to the port of an upper-layer protocol, you must use either `tcp` or `udp` in the ACL protocol field. If it says `ip` in the protocol field, you cannot filter on the port number of an upper-layer protocol. SMTP uses TCP.

16. D. If you add an access list to an interface and you do not have at least one `permit` statement, then you will effectively shut down the interface because of the implicit `deny any any` at the end of every list.

17. A. In solving this business requirement, we first need to create a deny statement from any source to destination host 10.10.1.110 equal to FTP or port 21. The second line is permit all other traffic. Option B is wrong because it doesn't start with the IP command.

18. C. A Cisco router has rules regarding the placement of access lists on a router interface. You can place one access list per direction for each layer 3 protocol configured on an interface.

19. A, C, E. IOS-based routers allow standard numbered, extended numbered, and named-based ACLs.

20. C. The NX-OS allows you to create only extended named ACLs.

Appendix C

About the Additional Study Tools

IN THIS APPENDIX:

✓ Additional study tools

✓ System requirements

✓ Using the study tools

✓ Troubleshooting

Additional Study Tools

The following sections are arranged by category and summarize the software and other goodies you'll find on the companion website. If you need help with installing the items, refer to the installation instructions in the section "Using the Study Tools" later in this appendix.

> The additional study tools can be found at www.sybex.com/go/ccnadatacenternetworking. Here, you will get instructions on how to download the files to your hard drive.

Sybex Test Engine

The files contain the Sybex test engine, which includes two bonus practice exams as well as the assessment test and the chapter review questions. The assessment test and chapter review questions are also included in the book itself.

Electronic Flashcards

These handy electronic flashcards are just what they sound like. One side contains a question, and the other side shows the answer.

Nexus Simulator

You can use the Nexus simulator to do all of the hands-on labs included in this book.

PDF of Glossary of Terms

I have included an electronic version of the glossary in PDF format. You can view the electronic version of the glossary with Adobe Reader.

Adobe Reader

I've also included a link to download Adobe Reader so you can view PDF files. For more information on Adobe Reader or to check for a newer version, visit Adobe's website at www.adobe.com/products/reader/.

System Requirements

Make sure your computer meets the minimum system requirements shown in the following list. If your computer doesn't match up to most of these requirements, you may have problems using the software and files. For the latest and greatest information, please refer to the ReadMe file located in the downloads.

- A PC running Microsoft Windows XP, Windows Vista, Windows 7 or Windows 8.
- If you are using a MAC, then you'll need to run VMware Fusion.
- An Internet connection.

Using the Study Tools

To install the items, follow these steps:

1. Download the ZIP file to your hard drive, and unzip to an appropriate location. Instructions on where to download this file can be found here: www.sybex.com/go/ccnadatacenternetworking.

2. Click Start.exe to open the study tools file.

3. Read the license agreement, and then click the Accept button if you want to use the study tools.

The main interface appears. The interface allows you to access the content with just one or two clicks.

Troubleshooting

Wiley has attempted to provide programs that work on most computers with the minimum system requirements. Alas, your computer may differ, and some programs may not work properly for some reason.

The two likeliest problems are that you don't have enough memory (RAM) for the programs you want to use or you have other programs running that are affecting installation or running of a program. If you get an error message such as "Not enough memory" or "Setup cannot continue," try one or more of the following suggestions and then try using the software again:

Turn off any antivirus software running on your computer. Installation programs sometimes mimic virus activity and may make your computer incorrectly believe that it's being infected by a virus.

Close all running programs. The more programs you have running, the less memory is available to other programs. Installation programs typically update files and programs, so if you keep other programs running, installation may not work properly.

Have your local computer store add more RAM to your computer. This is, admittedly, a drastic and somewhat expensive step. However, adding more memory can really help the speed of your computer and allow more programs to run at the same time.

Customer Care

If you have trouble with the book's companion study tools, please don't contact the author, but call the Wiley Product Technical Support phone number at (800) 762-2974, or visit them at `http://sybex.custhelp.com/`.

Index

Note to the reader: Throughout this index boldfaced page numbers indicate primary discussions of a topic. Italicized page numbers indicate illustrations.

G

N

R

Free Online Study Tools

Register on Sybex.com to gain access to a complete set of study tools to help you prepare for your DCICN Exam

Comprehensive Study Tool Package Includes:

- Assessment Test to help you focus your study to specific objectives

- Chapter Review Questions for each chapter of the book

- Two Full-Length Practice Exams to test your knowledge of the material

- Electronic Flashcards to reinforce your learning and give you that last-minute test prep before the exam

- Nexus Simulator to complete all the hands-on labs in the book

- Searchable Glossary gives you instant access to the key terms you'll need to know for the exam

Go to www.sybex.com/go/ccnadatacenternetworking **to register and gain access to this comprehensive study tool package.**

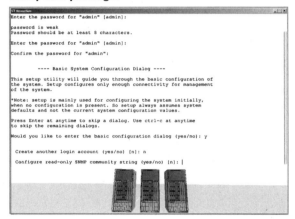

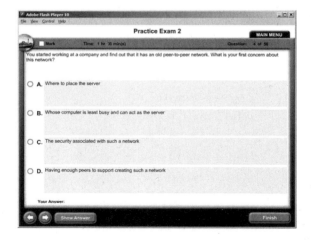